Friedelind Wagner

Friedelind Wagner

Richard Wagner's Rebellious Granddaughter

Eva Rieger

Translated by Chris Walton

THE BOYDELL PRESS

First published 2013
The Boydell Press, Woodbridge

ISBN 978 1 84383 864 7

The Boydell Press is an imprint of Boydell & Brewer Ltd
PO Box 9, Woodbridge, Suffolk IP12 3DF, UK
and of Boydell & Brewer Inc.
668 Mount Hope Ave, Rochester, NY 14620–2731, USA
website: www.boydellandbrewer.com

A catalogue record for this book is available
from the British Library

Printed and bound in Great Britain by
CPI Group (UK) Ltd, Croydon, CR0 4YY

Contents

Illustrations

Unless otherwise indicated, all illustrations are © Friedelind Wagner Archives with kind permission of Neill Thornborrow.

'A diffusely expanding family hydra. A selfish, pretentious mass with prominent noses and thrusting chins. An Atridae clan in which fathers castrate the sons and mothers smother them lovingly, in which mothers cast out their daughters and daughters condemn their mothers as heretics, in which brothers tread on each others' toes and brothers rise up against sisters as do sisters against brothers ...'

Nike Wagner: 'Die Familienbande' in Wolf S. Wagner 1976

Acknowledgements

My special thanks go to Gottfried Wagner, who gave me the idea of writing this biography, and to the owner and custodian of the Friedelind Wagner Archives in Düsseldorf, Neill Thornborrow, who gave me access to everything. They both kindly answered all my questions and offered their comments whenever I needed them. In contrast to the historian Brigitte Hamann, who for her biography of Winifred Wagner was afforded access to Wolfgang Wagner's private archives, I was unable to consult any of his materials. I am thus all the more grateful to the descendants of Wieland Wagner, who made it possible for me to consult their father's documents, held today in Salzburg. My particular thanks are due to Verena Lafferentz, Friedelind Wagner's sister, who placed Helene Roesener's letters to Winifred Wagner at my disposal and was happy to meet me for several conversations. She read my manuscript and offered her comments on it, which resulted in discussions that were not always easy for either side. Eva, Nike, Daphne and Iris Wagner also readily replied to my requests for information. Markus Kiesel, Harvey Sachs, Peter Konwitschny, Peter Pachl, Gisela Graf and Rainer Fineske generously allowed me access to their letters and provided me with further information. John Dew, Walfredo Toscanini (†), Joachim Herz (†), Muhai Tang, Michael Tilson Thomas, Martin Bernheimer, Anja Silja, Jonathan Dudley, Tom Lipton, Philipp and Evelyn Marfurt, Alfred Kaine, Doris Metz, Doris Stoisser, Dominique Modesti, Erich Singer and Patricia Sage all provided me with important information. Gudrun Foettinger, Helga Bahl, Nora Neese, Helga Dolega-Kozierowski, Peter Sommeregger, Roger Sims, Katia Fleischer, Charmian Brinson and Elisabeth Furtwängler kindly answered specific questions. Hannelore Abt and Christine Koschel edited and offered comments on the German text. The Editorial Director of Boydell, Michael Middeke, was of great assistance. Chris Walton worked on the translation with patience, empathy and came up with many suggestions, which made him wellnigh essential for the project. And last but not least I must thank Dagny Beidler, whose support and helpful comments aided me in shaping the final manuscript.

Abbreviations

AdK = Akademie der Künste (Academy of Arts), Berlin

AFB = Archive of the Society of Friends of Bayreuth

AGM = Archive of the Gesellschaft der Musikfreunde, Vienna

BB = Busch Brothers Archive, Karlsruhe

BG = Blandine Gravina archives in the Bayerische Staatsbibliothek, Munich

BH = Brigitte Hamann: *Winifred Wagner. A Life at the Heart of Hitler's Bayreuth* (see bibliography)

BHA = Bayerisches Hauptstaatsarchiv, Munich

DBA = Dagny Beidler archive (private)

ERA = Eva Rieger archive

FW = Friedelind Wagner

GGA = Gisela Graf archive (private)

GSt = Gertrud Strobel, diary (RWA)

HoF = Friedelind Wagner: *Heritage of Fire* (see bibliography)

HR = Helene Roesener

IfZ = Institut für Zeitgeschichte, Munich

Lebens-Akte = Wolfgang Wagner: *Lebens-Akte* (see bibliography)

LiS = Liszt Saeculum Vol. 46 (1991)

LS = Lieselotte Schmidt

MNH = Manx National Heritage Museum, Isle of Man

Monacensia = Literaturarchiv und Bibliothek München (EM M 144).

MUB = Manuscript Department, University of Basel (Zinsstag archives)

NA = National Archives, Kew, London (KV2/1914, KV4/141ff. and KV4/339ff.)

NTh: Neill Thornborrow archives (Friedelind Wagner archive)

NYPL = New York Public Library, Toscanini Legacy, Ted Shawn Collection

PA = Politisches Archiv des Auswärtigen Amtes (Political Archives of the Foreign Office), Germany

RWA = Richard Wagner Archive, Bayreuth

SA Luzern = Stadtarchiv Luzern (B 3.3/A 99)

SLB = Stadtarchiv und Landesgeschichtliche Bibliothek Bielefeld (Städt. Bühnen 107/6, Nr. 1063, 1625, 1669, 1684, 2044)

STM = Staatsarchiv München

VL = Verena Lafferentz

VLA = Verena Lafferentz archive (private)

WoWa = Wolfgang Wagner

WW = Winifred Wagner

WWS = Wieland Wagner Archive, Salzburg

Note on source material

Several of the people quoted in this book were bilingual, even multilingual. Both Siegfried and Friedelind Wagner occasionally mixed languages in their letters, while Friedelind and others adjusted their language of correspondence according to the mother tongue of their addressee. Friedelind also wrote in (American) English when this was her common language with the correspondent in question (most notably Toscanini). English-language sources have here been quoted from the original wherever possible and their grammar, spelling and punctuation (occasionally rather idiosyncratic) retained without further comment.

The Wagner Family

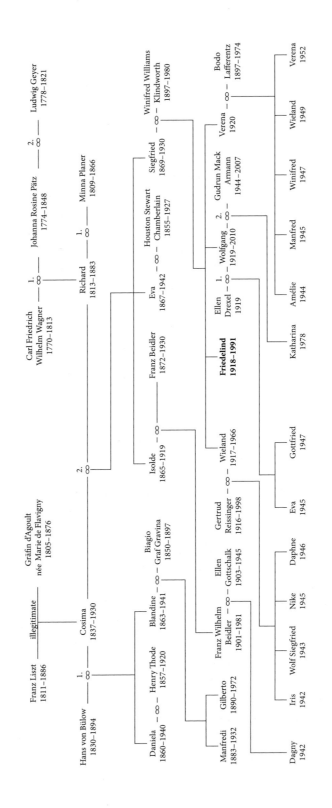

Introduction

RADIANT BLUE EYES, lips painted a garish red, dyed blond hair, flashy clothes: not everyone took a liking to Friedelind Wagner when she returned to Germany in 1953, after over a decade as an émigré abroad. Now a US citizen, she had come back to attend the Bayreuth Festival founded by her famous grandfather in 1876.

Friedelind Wagner, great-granddaughter of Liszt, granddaughter of Cosima and Richard Wagner and the daughter of Winifred and Siegfried, was a strong-willed personality who talked much: too much, some thought. Her arguments were loud and passionate, often undiplomatic to the point of tactlessness. Yet she exuded an aura that fascinated others. Certainly, Friedelind's profile was strikingly similar to that of her grandfather, whose oeuvre is among the most significant achievements in music history. But she also possessed a razor-sharp wit, intellectual agility and considerable charm, and all this had an impact on those around her. Nevertheless, hardly any other member of the extensive Wagner family has had to endure as much invective as Frie-delind, or so many untruths. These have ranged from the implicitly derogatory ('the Valkyrie of the jet age') to vulgar, threatening letters. Such attacks were undoubtedly prompted in part by her often rebellious manner and her fondness for making provocative statements. But they were equally a result of her opposition to much of what was held up as holy in Bayreuth. She took a stand against her mother, against the rehabilitation of ex-Nazis in post-war Germany, and against attempts by her brother Wolfgang to block the next generation of Wagners from directing in Bayreuth. It is hardly surprising that the Bayreuth establishment felt irritated by her, at times even under attack.

The erection of the Festspielhaus in 1876, high above the city, was the reali-zation of Richard Wagner's long-held dream of having his own theatre. Built according to his own ideas and plans, it would be devoted exclusively to his own works. It was constructed to perform his *Ring of the Nibelung* and he subsequently wrote *Parsifal* for it. Throughout his life he had endured a prob-lematical relationship with his public, but he had also exploited it extensively through his contributions to numerous journals and through making his views known in letters to journals, in poems and even in anonymous articles when-ever something bothered him. He cultivated his fame, but as it grew he had to accept that it drew with it all manner of wild speculation – about his possible illegitimacy, about his affairs with women, his relationship to Ludwig II, and much more besides. This difficult relationship with the public has been inherited by his descendants. The Wagners have become the 'ersatz royal family of Germany', of whom 'one can look under the bed covers at every opportunity'.[1] This is perhaps not so surprising, since the composer's descendants have always preferred indulging in their mutual vendettas in the public eye. In the case of Friedelind it was not so much her private life that interested the media, but rather her having turned her back on Bayreuth, along with her critical view of the post-war Festivals.

The criticism that flooded over her took as its starting point her memoir *Heritage of Fire*. Although it first appeared in print in America and Switzerland in 1945 and was published in several languages thereafter, no edition was published in Germany until 1994.[2] Her brother Wolfgang, at the time the Director of the Festival, wanted to have as little as possible to do with his sister and opponent of old. After the German edition appeared, an odd game of hide-and-seek took place at the bookstall in front of the Festspielhaus: "'Yes, we have the book," said the girl on duty at the desk, reaching beneath the counter. "But don't make it so obvious, Wolfgang Wagner doesn't like it".[3] In her film interview with Hans-Jürgen Syberberg, their mother Winifred had insisted that Friedelind had not even written the book herself, while Wolfgang brushed it off as 'subjective, creative yarn-spinning'.[4] He and his brother Wieland spoke of 'mistakes, instances of bad taste, slander' and of its 'mediocrity'.[5] Their chagrin was understandable. While they had believed in the 'Führer' to the last, Friedelind had long since cut herself off from him.

As is well known, the documentary value of memoirs is not necessarily greater than that of other sources, nor are they automatically closer to the truth. And Friedelind, too, often exaggerated in her book. But there is no reason to doubt her integrity. There are sufficient documents in her archives that show how her publisher arranged for her chapters to be edited and their English improved – but this suggests that the words were indeed hers. And there are parallel sources (such as letters) that can be regarded as authentic and which, in their descriptions of precise events, demonstrate that Friedelind stuck largely to historical truth (albeit with moments of elaboration here and there). Furthermore, Friedelind's intimate knowledge of the Nazi bigwigs who were constant visitors in Bayreuth affords the book a special documentary value – precisely because her siblings preferred to remain silent about it all. Her story of her own life is thus not just a biographical source, but also a testament to one of the darkest moments in German history.

Although her distance in time to certain events meant her memory was not always accurate, Friedelind is almost always reliable when writing of her own experiences. When she draws instead on what others have said, certain things become blurred or exaggerated, as in the case of a financial scandal in 1938 that she attributed to the Bayreuth finance manager Knittel,[6] but for which Winifred in fact was as much to blame. Friedelind could not know this, for her mother had simply not told her. What is crucial is Friedelind's sense of self-image, which comes through in what she writes. But in one point we have to admit that she intentionally erred, for she claims to have turned her back on National Socialism somewhat earlier than was the case. It was a long learning process that led to her becoming a committed anti-Nazi, and that process was also clouded by doubts that are all too understandable, given her background. As Jonathan Carr rightly states, 'That she of all the Wagners should then – in post-war Germany – regularly have been dubbed the "black sheep of the family" is a peculiarly shabby irony.'[7] But this also has to do with the unwritten laws regarding the depiction of people in the public eye. 'Deep mythic structures determine who is likeable and who isn't among the famous dead,' writes Janet Malcolm, who, more than just about anyone else, has investigated the traps into which biographers can fall.[8] This led to Friedelind being often described in the German press as a 'renegade' who was used by anti-Nazis 'as a propaganda object', who was full of complexes and who, with her book, had 'given vent to inferiority complexes and to her feelings of having been sidelined'.[9]

The patterns of life that men and women follow are in most cases vastly different. Thus women more often experience discontinuities and fractures that mark their lives and rob them of consistency. This makes it more difficult to establish an overarching biographical narrative. Furthermore, women are still regarded more critically than are men. Those women who carve out their own, independent path through life or who stand fast against established trends have often encountered particular difficulties. In Friedelind's case there is the additional fact that she took a stand against the reigning establishment in Bayreuth. There were times when her decision to leave Germany was seen merely as an outward act of inner rebellion against all conventions.[10] Her letters from exile were thus a symptom of 'sanguinary muddleheadedness', as her sister-in-law Gertrud once said.[11] But opposing opinions have also been offered in which Friedelind has been idealized into something quite different; according to some she was shipped off to 'various prisons and penitentiaries' and her personality was supposedly 'worn down or destroyed' by her mother and by her circumstances; she had also purportedly been subjected to 'psychological bullying, legal threats and financial coercion' in order to prevent her from publishing her second book (though in fact that book had never existed).[12]

The question remains whether it is worthwhile to document the life of a woman who can claim famous grandparents and great-grandparents, but who herself never ran a theatre nor achieved anything 'great' in the sense of some major historical act. But the stylization of significant people into 'heroes' is precisely what has often been criticized in gender research, and rightly so, because it ignores the many women who have acted in the background yet still achieved great things. In recent years there has been an increased interest in the social, everyday and historico-cultural aspects of a life. Friedelind's broad network of contacts, her fame, her friendships with important artists, her support for the young and the talented, her lifelong struggle to improve the quality of opera performances – all this makes her a fascinating person, one whose life merged with the political upheavals and events of her time. We cannot do her justice by merely casting a voyeuristic glance at the 'scandals' for which the Wagner family has long become known. All the same, any telling of Friedelind's life and work cannot exclude the struggles that went on for the directorship of the Bayreuth Festival, for the right to determine its future, for the inheritance of Siegfried and Winifred and for the rights of succession – struggles that time and again rent this large family asunder and were integral to her biography.

Friedelind's comprehensive archive was made available for the present biography and this access has allowed us to consider in detail the course of her life. The sources include letters, newspaper cuttings, her occasional journalistic work, lectures, drafts for her book, notes on the master classes in Bayreuth and Stockton-on-Tees, plans for her own opera group, quarrels with her family both legal and otherwise, and numerous photos. She kept everything. She was a passionate letter-writer – one of her letters, albeit admittedly in the very large handwriting for which she was always known – reaches no fewer than 34 pages in length. Sometimes she sat at her writing desk until three in the morning.

The task of the present biography was thus to take this mass of material and to filter out what of it had been of the most significance in her life. There were nevertheless serious gaps while reconstructing her story, for hers was a life that resists many of the usual categories. On the one hand she remained closely connected to the Festival that had so left its mark on her childhood and youth, but on the other hand she was an outsider who never really gained access to the inner circles of power. The contradictions in her character and in her life were deeply human ones, and they must not be ignored here. But who is to select what is significant, and with what intentions? The content and style of letters naturally depend on their addressee. They depend on their particular situation; the content of some may be overtaken by events shortly afterwards, or they may retain significance for the rest of a life. Is it not speculative to use them as a source of information? Is there not a danger that a biographer might slip into Friedelind's skin and adopt her dislikes and preferences? And, as someone coming long after the fact, is one not likely to try and harmonize this third-party life, to discover common narrative threads and to level out a conglomerate of assorted events so that a coherent picture results? Is there not a danger that the subject of a biography might have made a decision that his or her biographer regards as having been wrong, and that this might in turn lead the biographer to emphasize what intensifies criticism of the person in question?

It has long been acknowledged that historical material and oral statements can offer no direct access to historical reality and that all they say or report is itself constructed and filtered. Interviews with contemporaries of Friedelind sometimes resulted in contradictory reports.[13] It would thus be inappropriate to regard all sources as equally reliable. So however much the present interpretation of her life endeavours to locate the truth, it is nevertheless situated in a space between objective scholarly report and a representation that seeks to interpret what was real. We wholeheartedly agree with the words of the well-known literary scholar Peter von Matt: 'descriptions of history will never be able to exist without narratives.'[14]

Above all, what makes Friedelind a person of general interest is her direct family connection to Richard Wagner, whose work remains unendingly fascinating to this day. It is not just the sheer enjoyment of the music he composed that has allowed him to retain his undimmed popularity, but the multitude of interpretive possibilities in word, music and ideology that have occupied his adherents and his critics alike. The Festspielhaus and the ideas behind it – an incomparable venture undertaken by a single composer – further serve to confirm his unique status in western music and culture. The sunken orchestra whose sounds seem to emerge out of nowhere, the recourse to mythology in his opera plots, the mystic, cultic atmosphere – all this heightens the experience offered to those who attend his festival. The international media interest in the struggle for the Bayreuth succession in 2008 has shown that the name of Richard Wagner has attained a standing in our cultural life that is utterly without parallel.

At the same time, we can see clearly that the power struggles that began when Winifred took on the Festival have become far less subtle. This has consequences for Wagner's heirs. Friedelind engaged with Wagner's music at an early age, and it remained the prime determinant of the rest of her life. Whether she was planning performances, organizing master classes, giving lectures or supporting individual musicians: the music of her grandfather was always central to her undertakings, far more so than that of her great-grandfather, Franz Liszt, or of her father, Siegfried Wagner. She took on the role of Richard Wagner's granddaughter with gusto and made her commitment to his life and work the basis of her own livelihood in the USA. Later she also devoted herself to the work of her father, promoting it as best she could. The subjugation of Bayreuth to a nationalist, racist ideology in the end led to Friedelind's abandoning the place of her artistic dreams and was the reason why she never realized her greatest desire: to become an opera director. After the Second World War, her brothers ensured that she was completely excluded from the management of the Bayreuth Festival. And yet the master classes that she organized for several years launched major names into the theatrical world, thus proving her ability to recognize artistic potential and to promote it in the long term.

It remains for me only to mention an odd intersection of fate. When Friedelind was interned on the Isle of Man on 30 May 1940, she could not have suspected that one of the other women detained there on that same day was the pregnant mother of her later biographer. As the wife of a German pastor who had emigrated to England in 1930, Johanna Rieger had also been taken into custody. She was brought to the hotel next to that of Friedelind. The photos of the two women that were taken at the beginning of their internment show, in Friedelind's case, an open, almost inquisitive face, whereas the expression on my mother's face – she had three small children to look after and was expecting a fourth – is one of fear. Friedelind was taken to London two months before my own birth. She thus was never able to look into the face of the baby who many years later would go in search of her and commit her life story to paper.

Chapter 1

A 'giant Easter egg': Mausi's home and family

MUCH WOULD have turned out differently, had she been born a boy. Her dominant manner, her impulsive nature and her musical and artistic gifts made her stand out from her brothers even as a child – if she had been a boy, her pre-eminence among them would surely have been undisputed. Her 'bad luck', so to speak, was to have come into the world as a girl. Her grandfather Richard Wagner had in his day regarded his son Siegfried as the sole guarantor of the survival of his legacy, and Siegfried's birth had prompted an overwhelming sense of joy such as the composer had never before experienced. After the birth of his daughters Isolde and Eva, the birth of a male heir seemed to him to be an act of redemption and Siegfried was accordingly celebrated as a demi-god. 'O hail to the day that illuminates us, hail to the sun that shines upon us', cried Cosima Wagner, Richard's second wife, quoting the close of the opera *Siegfried* from the *Ring of the Nibelung*. Richard was going to build a house just for his son and he wanted him to have a wild, oat-sowing youth – quite in contrast to the staid fate intended for his sisters.[1] The birth of this son was immortalized in music in the *Siegfried Idyll*, composed by the proud father for Cosima and first performed on Christmas Day 1870. Siegfried Wagner, explorer, soldier, scholar, house owner-to-be: on his head rested all expectations, and the notion of a Wagner dynasty whose heritage was to be passed on from father to son (preferably the first-born) would continue into the next generations.

Siegfried abandoned any such notions when he left open the question of succession for all four of his children, even entertaining the possibility that Friedelind herself might become heir to the Festspielhaus (at least according to Friedelind's own recollection). Oddly, it was the women of the family themselves – first Cosima, then Winifred after her – who insisted on the male right of succession. They saw themselves as widows whom only sheer necessity had compelled to assume the mantle of Festival Director. But while Cosima retired from the post with dignity, Winifred would gladly have held the reins for longer than she did, even after the Second World War.

When Richard Wagner died in Venice in 1883, Cosima took on the directorship of the Festival on a provisional basis in order for it to continue. After two seasons had proven the finances to be sound, Cosima was ready to make her provisional directorship permanent. Her critics were highly sceptical about what she was planning – namely taking on the organizational, financial and artistic responsibility for a major cultural institution that could not be sure of receiving any subsidies at all. But Cosima was driven by the desire to give Richard's oeuvre the platform it deserved, and this helped her weather all storms. She had no ambition of her own, only to serve the work of her deceased husband. She held as firmly as possible to Wagner's own maxims, clad herself in a widow's black and sat in a concealed part of the auditorium from which she sent down little notes during rehearsals to suggest corrections. All this strengthened the idea of her as a medium, transmitting the wishes of 'Him' who really had the say in everything.

Yet Cosima was a good deal more creative than is usually supposed. In 1886 she designed the sets for *Tristan*, stipulated how it was to be lit and much else, basing her work on her experiences of the two productions that Wagner had himself overseen (in Munich in 1865 and in Berlin in 1876). Over and above this she engaged in an intensive study of the scores, giving much thought to both the stage design and the manner of singing and acting. In 1884, the conductor Hermann Levi wrote: 'The fact that this year's performances were so perfect is in large part thanks to the active intervention of Frau Wagner.' In the few days spent under her direction, he claimed, he had learnt more than in his twenty years as a conductor.[2] However, the finances remained precarious and Cosima survived thanks to help from a family friend, the banker Adolf von Gross.

After the performances of *Parsifal* in 1888, it could no longer be doubted that the Festspielhaus was now a stable, significant fixture on the German operatic scene. In 1891, Cosima produced *Tannhäuser* and, in the process, hunted out everything that had even a remote connection to the work. In 1894 *Lohengrin* was the next to be performed, and received good reviews in the press. *The Flying Dutchman* followed in 1901, and in 1906 Cosima staged a new version of her *Tristan* production. 'Behind the claim to authenticity there is in fact an individual style ... the history of theatre knows no woman who has achieved anything comparable in organizational and artistic terms, nor who has exercised anything approaching her great influence.'[3] In the course of 23 years of hard work, Cosima had succeeded in making Bayreuth a world phenomenon. Tens of thousands of visitors from Germany and from beyond its borders streamed into this little town to hear the music of Wagner.

At the same time, the 'Bayreuth circle' – a group of people whose stance was nationalistic, anti-Semitic and, generally, altogether racist – was busy trumpeting its ideology to the world. Cosima was a convinced anti-Semite and, although she participated little in the activities of the Bayreuth circle, she did not contradict the ideas they disseminated. All that mattered to her was the fame of her husband. She turned the festival into a kind of religious experience: a cult was erected around Wagner that ultimately turned him into a Messiah-like figure. The Bayreuth performances became acts of sanctification that were supposed to lead one into a realm of pure, uplifting 'spirituality' (and this despite the heady sensual impact of Wagner's music). The *Bayreuther Blätter*, the journal founded by Wagner in 1878, also did its part in emphasizing the magnitude and untouchability of Wagner's oeuvre. Thus Cosima shares with Richard himself the responsibility for shackling his achievements to a Germanic, ethno-conservative mindset that rejected industrialization and democracy as much as it idealized German nationalism; and in doing so, 'the Jews' were cast as guilty of the excrescences of the capitalist system.

It is hardly surprising that Cosima's daughters Daniela and Eva adopted this mendacious ideology. Michael Karbaum, one of the first to engage in a scholarly study of the history of the Bayreuth Festival, sees the heyday of the German nationalist Bayreuth circle as occurring between 1901 and 1912, and regards the 'Green Hill' itself as the rallying point of this reactionary grouping.[4] Like so many other Germans, Siegfried greeted the outbreak of the First World War with euphoria, composing an 'Oath to the flag' that he dedicated 'To the German Army and its leaders in enthusiastic gratitude'.

Heart problems caused Cosima to hand over the direction of the Festival to her son. It was no easy step for her, but she kept her stiff upper lip, refrained from meddling, and remained remarkably consistent in this attitude thereafter.

This was the environment in which Siegfried lived: surrounded by a strong-willed mother, two half-sisters (Daniela and Blandine) and two sisters (Isolde and Eva). He had originally wanted to study architecture and to this end moved to Frankfurt am Main, where Daniela had lived since her marriage and where he felt at home. But while he busied himself with his architectural studies, he was also travelling regularly to nearby Mainz for tuition in harmony and counterpoint from Engelbert Humperdinck. His fondness for Daniela shines through in his letters, which are humorous to the point of exuberance. Daniela was for him 'the most direct' link to his lover, Clement Harris. Although many a Wagner commentator has refused to believe it, it seems that she was well aware of the nature of their relationship, and she was possessed of a sense of humour herself. Thus Siegfried wrote to her on one occasion: 'Give little Clement my warmest greetings: during the days when I'm there, he should stay away from Parnassus as much as possible.' Siegfried was also on friendly terms with his mother's first husband Hans von Bülow and attended his concerts whenever the opportunity arose. Thus he wrote to Daniela in his typical mishmash of languages: 'If only your father would make better programmes! It was really empörend [shocking] last time, I am still quite dégouté [disgusted].' When she complained that he had not thanked her for sending him some music, he answered: 'You old Crocodil! [*sic*] What are you knausching! [being mean about] I give you a slap! Did I not thank you for the Missa Choir. If I did not, I'm a pig and beg pardon; it's already finished two days, also Lenau: Frühlings Tod [the death of spring]. Seiner süssen Schwester gewidmet. [Dedicated to his sweet sister] And if you are not yet pleased, I'll compose a symphonic poem: Daniela, your character-bild [picture].'[5]

In the course of time, Siegfried switched to music and became a conductor and composer – and then, as mentioned above, successor to his mother as the director of the Bayreuth Festival. The experience he gathered as stage director and designer meant he was well prepared for the tasks before him. In 1907 he took over the reins of Bayreuth with the goal of maintaining its position as a summer festival and he henceforth dedicated himself to directing his father's operas. He would receive much praise for his productions, especially for his use of lighting effects.

In 1913 the copyright ended on all of Wagner's works, meaning no more royalties. The outbreak of the First World War in 1914 then ensured that any thoughts of continuing the Festival were abandoned. And then another crisis engulfed Wahnfried when Isolde began court proceedings to establish her status as Wagner's biological daughter (although Richard's three children had all been born illegitimate, only Isolde was still officially a 'von Bülow'). Siegfried protected his own interests by opposing her and ensured that her desperate letters never reached their mother. Cosima was further sheltered from events around her by Eva and her husband Houston Stewart Chamberlain. Isolde lost – but never got over it. She died a few years later of pulmonary tuberculosis.

Since Siegfried was homosexual, the question as to who would succeed him remained uncertain for a long time. Only when his family insisted, did he decide he had to produce an heir. In the midst of the War he married a young English girl, Winifred Marjorie Williams. Her mother, Emily Florence, née Karop, was a half-Danish, half-English actress who had married the English writer and journalist, John Williams. Within eighteen months of Winifred's birth in Hastings in 1897, both her parents were dead and the orphaned girl entered a children's home. Its strict rules, combined with the apparently traumatic experiences she endured there, seem to have been the point of origin for the strange mixture of freedom and strictness that she later practised when bringing up her own children. Winifred's mother was a cousin of Henrietta Klindworth, the wife of Karl, a famous pianist, conductor and sometime friend of Wagner himself. Thus it was that Winifred was fostered by the Klindworths from 1907 onwards and later adopted by them. When Winifred was 17, Klindworth took her to the dress rehearsals at the Bayreuth Festival. This was where she first met Siegfried in early August 1914 just before the outbreak of the First World War and the Festival closed its doors for ten years.

Winifred was 18 and Siegfried already 46 years old when they married in 1915. Their big age gap – 28 years – reminds one of the gap between Cosima and Richard (24 years) and of the difference of 22 years between Winifred's own parents. Cosima was over the moon about her son's marriage. 'I think sometimes that I am dreaming when I see this graceful, youthful being walking at his side, brought up by our friend Klindworth in exemplary fashion, and bringing with her all the qualities that match Siegfried's person and harmonize with our house.'6 The balance in the relationship that Cosima seems to have seen between her son and daughter-in-law might have been in reference to their varied temperaments. Siegfried was friendly but shy of conflict, whereas Winifred was able to defend herself and put up a fight (traits that only gradually became obvious, however). It was a matter of course to her that her existence was to be geared primarily to serve her husband, just it had been for Cosima. 'My husband was more important to me than my children when they were growing up.'7

In 1917, Siegfried and Winifred had their first child: a boy, whom they named Wieland. To everyone's delight, Cosima went to the piano and played to celebrate the happy event. Bayreuth now had its long-awaited son and heir, for since Isolde had lost her court case, her son, the 16-year-old Franz Wilhelm Beidler, was in the eyes of the law no longer regarded as Wagner's grandson and was thus excluded from his inheritance.

One year later, when the First World War was still raging and its consequences were even being felt in Bayreuth, Wieland was joined by a sister. Winifred was taken to hospital by Dr Schweninger, the family doctor, on Maundy Thursday, 28 March, at six in the morning.8 The proud mother wrote from the hospital that 'the Easter bunny brought us a giant Easter egg on Good Friday at seven in the morning: a small, sturdy, red-cheeked girl weighing seven pounds and 300 grams. She is to be called Friedelind. I'm well, thank God – of course I'm lying out here in the hospital again and am mightily bored. But in eight days at the latest I'll be home again – I'll just have to bear it out till then!'9 One day later, Siegfried confirmed the happy news: 'On Good Friday at seven in the morning, Huschele's little sister Friedelind saw the light of day with a happy cry and little kicks of her feet. The mother is well. It all went a lot easier than the first time.'10 Engelbert Humperdinck received a postcard from Siegfried with a two-bar melody under which he wrote: 'A little girl has arrived.' And to this he added: 'On Good Friday, thus on the day when you wrote to me: I answer in B major! Friedelind is the name of the strapping little girl. Mother and child are well! Happiness reigns in Wahnfried! And happiness is something we need well enough in a world full of madness and hatred!'11

1 Winifred with the 'son of the muses', Wieland, who secured the succession, and Friedelind who was a year younger, born in 1918.

2 A family idyll: Siegfried with Wolfgang on his lap; Wieland standing; Winifred with Verena and Friedelind.

Siegfried also gave the name 'Friedelind' to the heroine of his opera *Der Schmied von Marienburg* that he was sketching at the time. Her name is derived from 'Friede', peace, referring to the yearning for an end to hostilities that was widespread at the time. In the family, however, she was soon called 'Maus' or 'Mausi' by everyone ('mouse'). The name stuck throughout her life, and is how she signed her letters to friends. Winifred took it upon herself to answer all the messages of congratulation that had arrived. The child's temperament was not long in showing itself: 'The little mouse screams Mama & Papa so much that she's quite hoarse by the time evening comes.'[12]

Wolfgang was born a year after Friedelind, and one year later came the fourth and last sibling, Verena. Their mother did not have much time left over for pampering and cuddling them, since she saw it as her duty to accompany her husband on his many trips. She loved to travel and often found life boring in 'Schilda', as Bayreuth was called in the family correspondence (after the mythical German town whose citizens are notable for their dull-wittedness).

The fact that the four children were all born in rather rapid succession meant that they played together a lot. They soon acquired the reputation of a 'gang of rascals',[13] always looking out for tricks to play on others. Friedelind seems to have slipped into her role as 'leader of the opposition' at an early age. In an undated letter, Winifred wrote of the christening (held for the first three children all at once) that 'Both boys were well behaved, but Friedelind commented on everything the vicar said, crying out "yes" or "no" and then calling out everyone's names! She doesn't seem to have much respect for the high clergy, because when it came to her own christening she stuck her tongue out at the vicar!'[14] This is actually reminiscent of Cosima's opinion of her daughter Isolde, with whom Friedelind would often be compared: 'Even today, I can still hear the laugh she gave when I returned home from my walk, at which she would sit up straight in her pram and neigh like a Valkyrie.'[15]

'The Germany in which I was born in 1918 was a chaotic, devastated land but Bayreuth, my own particular corner of it ... had suffered in especial ways. The Festspielhaus was closed. Singers and visitors alike had vanished.'[16] Thus Friedelind begins her memoirs, and it is not by chance that she mentions the cultural decline of her home town right at the start. Bayreuth remained a fixed point in her life, even later when she was the only one of Siegfried's family to take a stand against the Nazis.[17]

But 1918 was also a year of new beginnings. In Germany, a republic was declared and women were given the vote for the first time.

Right from the start, Winifred was enthusiastic for the goals of the German nationalists and the National Socialists – which might have been in part deter-

3 Wolfgang, Verena, Wieland and Friedelind (from left), in Wagner costumes
sewn by their Aunt Daniela. Friedelind got the role of quarrelsome Fricka.

mined by the fact that she early on became acquainted with Adolf Hitler in
the home of the Bechstein family. Acquaintance soon turned to admiration.
The desire for a real leader was one that she shared with many of her fellow
Germans, just as she held the same widespread opinion that 'the Jews' were to
blame for all the social, cultural and political evils of the land. Even after the
loss of the First World War and the ensuing economic crises, the dream of a
strong, nationalist Germany remained powerful in certain circles. The efforts
made to democratize Germany during the Weimar Republic were regarded by
many as doomed from the start. It is quite possible – as her granddaughter
Nike has suggested – that Winifred's feeling of rootlessness during her years
in the orphanage might have inculcated in her a fierce desire for stability that
extended for her to the political sphere.[18] According to Friedelind, Winifred
was attracted to everyone who spoke fluently and convincingly, and among the
men who fell into this category were Heinz Tietjen – who would later become
the artistic director of the Bayreuth Festival – and Adolf Hitler. 'Once she was
taken by someone, she remained completely blind to their faults and nothing
could change her opinion of them.'[19] Friedelind maintained that Winifred's

inability to recognize a person's character was the reason for the later discord between them.

Although Siegfried had a reputation for being apolitical, he shared his family's anti-Semitic leanings. Nor did he keep a discreet distance when observing his wife's ardour for the National Socialists in general, and Adolf Hitler in particular. He was concerned not to offend the Jewish visitors to the Bayreuth Festival, and for this reason remained uninvolved himself. But he gave his wife full rein to express her enthusiasms. As early as 1922 – when Friedelind was four – a local group of the NSDAP was formed in Bayreuth. And just a year later saw the famous handshake in Bayreuth between Hitler and Eva Wagner's husband, Houston Stewart Chamberlain. Chamberlain's writings had already made him one of the leading racial ideologues, and he took to Hitler with gusto.

Hitler was present when the annual 'German Day' celebration of the German nationalists was held in Bayreuth on 30 September 1923. He visited Wahnfried the following day, 1 October, and the reverence he showed to everything he saw was what one might expect from someone who had been a fanatical Wagnerite since his youth. August Kubizek, a friend of Hitler's in their younger days, later wrote of Hitler's admiration for Rienzi, the people's tribune in the opera by Wagner of that name. He also mentioned that Hitler had identified with the character and repeatedly attended operas by Wagner in Vienna. And Winifred Wagner reported that Hitler knew every bar of *Lohengrin* which, if true, suggests that his general level of knowledge of Wagner's oeuvre was indeed high.[20]

Although Friedelind was only five years old, she always remembered the first visit by Hitler that had meant so much to her mother (though she places it in spring 1923, whereas all other sources suggest that it happened in the following autumn, as described above). The whole family was present, she said, including two-year-old Verena. Wieland was allowed to skip school on account of the portentousness of the occasion. In later years, when she recalled that day, bitterness was dominant:

Looking back now ... I find it hard to realise that everything which has happened to me since stems directly from this short social call paid on the Wagners by a poor and practically unknown Austrian in a fancy dress outfit. I could not know at the time that this hungry-looking scarecrow would one day drive me from the very house into which he had just been hospitably received, tearing me from an existence which, by the accident of my birth, had afforded me a comfort and security denied to the average person, and in the process destroying all understanding

4 Friedelind (second from right) and Wieland (at the steering wheel)
with visitors, in 1924.

and affection between me and my family. I could not know that this man,
who on that day seemed like an opera buffo character, would eventually make an exile of me, drive me from country to country, in search
of a refuge; that he would dispossess me of all the precious things he
was then so obtusely admiring at Wahnfried; and that he would finally
condemn me to death for high treason and do his utmost to destroy
me.[21]

The Munich putsch took place a few weeks later. Hitler tried to organize a
coup to topple the government in Berlin, but failed and was instead arrested.
Siegfried and Winifred happened to be in Munich on the day for a Wagner
concert, and so were observers of the hullaballoo. Winifred gave the Bayreuth
branch of the NSDAP a summary of the events three days later. 'I let rip with
my soprano trumpet! A second Rosa Luxemburg!!' She knew full well that
she was publicly linked to Adolf Hitler, and she delighted in it: 'For me, the
9th November opened up a whole new field of activity, namely my passionate
support for Hitler and his ideas.'

Siegfried too was beside himself over the failed putsch. 'There has never
been such a despicable act of treason. But not even such pure men as Hitler

and Ludendorff are immune to such skulduggery.'[22] He saw Hitler's fanaticism as proof of his straightforwardness, and regarded him as the future saviour of Germany: the man who would restore the honour of the country. He was not just pleased that Winifred fought 'like a lioness' for Hitler: he found it 'grandiose'.[23]

Five days after the attempted coup, Winifred published a statement in the *Oberfränkische Zeitung* in which she confessed to having had an inner commitment to Hitler's work for years: 'This German man, who, filled with passionate love for his fatherland, offers up his life as a sacrifice to the idea of a purified, unified, nationalist Greater Germany ...' She praised his 'moral strength and purity' and stressed that she stood by him even in his present difficulties.[24] A victory for Hitler's party would also mean a victory for Bayreuth.

Indeed, Siegfried was well able to calculate how Bayreuth, too, would profit, if the Nazis were to grow in strength politically. Similarly, Hitler knew that the support of the Festival and the name of the Wagners would bring greater legitimacy to his cause.

The children were surrounded by people who were utterly convinced that Hitler was Germany's saviour: Chamberlain, Winifred, Siegfried, aunts Eva and Daniela, Hans von Wolzogen ('Uncle Hans'), their governess Lieselotte Schmidt and others. So it should not surprise us that the children soon shared their enthusiasm. One year later, a large-scale petition was launched from Bayreuth to demand Hitler's release from prison. More than 10,000 signatures were collected. It was even mooted that Hitler might be allowed to live in Wahnfried after his release.[25]

In 1924 Hitler was given a mild jail sentence that meant he spent only a few months behind bars. Winifred sent a woollen blanket, a jacket, socks, food and books to him in Landsberg Prison and organized a collection point for donations in kind, which she called 'love parcels for Landsberg'.[26] Nor did the children's aunt Daniela Thode make any secret of her enthusiasm for Hitler's cause and travelled to Munich to visit a wounded Nazi. After returning home she gave a report of her experiences in a Bayreuth restaurant. Chamberlain penned a message of solidarity in which he praised Hitler's purity and adjudged it 'a sign from God' that both Hitler and Ludendorff had survived the events of 9 November unscathed.[27] A copy of this message to Hitler, dated 1 December 1923, can be found among the correspondence of Winifred's friend Helene Roesener. It bears the names of Houston and Eva Chamberlain, Hans von Wolzogen, and Siegfried and Winifred Wagner.

Hitler's party had now been banned, but Winifred transferred her support to its new front organization, which called itself the 'Völkischer Bund' ('Nationalist League'). That same year, elections took place for the Reichstag and the National Socialists won a large share of the vote, joining the other nationalist parties in parliament. Hitler ascribed this electoral success primarily to the influence emanating from Bayreuth: 'I was seized by a proud delight when I saw the nationalist victory in the same city in which the spiritual sword was forged – first by the Master and then by Chamberlain – and with which we fight our battle today.' He could hardly have been clearer about how much his ideas owed to the inspiration of the 'Master'. The use of the sword metaphor allowed him an act of identification with Wagner's hero Siegfried: endowed with superhuman powers, he forges a sword (to the accompaniment of bombastic music) with which he overcomes all obstacles. Hitler continued by claiming that he had earlier hesitated to come to Bayreuth so as not 'to bring upon the house the enmity of those men under whose resentment your blessed father, the "Master" of us all, had been compelled to suffer so much' – which statement reminds us that he knew all too well the anti-Semitic writings of the 'Master'.[28]

In 1924, after the hyperinflation had passed, the Festival was opened again for the first time in ten years. For both financial and organizational reasons Siegfried was unable to present anything new, but everyone was satisfied to have revivals of earlier productions. Hitler came to the Festival in 1925, having now been released from jail, and as late as 1942 happily recalled this particular visit.

I really didn't want to go. I told myself that it would only make Siegfried Wagner's difficulties even greater, as he was somewhat in the hands of the Jews. I arrived in Bayreuth at 11 in the evening ... the next morning, Frau Wagner arrived and brought me some flowers. Things were really busy! There are lots of photos from that time that Lotte Bechstein took. During the day I wore my short uniform, and wore either an evening jacket or tails to the Festival performances. The free days were always wonderful. We drove into the Fichtelgebirge hills and to Franconian Switzerland. But otherwise, too, it was marvellous there. Even if I just went to the Eule restaurant, I straightaway had contact with all the artists. But at the same time I wasn't yet so famous that I didn't have any peace.[29]

Hitler's veneration for Wagner's works and his friendship with Winifred and Siegfried were a logical consequence of Wagner's own actions. For our purposes, we need only to sketch out in brief the direct links that exist between the composer and the ideology of the National Socialists. Wagner's legacy did not just comprise the cultural riches found in his operas which, with their recourse to myth and their appeal to all the senses, have continued to move and fascinate all subsequent generations of music lovers. Bayreuth also signified the dissemination of his ideas about 'Germanness', race and an exclusive German nationalism. Already in 1850 in his article *Jewishness in Music* Wagner had launched a diatribe asserting that people of Jewish descent were somehow biologically determined to be something 'other' and abnormal, and he had not hesitated to pepper his tract with numerous repellent details. In 1869 he had felt compelled to publish it again, in pamphlet form, even though Cosima's diaries make it clear she had been against the idea. Towards the end of his life, after having read the writings of Arthur de Gobineau on the primacy of the Aryan race, Wagner's own racist and German nationalist notions intensified and found further expression in his writings. He regarded his monumental oeuvre as a figurehead for an ethos that was both firmly (German) nationalist and anti-Semitic. His decision to derive his operatic topics from mythology – thus from the archaic origins of humanity – allowed him to touch deepseated emotions that were only intensified by his ability to sculpt his music to reflect their most subtle psychological ramifications. For most visitors to the Festspielhaus, all this made it into a temple of sensual pleasure and a source of intellectual debate. The composer believed that his oeuvre would be able to rejuvenate German art – indeed, his sights were set even higher, on the whole 'civilized world'. The Nazi's own newspaper, the *Völkische Beobachter*, recognized for its own purposes the relevance of his views when it declared that it foresaw the imminent 'practical fulfilment of the renewal of the German people in the spirit of Wagner'.[30]

In 1930, after the sudden, unexpected death of her husband Siegfried, Winifred Wagner was left to rely on herself. Her sisters-in-law regarded her as incapable of running the Festival. But just as she had helped Hitler in the 1920s, so he was now willing to help her. Her veneration for him outlasted the collapse of Germany, lasting beyond Hitler's suicide until the end of her own life, and she 'maintained her image of him as saviour resolutely and blindly'.[31] This utter misjudgement of historical facts, this lack of any personal sense of shame, was something for which Friedelind would never forgive her.

Chapter 2

The noisy child
1924 to 1931

WAHNFRIED MEANT HOME. Siegfried and Winifred spent time with the children whenever they were in Bayreuth, though they were often absent, travelling. Breakfast and lunch were eaten together and at 4pm there was afternoon tea, which was an extended ceremony following the custom of the English upper classes. Siegfried was good-natured and indulgent and, since he was barely involved in the upbringing of his children, he found Friedelind's cheekiness amusing, whereas Winifred's concern was to tame her rebellious daughter. Friedelind possessed a penetrating voice and knew how to use it, which soon brought her the nickname 'Krachlaute' (literally, 'racket'). Her brother Wolfgang wrote that she 'dominated with big words – often flippant ones', which 'amused my father, but often compelled my mother to reprimand her ... she always behaved flamboyantly and the volume of her voice alone drew the attention of all bystanders'.[1] This barely flattering depiction already hints at the close relationship between Friedelind and her father. The latter's liberal ideas of how to bring up children were different from the rigid notions of his wife, who was perfectly able to dole out corporal punishment and other punitive measures that Friedelind often had to endure. She was the only child to be smacked by Winifred, though it did little to change her.

Siegfried's easy-going attitude to his children was perhaps a reaction to the excessive supervision he had endured himself. The only thing that 'Mausi' could remember him forbidding her was cycling up the hill to the Festspiel-haus, for the simple reason that Siegfried thought it might damage her heart.[2] The children were even allowed to try out smoking, since Siegfried was convinced that they would then regret it – which indeed proved to be the case.[3] His strong-willed daughter instinctively sided with her father who, in turn, recognized her musical talent and her quick-wittedness and felt particularly drawn to her. 'My sister was a daddy's girl,' writes Verena. 'He loved her very much – her intelligence, her spontaneity, her cheekiness, her unchecked spirit.' If she came to table unwashed and with her hair a mess, he would whistle Ferrando's Cavatina from Act One of Verdi's *Trovatore* – 'A gypsy woman, terrible to see,' which had the desired effect: she would get up, laughing, and return untousled.[4] She liked to accompany him on walks in the countryside around Bayreuth, during which he would teach her French and English – languages that he spoke without an accent. He had even mastered Italian to the point

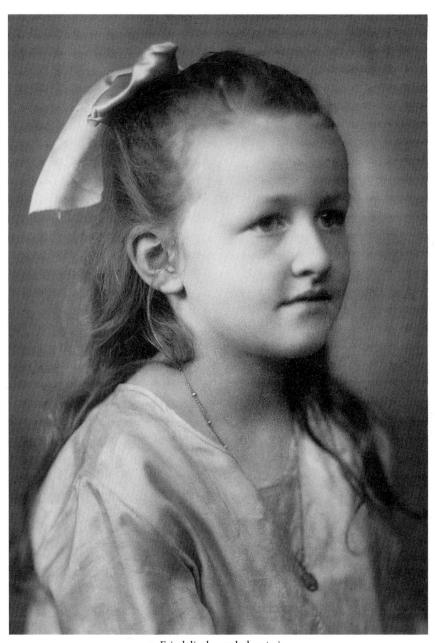

5 Friedelind, aged about six.

of being able to mimic dialects (he had, after all, often visited Italy with his father).

The Wahnfried villa, the family home, reflected the tastes of its creator, Richard Wagner. Innumerable objects were linked to his memory: furniture that he had designed himself, books that had been bound according to his instructions, letters that he had written and kept, mementos bought on his travels, portraits of him and his family, and a piano in almost every room. A screen featuring a parrot, embroidered by his first wife Minna, was especially prominent.

Whatever had a connection to Richard Wagner himself was treated as a relic. In the villa there were precious souvenirs kept under glass, scores were left open, two large portraits of Cosima stood on easels[5] – everything breathed history and tradition. In the centre of the house there was a large room, two storeys high with a marble floor covered in carpets. It had the air of 'something between a museum and an Egyptian burial chamber'.[6] The glass ceiling was so high that it formed part of the roof of the house, with the sunlight shining down through it into the salon below. Halfway up the walls was a gallery, and hanging underneath were oil paintings with images from the *Ring of the Nibelung*, all gifts from Ludwig II. Six marble statues on plinths, depicting characters from Wagner's operas, were also given by Ludwig. They were used at Christmastime to hang up pine wreaths. In the library, the silken wall hangings had been painted with flowers, and Aunt Eva once showed Friedelind the part of it that she had designed herself, though it had long since faded.

The cries of children echoed through the venerable old rooms of the house. Friedelind grew up in a wonderland of music, art and literature, her head full of stories of her forefathers and their traditions. The traces of this old world were still visible everywhere, and her grandmother Cosima was a symbol of her connection to it. The children were allowed to visit the old lady any time they wanted to, and she would tell them stories from Wagner's operas. They were often in her room, where they would gaze at the bust of their grandfather and play with Cosima, who frequently had to pretend to be sick so that they could nurse her. She laughed much with them, and when she asked Friedelind how it was at school and got the answer: 'I'm going to go to the humoristic Grammar School' instead of 'humanistic', she commented 'I hope it will always be that funny'.[7]

Concerned visitors to Wagner's grave in the garden were on occasion confronted by the frolics of four half-naked children. 'But Mrs Wagner, only poor children run about barefoot', Winifred was often told by horrified residents of Bayreuth when her children went about town yet again in clothes either torn or dirty, and no footwear. In her wildness, Friedelind most resembled her aunt Isolde – of that her aunts Eva and Daniela were sure. 'I send you a Loldi kiss, long and strong,' Cosima once wrote to Daniela, confirming the vigorous nature of her eldest daughter by Wagner.[8]

The old nanny, Emma Bär, looked after the four children. She allowed them much freedom and it was utilized to the full. Friedelind developed a mistrust of all authority early on, and so these first years were the most carefree of her life.[9] Since the name 'Wagner' was holy in Bayreuth, she grew up in the certainty of being something special. 'They tell anecdotes about the children as if they were the offspring of royalty in earlier days,' wrote one Bayreuth resident, who called Siegfried and Winifred 'The king and queen of Bayreuth'.[10]

Quite in contrast with her later self, Friedelind at this time showed a decidedly well-developed business sense. On the 400th anniversary of Albrecht Dürer's death she had collected hundreds of postcards and colour reproductions, and now hung them all around the walls of the gallery in the salon. She charged an entrance fee for those wishing to view them, got Wolfgang to man the cashbox, and organized guided tours. Verena took 10 pfennigs as a cloakroom fee. Friedelind shared her profit with her brothers and sisters, and they all went and bought *knackwurst* sausages at the market (because Winifred was at the time feeding them only vegetarian food).[11] In 1927, Wolfgang 'inherited' a chicken coop from his uncle Houston and began selling the eggs to his mother, with Friedelind this time given the task of treasurer. During the Festival, the children had the idea of fitting out a handcart with little benches, in which they offered visitors trips to Wagner's grave for 10 pfennigs a time. It proved quite popular, and one of their customers was Hitler's future propaganda minister, Joseph Goebbels.

The children enjoyed close friendships with those involved in the Festival, for at the time most of the artists stayed in Bayreuth for the whole summer. As an old man, the tenor Lauritz Melchior (1890–1973) still kept a photo of the four Wagner children who used to climb all over him in Bayreuth, and he remembered how their irreverence extended to shouting 'fatty pig' after him.[12] On the patch of grass next to their grandfather's grave, the four of them used to play football with children from town and in the process ruined the lawn, which Winifred had to have dug up and replaced. Friedelind liked to be the goalkeeper (presumably on account of her already being somewhat overweight). She also loved walking on stilts and was a master of the art of walking up steps on them.[13] The toy stove kept in the Wahnfried attic that could cook small meals did not interest her a whit.[14] She loved animals, however, and when the four children were each allowed to pick a pet dog from a litter, the others chose the strongest, while Friedelind took the runt. And when the family dogs produced a litter, she proved herself a first-rate puppy nurse.[15]

Wieland's later wife Gertrud Reissinger had got to know Friedelind in gym class at school, and described her as an 'elfish joker'.[16] The two girls became friends, and when Gertrud visited Wahnfried they would make fun of the family tea ritual. They sat in the dining room and, when Friedelind called down through the lift shaft 'Hey, Grete, what's for tea?' the lift would soon clatter up, with a tray laden with tea, milk, bread, buns, butter and jam. Friedelind would sit the two dogs of the house on the comfy armchairs, from where they would lick milk out of the porcelain cups and eat the buns off the plates, much to the amusement of the two girls. When one of the dogs was sick and refused to eat cod liver oil, Friedelind poured it over her pups, at which the mother licked them clean.[17]

'My bounding energy and unrestrained candour were always landing me in trouble,' Friedelind later wrote of herself.[18] Her 'big mouth', for which she became well known, was something she had in common with her brother Wieland. Both delighted in wordplay to the point of obscenity, not least in order to distance themselves from the Bayreuth residents whom they found terribly narrow-minded. Since she tended to put on weight easily, Friedelind's stockiness even as a child served to set her apart from her pretty, delicate sister Verena, and she sought to compensate for this with her high spirits and a get-up-and-go attitude.

As a young wife, their mother Winifred was hungry for adventure. She was depressed when Siegfried went away on his many trips and tried to find ways and means of accompanying him. 'I happily survived alone when he was in Danzig, but now I'm sitting here without a husband yet again ... I'll probably go along with him to Berlin because I can get away for a few days without having to wean the child. I'll pump out the milk and send it to Bayreuth in bottles. It's great, isn't it?'[19] An article that she tore out of the nationalist weekly *Die Sonne* in 1924, that she later sent her best friend Helene Boy (later Helene Roesener), was in praise of platonic love and presumably refers to the problems she faced on account of having a homosexual husband.[20] It was undoubtedly difficult for her to come to terms with Siegfried's sexual preferences.

But nor was Winifred herself a common or garden role model. She was a far cry from the supposed ideal woman, sacrificing her femininity for husband, household and family and was oriented more towards the image of the independent woman that became current in the 1920s. She took great pleasure in driving cars, in travelling and in getting to know new people and new places. Her sister-in-law Daniela once described her thus: 'She's young, quick, impatient and impetuous and all but laughs when one speaks in a way intended to appeal to the heart. Only what her intellect can comprehend has a chance of success with her.'[21] Winifred was attached to her children but had no desire to satisfy herself with the role of a demanding, enveloping mother. And so her offspring had to accept the fact that their mother was often away from home. At the same time, however, she could be domineering, even dictatorial – something that would often prove useful when she later had to run the Festival, but was bound to provoke resistance when dealing with a child as independent as Friedelind. As the 'undisputed sovereign lady of her household state, vast as it was, with all its many servants and the two cars … she was free and easy when young visitors called, and self-assured with the domestics that danced around them all. She could assume an assertive demeanour and knew how to use her powerful voice when she felt she had to. Half of Bayreuth could hear her when she called for her daughter Friedelind – "Mausi!"'[22] The fixed family eating times offer a prime example of how she united her strictness with a talent for organization. Whoever did not appear at 1pm on the dot was banished and had to be content with leftovers in the kitchen. The empty chair would then be given to the dog, the family schnauzer.[23] Winifred otherwise showed little interest in either the cult of bourgeois domesticity nor its emotional potential, but she did insist on taking meals together and on certain rules. Once she had to hunt for a new cook, and found one: 'a buxom woman who looks as if she might be able to keep that gang down there in order'; and she added 'whether or not she can cook is secondary.'[24]

In 1923, when Friedelind was five years old, the economic situation worsened and the period of high inflation began in Germany. The right-wing press began to agitate against the French occupying forces on the Ruhr. The Versailles Treaty was regarded as a great indignity and had imposed a harsh postwar economic burden on Germany. A feeling of impotence extended across all classes of society, and Adolf Hitler, with his rhetorical gifts, seemed to many to embody their last hope. When the annual 'German Day' was due to take place in Bayreuth that year, it was clear that Hitler would come and speak. Winifred stood at the entrance to the garden of Wahnfried in order to greet the participants as they marched past. Nationalist flags were waved, there was a parade on Castle Square, and that evening the Margrave's riding arena was fit to burst when Hitler spoke. He insisted on the 'authority of the personality' that must replace parliamentary democracy, and the idea sounded seductive to many.

As soon as he had finished his speech, Hitler drove to Eva's husband, the writer Houston Stewart Chamberlain who, with his abstruse theories, had helped lay the basis of Hitler's belief in the inequality of the races. Hitler was then offered an invitation to breakfast in Wahnfried, which he accepted. He arrived on 1 October 1923, but came – according to Winifred – as 'a reverential admirer of the German genius Richard Wagner, not as a political agitator.'[25] Nor would he have needed to agitate at all, for Winifred had long been in agreement with his political ideas. He was visibly moved when he viewed the relics of Richard and Cosima and the rooms where they had lived. Since childhood he had revered Wagner's music and had long succumbed to its addictive power. He identified with the heroes of Wagner's operas and found in them a parallel to the role he wanted for himself. He was received warmly and met Siegfried and the four children. Siegfried took a liking to their guest and offered him the familiar 'Du' term of address. 'Thank God there are still real German men!' he wrote about him. 'Hitler is a splendid man, a true example of the German folk spirit. He has to succeed!'[26]

In 1925 the Nazi Party was refounded after Hitler's release from prison. Winifred attended the first gathering in Munich, where Hitler spoke before an audience of 3000 listeners. Afterwards, 'Wolf', as Hitler liked to call himself, took her north in his new Mercedes to Plauen in eastern Saxony, where Siegfried was staying on account of a production of his opera *Schwarzschwanenreich*. Hitler wanted to thank him personally for his support. Because it was already late, Winifred suggested stopping off in Bayreuth on the way and spending the night in secret at Wahnfried, which they did. The unexpected death of Reichspräsident Friedrich Ebert the next day meant that the performance in Plauen was called off and Hitler had to leave. The children, infected by their parents' enthusiasm, now also began to call Hitler 'Wolf' and liked to listen to his stories. Arriving so late at night gave him a hint of something mysterious, and he embellished it all by telling the children how much danger he was in.

Shortly after this, Winifred and Siegfried visited Hitler in his small apartment in Munich, and he promised to come to the next Bayreuth Festival. This he did, seeing the *Ring of the Nibelung* for the first time that year. Later, when he was Chancellor, he would declare publicly that 'There is no more glorious expression of the German spirit than the immortal works of the Master himself.' Joseph Goebbels was also given a friendly reception when he visited Wahnfried in 1926. Winifred showed him Wagner's grand piano, his desk and assorted portraits of him while the children frolicked through the rooms. She seems to have complained about her husband, for Goebbels afterwards noted 'Siegfried is so limp. Ugh! He should be ashamed of himself before the Master.' He called him 'Feminine. Sweet natured. Somewhat decadent.' A few weeks later he had become friends with the children and noted in his diary that Friedelind (whose behaviour, Winifred claimed, was getting 'worse and worse'[27]) was in fact the most talented of the four: 'The oldest girl is the brightest ... march past in the afternoon. Flowers are thrown and people cry "Heil". Then I romp around in the hay with the Wagner brats. Such a delightful gang ... I have somewhat fallen in love with them.'[28] An undated photo from 1926 or 1927 shows Friedelind sitting on his knee.

For the eight-year-old Friedelind, a Siegfried Wagner Week held in Weimar was an event that remained unforgettable. The family travelled there in 1926 with a whole retinue of Siegfried's admirers. Besides a number of elderly ladies, these also included Friedelind's godfather Franz Stassen, who showed her around the museums in Weimar. She could in later years still remember the exciting atmosphere in the hotel, charged with expectation, surrounded as she was by the musicians, singers and guest conductors participating in the Festival. They visited Goethe's house in Weimar and also the court gardener's apartment where her great-grandfather Franz Liszt had lived. They rode on donkeys up to the Wartburg near Eisenach, the same castle that had inspired her grandfather Wagner to his *Tannhäuser*. Everywhere she looked, she saw the traces of her forefathers and was aware of being the heir to a great cultural heritage.

Friedelind's first ever school was in Bayreuth, where she was sent in 1924 – the same year in which the Festival had begun again after the hiatus caused by the First World War. 'With the reopening of the Festspielhaus in 1924 we children began to live in a fairy tale come true.'[29] She was fascinated by everything that happened on stage: she watched it, she mimicked it, she spoke with the artists, she mingled with them. She later claimed that from the beginning of this first post-war Festival to the day she left Bayreuth, she never missed a single performance or rehearsal unless it was absolutely impossible to be there. As the singer Anna Bahr Mildenburg had once remarked, 'The zeal and restlessness displayed in the work during those weeks before the Festival opens are incomprehensible to anyone who has not experienced it.'[30] The rehearsals with the singers had already begun a year in advance. Friedelind later wrote: 'We never had any doubts that our futures would also be totally absorbed, obsessed and dedicated to music theatre.'[31] Being both naughty and imaginative, Friedelind slipped under the curtain at the dress rehearsal of the second act of *Siegfried* to announce loudly to the perplexed audience that her father's next opera would be called 'The Cow's Tail'.[32] Once, when Daniela was making costumes for the children that were based on those for Wagner's *Ring*, 'Mausi' raced as Fricka through the garden – it was probably not by chance that Daniela had given her the role of Wotan's nagging wife.

Friedelind's first three years in school were to her liking. She went to a so-called 'seminar school' in Bayreuth that comprised four school years and was used for trainee teachers. In 1926, Winifred was able to write proudly to Grete Bie (the wife of the art and music critic Oskar) that 'Friedelind brought a fine school report home. 11 As + 4 Bs!'[33] But her delight was not long lasting. When

Friedelind's class was assigned an unfair teacher in her fourth school year, she protested, demanding to know why he didn't direct his spite at her, but instead at her innocent classmates. She also told him the answer: 'You know you wouldn't dare touch a Wagner.'[34] Despite her famous name, she insisted on being treated like everyone else.

Friedelind was made to repeat her fourth school year because of bad results, meaning she wasn't sent directly up to high school. This had a disastrous impact on her motivation. Instead of trying to do better, she spent her time annoying the teachers, which in turn prompted her mother to devise special punishments for her. But feeding her bread and water, sending her to bed early or withholding Friedelind's favourite things did nothing to break her rebellious will. Instead, this raft of measures merely nurtured a sense of enmity between mother and daughter that would become the foundation of their lifelong tempestuous relationship. The more the mother tried to subdue her refractory child, the wilder she became. '[I] dashed about with Verena (Nickel, we called her) on the handlebars and Wolfi on the back wheel of the bicycle, paying attention to everything except my homework.'[35]

When she was finally admitted into the 'Christian Ernestinum' grammar school, Friedelind found the syllabus undemocratic, for critical questions were frowned upon. The 'war guilt lie', as it was generally called, denied the sole guilt for the First World War that had been imposed as part of the Versailles Treaty, and it was emphasized at school in a one-sided, politically loaded manner that annoyed Friedelind. 'As always in Germany I was tormented by the feeling that I was being choked by a rope which was being tightened at both ends. The teachers complained; Mother was at the end of her wits ... again I was in open rebellion. My sessions at school became one long battle. The tension grew.'[36] According to Gertrud's recollections, Friedelind rapidly assembled a large band of followers at school, 'thanks to her aggressive, witty gift of the gab and her chummy affability'. Her gang of friends would go from school to the garden of Wahnfried, where they would play football. 'It was part and parcel of Maus's style of leadership that she didn't behave like "girls", but demonstrated the coarsest possible tomboyishness, including the expletives that went with it.'[37]

On her tenth birthday in March 1928, Mausi invited 15 children, her aunts Eva and Daniela and even her piano teacher, Miss Mann,[38] despite not being a particularly diligent pupil. Winifred praised Wieland, who could already transpose, and wrote 'Mausi is bone idle and for that reason fails to attain what the boy manages through a sheer sense of duty.'[39] Siegfried expressed it differently, however: 'Wieland is very musical. Mausi gets tempo diarrhoea and runs away with her crotchets. Verena sings sweetly and Wolf wants to learn the flute.'[40]

Winifred began to display a degree of helplessness: 'The brazen-faced Maus recently got an "F" in her maths. What on earth can one do with such a brat?'[41]

On 15 July 1929 Winifred drove to Munich with Wieland and Friedelind and then on to Marquartstein, a small spa town to the south, near the Austrian border and just twenty miles west of Salzburg. There Mausi was to spend the summer at the 'Landerziehungsheim', a grammar school for boarders. She later recalled her delight at the view from the castle in Salzburg itself.[42] The Landerziehungsheim was well known for its humanistic, liberal ethos, though Friedelind will hardly have noticed it at the time. She described the place as a 'holiday camp'. It is not quite clear why Winifred sent her there. Did she want to free herself for a while from the burden of an impertinent child? When a teacher took Friedelind to Munich to see a performance of *Lohengrin*, Winifred let her spend the night in the exclusive Hotel Excelsior, though gave her the name of a cheaper establishment where she should take her evening meal. Friedelind, however, insisted on eating in the pricey Excelsior where she downed a roast chicken with gusto – an early example of her later insistence on following her own will.[43]

Since the Nazi Party convention was taking place in Nuremberg on 4 August 1929, Friedelind was allowed a brief visit back to Bayreuth to attend the so-called 'consecration of the flag'. Her three siblings, their mother, their governess Lieselotte Schmidt, their housemaid Emma and Eva Chamberlain all set off at six in the morning and took up residence in the Deutscher Hof, next to Hitler's rooms. For the parade – which lasted four hours – they were given the best seats at the central market square. The general enthusiasm was palpable. Two days later, several leading Nazis came to Bayreuth, Goebbels among them. Lunch was provided for twelve people and afterwards everyone stayed and chatted for several hours in the main hall and in the garden. The Nazi elite and the Festival management were thus wedded together as closely as could be.

Friedelind was then shipped off back to Marquartstein, but in her letters gave such a desolate, mournful account of her homesickness that when Winifred and Siegfried left on a five-week trip that same August, they fetched her and let her spend part of her holidays alone with them – for her siblings were already on holiday by Lake Constance. Friedelind and her father wandered through the Bavarian and Tyrolean Alps, stopping off at country pubs along the way, and together they admired the spectacular views of the mountains. Friedelind enjoyed it all to the full, wishing that the summer would never end; these weeks were some of the happiest she had ever spent.

Back in Bayreuth, her problems with school resumed. Latin now appeared on the curriculum. So Mausi went on strike, spending her time devising new antics to annoy the teachers. The principal threatened to expel her. Winifred wanted to avoid any such scandal, and since she regarded the ability to speak English as more important than Latin, she and Siegfried agreed to send Friedelind to England for a year. Their plan was that she could then switch smoothly into the 'Lyzeum' afterwards, where a knowledge of English was a prerequisite. The otherwise obstreperous Friedelind found the idea of a trip abroad exciting, and it would not disappoint her.

In 1930 Winifred travelled with her to Cologne. There they met up with Siegfried, who arrived from Danzig. Together they travelled to the Channel coast, then across to England where Siegfried had concert engagements – first in Bristol, then in Bournemouth. The latter, he noted, was a place 'full of old spinsters with pinces-nez'[44] – which echoes remarks made by his father when conducting in London 75 years before, where he had been angered by the ladies in his audience ('Often you see a vast, luxuriant coiffure, with roses and curls, and in front of it a pair of spectacles on the nose'[45]). They stayed 'in the best gourmet hotel in London'.[46] Then Winifred accompanied her daughter to Brighouse in Yorkshire, a town of some 20,000 inhabitants, five hours by train from London. The lady principal of Brighouse High School, Miss Ethel M. Scott, had once been a teacher of Winifred's, and so Friedelind was given special treatment. She was allowed to live in Miss Scott's house and had free use of her letter-headed paper when she wanted to write home. Friedelind liked it there, and she learnt English with ease. One of her teachers recalled that she was a happy child, had many friends, loved to play jokes and had a healthy appetite. 'She was very pro-Hitler in those days and went about giving the Adolf Hitler salute, much to the amusement of her classmates.'[47]

It was a happy time for Friedelind. She did not suffer from homesickness, but wrote Winifred 'chirpy' letters: 'It's much better here than at home – I never have school on Saturdays and can always go away with Miss Scott.' For her part, Winifred was glad to be free of her: 'Scott is bearing a heavy load – and yet it seems to be working. I'm paying in total 100 marks a month for board and lodging – actually it's charmingly decent, isn't it?'[48]

When Cosima died on 1 April 1930 at the age of 92, it prompted international interest. She was already a legend. For the children it was an occurrence that had no real sense of tragedy, for their aged grandmother had long shown little will to live. She had become for them something of a lifeless character who was wheeled around in her bath chair. Cosima had instilled greater dread in the adults of the household, for she symbolized everything that was connected to the 'Master', around whom the whole Festival was centred. Be that as it may, Friedelind, so far away, felt a need to return home to attend the funeral ceremony.[49]

Siegfried suffered a heart attack just four months later, during a rehearsal of *Götterdämmerung*, and was already in a hopeless state when he arrived at the hospital. Friedelind was by now back in England, her siblings away on holiday, but she was the only one they fetched home, for they all knew how close she was to her father. But she would never forget her distress at being prevented from entering his hospital room – the doctors had forbidden Siegfried any kind of agitation. She walked up and down outside his room for days until she was finally informed that he had passed away. He was just 61 when he died, and his death was a heavy blow to her. She went to her Aunt Eva to seek comfort, and there met the conductor Arturo Toscanini. He embraced her and assured her that he would look after her. She never forgot his promise.

Siegfried's will named all four children as his heirs. He also appointed Winifred as Festival Director, but only for as long as she did not marry again. The day after his death, Winifred was already back at her desk, now doing the work of two and determined to continue with the Festival. 'Wolf' had presumably given her his blessing, which would have imbued her with both self-confidence and a sense of security. In 1930, the year of Siegfried's death, the Festival that he had prepared was a success, both artistically and financially. Winifred then plunged with renewed vigour into planning the Festivals for the ensuing years.

Friedelind now had no father to protect her and at times felt ostracized. According to her sister, she remained inaccessible to all endeavours by their mother or siblings to comfort her, to caress her and to draw her into the family.[50] After Cosima's death the children were given the rooms that her staff had occupied. Friedelind and Verena now moved into a room with biedermeier beds and a white four-poster bed hung with white gauze. The children's main room was furnished with desks, a piano, a couch, comfy chairs and a table with enough spaces for guests. Friends were now allowed to visit more often in order to provide company for the four fatherless children. Winifred set up her 'command centre' on the ground floor and from there she organized everything, wrote letters and had meetings with the staff.

In 1931 Winifred organized her first Festival. The flood of work that this brought upon her meant that she still had little time to bring up her children. Thus they were often left to their own devices and, as the soprano Frida Leider recalled, no one was able to instil any kind of order among them. 'Wagner's four grandchildren knew no discipline in their lives and with their antics they were as popular in Bayreuth as we singers were.'[51] Furtwängler's secretary Berta Geissmar had similar experiences: 'No one was safe from them, and no one knew what they would do next ... I always had a lot of time for "Maus", as she was called. Her contradictory spirit, her quick wit and her natural musicality attracted me. She was twelve years old when I came to

Bayreuth for the first time and she was the naughtiest, most amusing child that one could imagine.'[52]

They swam, they played tennis, they read aloud, they read in bed, they argued about who could practise the piano first, and often they listened to newly released records – such as a *Tannhäuser* issued in February 1931. 'The children listen reverently,' wrote Lieselotte Schmidt.[53] They went to concerts – such as a piano recital by Elly Ney – and also went now and then to the cinema. The children learnt to take photos and often visited friends or invited them back home. One favourite game was called 'picture guessing': Wieland would show them a painting from a book on art history and they had to guess the artist. At Ascension they drove to the Riemenschneider exhibition in Würzburg. Their holidays were spent in Nussdorf by Lake Constance, where Winifred had bought a house near the water's edge and where she was able to take time to have the children just to herself. After breakfast the children would race down to the lakeside. They spent two happy weeks there again after the Festival was over.

In these years, the children experienced their mother as a strong woman who knew how to run the household with a firm hand, in control of all its minor organizational details; she typed innumerable letters herself and was often travelling away from home (on one occasion, after having to go to Milan to negotiate with Toscanini, it took her 24 hours to reach Berlin by train). 'Tonight we're expecting Mummy, then things will be lively once more and she'll no doubt bring a pile of work with her again,' wrote Lieselotte.[54] Winifred probably found release on her travels, but they were also undoubtedly undertaken out of a sense of duty, as she needed to put the Festival on a proper footing. She was in urgent need of a professional adviser, for there was uproar in the press. The 71-year-old Karl Muck had resigned, and Winifred had instead called upon both the conductor Wilhelm Furtwängler and Heinz Tietjen, the General Director of the Prussian State Theatre in Berlin. Muck had decided to take his leave from Bayreuth after Siegfried's death, but it was rumoured in the press that in fact he had withdrawn because he was against engaging Toscanini for the Festival. Hitler took an interest in all the goings-on at Bayreuth and was horrified at Muck's withdrawal. 'Yesterday afternoon Wolf was with me from 3 to 6 – he is so beside himself because of Muck that he wants to go straight to him – but it won't achieve anything!!!' wrote Winifred,[55] and Lieselotte wrote to her parents that: 'It is so interesting to be right at the source of things. Frau Winny is so sweet. I saw the comments in all the papers – some stupid, others spiteful.'[56] Winifred remained undeterred by the flurry of concern in the media – a trait that her daughter would obviously inherit from her.

In Tietjen, Winifred gained a manager whose position at the head of the Prussian State Theatre gave him the advantage of ready access to a large number of artists and technical personnel. He closed down the progressive Kroll Opera in Berlin in 1931, presumably because the Nazis saw it as a 'communist-Jewish cultural institution' and had protested loudly against it.[57] His virtuosity in adapting his stance according to where the wind blew was something for which Friedelind would later detest him. But the final rehearsals for the 1931 Festival were proceeding well. No new productions were planned, though there was still much that had to be organized. Furtwängler was rehearsing *Tristan*, Toscanini *Parsifal*. The children spent every free minute they had in the Festspielhaus. On their mother's birthday they presented her with money from the period of hyper-inflation, wrapped up in various envelopes and bearing witticisms such as 'for purposes of debt repayment'. Two concerts were organized for the first anniversary of Siegfried's death, one of which was conducted by Toscanini. In a morning matinée, Friedelind demonstrated her increasing musical prowess in an arrangement of the *Siegfried Idyll* for two pianos in which the other part was played by the répétiteur Karl Kittel.

Winifred was delighted with the landslide victory that 'Wolf' had won in the elections of September 1930. In order to avoid gossip, they did not greet each other officially at public events, but he already practically belonged to the family. He sent large bouquets of carnations when Wieland and Friedelind were confirmed, and this prompted a flurry of tittle-tattle as it was assumed that they must be for Winifred. Whenever possible, he and the family came together. When Hitler announced that he would be attending a meeting at the Hotel Behringersmühle near Bayreuth in May, the whole family went along on the hour-long drive that took them there. 'He did not talk a lot at first, but you could see how above all it was seeing the children again that he found almost moving, for they idolize him and he is very fond of them … he was sweet-tempered when the children took photographs of him from just about every angle.'[58] Winifred felt that Hitler enjoyed their company precisely because he barely had anything like a family himself.[59]

Friedelind's weight problems meant she had to spend three days in a sanatorium in Jena and after that she was transferred to the head of the University Medical Clinic, Professor Veil, to whom she developed a deep aversion. Years later she claimed that he had diagnosed her incorrectly with a 'fatty degeneration of the brain'.[60] He then moved Friedelind – now almost 14 years old – to Wiggers Sanatorium in Garmisch-Partenkirchen, where she was to spend two months. Contrary to her expectations, she rather enjoyed her stay there. She was the only child in the clinic, so she made friends with the adults, went skiing and on other excursions with them, and shared the giant cream puffs that they ate up on the alpine pastures (they were so huge that there was always something left over for her). She wrote to Gertrud that she hadn't yet thought about what she wanted as a confirmation present: 'We'll surely get hymn books from our aunts!' Then she turned to politics: 'I still doubt whether Hitler will come to power now. The right-wing parties aren't yet united. They all want to put forward one man. But Hindenburg won't be up top for that much longer. I don't know if I'm being too pessimistic! But I would be wildly happy if he [Hitler] succeeded.'[61] She would have liked to take a ride up the Zugspitze mountain, but didn't dare spend the 25 marks that was the price of a ticket for fear of the maternal anger it would provoke (her weekly pocket money at the time was just 50 pfennigs). She fulfilled her wish a quarter of a century later.[62] On the journey home, she wrote, she would stop off in Munich and visit the Braunes Haus, the 'Brown House' that was being renovated as the party headquarters of the National Socialist party. It was a sign of her independence, but also of her continued enthusiasm for the Nazis.

Chapter 3

'She should learn to cope with drudgery'
At boarding school
1931 to 1935

'I WANT TO DO half an hour of maths with Maus. It's urgent because of the schoolwork she's facing. She simply doesn't want to. But after a strenuous exchange I leave the field as victor (which is quite something when you're up against Maus) and we plod through it for three quarters of an hour.'[1] According to her governess Lieselotte Schmidt, Friedelind either didn't do her homework at all, or 'at best, five minutes before the deadline'. These problems could be overcome, as in this case. But what really bothered Friedelind so much about school was the manner in which knowledge was presented. Years later she had nightmares when thinking back to her school years in Germany, whose education system seemed to her the epitome of 'narrow-mindedness, intolerance, dogmatism. It was a systematic act of poisoning everything beautiful. Hate and revenge were the basic tenor of almost everything in school education after the First World War.'[2] Even if one has become accustomed to Friedelind's turn of phrase, her vehement dislike of school remains striking.

Mausi's annoyance at her teachers finds expression in a letter written in 1931 to a 15-year-old girl who had asked for more information about her.

I am 12 years old and I'll be 13 in March. As you will know, I've not got what you'd call a slender figure. I attend the girl's Lyceum here in Bayreuth. We call it the 'broom cupboard' because it's full of apes, though I don't count myself among them ... We've also got the most stupid teachers that exist. Our class teacher looks like a witch and she is one too, because she's dreadful to us and no one likes her, she's even at loggerheads with the other teachers. Well, I don't want to describe all the teachers, because it wouldn't interest you. Singing classes with Prof. Kittel are the nicest, and we all like him too ... But now I have a request: don't address me as 'Sie' [the German polite form], but as 'du', which suits me much better, and I prefer it by far. And don't write 'Miss' ['Fräulein'] to me, just 'Dear Friedelind'. I've got nothing of a 'Miss' about me, so the title doesn't fit at all.[3]

These lines tell us much about her general attitude. As if able to muster strength from her contrariness, she self-assuredly lists her two deficits ('not what you'd call a slender figure' and 'nothing of a "Miss" about me') and thus both commands appreciation and confirms her self-esteem. It was probably this same confidence, worn on her sleeve as it were, that sent many a teacher into a rage. But Friedelind's life was hardly easy, for she had to endure much teasing. While Verena was regarded as a beauty by everyone, Friedelind suffered from being overweight. She drew strength from the belief that she was part of a special tradition and destined for great things.

This belief was fostered from childhood onwards. Thus the family asset manager Albert Knittel once wrote to her: 'Think on your duties to the house of Wahnfried, to Siegfried Wagner's heritage. Stay true to it in your actions, just as outwardly it has found in you its fullest manifestation.'[4] Such a sense of moral duty, instilled at an early age, was bound to leave its mark on her identity. Whereas the other children of famous parents often drifted into crises, Friedelind veritably grew under her burden. She was artistically gifted and keen to learn, but she still came into conflict with the school system because it did not allow her abilities to shine. It is a common phenomenon that creative people are often bored at school and compensate for it by playing pranks or provoking conflict. Only with difficulty are they able to adapt to their circumstances. Punishment has little impact on them and can serve to increase their contrariness.

Friedelind's weight problem remained with her throughout. During her childhood and youth she was repeatedly sent off to lose weight. This gradually accustomed her to being wrested out of her home environment at regular intervals. Perhaps this was also partly responsible for her later restlessness. While she was packed off to a diet clinic in Garmisch-Partenkirchen her siblings were allowed to stay at home, trying out the radio set that was their latest source of entertainment. But since Friedelind was absent, she at least did not have to sample the delights of the latest puppet play by 'Uncle Hans' (von Wolzogen). It was called 'Princess Bulette' and was written for Wolfgang. A milkmaid loves her boyfriend Peter, 'but then a disgusting Jew turns up, whom she sends packing with a box to the ears. Kasperle then offers an epilogue that closes with "Heil Hitler".'[5] Thus the children were systematically fed Nazi ideology. And since they loved their Uncle Hans, his influence on them was considerable.

Hans von Wolzogen (1848–1938) had been brought to Bayreuth in 1877 by Richard Wagner and had become a friend to three generations of the family. Posterity knows him as the governing authority behind the Bayreuth ideology, though he had based his own beliefs on those of Wagner. Von Wolzogen edited Wagner's journal, the *Bayreuther Blätter*, penning many articles for it himself.

The family was looking forward to Friedelind's return. 'She was quite an angel! Is it because of the 23 pounds she lost?' asked Lieselotte, who found her slender and pretty.[6] When Franz Stassen invited the children to visit the German Museum in Nuremberg, Verena and Wieland respectfully declined. But Wolfgang and Friedelind accepted gladly and spent three hours in the Museum without getting bored. 'Afterwards they ate with us at the Württemberger Hof and were as well-mannered as they were polite. They had the greatest fun at the zoo,' wrote Lieselotte.[7] When she wanted, Friedelind could fit in perfectly.

The children began the new school year with appropriate enthusiasm, and even Friedelind – who had to repeat a year – worked punctually and hard. To Lieselotte's astonishment she had become unusually polite, 'perhaps it's thanks to her time in the clinic?' When they attended a song recital with Gunnar Graarud in April and Friedelind saw the title 'Prometheus' by Schubert on the programme (a name otherwise familiar as an electrical goods manufacturer), she asked if that was a vacuum cleaner. 'She's hilarious,' wrote Lieselotte, who remained ever able to appreciate Friedelind's witty side.[8] But her 'polite' phase did not last long before her wilfulness came to the fore again. In confirmation classes at church she wore a swastika necklace in order to annoy the vicar, who was a social democrat. Her mother had arranged classes for her during her stay in Partenkirchen, but she had skipped them and Winifred had to exert much pressure on the Bayreuth vicar to have Friedelind confirmed despite her lack of knowledge. Friedelind protested, declaring that she wanted to be sent away from Bayreuth to another school. It would have been wiser for her to hold her tongue, for Winifred took her at her word and promptly went looking for a new boarding school.

In early May 1932, Winifred rang home from Plauen, asking Lieselotte to arrive at Berneck by nine in the evening. The 'Führer' wanted to meet them. The 13-year-old Friedelind said in the car on the way: 'If Goebbels is there, let's chat him up properly, so he doesn't think he's the only one in the Party who's got a mouth on him!' At 9.30pm two cars arrived with Hitler, Goebbels and his wife, and several other Nazis. Hitler had not seen the children for a year and gossiped with them for a long time. Then he drove off with Winifred, who presumably took the opportunity to tell him about her concerns in Bayreuth.[9] Despite her protestations after 1945 there can be no doubt as to the extent of Winifred's engagement with politics, as we can see from a letter written to Helene Roesener during the Festival just a couple of years later:

Hitler left at 9 this morning. The last thing he did was to place flowers on the grave. He was very happy here and the same as ever – he asked about you and reminisced about being in Würzburg with you!! – He is utterly enthusiastic about the performances and wants to help me financially wherever and whenever he can. He was thrilled with the extension to Wahnfried. Yesterday afternoon he was *en famille* with us (Heinz dodged it, sadly), he stayed until four, had Verena photographed etc. In the evening I had all the soloists at home – a cold buffet and all the usual hullabaloo – he came along too – he was touching with them and gave a proper lecture about the new production of *Parsifal* etc. etc. I think I have pulled off a complete victory and the aunts are out of it!!! – He quickly made sure – without my asking him – that Pretzsch was removed from the *Fränkisches Volk* (newspaper), where he was making trouble, toeing the line of the aunts. Daube will now report on the Festival. Lovely, isn't it? – he's living in the house on the Parkstrasse where Heinz stayed in 1931 – and he liked it so much that he is thinking of buying it so that he would have a permanent apartment in Bayreuth. With me he was the same as ever.[10]

The children were fed 'German' culture. A car trip that Winifred made in May at Whitsuntide was presumably intended to serve educational purposes. It began in Würzburg and continued in Wertheim and Miltenberg, where Lieselotte shared a double bed with Maus. 'That's huge fun for us both every time,' wrote the governess. In Amorbach they went on a hike to the Wildenburg, which had, at one time, been the knightly seat of Wolfram von Eschenbach. They visited the castle in Heidelberg and in Karlsruhe went to a performance of *Rienzi*. The next day they were in the museum to see 'the Thomas and the Feuerbachs'.[11]

Winifred travelled much, causing considerable commotion wherever she went – though her relationship with Tietjen perhaps played a role in this. It did not go unnoticed that she was much happier whenever he came to Bayreuth to hold rehearsals.[12] She often felt that she was stagnating in Bayreuth and so she accepted many invitations elsewhere, as she wrote to Helene Roesener:

Hoesslin was here on Thursday and Friday – yesterday it was the Benckers and today I'm expecting Edwin Fischer, who has a concert on Tuesday. On Thursday I have to dash to Chemnitz to the founding of a local Wagner society and on Friday to Würzburg, where Zilcher has a lecture at the local society on Goethe and music. And then we'll see each other in Heidelberg![13]

Yet she still had to find time to carry out her organizational tasks as Siegfried Wagner's successor.

Heinz Tietjen was now appointed Friedelind's guardian. Since she did not like him, it came as a shock to her. Verena recalled his malign influence many years later, maintaining that he had played them all off against each other. 'That split the family.'[14] But Winifred did not yield, and her elder daughter had to accept her *ersatz* father for good or ill. Her autobiography has barely a good word to say about him: 'In no time at all he had Mother in his pocket and the entire staff of the festival by the ears.'[15] Tietjen took Friedelind's friendship with a girl called Susi Wieger as an opportunity to accuse her of lesbian tendencies. 'I hope that Heinz is wrong in supposing that the child, Maus, is sexually abnormal!' Winifred complained to her friend Helene, 'It would be too abominable – but irreversible. Her behaviour is strange, after all.'

It was also Tietjen who convinced Winifred to send Friedelind to a school with a particularly rigid regime. 'Mausi is behaving so scandalously that Heinz insists on her being sent to a very strict boarding school after the long holidays,' she wrote. 'I'm looking for something in Dresden after the manner of the 'Englische Fräulein' so that she can learn a bit about cosmopolitan manners. She has no idea about it yet – but it *has* to be – things can't go on like this.'[16] She had given her children a very liberal upbringing, but in her sense of helplessness she was now lurching to the other extreme. Nor did she only call on Tietjen to help with Maus, but Albert Knittel too – another man to whom Friedelind had developed a deep aversion. This time it was on account of a scandal that Friedelind had set into motion. She had discovered nude photos that Wieland had taken of his girlfriend Gertrud Reissinger. But instead of showing them to her mother, she decided to use them 'to score a victory against her mother and "Heinz" who had inveigled his way into her father's bed', as Gertrud recalled several years later.[17] So Friedelind gave the photos instead to the head of the local Bund Deutscher Mädel (the 'BDM', the girls' equivalent of the Hitler Youth). She in turn promptly expelled Gertrud from the Bund. In fairness to Winifred, it must be said that she took Gertrud's side when it all came out. She even allowed her to continue seeing Wieland.

Winifred and Knittel now travelled together to look at the boarding school in Heiligengrabe, some 50 miles north-west of Berlin, halfway between the capital and the Baltic coast. The school uniforms, its strict daily routine and its nineteenth-century ethos of discipline and order will have been obvious, so on a subconscious level they must have intended it as a punishment for Friedelind. 'She is a strange child and a source of great distress to her mother,' wrote Lieselotte on one occasion.[18] Friedelind was a hyperactive, strident, disobedient child. But she was also imaginative, lively, highly interested in artistic matters, and talented too. So putting her in a strict, spartan convent school such as Heiligengrabe, with its insistence on submission and knowing one's place, can only have been intended to break her will – with force if necessary.

Before her departure, however, Friedelind enjoyed another carefree summer at Lake Constance with the rest of the family. After breakfast they went swimming in the lake. They also learnt to row, sailing off in all directions. Hans von Wolzogen was sent a postcard showing Friedelind in her confirmation dress: 'This [photograph] was made at home on Sunday. I was under orders to wear my confirmation dress, so it looks rather ...!' She drew a swastika underneath and wrote 'Heil Hitler!' next to it.[19] In September 1932 she was then packed off to what she later described as 'Germany's most reactionary school ... in the darkest reaches of Mark Brandenburg'.

Heiligengrabe lies in the Prignitz region of Brandenburg, between Wittstock and Pritzwalk. Even today it lies almost hidden, for it is situated in a hollow off the beaten track, surrounded by trees and fields and at some distance from the two main roads. It had been founded in the thirteenth century as a Cistercian convent and had once been a well-known place of pilgrimage. Its history was turbulent. After the Reformation it was turned into a Protestant convent and was for many decades a school for daughters of the nobility from the estates of Pomerania, Mecklenburg, Silesia and the Mark. In 1930 the school was still primarily an educational establishment for the female aristocracy and in its ethos was rather like the old military schools that had since been dissolved. It was slow to accept teachers and pupils from the upper echelons of the bourgeoisie. A sense of duty, readiness to help, subordinating one's needs to those of the group – that was the Prussian system to which the Wagner family's prime individualist was now to be subjected.

The strict regime in Heiligengrabe was a real burden to a girl as independent-minded and unconventional as Friedelind. We can get an idea of its atmosphere from reports of similar schools from the nineteenth century, or from German films such as *Mädchen in Uniform* ('Girls in uniform', 1931, with two remakes in 1950 and 1958), or the play *Ritter Nérestan/Gestern und heute* by the German-Hungarian writer Christa Winsloe ('Sir Nérestan/yesterday and today'), premièred in Leipzig in 1931 and produced in Berlin in 1931. Winsloe also adapted the topic for a novel published in Amsterdam entitled *Das Mädchen Manuela* ('The girl Manuela'). Her autobiographical account of the time she spent at the Empress Augusta convent school in Potsdam makes it evident that she was drawing on her own experiences:

> In dark, heavy dreams I find myself there again, wandering around in the long white corridors, woken from a deep sleep by the shrill bell and by commando-like voices. Attending prayers while hungry, hurriedly

gulping down a watery cup of cocoa – I feel once more the sense of strid-
ing along in rows of two, always afraid of being stepped on from behind
or of stepping on the feet of the girl walking ahead of me. Those empty
Sundays return to me, where we would seek out the strangest nooks just
to be alone or with a friend for just one, single time.[20]

Reports written by the pupils of Heiligengrabe correspond to Winsloe's scenario. There were 80 girls at the school. The strict discipline began with the
ritual of kitting out after they arrived. Any and every visible hint of prettifica-
tion or vanity was expunged. Mothers were instructed to have numbers sewn
into their girls' underwear, and these served instead of names. 'You were a
number, embedded in a larger whole into which you then had to merge, and
you were not to oppose it', recalled another former pupil.[21] Because of her full-
ness of figure, Friedelind did not have to wear a worn, second-hand uniform,
though she found her new dress no less awful for it. Over this the girls wore
an oversized apron made of alpaca wool. It was used to wipe away excess
ink when writing and was put aside during mealtimes. It was tied around
the waist, which at least allowed a semblance of feminine form. The bluntly
tailored, unpleasantly coloured, red-blue chequered uniforms were called
'blood sausage dresses' or 'sacks' by the girls. In the summer they wore green
cotton dresses, in winter woollen dresses with thick grey socks underneath.
On Sundays they wore blue skirts with elastic waists and black-and-white
striped blouses that were too big and generally unprepossessing. The school
brooch was important – whoever forgot to wear it was given a black mark
in their house report. Three such marks brought a reprimand that entailed a
severe talking-to. Since the abbess had once been a lady-in-waiting at court,
royal etiquette was practised: 'You entered the holy of holies that was the Lady
Abbess's room with a deep curtsey, you remained at an appropriate distance
and afterwards left the room backwards with a similarly deep curtsey.'

Friedelind did not sleep in the dormitory but in a tiny cell that they called
the 'Mausloch', the 'mouse hole' or 'Liliput'. It was the only such room and had
just two beds in it, which was a sign of her privileged status. She lived there
with another girl who later admitted that she had been put there 'to keep an
eye on her'.[22] Letters were received while giving another deep curtsey. Those
sent by members of the opposite gender were opened before being handed
over. As for outgoing mail: only letters sent to parents were allowed to be
sealed by the girls. Everything else was read before being sent.

The 'merciless pealing of a cowbell' was what the girls heard first on a
morning. Breakfast was at 6.55 and was a piece of black bread with malt coffee.
The girls had their weight checked every week. If they had lost weight, they

were sent to the soup table in the morning to eat a large bowl of porridge. Food parcels from home were only allowed on birthdays. 'Then we had fruit salad in the dormitories that we ate out of our washing bowls and we told wonderful tales about our lives at home – about horses, hunting and our big brothers.' After breakfast they got ready for the inspection of their sleeping quarters. It usually smelled bad because their clothes were rarely washed. 'Changing our collars was the job of Dippi, the woman with a limp and a lisp in charge of our clothes, but this was unable to prevent the smell of pubertal sweat emanating from the girls.' The woman in charge of the dormitories was greeted with a curtsey. She then assured herself that they were wearing warm underpants and clean shoes. The washing room next to the dormitory was unheated and had tin bowls at which the girls stood in their panties. Lessons began at 7.45 and break-time saw bread and cocoa served. At the beginning of the school year the girls were allowed to stipulate how many slices they wanted and whether they wished them to be accompanied by sausage, butter, ham or lard, and this enabled a busy exchange to take place during the rest of the year.

Lessons lasted for five hours, after which they returned to their dormitories to exchange their 'morning horrors' for their afternoon attire. Then they were let into the dining room. Once all the girls were at their places one of them called to the Abbess: 'Lady Abbess, the meal is served!' The girls curtseyed when she entered, then she sat at the head of the table on a comfy chair decorated with petit-point embroidery. Lunch largely comprised potatoes. Only on Sundays did they get any meat; there were never any eggs, nor was there milk or fruit. After lunch every pupil had to curtsey before the abbess as gracefully as possible so that the hem of her skirt was extended to its full breadth. On Sundays the mattresses were turned, the bed linen changed and the cupboards tidied. The girls were able to bathe once a week. The bathroom had three tubs in it, and the girls were called up in groups of three. A nurse kept guard to ensure that everything went according to plan and with the necessary decorum. After they had eaten, the girls went for a constitutional, in rows two abreast. They chose their walking partners by the peculiar method of asking another girl if she already had 'a man'. Sometimes a pair would sneak off during a walk in the woods in order to smoke or to engage in other similarly forbidden activities, and then sneak back to join the rows of two when they were on their way home. In the common room they then had 'tea', which was in fact a malt broth accompanied by a dry bread roll and black bread with plum jam. They then had two hours in which to do their homework or to take their weekly bath. Talking was forbidden during their evening meal, but the girls were allowed to communicate by gestures. On Sundays they were allowed to write letters in the common room, during which they would arrange family photos from home around themselves. After dinner prayers were said and hymns sung. Bedtime was at 9pm.

To be sure, this ascetic, authoritarian regime also offered a varied general education. The range of subjects offered was no longer restricted to those few that until the early twentieth century had been regarded as necessary for young girls. They were given lessons in German, French, physics, art, drawing, maths, gymnastics and handicrafts. Some subjects fascinated Friedelind, but one can easily understand how much difficulty she had in sitting still for long periods, and how the minutiae of embroidery bored her. She protested against the dancing lessons, and orthopaedic gymnastics drove her to the point of tears.[23] Her piano lessons were presumably taken with the daughter of the famous piano pedagogue and minor composer Theodor Kullak (her irreverent nickname among the girls was 'the cow').

Friedelind was able to make her mark in the school plays. Thanks to her background, she was entrusted with stage design and direction. She applied stage make-up to her fellow pupils, and Tietjen let her order costumes from Bayreuth and Berlin. Her clear diction and powerful voice meant she was also able to take on numerous roles.[24] The plays that they produced were demanding, such as *Le trésor* by François Coppée in 1933. Sometimes there were class excursions, as in October 1932 when they travelled to Weimar to spend three days at the Goethe Festival organized by the Schiller Society. That same year there was a large bonfire on Midsummer's Eve (the festival celebrated in Wagner's *Meistersinger*) for which the girls had great fun 'dragging down half the forest to build a fire'. They also travelled to the local history museum in Havelberg and visited the cathedral there. On one occasion they put on a version of *Faust* with puppets that they had made themselves, while on another there was a slideshow about Rumania. The girls were also able to visit the excavations of a Bronze Age burial ground. Every year there was a school excursion after the long summer holidays. During Friedelind's time they went once by train to Neuruppin, then by steamer past Altruppin to the Tornow Lake, passing through a series of beautiful little lakes in the region known as 'Swiss Ruppin' ('Ruppiner Schweiz'). They then hiked to Binenwalde, a little village with a lakeside castle, and afterwards returned to Neuruppin by steamboat and took a bus back to school.

Politics slowly began to make their impact on school life. In 1932, when the abbess Elisabeth von Saldern required the upper classes to take an active interest in political matters, one of Friedelind's fellow pupils noted her energetic support of 'Hitler's party'. Having got to know and love 'Wolf' back home in Wahnfried, she presumably enjoyed a special status among her peers. In

September 1933 the Nazi Party organized an autumn harvest festival and the school invited 500 members of the SA to a stew in the cloisters. In early 1934 the girls hoisted the flag of the Hitler Youth at the school and in early September commemorated the victories of Sedan and Tannenberg. The 120th anniversary of the Battle of Leipzig was also celebrated in Heiligengrabe, and the girls offered singing and speaking choruses at a memorial for the fallen in Hitler's Beer Hall Putsch of 9 November 1923.

Friedelind herself testified years later that several of the teachers had been decent and sincere in their views. On evenings she occasionally went to chat with two of them who lived in little houses next to the school – further proof of her independent spirit, but also of her privileged position. As a whole, however, the ethos of the school, founded as it was on obedience, was excruciating to her. 'Now Maus has been a whole day in her exile,' wrote Lieselotte. 'The little shrew hasn't had it easy and she is rebelling mightily against the coup d'état against her. She had thought it impossible. But it's the only right thing to do, and the little agitator's absence is already having a pleasant effect on the behaviour of the others. Nickel has become much more composed during the holidays and up to now has behaved faultlessly. And she is so keen at school and at the piano that it is a real joy … everything is only half as difficult with that little goat out of the way.' She felt a certain malicious glee at how Friedelind had to give a deep curtsey to the abbess and kiss her hand: 'That must be hilarious from the little rebel.'[25]

Agitator, shrew, goat, rebel: Friedelind's habit of protesting loudly at instructions from adults had carved her a clear role. Her fellow pupils recalled her receiving forbidden food packets from home – presumably it was Lieselotte who showed mercy on her. When she wrote home, she gave her address not as 'Heiligengrabe' – 'Holy Sepulchre' – but as 'im Grabe' – 'in the grave'. She told her family that she couldn't stand her school and begged for a diary that she could lock. She also had them send her copy of the book *Raiders of the Deep* – rather warlike fare for a 14-year-old girl. This novel by Lowell Thomas, who had written the bestseller *With Lawrence in Arabia*, describes the submarine warfare of the First World War. Friedelind asked for silk stockings from home,[26] even though these were forbidden – perhaps it was an endeavour to achieve some degree of femininity from which she felt otherwise excluded on account of her excessive weight. 'I can still hear that incessant "You're stupid", "You're ugly", "You mustn't want to be pretty", "Vanity is a sin", "It's your duty to be in the wrong", wrote Christa Winsloe. 'That stuck with me throughout my life. Later, they call it inhibition and inferiority complexes, and it's treated like a disease. Oh, how sinful we felt when she combed over our ugly, compulsory haircuts, when we looked at our décolletés in the mirror and checked each other out – is she pretty or not? – that ugly, sad uniform only made us desire extravagant clothes. I left the school at the age of 16 without a clue as to how to dress, without knowing anything about running a home, unworldly, timid and frightened, shy to the point of misanthropy, weighed down by a sense of my own inadequacy.'[27]

These experiences at boarding school could not dampen Friedelind's independent spirit. When she returned home at Christmas she demanded her own room and went of her own accord to visit Eva, Daniela and Hans von Wolzogen. Winifred was amazed: "'Go, I can't stop you" – that's what I have to say – I can't help it if she prefers things elsewhere to what's at home.'[28] She spent her holidays in Arosa, where she practised her ice-skating with Verena. Wieland and Friedelind drew up a contract that stipulated that she would receive 100 marks from her brother if she remained unmarried throughout her life. Friedelind for her part would have to pay Wieland 100 marks if she went on honeymoon. This contract was to be valid until 29 March 1968, her 50th birthday, and is perhaps a sign that even now she already had no interest in marriage.[29] When her brother once wanted to marry her off to 'an East Prussian landowner', she replied that 'He could not find a less interested wife'.[30]

While the children were passing their time with assorted japes, the situation on the political front was worsening. The Nazis' assumption of power in early 1933 meant that neither Jews nor those possessing liberal convictions could move about freely in Germany any more. Goebbels's call for a boycott of Jewish businesses was approved by Hitler's cabinet. This action was led by Julius Streicher, the editor of the anti-Semitic smearsheet *Der Stürmer*, and it was directed not just against Jewish shops and goods but also against the activities of lawyers and doctors who happened to be Jewish. On 1 April, the day of the general 'Jewish boycott' in Germany, Friedelind and her mother were invited to lunch in the Chancellery of the Reich. Winifred wanted to know from Hitler whether she could still engage Jewish singers in Bayreuth. But, despite sitting next to him, she did not get around to asking the question. The dining hall was massive. There was noodle soup, served in silver dishes bearing coats of arms. According to Friedelind's recollection, political events were not mentioned.

In the evening they went to the Berlin State Opera. Two Jewish musicians were involved in the performance of Mozart's *Magic Flute*: the conductor Leo Blech and the singer Alexander Kipnis. Both were given rapturous applause. Despite this demonstration against the boycott it was clear that the Nazis would have their way. Jewish artists were soon banned from performing and so left the country or made preparations to do so. Otto Klemperer and Bruno Walter were among them, as was the Busch family (who were not Jewish, but left for political reasons). Numerous other musicians did the same. Franz

Schreker and Arnold Schoenberg were removed from their posts in Berlin at the Music Academy and the Prussian Academy of Arts respectively. Paul Hindemith was denounced. The 'Cultural Association of German Jews' was set up as a *de facto* ghetto for Jewish musicians. Their activities were watched and closely controlled. Germans were deprived of their national identity and their rights, just because they happened to be Jewish. It was in this year that the great stream of refugees began leaving the country.

The 16-year-old Wieland wanted to give Hitler a present on his birthday, 20 April 1933, by playing Wagner's *Faust Overture* in a piano duet version together with Tietjen. 'If it can be arranged, I'll give the boy the pleasure of doing it,' wrote Winifred. Hitler agreed. Winifred: 'We'll probably drive to Berlin as a fivesome – Wieland can play to Wolf on his birthday and I will take all the children to him, as an Easter gift to them and as a birthday surprise!!!'[31] This year, Winifred also made public her intention that Wieland would one day succeed to the management of the Bayreuth Festival – despite this being in contradiction to Siegfried's will. She did this in an open letter to Tietjen for the book *Bayreuth in the Third Reich*, which ended thus: 'Aid me with your faithful cooperation and lead my son Wieland step by step to the task that life has set for him: to be the worthy successor to his father in the service of Bayreuth.'[32]

It was a shock to Winifred when Arturo Toscanini withdrew from conducting in Bayreuth on account of the political situation. She immediately contacted Hitler, who sent the conductor a telegram followed by a personal letter. But Toscanini remained true to his principles. Winifred hoped for further assistance from the 'Führer' for Bayreuth: 'Our work here proceeds magnificently. In artistic and financial terms it looks bad, but I've gathered together all the cancellations made on political grounds and will take them to the government and go soliciting!'[33] The town of Bayreuth was full of Brownshirts during the Festival and Hitler arrived in a large black car, surrounded by a bodyguard of SS men who stood on the footboard. The whole atmosphere of the place had changed.

Friedelind was not allowed home during the autumn holidays in 1933, since there had been cases of polio near her school and no child was allowed to leave. Instead, Winifred came to Heiligengrabe to see her on 8 October. Despite the quarantine, she was allowed to take Friedelind away with her. But they went only to Berlin, where she met her siblings for a few days. 'Mausi is behaving very nicely – runs to the theatre alone every evening – can't get enough of it,' her mother wrote. Among the operas she saw were Bizet's *Carmen*, Verdi's *Sicilian Vespers*, Pfitzner's *Palestrina*, Strauss's *Rosenkavalier* and 'the scandalous *Tannhäuser*'[34] – Otto Klemperer had dared to conduct a production that was interpreted as an attack on the Nazis and served to accelerate his own process of emigration. All these theatre evenings were quite an achievement for someone only 15. But even this was not enough for her. With her brothers and sister she attended the ballet and variety shows, saw George Bernard Shaw's *Pygmalion*, the comedy *Das Glas Wasser* by Eugène Scribe and went to museums. Their mother had not failed to notice that the children were in the midst of puberty. 'Mausi flirts to her heart's content with Lorenz – Nickel is teased about her infidelity to Heinz and receives many an embarrassing letter – Wieland buys amber necklaces for his Gertrud and only Wolfi remains true to his family – in other words his mother!'[35] Friedelind had fallen in love with the tenor Max Lorenz who, along with Lauritz Melchior, was one of the top artists at Bayreuth. He was both gay and married, but none of this served to dampen Friedelind's gushing passion – and perhaps it was his subtle art of keeping his distance that she found appealing.

Back in Heiligengrabe, Friedelind received 'a glutton's Advent package'. She was finally allowed home at Christmas. Her return to school in the New Year will have been hard on her. Lieselotte wrote with merciless humour that 'She was yesterday put under lock and key again', and that is surely how Friedelind felt about it too.

The political machinery was all the while running relentlessly, and schools and other teaching institutions were being brought into line with Nazi policy. The 'Enabling Act' of March 1933 had allowed Hitler to set up his dictatorship. All political parties were dissolved except for the Nazis, making the Reichstag a one-party parliament. Every (male) youth organization was incorporated into the Hitler Youth. In May 1934 a section of the Bund Deutscher Mädel was inaugurated at Heiligengrabe and was promptly joined by 30 girls. In the middle of the year, the local vicar and one of the canonesses denounced the school to the Nazis, so two school inspectors were dispatched to investigate the ideas that the school was propagating. Lessons in 'genetics' now had to be given – they had hitherto never figured on the curriculum. During the inspection the schoolgirls tried to help the teacher who was under suspicion, and Friedelind eagerly did her part. In history classes the teacher asked questions from a Nazi perspective – and since she had learnt all about that at home, Friedelind knew the answers and proffered them eagerly. And when questions were asked about the time before the Great War, Princess Herzeleide of Prussia helped out – she was the daughter of Prince Oskar of Prussia and thus a granddaughter of the former Kaiser. 'I had Herzeleide as my "roaring companion". And we put on a competition for who could out-shout the other, because she also seemed to notice what it was all about.' The teacher was saved for the moment.

Although Friedelind and Herzeleide were friends, there were nevertheless

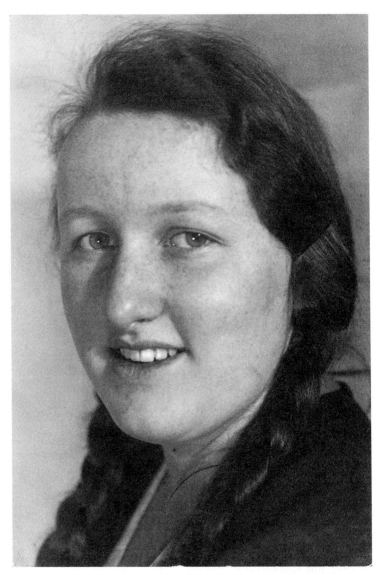

6 Friedelind in her teenage years: the world her oyster.

occasional bitter disputes between them when it came to history lessons and the First World War. Whereas Friedelind insisted stubbornly that the Kaiser was to blame for the War, had run away cravenly at the end of it and thus had to bear responsibility for the subsequent collapse of the state, the Princess protested vehemently in defence of the honour of the House of Hohenzollern.[36]

The conclusion of the inspection by the school authorities was that Abbess Elisabeth von Saldern was 'not capable of adjusting completely to the circumstances of today's times' and was thus unsuitable for a teaching position from a National Socialist perspective. She promptly wrote to Winifred to ask for support, and Winifred reacted immediately.

'As one of the first women in National Socialism I find it deeply outrageous that lies and denunciations have served to depict this place of exemplary youth education as reactionary and as a "foreign body" in our state today. My children are happy to know nothing other than a National Socialist world view. Friedelind is extremely critical and observant of her environment and – inasmuch as it can be said of a child – she is politically committed; yet never has she found any reason to complain about anti-Nazi feeling in Heiligengrabe.'[37] When the 'Führer' called on her again on 3 October for a 'really cosy visit from quarter to seven in the evening until half past midnight', she spoke to him of her concerns for Heiligengrabe. 'Completely alone. It really has been a long time since he was so relaxed and human and touching. We discussed the whole Wahnfried inheritance problem with him.'[38] She was trying to have Wieland declared the sole heir, referring in the process to the 'Imperial Hereditary Farm Law' of 1933 according to which it was not permissible to divide up an estate, which should instead be given over to a single inheritor. The law furthermore preferred men above women in matters of inheritance. Winifred suspected that the succession issue could become problematical precisely because of Friedelind, who later recalled that she had in these years become aware of her duty to maintain the Bayreuth Festival tradition: '... the vague purpose that was struggling inside me ... quickened my consciousness of my responsibility not only then, but for the future.'[39]

Hitler rejected Winifred's request. In any case, her problems with her eldest daughter were not diminishing. Winifred knew that she was not happy at school. 'She inwardly held all those years in Heiligengrabe against me because I had put her there.'[40] Nor was it always harmonious at home. Winifred complained to Helene Roesener that she wanted to take Wolfgang to the Erz Mountains as he had undergone an operation on his tonsils and needed to recuperate. But she had to take Mausi along too. 'If I leave her here on her own, everything goes wrong. I am still having a difficult time with the child. Since yesterday I've had a rule that if she isn't down for breakfast by nine, then she gets nothing. Yesterday she was punctual, but not today – so she gets nothing. For the first eight days she was again sleeping until all hours – which, given her state, is not necessary.' Furthermore, her school report was 'miserable', at which her mother made quite clear to her that another year at Heiligengrabe would ensue if she did not pass her exams.[41] Winifred also refused to take her to her apartment in Berlin: 'On 2 October Mausi starts her holidays, until the 18th. She had again imagined that she would spend the whole time in Berlin, meeting her artists day in, day out and sitting in the theatre every evening while I'm allowed to cook for her, wash up for her and generally be her servant. Since I have no desire for all that and since she spent the summer holidays swanning around in the company of the whole rabble, I'll have her brought here and she can mope around for the full 14 days at home.' In any case Winifred did not want to be in Berlin, for Tietjen was directing *Parsifal* and had no time for her; furthermore his wife Nena was sick. 'As for acting as a lady's companion to Nena,' wrote Winifred, 'no thanks.'[42]

On 10 and 11 December 1934, Tietjen invited Friedelind's school class to Berlin for two days to see Kleist's *Hermannsschlacht* at the State Theatre. The girls were spoilt at every turn and the whole trip was undoubtedly a triumph for Friedelind, who was the centre of attention. Her final exams seem to have gone well, too, for Friedelind was writing with unusual frequency to her mother: 'I'm astonished by Mausi – she's writing at least every two days to me, really nicely and at length!'[43]

Friedelind was highly aware of her special status as Wagner's granddaughter and as one of the heirs to Bayreuth. We can see this clearly in a remarkable document that she wrote in her youth to an unknown addressee, and in which she situates herself clearly on the same level as the recipient of her letter:

Do you truly believe that anyone here is quite intentionally treating you badly? I can't imagine it. And if T[ietjen] or Mama are sometimes nonchalant or unfriendly towards you, just remind yourself, please, what the two of them have to cope with! Behind the scenes things don't look so simple! So just swallow any disappointment that you might experience with the two of them. We children don't have things any differently. Or do you think I find it ideal that I have to stay clear of trouble when I'm already away from home all year? And just who do you think is 'cutting you out'? Don't go imagining things! You say that no one is paying attention to you! For one thing, 'paying attention' has to go both ways in my opinion. If you are referring to either of the two bosses, then again I can only say: just think about all the people to whom the bosses have to pay attention! Many people are often happy when they see that anyone from the family is there to represent them. All four of us are still children, but aren't we all at least still Wagners? And one of us will one day also be the 'boss' of the business. Can't you see us as junior representatives of our mother? And can you still then tell yourself that no one here in Bayreuth is paying attention to you?[44]

A strongly developed sense of self-awareness shines through these lines: a knowledge of tradition and the duties that it brings with it. This direct, spirited tone of address is something that Friedelind kept her whole life long whenever something did not appeal to her.

After her final exams in Heiligengrabe in 1935, Winifred organized a little reception for Friedelind's 17th birthday in Berlin. But Friedelind did not have much time to enjoy herself, for two weeks later she was sent to an agricultural domestic science school in Grosssachsenheim near Stuttgart. 'Mausi has been accepted in Grosssachsenheim! She's muttering about it of course. But she's got to come to terms with it!' wrote Winifred with a hint of triumph.[45] She had first planned to send her to a different school, but had rejected it for being too 'intellectual'. 'She should learn to keep house and to cope with drudgery.'[46] And drudgery it was. The school courses included *haute cuisine* cooking and baking, greenhouse gardening and poultry farming. Its imposing three-storey building had been built in 1913 using charity funds. Its aim was to offer a diploma course for girls, teaching them the art of running a home. Since 1908 the site had belonged to the 'Reifensteiner Association' created by Ida von Kortzfleisch (1850–1915). She had founded the first school on the premises in 1897 and had intended on the one hand to offer qualifications for girls in agricultural and domestic matters, and on the other to educate them to be independent, responsible citizens of society.[47] In 1900, that had been a thoroughly progressive, even reforming goal.

Friedelind found the course content so foreign that she inwardly railed against everything. Although she loved animals and at the beginning was 'happy to be with my hens,'[48] since the onset of puberty she had occupied herself intensively with theatre, opera, concerts, museums and books. Her thoughts and fantasies were all focused on intellectual and artistic, cultural pursuits. 'After two and a half years in a school for princesses in which the diet was designed to give one anaemia and the most strenuous exercise provided was an afternoon walk, I was suddenly introduced to the hardest kind of physical labour. It was not surprising that my health gave way,' she later wrote in her autobiography.[49] She took ill and had to spend most of her time in bed until the summer holidays.

Friedelind had up to now attended a boarding school for aristocrats and

royalty; perhaps Winifred sensed that she had failed in her daughter's upbringing and so now went to the other extreme, placing her instead in an institution
where she would learn poultry and pig farming and how to grow vegetables.
The older Friedelind became, the stricter was the treatment meted out to her.
Was Winifred unable to cope with her impudence and with the liberties she
took, or did she just want her rebellious child out of the house so that she
could continue her relationship with Tietjen in peace? Or did she need more
time for her job running the Festival? To be sure, Friedelind did not subject
herself constantly to the horticultural harassments of Grossachsenheim, but
sought outside entertainment whenever possible. 'I only get funny letters
from Maus,' wrote an irritated Winifred, 'it's a mystery to me when she's actually in Sachsenheim.' Friedelind had just been to Stuttgart, attending a dress
rehearsal at the opera, then taking tea with the family of a friend and going
to *Aïda* in the evening. Another time she was travelling to Tübingen to visit
Prince August Wilhelm (nicknamed 'Auwi'), a friend from Bayreuth. He was
the fourth son of the former Kaiser Wilhelm II, a supporter of the Nazis and
himself a Standartenführer in the SA (later an Obergruppenführer). While in
Tübingen she made some new acquaintances and was promptly invited to the
winter dance at the university. 'But I'm not asked for permission, she just goes
there and I'm allowed to know about it afterwards when she asks for money!'[50]

Since Mausi was too fat and Nickel supposedly too thin, Winifred sent them
both to a clinic in Törwang in Upper Bavaria. Mausi was to be 'put through
her paces (going walking etc.), and Nickel must be fattened up.'[51] Mausi lost
28 pounds at the clinic: 'You can barely see me any more!! We've got snow
and ice now. I'm sticking to the ice because the snow is still a bit too thin on
the ground and I'm fearful for the noblest part of my anatomy, which is still
in good shape. I wish I'd lost more weight down there!'[52] Verena did not want
to gain any weight at all, so had a girlfriend send her laxatives. In order not to
draw attention to herself when being weighed, she sewed lead tape into her
clothes and drank as much water as possible beforehand.

Wieland liked taking photographs and his interest in it extended beyond
a mere hobby, into the aesthetic and artistic. He earned a pretty sum from
taking photos of the 'Führer' and selling them as postcards. In 1935 Hitler gave
him a Mercedes as a gift – proof enough of the expectations that were placed
on the young man. Wieland and his brother travelled to Munich to pick up
the car and spent the night in Hitler's apartment. Wieland slept in Hitler's bed
because the latter had to travel to Berlin.[53] At Christmas the family was united
again in Wahnfried. The 'Führer' sent presents for the children: jewellery for
Nickel, a book for Wieland and a stereoscope machine for Wolfgang. For her
part, Winifred organized a messenger who took copies of the letters between

Wagner and Ludwig II to Munich, where they were presented to Hitler.[54] It seems that Hitler had expressed an interest in reading them.

Just three months before, Hitler had passed the infamous 'Nuremberg Race Laws' that forbade all non-Jewish Germans from marrying Jews and whose further aim was to drive all Jews out of their positions in the state, industry and culture. But this did nothing to alter the festive, Christmas mood in Bayreuth. Nor was anyone interested in knowing that Richard Wagner's other grandson, Franz W. Beidler, had married a Jewish woman, Ellen Gottschalk – the daughter of a Berlin gynaecologist – and that they had together emigrated via France to Switzerland. Having such a Nazi-critical relation would in any case only have been a disagreeable embarrassment to Winifred.

Friedelind's experiences at her two schools had strengthened her in her determination to stand on her own two feet as soon as possible. She also instinctively grew closer to her aunts Eva and Daniela. It would be her intellectual discussions with them, combined with her own experiences while on foreign travels, that would help her find her way back to her own true interests and needs: namely art, music and a natural interaction with her fellow human beings.

Chapter 4

'Impudent, endearing and witty'
Friedelind and her aunts
1936 to 1937

IN HER TEENAGE YEARS Friedelind enjoyed an especially close relationship with her aunt Daniela Thode, the first daughter of Cosima's marriage to Hans von Bülow. It was a friendship which continued into the years of Friedelind's early adulthood. Daniela was generally regarded with some contempt as a fossilized old maid. But she was clever and spirited, even passionate. 'She was continually exploding, wrecking everything about her, continually repenting and flagellating herself for her outbursts,' recalled Friedelind.[1] Cosima had brought up Daniela firmly within the narrow bounds that were normal for girls at the time, so she had been unable to develop her intellectual and creative abilities to their full potential. Heinz Tietjen claimed that Daniela was 'stubborn and dangerous' and tried, without success, to drive a wedge between her and her niece by insisting that Friedelind show solidarity with Winifred. 'We have to protect your mother,' he said.[2] Friedelind resented such pressure and remained attached to her aunt notwithstanding all her eccentricities. She also drew close to Eva, Richard's second child. After both aunts had lost their husbands (Daniela through divorce, Eva when her husband died) the two of them moved close to one another in Bayreuth and often went on trips together.

Given Siegfried's advanced age when he started a family, there were essentially two generations separating his sisters from their niece Friedelind. This gap was particularly obvious in matters of upbringing. Friedelind and her siblings enjoyed ample freedom during their childhood, with little disparity between how the boys and girls were treated. This was very different from Daniela's early years. Cosima and Richard had invested so much in Siegfried's nurture and education that his sisters understood from the start that they belonged to the 'second gender'. They were raised to be cultured and to show an interest in intellectual matters, but the aim of their education was to prepare them specifically for their future role as subservient wives. Richard Wagner once caught the 19-year-old Daniela at the piano, setting a poem to music – and promptly forbade her to do so, explaining that he did not want his children to be subjected to the same misery as a composer that he had been compelled to endure. None of the daughters was given a proper chance to develop her talents.[3] When Daniela asked for permission to have visiting cards printed, Cosima refused point blank: 'If you have visiting cards, then you're emancipated, like an ugly 30-year-old woman.' Printing one's name gave one subject status in Cosima's opinion. That was at best unseemly, at worst offensive. She advised her daughter – 21 at the time – to keep her 'maidenliness', to be 'modest' and to 'subordinate herself'. Even when Daniela reached the age of 25 she was only allowed among company when accompanied by a married woman.[4] Thus she was taught what was seemly for the fairer sex.

But Daniela was different. She would gladly have undergone a professional training to find a field of activity that satisfied her. It was denied her, and the impact of that denial contributed to the general picture of her as a bitter, grumpy old woman (though as it happened, it was a picture that was at times not far from the truth). Yet within the boundaries assigned to her she acquired a considerable knowledge of literature and art history. She read widely, went to concerts and practised the piano for two hours each day. In 1886 she married Henry Thode, a banker's son who had taken his doctorate in art history, was interested in Bayreuth and in Wagner's music, and was appointed to a professorship in art history at the University of Heidelberg in 1893. But in 1914 irreconcilable differences led to their divorce, after which Daniela returned to Bayreuth, wounded and disappointed.

Daniela was particularly interested in costume design. In 1909 she took over the management of the costumes at Bayreuth from her half-sister Isolde, though she insisted that the latter possessed a 'brilliance' that she would never match.[5] She was tentative at first, but two years later engaged in historical research for the *Meistersinger*, orienting herself on works by German Renaissance artists. She copied portraits by Dürer, Holbein, Grien and others and adopted certain details with regard to the cut of clothes and caps, the colours and hairstyles. She displayed her knowledge of art history by drawing on influences from the Symbolist movement in her costumes and matched the colours of the Masters' robes to their respective guilds.[6] In *Tristan* in 1927 and 1928 she had all jewellery, ornaments, weapons and equipment fashioned after Celtic models. For a *Tannhäuser* production, on the other hand, she spent two years studying sources from the Ancient world and from the German Middle Ages, taking the illustrations from the Manesse Manuscript as the model for her costumes. She also became involved in several book projects: she translated dialogues of Dante and Goethe that had been collated by her grandmother Marie d'Agoult; and published 'Sayings about music and musicians' by Richard Wagner, a German edition of Valérie Boissier's 'Franz Liszt as Teacher' for Zsolnay Verlag, letters of her father Hans von Bülow, and much more besides. She was an excellent pianist, as her mother had been, though of course neither had trained professionally with a view to giving public performances: 'On the 18th I brought my friends together at my home, offering Bach, Beethoven and

7 Friedelind's aunts Daniela Thode (left) and Eva Chamberlain,
to whom she became bound by a strong mutual affection.

Chopin instead of tea and sausages.'[7] She gave concerts for private associations and occasionally even in public. In 1938 she performed Bach's Chromatic Fantasy and Beethoven's *Eroica Variations* – a demanding programme by any standards. She gave lectures on her travels, preferably about her grandfather Franz Liszt. Eva and Daniela also delighted in reading to each other from Plato, Plutarch, Shakespeare, Lessing and Goethe.

The close relationship between the 18-year-old Friedelind and her 76-year-old Aunt Daniela was rooted primarily in their similar characters. Decades before, Cosima had scolded Daniela for her 'tendency to extreme tempestuousness'[8] such as Winifred also experienced in Friedelind. Daniela will have recognized Friedelind's curiosity in the world despite all 'feminine' constraints and educational maxims, and wanted to encourage her.

Winifred's conflict with Daniela and Eva became more intense after Siegfried's death. For as long as Cosima was alive they remained undisputed nabobs in her house, though Winifred was all this time acquainting herself swiftly with the organization of the Festival and making herself indispensable. She was highly power-conscious – a character trait that neither Eva nor Daniela had inherited – and possessed of a hands-on nature: if her car needed repairs she would don trousers herself and disappear beneath it, emerging afterwards with her hair loose and her clothes and hands besmirched with

oil, all of which must have struck horror in the hearts of her two elderly, conservative sisters-in-law. After Siegfried's death they felt completely displaced.
Daniela came to believe that Winifred was spreading rumours about Toscanini
being responsible for Siegfried's death and so she wrote an article to deny it.
'Truly, her revenge is terrible!' she wrote furiously to her sister Blandine,

> We know Siegfried's will, and he gave not a hint of making Winifred
> the director of the Festival ... but because she is the sole heir and the
> Festspielhaus is private property she has vehemently seized the director-
> ship of the Festival too, and she is gradually ruining it. He also knew her
> lust for power and her jealousy, which both verge on madness and were
> bound to make any collaboration impossible. All this is fate. I have with-
> drawn from everything, also from any further polemics, and endeavour
> to do so without rancour and bitterness.[9]

Winifred was in fact only nominated a 'preliminary heir' in Siegfried Wagner's
will, with her four children the reversionary heirs 'in equal shares'.

The older ladies suffered under the claims to leadership exercised by their
sister-in-law, and the changes that she introduced and enforced were felt
by them to be an attack on the 'holy' traditions of the Festival. Productions
were altered in contradiction to Wagner's own stage directions (Daniela complained about the 'transformation of the Temple of the Grail into a convention
hall, or worse, a hotel lobby'), the media were given access to the Festspielhaus, flashy cars drove up to the Festival, and everything sacred seemed to
have been made profane. Daniela lamented 'the mercantile spirit, the irreverence, the impiety, the lack of tradition both on stage and in the house'. The
'spirit of Bayreuth' that Cosima had insisted must focus solely on the Master's
works in order to elevate his audience was now, so Daniela believed, on the
verge of being lost altogether. Daniela was a convinced supporter of the Nazi
Party that she hoped would be the 'salvation' of Germany. So it is not a little
ironic that in 1933 she complained about 'the politicization of the Festival that
[Winifred] has so long striven for'. Winifred had namely postponed the third
act of the *Walküre* by some two hours at its second performance so that an
election speech by the 'Führer' could be broadcast from loudspeakers set up
at the Festspielhaus; it ended with the thronged masses on the Festival hill
singing the German national anthem and the Nazis' own anthem, the 'Horst-
Wessel Lied'.[10] Daniela and Eva were also hurt because Winifred had cancelled
their portion of the box-office takings that Siegfried had always granted them
out of sheer kindness.[11] In conversation with one of her girlfriends, Winifred
dropped all hint of respect when talking about Daniela: 'Today we're having

8 Wieland, Wolfgang, Friedelind and Verena standing behind their mother.

a performance by the 76-year-old child prodigy Daniela – along with three others she's hammering out a concerto for four pianos by Bach! I'll take the evening off because "good old Schmidt" and his amateur orchestra get on my nerves too much.'[12]

Friedelind was busy acquiring greater freedom from all maternal constraints. But Winifred's complaints about her renegade daughter merely increased. 'Mausi is travelling to Stuttgart on Monday to see a friend – it's quite superfluous, as they already spent the whole year in Sachsenheim together,' she wrote. 'All my suggestions of work for her – piano lessons or learning stenography or touch-typing – are always met with a stony silence. So I have decided to do nothing with her at all. I just let her go – after all, she is old enough to know what she's doing. There's no talk of her helping me in any way – a strange child! – I couldn't stand doing nothing all the time.'[13] Friedelind turned 18 in April 1936 – a moment for which she had yearned – but coming of age changed nothing for her. The conflict intensified. Sometimes her mother would treat her as an equal, even as a friend, but at other times she would revert to the exact opposite: 'Something that set her on edge always made her return to the role of dictator,' wrote Friedelind. 'Then she would hurry from the room to avoid a scene.'[14] In moments like that, Friedelind regretted that there was no one around to mediate between them.

But Friedelind now began a prolific correspondence with Daniela ('Aunt Lulu'), by whom she felt accepted and loved. 'Farewell, then. Know that everything of Mausi's will be met with our wide open interest. Your faithful Aunt Lulu embraces you with all her heart,' she wrote.[15] The conflicts that they both had to endure with Winifred were left unmentioned in their letters, for Daniela did not want to be accused of exerting a negative influence on her niece (and nor, for her part, did Eva). Up to 1939, the year of crisis, their correspondence dealt almost exclusively with cultural experiences and plans for the future. The 18-year-old Friedelind wanted to become an opera director, but how she should achieve her goal remained unclear to her. She considered writing a biography of her grandmother Cosima – perhaps in order to familiarize herself with the Festival tradition – and asked Daniela to tell her as much as she could about her. But Daniela refused for the moment, claiming a lack of time:

> I know many a thing that is not in any biography ... so please have patience and indulge me. Sometime, when I see that I have the time, I will gladly write something for you – things that others don't know yet. You have no idea of the things that incessantly call upon me with regard to our common cause, our family etc. etc. [...] I often do not know how to keep the two hours for my piano playing that are a vital need to me.[16]

Regrettably, the promised revelations from Daniela were never forthcoming.

In March 1936 Winifred went off again to be with Tietjen in Berlin. She had rented an apartment there for the purpose, but he was too busy with his semi-invalid wife Nena to have time for his lover. Winifred's patience came to an end when Friedelind decided to abandon a trip she had planned to Rome and come to see Heinz in Berlin instead.

> That's all well and good – it's my own daughter – but he then more or less casts me out and lets Maus come. He claims to have time for her, but he never has time for me! – I blew up completely and told the child and Heinz what I thought. Now I don't know what will happen, but in any case she's not coming to Berlin and she seems to be trying to set up the Rome trip again.[17]

The competition between mother and daughter for Tietjen's attention continued up to Friedelind's departure for England. Friedelind claimed not to like him, but he possessed a firm power base and in artistic matters was able to

9 From left: Friedelind, her godfather the artist Franz Stassen,
and Richard Strauss, ca 1934.

do whatever he wanted. Furthermore, Winifred was dependent on him – and that made him interesting.

Bayreuth had by now become a hive of National Socialism. In the newly built 'House of German Education' one could admire a nine-metre-tall statue of 'the German mother'. The town had been made the seat of the regional administration and of the SA Group 'Bavaria East', and was now also home to assorted party offices and the Imperial Directorate of the Nazi Teachers' Association. The Nazis did not meddle with the Festival directly, but the arts were becoming more and more a plaything of the Third Reich and Bayreuth an artistic flagship for Nazi Germany. Reichsminister Goering, Propaganda Minister Goebbels, the 'Gauleiter' Wächtler, Streicher and Koch, ambassadors von Ribbentrop and Minister von Papen – the highest-ranking National Socialists attended the Festival in great numbers. Winifred consulted Adolf Hitler before making her most important decisions, and he supported all she did – much to the astonishment of Daniela and Eva, who had hoped to find in him an advocate of the unaltered retention of Wagner's own productions. The Bayreuth archives make it clear that from 1933 'almost no important decision was made any more without the approval or the knowledge of the Führer'.[18] This can also be explained by the fact that the Nazi policy of centralized, 'enforced conformity' ('Gleichschaltung'), coupled with the reigning institutional chaos, served not to weaken Hitler's personal authority, but to strengthen it.[19] This was also to Winifred's advantage. Hitler's word was far weightier than that of the Party itself, where hers was in any case often a dissenting voice.

In collaboration with the stage designer Emil Preetorius, Heinz Tietjen now created a series of remarkable productions in Bayreuth. They succeeded in combining the music and the scenic aspect into a single whole – in other words, depicting the music in the form and colour of the stage design. Friedelind saw how they employed Wieland's designs for *Parsifal*, and she also heard Tietjen discussing many things by telephone with Goering. Furtwängler conducted *Lohengrin*, and praise was heaped on the musical successes of the Festival. Maria Müller, Josef von Manowarda, Margarete Klose, Herbert Janssen, Jaro Prohaska and many others sang at Bayreuth in these years. Frida Leider was a superb Brünnhilde, and Max Lorenz her equal as Siegfried.

In 1936 the Festival was divided into two halves – an unusual step, necessitated by the Olympic Games. The first half ran from mid-July to the end of the month, then the second half, after the Games, from 18 to 31 August. After the first Festival cycle, Friedelind and Verena travelled to the Games in Berlin, for Hitler had placed complimentary tickets at their disposal. The Bayreuth Festival Chorus took part in the opening ceremony, singing the Olympic Hymn by Richard Strauss under the composer's baton along with Handel's 'Hallelujah Chorus' from the *Messiah*. Friedelind enjoyed her trip to the metropolis in every way possible. 'Maus has rented a room next to [Frida] Leider and we don't hear a squeak from her!' said Winifred, who found it 'touching' that Hitler invited Friedelind and Verena to lunch in the Imperial Chancellery when they were the only women present.[20] Surprisingly, Friedelind refrains from mentioning this visit in her autobiography, though she did so in a later radio broadcast.[21] Friedelind liked the fact that Frida Leider took her seriously and praised her when she dressed nicely. 'The words were balm to the hurt that Mother was always deepening, making me feel like an awkward ugly duckling.'[22] Her corpulence clearly troubled her more than she would admit, and it must have hurt her even more to find her sister's portrait reproduced as a paragon in a book entitled *Nordic Beauty: its Ideal in Life and Art*, in which 'mixing and the intrusion of foreign blood' is also denounced, all in line with the racial theories promoted in Nazi Germany.[23]

After the Festival the family went to Nuremberg to attend the *Meistersinger* that opened the annual Nazi Party rally. They subsequently listened to 'Wolf's' monologues into the early hours. But autumn 1936 brought family problems to a head. Friedelind's desire to have an artistic role in the Festival had grown more intense and she had the support of both her aunts. She insisted on being allowed to participate, but Wieland was against it. He was obviously aware of the energies that his sister could mobilize and that she might dispute his future claim to dominance over the Festival, so he made sure to have their mother on his side. Winifred was of the clear opinion that a male heir should take over the Festival. 'Frau W[agner] and Wieland would not allow Friedelind to have any role in the Festival until Wieland was ready,' wrote Gertrud Strobel just a few years later, in the light of letters that her husband Otto (the Wahnfried archivist) had read from Tietjen to Friedelind.[24] That was Verena's opinion, too: 'For my mother, Wieland was the crown prince, so to speak. We all had our own very minor duties to fulfil, and Wieland and Friedelind both naturally also wanted to be active on the artistic side of things. But my mother wouldn't allow it back then.'[25] The 'Führer' also played a role in furthering the ambitions of Wagner's eldest grandchild by freeing him from military service in late 1937. This enabled Wieland to direct two operas by his father: *Sonnenflammen* in Düsseldorf and *Der Bärenhäuter* in Cologne and thus gain his first hands-on experience as a theatre director.

In order to get away from home, Friedelind applied to participate in the women's labour service near Berlin, where she lived in a house with 40 girls. It was a poor decision on her part, for she was once again confined and had to follow orders, just as at boarding school. All the girls sang for an hour every evening, they practised folk dances and underwent lessons in Nazi ideology. The work itself was physically tough and, after just a few days, Friedelind took ill with a sinus infection. Her mother sent orders that she be sent to the rheumatologist Professor Wolfgang Veil in Jena. Friedelind protested, but in vain and underwent six weeks in the clinic without her condition improving. In her desperation she toyed with notions of suicide, eventually overcoming them through a form of self-therapy: she told herself that it was a great act of cowardice to want to die and thereby supposedly succeeded in banishing all dark thoughts. Her dreams of becoming an opera director and of starting her career with a production of *Tristan* were what spurred her on. This was a mental strategy that would also later help her cope in the time she spent as an internee in England. Her will to live now gradually returned. Her aunts sent her flowers, books to read and newspapers, and this also buoyed her up. 'Mausi isn't writing to me at all!', complained Winifred, however.[26] When Wolfgang Veil carried out blood transfusions without Winifred's consent, she finally went and fetched Friedelind in order to celebrate Verena's 17th birthday together on 2 December in Dresden.

Despite her dreams of directing, Friedelind still lacked any real sense of what her career options were, and these were the topic of a long letter Tietjen sent her. He took pleasure in playing people off against each other – and now he stopped siding with her mother. Winifred had recently visited him in Berlin, of which he wrote to Friedelind: 'Your mother was here just once, briefly, in all this time, and everything ended in an argument, as you have often experienced yourself.' Friedelind had left with him all her clothes and the things she needed in Berlin, but her mother had now gathered up everything and brought it back to Bayreuth. Tietjen continued: 'I have observed how it has highly impressed your mother when a girl of your age, either from your circle of acquaintances or from hers, has made herself independent. I see this as the only way to get out of the whole confusion and to extract yourself from your irreparable relationship with your mother. Well, – then there's the inheritance.' He was having his own problems with Wieland, and he now placed Friedelind's brother centre-stage as her potential adversary. To underline what he meant, he continued: 'I think your hopes are in vain of participating in the Project.' He proposed that she should go and live in the countryside and make a career for herself there, 'as a kind of secretary to the manager of an estate, as the independent manager of a small livestock farm where there are no women, or as an assistant in forestry management.' He closed by urging her to set herself free from Wahnfried.[27]

What drove Tietjen to suggest such an inappropriate career for her, when for years he had known of her passion for the theatre? His proposition was also doubly odd when one considers that he had himself offered to teach her the art of opera direction in Berlin in the late autumn and winter. His letter in fact reveals his tendency to treat his fellow human beings like pieces on a chessboard, without regard for their true needs or talents. This was why Friedelind later passed such harsh judgment on his character in her autobiography. On this occasion she rejected his ideas on the spot. But nor did she want to continue sitting around in Bayreuth, doing nothing. So she decided to travel to Berlin, even though this presumably meant that she missed Daniela's official speech on Cosima's 100th birthday, given in the Ludwig-Siebert Hall in Bayreuth.

Winifred would only allow Friedelind to return to Berlin if it were for some kind of vocational training, so she organized a course in touch-typing and stenography for her at the Rackow School. But Friedelind only attended it sporadically. Her connection to Tietjen meant that she could get free admittance to all the theatres and concert halls in Berlin, and that was far more enticing. His advice to find a career in agriculture had been rejected, so instead he gave her tuition in score-reading and conducting. Tietjen was by now estranged from Wieland, so he presumably wanted to build up Friedelind as a possible competitor to him. She learnt how to judge voices and was particularly proud that Tietjen trusted her opinion when she reported back to him on singers whom she heard when away from Berlin. It was a skill that she continued to develop throughout her life. But most of all: now she was free at last.

10 Verena and Friedelind arm in arm with the 'Führer',
photographed by Wieland.

The touch-typing course nonetheless bore fruit, for to Daniela's delight she now received a typed letter from Friedelind 'though the handwriting on the envelope that once had the lines of a Fafner have given way to a Freia-like grace, shining out upon us' (in other words, her spidery script had mutated from something akin to a dragon into the delicate lines of a goddess). 'If God will,' wrote Daniela,

> we shall see you again soon, then we shall chat happily and candidly with each other as if there were no grief in the world, about books and pictures, music and theatre, people and animals, and we shall love one another. For the time being enjoy to the full all that is beautiful that Berlin offers you in all its life and richness.

She asked her niece to greet Hitler from her:

> We also assumed that you were in the diplomats' box when Hitler gave his mighty speech, his frank, open, strong appeal to the whole world – it made such a great impression on us. And at its close, when it became so personal, it moved me deeply. I would have liked to have telegraphed him, as I too always enjoy a gladdening answer, but he is so busy. But please tell it to him, from me, if you should happen to see him.[28]

Friedelind had in the meantime developed a deep aversion to Hitler's 'rasping, barking fusillade of words'.[29] And yet his contact with the family was closer than ever. At Christmas Hitler gave gold watches to the brothers, while Friedelind and Verena received golden bracelets and Winifred a portrait photo with dedication.[30] Daniela was attached to the 'Führer', but was not uncritical in her opinions. 'Oh, if only he had not offended religion and the churches, especially our beloved Evangelical church, and if only he had not dealt with the Jewish question in such a foolish, false manner that has made enemies for us of more than half the world! He will be forced to regret it, and Germany with him.'[31]

Whenever she had the time, Friedelind went out and about to sample Berlin's cultural riches. She wanted to see Shakespeare's *Richard III*, though Daniela had warned her that she would be unable to sleep afterwards ('it offers a terrible vision of the abysses of the world and of the human heart'). She saw Shakespeare's *Hamlet* and Mozart's *Magic Flute*, and Daniela remembered that Wagner had particularly loved Pamina's aria 'Ach, ich fühl's'.[32] Friedelind discussed the Berlin interpretation of the *Fliegender Holländer* with her aunts. The Senta in Berlin, Marta Fuchs, had studied the role of Kundry with Daniela in Bayreuth and the latter praised her ability. For the first time ever in her life, Friedelind was able to wander the streets of Berlin on her own, rummaging through book shops new and second-hand, and visiting museums and galleries. Against her mother's wishes she had her hair cut short and was now allowed to buy her own clothes too. She was gaining her independence. 'This was the first time I had ever lived in a big city with freedom to wander about the streets, poke into book and art shops – the museums, the lovely surrounding country where we often went for Sunday drives with Tietjen, the opera, the theatres, the fashionable shops and hotels.'[33] Did he perhaps want to play her and Winifred off against each other?

When Winifred visited Berlin, she discovered that Mausi had been skipping the courses in which she was enrolled. She could not understand that her daughter wanted to make her own decisions and was keen to educate herself in as many topics and in as many places as possible. Reading, listening to music, going to performances and judging them, getting to know art history, learning languages, meeting artists and making new contacts in artistic circles – all this gave her the wide-ranging competence that would serve her well, were she ever to manage the Bayreuth Festival. But Winifred could not see her potential. Perhaps she was just pushing it to the back of her mind because she was unable to contemplate anyone but Wieland as the head of the Festival, and because as a mother she could not comprehend Friedelind's apparent lack of direction. 'One just doesn't know what will become of Mausi,' she wrote when airing the idea of setting up a home near Tietjen in Berlin – a home that was intended to be *sans* Friedelind.[34] When Mausi said she would like to travel to England, Winifred allowed it on condition that she pass the final exams at the Rackow School. This she did, effortlessly.

Since Frida Leider (1888–1975) was to sing at Covent Garden in London that coming Easter, Friedelind did not want to wait any longer before going. Winifred thought it too risky to leave her 19-year-old daughter to her own devices, so she asked the singer to take her to England with her. Friedelind had struck up a friendship with Frida as far back as 1928. She had been resting on a sofa in her dressing room after a performance when Friedelind, then a ten-year-old with long blond pigtails, appeared in the room and sat opposite her, her hands folded in her lap, just looking at her inquisitively. She will have heard her sing and was presumably already fascinated by her[35] – Leider was among the most important Wagner singers of her time. With her slender, beautiful soprano and her intelligent art of interpretation, she had proven that a woman did not necessarily need a huge voice in order to sing dramatic roles. Over the course of the years the two women became close, and a lifelong friendship blossomed.

Friedelind was registered at Tortington Park School near Arundel in the

South Downs of West Sussex. It was intended for children up to the age of 16, but since she did not want to delay her visit any longer, Friedelind agreed to go there despite being two years over the limit. The school was an old brick building in a picturesque setting amidst forests and meadows. It lay just a couple of miles from the sea, and soon Friedelind was swimming there every day. She borrowed books from the school library to improve her knowledge of English. She was allowed to travel to London to see Frida on stage, and in between performances Frida found the time for them to wander through museums and galleries. Friedelind also became friends with Lauritz Melchior's wife, 'Kleinchen', for he too was now singing at Covent Garden. Winifred had not envisaged that Friedelind would meet opponents of Hitler during her stay. But she did. Furthermore, Friedelind now noticed that current events were portrayed very differently in the English media. All this laid the foundations for her slow withdrawal from the Nazi adulation that was the norm in the rest of the family. Aunt Eva had no inkling of what was going on, however, and wrote to Friedelind: 'If you can succeed in offering the English a different, correct picture of National Socialism, then you will have fulfilled an important mission and you will surely be given a big diplomatic post! You see, I can still be cheerful, even if many a thing oppresses my heart.'[36]

In 1937, nonetheless, Friedelind was situated in political terms somewhere between indifferent and uncritical, as is proven by a remark she made to her aunts:

> I am just as happy about the three kisses on the hand that the Führer gave you – the dear man – ! It is good to have a government whose attitude isn't that of a cow at a five-barred gate as it used to be. That means Wieland's whole future looks far happier and promising. He can always expect understanding and help from our great friend – and not just empty words or even opposition like it sadly always used to be![37]

She seems to have accepted as a given that Wieland would manage Bayreuth after Tietjen's departure – though she naturally also anticipated playing a considerable role herself. In any case, she had other things on her mind right now. Galsworthy, Thackeray and Shakespeare were on her reading list and she was planning to move to a college in London in the autumn. Friedelind also visited Berta Geissmar in Covent Garden, Furtwängler's former long-time secretary. She had been hounded from Germany on account of being Jewish and had been fortunate enough to find a similar position in the service of Sir Thomas Beecham. Geissmar remembered Friedelind as 'one of the most amusing, wildest of children' in Bayreuth, one whose 'rebellious spirit, quick powers of comprehension and natural musicality' had always appealed to her. Friedelind had missed the London performances of the *Ring* with the same soloists as in Bayreuth, but she saw *Holländer* and *Tristan* and found Frida Leider to be 'perfectly, heavenly beautiful, such as I had never yet experienced her.'[38] During one visit to the opera she was escorted to the royal box to be presented to Princesses Marie Louise and Helena Victoria; both were grand-daughters of Queen Victoria and had known her grandmother Cosima well. Friedelind asked Berta Geissmar for help when press photographers wanted to snap her in the royal box, because she was afraid of any photos of her reaching Germany. She was supposed to be at school, not hobnobbing at the theatre with the English ruling classes.[39]

Friedelind was determined to meet Arturo Toscanini, not least in order to impress Daniela and Eva. Both aunts went into raptures over the 'Maestro'. They regularly travelled to see him in Salzburg (just as they would later go to see him in Lucerne) and they devoted page after page to hymns of praise about his conducting.[40] Friedelind, too, capitulated before the magnetism that he exuded, and Daniela spurred her on:

Hurry straightaway into the artist's dressing room to the dear Maestro – it's best in the interval, because the poor man is so surrounded by the masses at the end of a concert. If you greet him from me you'll have a key to his heart. But you won't even need it, he will be happy to see you, for he embraced you so lovingly when you were all left alone![41]

Friedelind took the opportunity to write to him, and his wife Carla invited her to attend his rehearsals. He was conducting Beethoven's Ninth Symphony, and it seemed to Friedelind as if she were hearing it for the first time in her life, 'because I *experienced* it here for the first-ever time!' She bought him a little bouquet of violets, mustered up her courage, and, after a 'wonderful' Chopin recital by Alfred Cortot, she joined Toscanini and Stefan Zweig in the ante-room to the artist's dressing room.[42] The conductor embraced her, kissing 'cara Mausi' time and again, and asked after her family.

After this encounter he sent her a letter in broken English that she proudly copied out and sent to her aunts. He wrote that Daniela had often praised her to him and that the two old ladies deserved her affection. 'Now that I met you – spoke to you looking at your beautiful face I can say that I was able to read in your eyes the goodness that your heart conceal [*sic*].' He called Bayreuth 'the deepest sorrow of my life'. Everything to do with Wagner filled him with passion, and his break with Bayreuth repeatedly occupied his thoughts.[43] Frie-delind wrote to her aunts excitedly: 'I had an unbelievably wonderful time – I was really with the Maestro and no one else, and he was sweet and touching and loving – in short – everything! I wallowed in music day after day and was in every rehearsal from start to finish.' He rehearsed for an all-Wagner concert – it was as if he had chosen it just for her – and he took her to lunch. In the concert she 'dressed as beautifully as possible and had my best hair-do' and sat next to Toscanini's wife. Afterwards Madame Rothschild gave a supper 'to which I naturally couldn't go, in spite of all my love for the Maestro!' Instead she went to a 'highly cultivated Lord and his wife'. Turning down the (Jewish) Rothschilds was in line with her racial beliefs, acquired from Chamberlain's writings and elsewhere and as yet still virulent. Her doubts in this regard would only come later. But when she was invited to the estate of Lady Sybil Cholmondeley (1894–1989), which was well-nigh feudal in its grandeur, she accepted – despite knowing that her hostess was Jewish. So she was hardly consistent.[44] Toscanini made her promise to write regularly. She looked forward to the following October when he was due to return, and she took her leave from him when he set off for home in Milan.[45]

Daniela offered a typically ecstatic commentary:

I can't tell you how happy I am about your relationship to our dear friend, this incomparable artist, and how his tender love for you touches me – and if a drop of jealousy is here I would have to think of Wotan's words: 'to yield in gladness to the ever-young',[46] and would only feel joy. Youth is the ray of hope in his ageing life, so rich in sadness – and in your lovely appearance a living part of that Genius approaches him that he has honoured throughout his great life as an artist.

She was right in this, for Toscanini loved to talk about the Wagner family. Friedelind's close familial relationship to his revered Master fascinated him, as did her facial resemblance to Wagner. Toscanini had first experienced Wagner's music in 1878/79 in Parma when he heard the overture to *Tannhäuser*. When Bologna became the first Italian city to perform *Lohengrin*, he was a cellist in the orchestra pit. 'From that first rehearsal onwards – even, really, from the first bars of the prelude – I was overwhelmed by magical, celestial emotions; the heavenly harmonies revealed a new world to me', he wrote.[47] In 1889 he visited the Bayreuth Festival for the first time, together with the impresario Giulio Gatti-Casazza. But it would be many years before he could conduct there on account of protests from Daniela and Eva – the very same women who later became his most passionate supporters. They still had influence in Bayreuth back then, and had preferred Karl Muck above him. But by 1929 Siegfried finally decided to invite the world-famous Italian all the same.

Daniela attended his rehearsals, which he conducted from memory, and in which he revealed details that others missed. Soon her enthusiasm knew no bounds. In August 1937 Daniela attended his Salzburg performance of *Die Meistersinger* that has since entered the annals, and just a few days later put her impressions down on paper:

> I can find no words for the experience. It was for me the fullest revelation of this divine work because it was a creative act that emerged from the spirit of the work itself. Its sublime grandeur, right up to its very apotheosis, had been experienced by none of us to such a shattering extent. And then these subtleties, these tender moments, this clarity, transparency; and all the artists were of a precision such as one never finds, inspired by this leading genius and all raised up above themselves by him.[48]

*

How was it possible that Friedelind could so revere a man who was over 70 years in age? Toscanini was regarded at the time as the most brilliant conductor in the world, and even today his fame is unrivalled. His aura was legendary, he was handsome, and he always dressed impeccably and stylishly. Orchestral musicians and listeners alike have endeavoured to explain the fascination that his performances exuded. The violinist Samuel Antek, who played for years under him, wrote that his musicians felt like individuals, not mere subordinate orchestral players.

> This meant that everything you did, every note you played, possessed the same intensity and the same expression as if you were playing for yourself alone. He fired you up, he challenged you to give your best. Making music under him became once more a holy calling … we put up with the terrorizing and the curses that Toscanini screamed at us, bearing with them because they had their origin in his own humility, his own sincerity and his love for music.[49]

Toscanini was not just an outstanding artist, but had a personality able to cast a spell over others. Both the artist and the man made a huge impression on Friedelind. She had early on developed a sensitivity to the talents of others and immediately recognized his genius. She also remembered with great affection his performance of the *Siegfried Idyll* at her father's funeral.

Friedelind kept her two aunts informed of her experiences and her feelings in the words of a smitten teenager. 'Where is He now, perhaps?' she asked, the capital letter essentially raising 'Him' to divine status. 'You just want to hurry after him – on wings – only very quickly – close to him, you feel so protected and strong – safe from every storm ...! May the heavens bless him – the good man – the beloved – the great man!'[50] Together with two girlfriends she listened to his broadcast of Verdi's *Falstaff* on the radio, though the reception only worked when they held the radio cable in their hand as an antenna. 'And so I sat with my two friends – Norns at work!'[51]

Friedelind did not just attend Toscanini's concerts. She was enjoying London's music life to the full and so declined to return for the 1937 Bayreuth Festival. Numerous German artists were performing in London, including many who had been driven out because they were Jewish. Performances of the *Ring* in Covent Garden featured Frida Leider, Maria Müller and Max Lorenz in the first cycle, with Lauritz Melchior and Kirsten Flagstad in the second – Flagstad was giving her debut there as Brünnhilde. On one occasion Friedelind sat in the same box as Anna Mahler, the daughter of Gustav, but no further contact resulted.[52] Furtwängler also brought the Berlin Philharmonic to London. At a Toscanini rehearsal in June Friedelind got to know the pianist Isabella Valli (later Isabella Wallich), the niece of the recording pioneer Fred Gaisberg, and the result was a lifelong friendship. A voice next to Isabella exclaimed suddenly: 'What on Earth are you doing here? Nobody is allowed to be at the Toscanini rehearsals.'[53] Friedelind calmed down when she learnt that Isabella too belonged to the chosen few. Through Isabella, Friedelind and Frida Leider also got to know Colleen ('Coggie') Margetson, who later became known as an artist and a caricaturist. After their first meeting, Isabella took Friedelind in her father's spacious limousine on a day trip to Oxford, along with Yaltah Menuhin (the sister of the world-famous violinist Yehudi), who was in London, and bored. A chauffeur drove them to visit Isabella's brother Mondy. Another student by the name of Jobst von der Gröben was very keen to meet Yaltah, so invited her into his rooms to show her his grand piano – at which she sat down and played Beethoven's Fifth Piano Concerto including all the orchestral passages.[54] Friedelind reported nothing of all this in her letters to her aunts; did she perhaps want to remain silent about having met Jewish musicians?

Friedelind had planned to visit Paris and this she did indeed convey to her aunts, though she asked them not to mention it to anyone else. 'I'm only going to write to Mama when I have all the necessary documents, otherwise she could put a stop to it all because she thinks it's too daring.'[55] Daniela found her plans 'risky, rushed and a little adventurous', but closed her letter in conciliatory terms with a quote from Beethoven's *Fidelio*: '"But I'm courageous" – you can sing lustily along with Leonore's words ... so now, lucky child – good luck for Paris! Greet Blandine, Leonardo, Rembrandt and Raphael in the Louvre

and don't let yourself be led astray by the powder pots of the perverse Paris-
ian ladies!'[56]

Friedelind scraped her last money together and risked the trip to Paris in
September 1937, later describing it as 'the most wonderful seventeen days of
my life'. She stayed with the French composer Gustave Samazeuilh (1877–1967)
who also wrote about music and translated, and had made a French version of
the text to Wagner's *Tristan*. When the Berlin State Opera came for guest performances in Paris, she spent all her time with the members of the ensemble.
She roamed the streets of the metropolis on the hunt for things worth seeing.
Daniela took an intense interest in Friedelind's impressions of the city, advised
her to take her time and suggested that they should visit Venice together. Rus-
kin's *Stones of Venice* would be good to prepare them for it.[57] For Friedelind's
return to England she recommended seeing important pictures: 'In the print
Room of the British Museum, and also in the Malcolm Collection, you will
find innumerable drawings and studies by Michelangelo.'

At home, Daniela was busy giving her critical opinion of Wieland's stage
designs for a new production of *Parsifal*. She was convinced that Wagner's
own staging should be maintained 'as part of a holy tradition dating back 50
years'.[58] When Wieland rejected her criticism she found him 'brusque, almost
impertinent, without any respect, and without any warmth of heart'.[59] But her
niece defended Wieland, stressing that the music drama would not be des-
ecrated if the grandson of the Master went about his designs with due seriousness. 'After all, we are the same family – and the same blood – and so mutual
understanding – if only through small compromises – should be possible!'[60]
In this instance, Friedelind showed a serious desire to smooth out conflict.

When did Friedelind decide to leave Germany for ever? Looking back, she
herself situated her inner decision in the year 1937 and called it 'a conscious lie
from a certain source' to claim that she had emigrated only later.

> I left Germany on 7 May 1937 – the day before was the Hindenburg dis-
> aster – but I had to show my face again in the summer of 38 because I
> was not yet of age and they could have brought me back by force if they
> had known that I would stay away. The pretty face my mother and Hitler
> made when they were informed was captured on film by my brother
> Wieland. Already back then I wanted nothing to do with those criminals
> – nor do I want to have anything to do with today's far-right mafia …[61]

The photo in question shows Winifred and Adolf in a bad mood, which could
indeed have been prompted by news of Friedelind's departure. But we must
nevertheless doubt this version of events, for Friedelind's letters of the time

remain as yet uncritical of the regime. Only towards the end of 1938 do her political doubts surface.

Friedelind's brothers were meanwhile busy at home with their further education, and Winifred was still meeting 'Wolf' every now and then ('The Führer let us know he was coming – and I had him all to myself from two to six, all perfectly cosy – it was so lovely – because with me he can touch on very intimate, personal things that really got to him in Braunau and in Linz – I know both towns – and on his experiences there in his earliest youth!!!').[62] Friedelind, however, was still happy to be abroad. Her family name opened the doors of opera houses and concert halls and gave her unhindered access to both dress rehearsals and the artists themselves. Her desire to train as an opera director was undimmed, as was the urge to step out of her mother's shadow. Perhaps it was not just her problems with her mother, but also her conflict with Heinz Tietjen and with the family's financial advisor, Albert Knittel, that drove her away from Bayreuth.

In late 1937, Hitler told the generals of the Wehrmacht that Germany needed 'Lebensraum', 'living space' in the east, and would have to acquire it by force. In February 1938 he replaced the heads of the army. The majority of Germans still stood by his one-party state – and, after all, Adolf Hitler had repeatedly stated his supposed desire for peace. It did not bother most people that human rights were being eroded. The invasion of Austria on 11 March 1938 was accepted by many as a positive event – not least thanks to the weekly newsreels showing the jubilant masses. Not until the invasion of Poland over a year later did Germans begin to realize that contravening international law would sooner or later have consequences. But by then it was too late to react, for all opposition was being violently suppressed. Most Germans also chose to ignore the increasingly unscrupulous persecution of the Jews. The success of the Olympics in 1936 had underlined Germany's international importance, while the building of the Autobahn and the many seeming successes proclaimed by the regime all served to mute any contrary voices. And what was more: many of the country's citizens did not just tolerate state-sanctioned racism. They positively welcomed it.

Chapter 5

'Is it German, what Hitler has done for you?'
1938 to 1939

WHILE VERENA was lunching with Hitler on a trip to Berlin in January 1938, her sister was still in England. Far away from events in Germany, Friedelind was brimming with initiative and living on a generous 200 marks a month. Life was good.

Winifred was glad to have enough hard currency to keep her uncomfortable daughter at arm's length. 'Every month in England is a relief to us. Geissmar says she is always there during office hours and helps her out a lot with correspondence. That's a strange child! She won't help Bayreuth and her mother, but she'll do it voluntarily for the Jewess!!!!'[1]

Friedelind's intellectual exchange with her aunts continued unabated. Daniela and Eva read Shakespeare's *Coriolanus*, a work that according to Eva 'was a particular favourite of your grandfather's'. They also started on Balzac's novel *Illusions perdues*, which depicted a Paris – according to Daniela – 'where the beast and the devil reign in the shape of man, along with poverty, vice and despair (it's nothing for the young like you!)'. Friedelind replied cheekily that the youth of the day was enlightened, 'while you were probably as innocent as lambs at the age of nineteen ... and a little nine-year-old squirt probably knows more than both of you at 77'.[2]

In February, Furtwängler conducted two concerts in London that Friedelind criticized cockily ('the Brandenburg was as weak and characterless as the whole man himself').[3] Daniela defended him, despite her overbearing love of Toscanini:

> You're unjust towards Furtwängler with your harsh, brusque judgement. To be sure, I know what he lacks: in Bach the strength of characterization and the fervour of religious feeling, and in Beethoven the frisson of the daemonic, mysteriousness and the ecstasy of delight. Yet I once heard an extraordinarily beautiful Eroica from him, crystal clear in its structures, while another time the Andante-Adagio of the 9th Symphony was almost heavenly in its beauty, so much so that I wrote to your father back then to say that if Toscanini's star had not risen in our firmament, then Furtwängler could have been the right man for *Parsifal*.[4]

Concerts followed with Willem Mengelberg and Felix Weingartner on the podium, then a solo evening by Fritz Kreisler. Eugene O'Neill's play *Mourning becomes Electra* overwhelmed Friedelind; a performance of Shakespeare's *Othello* made less of an impression, however. She was also impressed by an exhibition of paintings from the seventeenth century, and spent many hours in different art galleries.

England was full of artists who had left Germany for fear of the political situation. They included the lied singer Elena Gerhardt (1883–1961), with whom Friedelind now took lessons. Gerhardt's husband Fritz Kohl had been chief administrator of the Mitteldeutscher Rundfunk (the 'Central German Radio'), but had fallen into disfavour with the Nazis and was arrested in 1934. His wife thereupon fled to England. After his release from custody he also came to London, where his wife was establishing herself as one of the most important interpreters of the German lied.

Friedelind continued to visit Lady Sybil Cholmondeley, who often invited artists to her splendid house in Kensington Palace Gardens (nicknamed 'Millionaire's Row' by the locals). Lady Cholmondeley was the sister of the politician Philip Sassoon and a friend of Winston and Clementine Churchill; she would be appointed Chief Staff Officer to the Director of the Women's Royal Naval Service in the Second World War. Musicians were allowed to practise in her home, the Toscaninis were often house guests, Arthur Rubinstein held his wedding reception there and, before the outbreak of war, Friedelind, too, was on occasion invited to stay the night. Since Lady Sybil's husband consistently went to bed at eight in the evening and never showed his face at her dinners, Lady Sybil's marital life was not without its frustrations, as she once admitted to Toscanini.[5] She belonged to the large circle of women who fell for the charms of the conductor, as several of her letters confirm. Toscanini enjoyed the attention she gave him, but did not take her overly seriously, once writing of Lady Sybil that 'I've tried to give her paternal advice, but it's all been futile.'[6] Friedelind's own tendencies to romantic rapture thus found a receptive environment in London.

The quarrels between her aunts and her mother smouldered on. Eva drafted a letter to Winifred to announce that she would not attend the first series of operas at the forthcoming Festival and would place her box at the disposal of others. 'As the daughter of the Master, a well-nigh degrading state of things has come about on the hill that was once so familiar to me,' she wrote.[7] It was presumably the failure to observe old hierarchies that bothered her, for Winifred held little regard for the supposed higher status of someone who just happened to be a daughter of Richard Wagner. Eva had to suffer being pushed to one side by a 'mere in-law'. Daniela was mourning the loss of her villa in Gardone in Italy that had once belonged to her and her husband Henry Thode and which had been confiscated. Friedelind also learnt that Daniela wanted to visit her 'noble Jewish friend' Max, Baron von Waldberg (1858–1938), in Heidelberg, who had in 1933 published Cosima's letters to her. He was a former professor of German who had taught at the University of Heidelberg from 1889 until he was forced into retirement in 1933. This phenomenon of classifying Jews en masse as 'inferior' human beings while repeatedly making individual exceptions was nothing unusual in the family. Richard and Cosima had done the same, and Winifred would follow in their footsteps.

In March 1938, Friedelind flew to Berlin to attend a production of her father's opera *Der Schmied von Marienburg* ('The Smith of Marienburg'). Her mother had provided the air ticket. She partied throughout the night, returning to her hotel at half-past six in the morning to take a bath and eat breakfast, 'and then the next full day started'.[8] For her attendance at the opera the 19-year-old Friedelind took great care with her appearance. She wore an embroidered black silk dress with a train and on top of this an evening coat of lacquered silk, ornamented with brightly coloured and golden flowers that Frida Leider had given her as a gift. And she wore red polish on her toenails.[9] At last she wanted to put behind her the image of an overweight tomboy and be accepted instead as a pretty, even elegant, young woman. Winifred thought she looked 'like a mannequin in the window of a hairdresser's – we'll get that out of her system bit by bit'.[10] She clearly thought she would still be able to impose her discipline on a daughter just weeks shy of her twentieth birthday. But Friedelind had long been experimenting with how she looked and would listen to no one's instructions any more.

While staying in Berlin she made a brief trip to Bremen in order to hear her adored Frida Leider sing Isolde there. Friedelind was yet again thrilled by her performance, both vocally and dramatically.[11] Afterwards, the two of them sat together into the early hours. The German army had marched into Austria on 12 March, which meant that Frida's Jewish husband Rudolf Deman was no longer protected by his Austrian nationality from the Nazis' anti-Semitic agitation. 'Our life had become a lingering crisis,' Frida Leider later wrote of this time.[12] Friedelind's doubts about the nature of the Nazi régime can only have increased during these weeks and months.

She stopped off in Bückeburg on her way back to Berlin in order to visit Verena at her school. In mid-March she returned to London where she heard the Menuhins play, and Rachmaninov too – his performances proved unforgettable. By sneaking into rehearsals she was able to hear these programmes several times. Friedelind was also determined to hear Toscanini's London concerts in May and June and wanted to try and find a job at the Royal Opera House.[13] But nothing came of this, and the opera house was in any case closed just over a year later when war broke out. For Friedelind, a job at the Royal Opera could have changed everything; she would surely never have left later for America, but would have remained in Europe to train professionally as an opera director.

In June 1938 Friedelind travelled back to Bayreuth from London, albeit under some duress. She now felt uneasy about the increasing impact of politics on the Festival, about propaganda initiatives such as selling huge batches of tickets to the Nazi leisure organization 'Kraft durch Freude' ('Strength through joy') and also about the many swastika flags that flew in the town. But the arts in Germany had long succumbed to the influence of politics. This was also the year when the notorious exhibition of 'Entartete Kunst' ('degenerate art') took place in Düsseldorf. Composers were attacked there too – among them Schoenberg, Weill, Krenek, Hindemith and Stravinsky. The music of Mendelssohn, Meyerbeer, Offenbach and Mahler had disappeared from the concert halls and opera houses and, from 1933 to 1941, musicians and composers who happened to be Jewish were forcibly ghettoized by being represented by the so-called 'Jüdischer Kulturbund' or 'Jewish Cultural Association' set up by the Nazis. In Berlin, Friedelind saw graffiti scrawled on the windows of Jewish-owned shops. So she could not remain unaware of the social, moral and legal calumny and the general chicanery to which her Jewish fellow citizens were being subjected.

The situation was also escalating in Bayreuth. Many artists had already emigrated. Frida Leider was under intense pressure and unable to cope. She experienced a nervous breakdown and called off her performances as Isolde. Her husband Rudolf Deman took it upon himself to tell Heinz Tietjen and, in the ensuing argument, the latter hurled insults for which Frida Leider could never forgive him.[14] Friedelind heard the shouting from the next-door room and was shocked at Tietjen's bullying. Frida Leider returned towards the end of the season to sing Isolde twice more, but thereafter broke off all contact with Tietjen for good. Friedelind also made it clear to him that his behaviour was unacceptable, and he later complained that 'after I threw out Deman, Maus never spoke to me again. She avoided me, pursing her lips. Up to the moment that she fled to Switzerland, she cut me off completely.'[15]

'Wolf' was back in Bayreuth again. Winifred was called to him in every free hour she had, whether after performances or at lunchtime, and Lieselotte Schmidt was impressed. 'She copes with everything with the strength of the gods. She goes under the sunlamp to make sure she looks good and, despite everything, she's kept her sense of humour. One can only marvel.'[16] Friedelind became bored at meals with Hitler because of his endless tirades and would yawn loudly to try and make him bring the meal to a close. She later claimed that when he gave a monologue about possible punishments for Kurt Schuschnigg, the chancellor of Austria up to its annexation by Germany, she had dared to suggest that a severe punishment would only make him a hero and a martyr. This did not go down well.[17] On the last day of Hitler's visit to Bayreuth they celebrated Wieland's acceptance into the Nazi Party, and in the evening Hitler invited all the artists to a reception. Friedelind also found time for frequent visits to the artist's pub the 'Eule' (the 'Owl'), and in reference to the two birds featured in *Parsifal* she wrote in its guest book 'from the swan to the dove to the owl! Friedelind Wagner'.[18]

Another young woman was also visiting the Festival in 1938: Unity Mitford (1914–48), an English aristocrat, sister-in-law of the British fascist leader Oswald Mosley, and herself an ecstatic disciple of the 'Führer'. Friedelind had heard of her and now got to know her in person. After a performance of the *Walküre*, Hitler took Unity with him in a special train to Breslau where they stood for hours, watching the march-past of participants from all over German-speaking Europe. They came from within the *Reich* and without it, including Germans from the Sudetenland (which was still part of Czecho-slovakia). When the crowds dispersed, Unity watched how masses of people ran to throng around Hitler: 'They were all sobbing & stretching out their hands & some of them managed to shout in chorus "Führer, wir schwören Dir aufs Neu, wir bleiben Dir auf ewig true".' ('Führer, we swear to you anew, we will remain eternally faithful to you.')[19] According to Friedelind, Unity spoke badly of England in Hitler's presence, though he did not take her too seri-ously. When war broke out between Germany and England in 1939, Unity shot herself in the head with a pistol. Although she survived her suicide attempt it left her severely brain-damaged; she was taken home to England where her mother looked after her until she died in 1948.

Daniela and Eva were not able to afford a trip to the Salzburg festival this year, and did not want to beg Toscanini to help them out.[20] So they decided instead to travel to Tribschen near Lucerne, where the 'Maestro' was also giving a concert. Not long after Austria's annexation, Toscanini was asked by leading members of the Swiss establishment to conduct at a small music festi-val in Lucerne. It had already been planned a year earlier, so was by no means intended as a political demonstration against Germany, as was often claimed later. All the same, the number of Jewish musicians taking part in the Lucerne Festival could only offend Nazi sensibilities.[21] To the surprise of everyone, Toscanini had agreed to take part in the Festival. Daniela wrote to Friedelind: 'Oh Maus, this is a farewell – for on the 21st I will leave here and meet Aunt Eva in Tribschen on 2 June. Will you perhaps think of the "good old ladies" there who have seemingly disappeared from your view for so long?'[22] She had not reckoned on Maus turning up there to surprise them – though this was precisely what she planned to do. Most of all, of course, Friedelind wanted to see and hear Toscanini. However, it was getting ever more difficult to organize an exit visa. Her opportunity arose when Gerta von Einem, the mother of a répétiteur in Bayreuth by the name of Gottfried von Einem, invited her to accompany them on a trip to Venice, via Switzerland.

Gottfried – who achieved fame as a composer after the Second World War – had fallen in love with Friedelind. He claimed to have received 'hundreds of letters' from her, so we can probably assume that his passion was at least for a while requited (the letters would be burnt by his later mother-in-law).[23] Both Winifred and the Baroness von Einem approved of the liaison. The latter was wealthy, travelled in a large English automobile with chauffeur and promised to cover all of Friedelind's costs outside Germany. This made the Baroness ideally qualified in the eyes of her adventurous young female companion. They agreed to meet in Zurich, and Friedelind arrived first. She ordered lunch in the hope that the Baroness would not break down on the way but would turn up in time to pay the bill – which luckily she did. Friedelind and Gottfried then travelled to Tribschen in good time for the dress rehearsal on 21 August, and there spent two 'extremely happy days'. Daniela was surprised and delighted to see her niece.

Toscanini was spending the summer weeks in Lucerne and, as usual, attracted other top-class artists too. The pianists Vladimir Horowitz and Rudolf Serkin performed at the Festival, as did the cellist Pablo Casals and the violinists Enrico Polo (a former classmate of the conductor), Adolf Busch and Bronisław Huberman. Toscanini conducted several concerts in Lucerne itself, in the art gallery and in the Jesuit Church. He also planned to conduct a concert in the park beside Wagner's former villa in Tribschen; Serkin had checked the venue out in advance and found it suitable. Comprehensive preparations were necessary to ensure that everything ran smoothly, not least because the conductor was extremely sensitive to noise and everything humanly possible had to be done to avoid any extraneous sounds. Car horns were forbidden in the vicinity, the steamships were diverted via Seeburg and the neighbouring farms had to lock away their chickens and their dogs. Ellen Beerli, the custodian of Tribschen, joked that even 'the ducks on the lake had their beaks tied together so that they wouldn't quack'.[24] Carpenters built a pavilion for the orchestra and set up chairs for the audience, some of whom had travelled from afar to be there.

Daniela had a shock when she saw an unknown woman in Toscanini's car as he drove into Tribschen; it caused the 78-year-old lady 'great emotional torment', according to Ellen Beerli.[25] It was a lovely summer evening;

the Maestro conducted an elite orchestra of assorted illustrious musicians including Adolf Busch as concert master. They played an overture by Rossini, Mozart's Symphony in G minor, Beethoven's Second Symphony and the Prelude to the third act of Wagner's *Meistersinger*, plus the *Siegfried Idyll* as a special homage to Tribschen, since Wagner had composed the work there as a birthday present for Cosima after the birth of their son Siegfried. The concert was broadcast by the National Broadcasting Company and 80 associated radio stations, and was beamed direct to America and elsewhere. Regrettably, the evening ended in discord when the conductor refused two giant bouquets with the words 'I'm not a ballerina' and rushed out of his dressing room. His entourage was used to such sudden mood swings, but it still served to ruin the otherwise pleasant atmosphere. Ellen Beerli commented laconically: 'That was a nasty reverse to my enthusiasm for this king of the baton, because you don't end such a great event with whims like that.'[26] The *Siegfried Idyll* in particular made an unforgettable impression on Friedelind, for Toscanini had conducted the same work at the funeral service for her father. To her, Wagner's musical homage to Cosima belonged first to her family, and only then to the general public.[27]

After Tribschen, Friedelind travelled with Gottfried and his mother via Milan to Paris, and then on to Venice. In the Hotel Daniele, Friedelind and Gottfried had separate rooms that were (so Gottfried later recalled) connected by a door.[28] From time to time Baroness von Einem sent up a chamber maid to spy through the keyhole to see if anything was happening. Since Friedelind later claimed that only Gottfried had been in love with her, not she with him, then one of them was clearly being less than wholly truthful.

Once back in Germany, Friedelind went to Berlin to apply for a visa that would allow her to travel again to Paris. Then she returned to Bayreuth. Winifred was away, so for a few days she was alone and left to her own devices. She was an adult now, a 20-year-old woman with as yet an unclear future. 'Those were magical days, mixed with a soft, melancholy undertone,' she wrote. During the day she would peruse books in the large library once owned by her grandfather, or wander deep in thought along the chestnut-lined path in Wahnfried's garden, recalling many childhood memories. In the evening she dined with her aunts who had meanwhile returned from Lucerne, and she will surely have intimated to them that she wanted to leave. She packed her most important books and music, though she left some clothes behind to avoid giving the impression that she had fled. When Winifred let her know that she would be returning home earlier than planned, Friedelind was taken by surprise. For safety's sake she hid her passport in the neckline of a dress.

At first, all went smoothly. Winifred was indignant when she learnt that

Friedelind had met Toscanini in Tribschen, for Lucerne was to her a city where Jews and the enemies of Germany congregated. Furthermore, Toscanini had refused to conduct in Bayreuth. This time, Friedelind did not keep her conflict with Winifred to herself, but wrote to her aunts to tell them of it. 'There was a terrible thunderstorm at home yesterday evening because of Lucerne!! But what does it matter afterwards!!! I reckoned with this, after all!'[29] Nor did Friedelind's proposed trip to Paris please her mother. She was keen to project a picture of a harmonious family to the outside world and felt that her daughter's behaviour was bad publicity for the Wagner name. Friedelind could only get out of the situation with a white lie: she said she had to travel to Berlin to see to various matters within the week. But she actually wanted to use the trip as a means to get away altogether. Her mother finally relented and let her go.

Friedelind did indeed travel to Berlin, and from there made a brief visit to Heiligengrabe. She even felt a certain nostalgia for the school that she had formerly hated so much: 'It's always like coming home – everything has stayed the same, with the same teachers' faces ...' But over everything hung the shadow of war. She soon left for Paris, and after arriving she wrote to her aunts that 'The political situation is rapidly getting worse – from hour to hour, one can say – and God knows what will come of it!' She continued: 'I am not very comfortable about sitting in a foreign country under these circumstances. Yesterday there were seven more murders in Czechoslovakia – Sudeten Germans and Czechs. Everything now depends on the Führer! King Heinrich's words must be my motto: "Lord, let me be wise"!!'[30] Despite all events, she still trusted Hitler to put things right.

In Paris, Friedelind stayed in the Hotel Bedford and from there she looked for an apartment. She visited Germaine Lubin, who had given a successful debut as Kundry in Bayreuth. Germaine invited her to the house she owned in the Auvergne, and there Friedelind spent a wonderful week in the countryside. The political situation remained tense, and the danger of war increased as Hitler's plans for Germany's expansion took on more concrete form. The Czechoslovakian Republic had existed only since 1918. A large number of ethnic Germans lived there, primarily in the border region known as the 'Sudetenland', and it was Hitler's aim to 'liberate' them. Friedelind was urgently advised to leave France 'until one can see how the situation will develop'.[31] She decided to travel first to Zurich in order to meet Frida Leider and other friends in the Hotel Dolder, after which she could spend several days in Tribschen. She begged her aunts not to let her mother know she was in Switzerland.

In late September 1938 the heads of government of Britain, France, Italy and Germany signed the so-called Munich Agreement that was believed by many to provide a solution to the festering international crisis. No representatives from Czechoslovakia were invited, and the Agreement gave Hitler permission to annex the Sudetenland. So on 1 October 1938 the Wehrmacht marched in. There were mass demonstrations against the Nazis in Czechoslovakia, and afterwards the windows were smashed of Jewish and Czech citizens in an act of reprisal.[32] Friedelind thought the Agreement had solved the conflict peacefully, and so by 3 October she was back in Paris. She did not suspect that just five and a half months later the Wehrmacht would march on Prague and annex the rest of Czechoslovakia.

For the moment everyone breathed a sigh of relief, as the threat of war seemed to have receded. Friedelind was among them: 'But now it's peace – unbelievable, incredible! What a blessing for the whole world!' she wrote on 3 October. She went to see Gluck's *Alceste*, listened to French music, and heard *Tristan und Isolde* with Kirsten Flagstad and Carl Hartmann in the title roles (Hartmann had that same year been the second Tristan in Bayreuth). Her assessment of Flagstad as Isolde reveals her increasing experience:

> Flagstad's voice is wonderful – fresh and youthful, possessed of magnificent clarity – metallic and luminous. Her top notes in particular are flawless and offer everything – more than is necessary – whereas she has almost no low register. As an actress she has nothing – she does not understand her role (she just sings the words) and can't manage it all on her own, meaning that she comes across as terribly cold. One could do wonders with her! Tietjen dropped her in 34 – sadly! A great loss![33]

Friedelind was living in a small one-room apartment on the Rue Mansart that belonged to the singer Norma Gadsden, whom she knew from Bayreuth. It was on the edge of Montmartre, and from there she could look out over the rooftops to Sacré Coeur. The Opéra gave her a permanent free pass and she made full use of it. When she wasn't wandering the streets of the city she took French lessons (in which language she made rapid progress), went to concerts, took courses and studied scores. In November she received a surprise visit from her two English friends Isabella Valli and Colleen Margetson, and together they 'turned the apartment upside-down': Friedelind played the piano and they all sang, sometimes mimicking others. They spent hours playing through *Tristan* at the piano, singing all the roles. Friedelind had a particular success with her portrayal of Kundry in the first act of *Parsifal* and with her Brünnhilde, using a cooking pot as a Valkyrie helmet. Then she arranged her hair like her grandfather Richard and put on a beret that merely heightened her physical resemblance to him, prompting yet more laughter. At midnight they sang and danced from *Carmen* in the hotel, and in the taxi they moved on to the *Meistersinger*. They also sampled the city's cultural highlights. They went to the Louvre at night – for twice a week the Greek, Egyptian and mediaeval departments were specially lit up – and they wandered in and out of antique shops and ate in fine restaurants.[34]

But political events could not be ignored any longer. On 9 November 1938 the Nazis organized the so-called 'Kristallnacht', a night of terror against its Jewish population in which the general public was also partly mobilized. They smashed shop windows, plundered businesses, destroyed synagogues, arrested 20,000 Jews and murdered others. Friedelind's negative view of Nazi policies now found new confirmation and intensified her desire to remain out of Germany. In late 1938 Hitler revealed his true intentions in a speech to journalists. He wanted to make clear to the people that some things could not be resolved peacefully. He had always spoken of peace before, he said, but now he had to 'shed light on certain occurrences so that in the mind of the broader masses the conviction gradually but automatically takes hold that if things cannot not be remedied for the good, then they must be remedied by force'. Preparing the population for war had been 'begun systematically, continued systematically, and has intensified'.[35] It was unimaginable that Winifred knew none of this. But in later years she remained unchallenged in her insistence that no politics had been discussed at Bayreuth. Instead, right now, she was enjoying a new Mercedes that the 'Führer' had given her as a Christmas present.

When Furtwängler came to conduct in Paris in December 1938 he met and spoke with Friedelind. He mentioned his own conflict with the Nazi regime and admired her decision not to return home. But he ignored her suggestion that he should remain abroad. She also learnt from him that she was believed to be involved in a scandal surrounding Baroness von Einem, who was under suspicion of having worked as a spy. Friedelind found this ridiculous and wrote an angry letter to her mother to complain about it. Winifred's reply was so harsh, and Friedelind's reaction to it so furious, that she decided not to write to her mother at all for a while. Winifred tried to maintain contact and even went on a trip to Paris with Wieland to celebrate Friedelind's 21st birthday in spring 1939.[36] She tried time and again to stop her family from drifting apart. In June 1939 she asked Friedelind to send her at least a sign of life. 'Telephone calls, response telegrams paid for in advance etc. all remain unanswered – your former concierge in Paris does not know your address, meaning that no post can be forwarded. Madame Lubin let me know that you are in London, but I have no address …' wrote Winifred. And she asked point-blank: 'Are you mentally ill, my darling?'[37] Since the aunts also complained to Friedelind about her silence, she became convinced that her post was being intercepted by the state, and wrote to them: 'For weeks I've been trying to find out the secret behind the correspondence business – and I only have one conclusion. You'd better go and fetch the letters from Herr Himmler.'[38]

Friedelind now returned to London after a long absence. There she saw her beloved Toscanini again and attended his concerts – of which she constantly kept Daniela and Eva informed. She visited museums and went to concerts, plays and operas. She was particularly impressed by a performance of *Electra* by Sophocles given by a Greek theatre group and became acquainted with the actress who played the title role, Katina Paxinou (1900–73), who, with her husband, belonged to the ensemble of the Greek National Theatre in Athens. A few years later, Paxinou would become world famous as the gypsy Pilar in the film *For Whom the Bell Tolls* (1943).

Friedelind's stay in London also had a serious purpose, for she had gone there primarily to prepare for emigration to New York. She had even decided on the ship that should take her there – but was prevented from taking it because by then the Germans had invaded Poland. 'So I had to postpone it – but I'm not giving it up!'[39]

Friedelind will have learnt from the press that her mother had been awarded the 'Cross of Honour' created by Hitler for German mothers with large families and which, in this case, was bestowed by him in person. Friedelind did not go to the Festival in 1939, however, for she had inwardly already turned away from it. Hitler went, accompanied by Goebbels and 'Reichsleiter' Martin Bormann. Fifteen men from the band of the SS division 'Leibstandarte Adolf Hitler' played the traditional fanfares from the balcony of the Festspielhaus. Since Hitler had celebrated his 50th birthday just a few weeks before, a giant photo of him hung above the main entrance to the Festspielhaus, the so-called 'Königsportal', the 'king's portal'. He was planning big things for the town, and when its Lord Mayor Fritz Kempfler showed him the current plans for its 'Gauforum' – which included a building for the regional government, a hall for 10,000 people, a city theatre and a sports field – Wolfgang was there as well.

When Friedelind learnt that her aunts would be back in Tribschen that summer she decided to go there, too. In fact, Toscanini had expressly invited her (writing, as usual for them, in English): 'Why don't you come here I think it is worth while come come we are all waiting for you your old friend = Toscanini.'[40] When she heard the news, Daniela wrote to Friedelind in July 1939: 'Dearest Maus, as always you're cheeky, endearing and original – we expect you with the greatest pleasure on the 28th at the latest. Your bed is made, Italian grammar will land in the waste paper bin, calligraphy lessons suspended, but stage directions by the Norns will be guaranteed.' Friedelind wanted to 'talk over a lot and study a lot' with Daniela because she had closely observed Cosima's productions in Bayreuth. In keen expectation of a few care-free summer weeks she wrote to her aunts from London to invite them to visit an exhibition of Spanish artists in Geneva. Daniela became the butt of her mockery, for whenever something did not appeal to her, she would claim to be too old for any such adventures; but when something indeed took her fancy, she would 'hop like a weasel'. 'She'd probably swim to New York to hear the Maestro – but she is too old to take a taxi from the Lisztstrasse to the Festspielhaus when Mr Tietjen is massacring the *Ring* (I don't blame her!). I'm just comparing how relative old age can be!'[41]

On 31 July 1939 a telegram arrived in Tribschen at eight in the morning: 'arrived, Maus'. Ellen Beerli had barely told the two delighted aunts the news when Friedelind was standing at the door: she had sent the telegram from Lucerne Station just half an hour beforehand.[42]

The political situation in Europe had worsened again. Toscanini would conduct just once more in Europe before the outbreak of war, and Lucerne again enjoyed the active presence of prominent guests such as Sergei Rach-maninov, Vladimir Horowitz, Pablo Casals and Bronisław Huberman. Besides Toscanini, the conductors present included Bruno Walter, Sir Adrian Boult and Ernest Ansermet. After a performance of Beethoven's Violin Concerto by Adolf Busch, Toscanini invited Friedelind to dinner in the traditional Lucerne restaurant of the Hotel Wilder Mann, where she sat with the two Busch broth-ers, the Serkins, the composer Samuel Barber, Enrico Polo and the unavoidable Eleonora von Mendelssohn[43] – an actress who was a descendant of the philo-sopher Moses and thus also a distant relation of the composer Felix. She was in love with Toscanini, boasted to have slept with him and had now arrived to pester him and his wife ('this woman behaves like a hotel guest in my house,' Toscanini wrote of her). The theatre director Max Reinhardt and the actor Rudolf Forster were two other beneficiaries of her insistent devotion.[44]

Toscanini's four concerts in the Art Gallery and two performances of Verdi's Requiem in the Jesuit Church were complemented by a conciliatory gesture on his part when he organized a special concert on the steps of the Villa Trib-schen, conducting a chamber orchestra of 15 players in the *Siegfried Idyll*. A small group of friends and relatives were invited. Friedelind had shut the aunts in their rooms during the preparations for it, and the surprise to them was complete. After the performance the two old ladies kissed Toscanini; without speaking a word he turned away, got in his car and drove off[45] – no doubt in full awareness of the impending European catastrophe.

From April to August the Soviet Union had been negotiating with England and France on the one side and Germany on the other. After Germany annexed Czechoslovakia, the mood changed. England was determined to accept no more German expansion by force, and since both England and France now gave a guarantee to maintain Polish sovereignty, Germany – eager to avoid a war on two fronts – began talks with the Soviet Union. On 24 August 1939 the foreign ministers Ribbentrop and Molotov signed a non-aggression pact in Moscow in the presence of Joseph Stalin that assured each party of the other's neutrality in case of war. A secret appendix to the pact agreed on a division of eastern Europe in respective spheres of interest, should a 'territorial realignment' of the region come about.

Friedelind, Eva and Daniela were still together in Tribschen when the Germans invaded Poland on 1 September and triggered off the Second World War. It was described in the Swiss press for what it was: an act of naked aggression. On 1 September the main Swiss newspaper, the *Neue Zürcher Zeitung*, ignored the propaganda claims of its big northern neighbour by writing of Germany's 'need to make Poland appear the aggressor'. The Swiss Federal Council ordered the mobilization of the Swiss army. Shortly after this, the government in London ordered the evacuation of mothers, children, the sick and disabled from the cities.

Toscanini and his wife Carla advised Daniela and Eva to stay in Tribschen for the duration of the war. But both felt compelled to return to Germany and did everything they could to get Friedelind to join them. On 24 September Arturo and Carla Toscanini travelled to New York on board the *Manhattan* from the French port of Le Verdon, accompanied by Igor Stravinsky and the doting Eleonora von Mendelssohn. Friedelind decided to stay in Tribschen until she had worked out an alternative. 'Toscanini knew that I would never in my life return to Nazi Germany. He was the only person who supported me in my decision and it was then he who helped me to enter the USA.'[46]

It was a difficult, undoubtedly painful process, turning from a supporter of the Nazis into their opponent. Contemporaries of Friedelind who also underwent such an inner conversion have described it as laborious and protracted.[47] But the invasion of Poland had finally opened her eyes and she now did all she could to convince her aunts of the rightness of her stance. According to Ellen Beerli, the custodian of the Wagner villa, there were dramatic scenes when the political situation was discussed. 'Our normally so solemn, quiet house had become very lively since the appearance of the "enfant terrible". Friedelind repeatedly brought up the matter of the persecution of the Jews, but her two aunts were not ready to abandon their unconditional admiration of Hitler. Although even these two staunch adherents could have harboured no doubts that this new war was one of aggression aimed at enlarging the Reich, they could not bring themselves to see Hitler as a criminal. 'Strong people like Mussolini, Hitler and Chamberlain are doing everything in their power to avoid this misfortune and to defend us against the terror of Bolshevism with that Jewish bloodhound Stalin at its head, and against the Jewish war mongers Roosevelt, Eden and innumerable others. As strange as it sounds, the terrible military build-up is in the service of peace, and the calm, prudent Ch[amberlain] has a firm grip on the balance of peace in Europe – let us trust him!' wrote Daniela. She seriously believed that 'the Jews' wanted world domination, and that

> ... they have already largely achieved it for a long while now. To be sure, I too have friends among the Jews – noble, benevolent, highly educated Jews whom I love and appreciate – and I also know that their mixing with the Aryan race has brought forth many an important, illustrious, endearing personality. But I would never misjudge the immense danger that the intrusion of this foreign race has brought and brings to every other people and whose modern, monstrous spawn is that Bolshevik against whom Hitler will fight to the death. But will he succeed?[48]

Their political squabbles continued almost daily. Once, when Friedelind rowed Daniela across Lake Lucerne, they had a loud argument at which Friedelind warned her: 'One more word and you'll be walking home!'[49]

When Daniela left Lucerne on 13 September 1939 – Eva had already left – Friedelind and Ellen accompanied her to the station. The scene was one of high drama. The aunt and her niece sensed that they would not see each other for a long time – perhaps never again. Daniela leaned out of the window of her railway carriage and said to Ellen: 'Carry on fighting for truth and justice as always!' These were astonishing words – had perhaps Daniela understood the truth, but was only able to acknowledge it in the intensely emotional moment of farewell? Daniela had often criticized Friedelind for using make-up, so Friedelind now took the edge off the situation by calling to her: 'Wipe your face, my kiss left lipstick on you!' 'Mausi, how could you?' cried Daniela, her indignation turning to laughter as the train rolled out of the station.[50] They would never meet again.

Daniela admitted to a friend:

> Our Friedelind, in whom you only see reflected all the pointless fads in which today's women are ensnared, has been a dear companion to us here. She is a splendid woman with a golden heart, great intelligence and talent – in whom, to be sure, many a rough edge must be filed away in order for her to attain harmony of being – and she is pursuing a straight path under highly difficult circumstances. She is in a well-nigh desperate situation with regard to her mother and the Bayreuth of today.[51]

Friedelind visited Frida Leider in Basel. Her husband had been living in a hotel for ten months because as an Austrian Jew he could not return home, nor did he want to. 'But no one may be allowed to know that we were here together,' wrote Friedelind to her Aunt Daniela, 'for all our dear friends in Berlin and Bayreuth would use it against us again!' Their mood was sombre, and Frida – according to Friedelind – was 'a bundle of nerves',[52] though she succeeded in cheering up the singer every now and then and was nicknamed 'the monster' by her (Daniela and Eva had already given Friedelind other nicknames – 'Oceana' and 'Ogre').

Friedelind did not want to remain too much longer in Tribschen. After the beginning of hostilities she had started to put out feelers to British politicians and to the British government. She was now ready to take a public stance against the Nazis. She wrote to the Conservative MP Sir Arthur Beverley Baxter (1891–1964), who was also an active theatre critic. He recognized Friedelind's potential propaganda value and made representations with the Foreign Office to get her permission to enter the country. It was, in the end, the chief civil servant Sir Robert Vansittart who gave the order to allow Friedelind into Britain.[53] Vansittart was an active opponent of appeasement and was one of the few who had acknowledged early on the danger that Hitler posed. He immediately agreed to Friedelind's request. Ever in good spirits, Friedelind was convinced that a combination of hard work on her part and the support of friends would enable her to earn a living.

Friedelind needed a French visa so that she could travel to Britain through France. This could not be arranged quickly so, to while away the time, she visited various events in Lucerne, including a concert by the world-famous contralto Sigrid Onégin (1889–1943), whom she met afterwards, and a charity event in the Hotel Schweizerhof, at which Albert Ferber (1911–1987) played the piano. She invited him the next day to a lunch that she cooked herself. Her thoughts strayed continually to Toscanini, whose refusal to conduct in Bayreuth and Salzburg now made him a role model to her. She poured out her heart to him in long letters and told him how it hurt her to have to leave her 'safe harbour', but that in the current situation she could not stay, since she would otherwise have to despise herself. Her current, oppositional stance, combined with the close ties between Bayreuth and the Nazi Party, now led her to believe that she was predestined to run the Festival in future:

Please, my dearest Maestro, do not worry about me – or think I do the wrong thing. Just think how *you* would react if you lived in my place …! I must do it. I cannot stop and dream. I must act. Every positive little thing I can do now – is already a stone for the future – for Bayreuth too! Who shall do it – if I don't???? The others are weak and will look at the moon all their life if they can help it. They are charming and beautiful and intelligent – but they have no backbone and no temperament and are so content in their comfort. They do not even know what Bayreuth is ...!![54]

Her undimmed self-confidence shines forth again here, encouraged by the example of the conductor to whom she owed the strength to break with her family.

Friedelind wanted to keep her future location secret from her mother, and Daniela promised to help. As a precautionary measure, letters to Verena were sent via Daniela, who would then invite her round to her Lisztstrasse home and pass them on.[55] But things still trickled through. Eva found out about Friedelind's intended country of residence in September, and wrote to her: 'Once more, fare well in your island refuge.' But it was difficult for Eva to avoid gossip among the family, and she admitted to her niece that 'your mother might possibly know about it already today.'[56] Winifred was annoyed at Friedelind's absence during the Festival, but was alarmed even more by her plans to stay away altogether. She complained that while the Festival was on in Bayreuth, her daughter was participating in 'anti-German cultural events ... that Jews and emigrants are organizing in Lucerne.' She wrote to Friedelind of her disappointment that she could place herself 'outside your family and your national community' at difficult times such as these.[57] Her stereotypical Nazi vocabulary sounds not a little ironic when we recall that Friedelind's aunts, neither of whom was averse to anti-Semitism, had also attended concerts in Lucerne. Friedelind now began to express herself more clearly. She answered that she wasn't mad enough to return to a place where friends were being arrested, and advised her mother to ship her own valuables to Switzerland for safe-keeping. Winifred now recognized the potential explosiveness of the situation and so, as a precautionary measure, sent her 'nice, gentle'[58] daughter Verena to Tribschen with the task of convincing Friedelind to come home. The two sisters had always been close, but Friedelind's will was stronger and she did not budge. Nor were Verena's efforts particularly convincing, for she sympathized with her. Their leave-taking was difficult for both of them, for they knew full well that it might be for ever. Friedelind compared her situation with that of her grandfather Richard Wagner, who had fled to Zurich for political reasons after the failed revolution in Dresden. She was convinced that she would be able to support herself by giving lectures.[59] The situation became more intense when Friedelind began to write accusations to her mother: 'At the same time that you are sending me proof of motherly affection, your best friends are allowed to slander me over and over again.' The gossip surrounding

Baroness von Einem was still niggling Friedelind. When she had travelled with the Baroness and Gottfried von Einem to Venice the year before, she could not have known that the Baroness was under surveillance. This in turn brought Friedelind under suspicion of being a spy. In fact, in 1939 she helped Gottfried to get out of Germany and enter Switzerland by inventing an uncle for him, and by forging a letter in which this 'uncle' assured the authorities that he would look after his nephew because he needed urgent medical treatment for tuberculosis. Gottfried had smuggled jewels from his mother's collection into Switzerland and now gave them to Friedelind for safe-keeping. They would cause Friedelind much trouble after the war.

Friedelind was now determined to ignore all warnings from her mother. The extent to which she had already distanced herself from her family's Nazi devotion can be seen in her exchange with Adolf Zinsstag, a jeweller and amateur musician who had been involved in maintaining Tribschen and had lobbied for the Wagner family to be given visiting rights to the house. Zinsstag sent her a copy of a letter from Siegfried Wagner to August Püringer in which Siegfried had argued against excluding Jews from Bayreuth. Püringer, the chief editor of the *Deutsche Zeitung*, had demanded that membership of the Festival Foundation – which was responsible for gathering donations – be denied to 'non-Aryans'. Siegfried had rejected the idea, for he did not want to alienate Jewish Wagner fans. Friedelind was delighted with the letter, and grateful to receive a document that seemed to exonerate her father from any charge of anti-Semitism. She wrote to Zinsstag to say she would very much like the international press to take note of it too:

> It is of great importance, especially for the future – when this dark nightmare is at an end – and we can hopefully – if God wills it – go to the rebirth of Bayreuth. It might sound fantastical – but I believe so wholeheartedly in it – and will not rest until it comes about. And this letter, thank God, has confirmed the rightness of my conviction – that I expressed loudly all those years – but of course people ignored 'the stupid blabberings of a child'![60]

She would later use the letter in her book.[61]

In December, Friedelind chatted to Zinsstag of her plans for the future over a meal of 'sauerkraut, Christmas songs and red wine', and he reported it to Daniela. She, in turn, passed the information on to Bayreuth, presumably also to Winifred. Back in 1930, Adolf Zinsstag had started a major protest against the changes to Wagner's Bayreuth *Parsifal* production and had been supported by Friedelind's aunts. So his name was enough to send Winifred into a rage. Friedelind in turn was furious at Daniela's 'betrayal', and wrote to her angrily that 'Now people will say of me that I'm conspiring against Bayreuth and goodness knows what. You had to know the effect that a letter from him would have! I really don't understand you.' She could not be pacified:

> You knew about all my plans and they can't have astonished you. I could not have imagined that with your intelligence you would repeat all the rubbish that the Propaganda Ministry bombards you with. All the letters that I get from Germany are the same – the way such lively minds allow themselves to be dumbed down really amazes one, if one isn't used to repeating everything mindlessly like a parrot![62]

The German High Consulate in Bern was watching Friedelind, and on 10 November 1939 a Swiss spy reported that she had repeatedly 'expressed herself in spiteful terms about the Führer and about National Socialist Germany. In particular, a few weeks ago, she said literally: "It won't take half a year, and this Hitler will be brought down." Furthermore, she has made secretive references to the fact that her earlier stays in England had provided her with good connections there and that she "could become English any time at all".'[63] Hitler will hardly have been pleased when he received information such as this. Verena was in Berlin, training to become a nurse, and met the 'Führer' there twice. The first time they talked mostly about her tasks in the clinic and about her exams, but on the second occasion she asked him to be indulgent towards Friedelind. Hitler replied that she had to remember that Friedelind was a traitor to her country, and so he could no longer protect her.[64]

Daniela made a last attempt to change the mind of her beloved niece. 'You must have known that Zinsstag would write to me after he visited you on Sunday a week ago, and you must have known too how much his news would disturb us and scare us ... Verena came to me late on the evening of the 5th of January, pale and crying dreadfully after what seems to have been a stormy scene in Wahnfried – and I was more or less able to calm the lovely, gentle child that loves you so much. Everyone is suffering.' Daniela then decided to travel to Friedelind together with Verena in order to talk through everything with her once more and 'to explain the desolate, calamitous consequences that your decision will bring if you estrange yourself from your father's house and family, fatherland and native country, and seek your fortune in foreign parts'. But her plan proved impractical – and presumably she was denied an exit visa. 'To go to England now, that heinous, embittered enemy of Germany – a German woman, a Wagner, who will perhaps only be used and exploited by the Jewish Internationale over there, used as a figurehead for their anti-

German plans and then cast aside! ... And then South America! To become a director at a big theatre!' At Toscanini's suggestion, Friedelind was now planning to direct operas in Buenos Aires. Daniela listed all the demands that would be made of her there: 'An immense knowledge of music, literature, art history, experience in stage technology, knowledge of the laws of optics, symmetry, harmony, logic, style,' as well as the ability to deal with people. She cited the example of Cosima, who had been 50 years old when she first directed an opera, 'and what an education and what experiences she had undergone, she who was born with genius. But you, despite your great intelligence, your sharp, critical mind, your healthy judgement, your artistic gifts – you lack all these prerequisites, and you also lack the strict self-discipline that every activity demands. Aren't you running straight towards a bitter disappointment?' And to finish with, she played what she thought was her trump card, for she knew that Friedelind trusted Toscanini unconditionally: 'Think of the beloved Maestro, who called you his daughter – and urgently advised you against travelling to America!'[65] But this could no longer do any damage, for Toscanini was now supporting Friedelind in her decision.

Daniela also wrote in some agitation to Adolf Zinsstag, insisting that Friedelind's 'brothers and sister are suffering under the current circumstances'. One way out, she felt, was for Friedelind to stay in Switzerland, where she could learn Italian or study the writings and letters of Richard Wagner in order to be useful to the Bayreuth cause. But she sensed that her niece would not bend. 'You see, dear friend, I am powerless – I can only hope with all my heart that the path through life for Siegfried's dear child will still shine forth for her, despite all the current darkness and confusion.'[66]

Zinsstag replied: 'I believe you will understand that I can arrange nothing according to your wishes here, and that Friedelind is for the time being in good hands and has become so fond of our Swiss, democratic nature that it is impossible for her ever to find her way back to the dictatorship in her homeland in which her beliefs and conscience would be subject to compulsion.'[67] Zinsstag's stance must have been a shock to the family back in Bayreuth. He also defended her decision to travel to England:

> She could simply do nothing else. She had to give expression to her emotions, which are quite contrary to the Third Reich, and live her life in a different direction, regardless of all the consequences. Here the implacable nature of her grandfather has found expression, for he too sacrificed everything for his ideals and for what he recognized to be right ... and his granddaughter today is acting in a quite similar manner. She, too, could have a good life, a brilliant life, enjoying all the favours of high-

ranking personalities – indeed, of the highest-ranking – and she could enjoy all the advantages of belonging to the Party, just as her siblings and her mother do. Instead she prefers to choose a completely unpredictable, insecure, even dangerous future, all for the sake of one, great thing: to give expression to her conviction, a conviction that was not imposed upon her by anyone, but which has come about of its own accord through her personal contact and acquaintance with a whole host of representatives of those powers that now hold the fate of Europe in their hands and that have manoeuvred the German people into the most terrible of wars ... one can think of her what one will, but she has thereby shown that she has character and would rather have a difficult, uncertain life than live within the constraints that would be demanded of her if she were compelled to return.[68]

Chapter 6

'It's precisely because I'm German that I'm not living in Germany'
The farewell
1940

FRIEDELIND HAD made up her mind. 'I won't let myself be ground through the mill if I can avoid it. And I will fight my whole life long for the truth only, for the good, the great and the divine – not for dirt and crime.'[1] These words, somewhat lofty but no less serious for it, were directed to Daniela while Friedelind was preparing for her departure to England. Once she had switched countries, she was emboldened in her sense of radical opposition to Nazi Germany and able to take a public stance in newspaper articles. She wanted to show the world – especially her mother – who was right in the coming battle. And she wanted the outside world to know what Wagner's granddaughter stood for. She had inwardly said farewell to her family and to their adulation of Hitler. Half measures were not for her. 'I now stand on a different shore from you all – and I have learnt to love and appreciate "Germany's arch enemies or mortal enemies", as you call them,' she wrote to Daniela. 'And I know that they don't want to destroy Germany. In fact, they want to save what can still be saved of its great human values. But it means sweeping aside the criminals, murderers and rabble-rousers who have caused immeasurable suffering in the whole world. Is it really German, all that Hitler has brought you??? Hasn't he turned the world into a miserable heap of rubble and doesn't he have the lamentations and tears of millions on his conscience – the death of the best of our youth and the greatest of our men?' The admiration that she had once felt for Hitler had now turned to loathing and hatred. She was well-nigh prophetic when she wrote to her aunt: 'Believe me, the day will dawn when you will all see the rightness of what I do, and perhaps sooner than you now think. Germany cannot win this war, because justice is not on its side. And since you went through all this just a quarter of a century ago, I am amazed how you can again rush blindly to your own destruction.' And she continued, referring to the Molotov-Ribbentrop Pact between Nazi Germany and the Soviet Union: 'I would under no circumstances want to deprive your National Socialist, Stalin-sodden beliefs of their glowing fanaticism – but I would just like you to allow me to hold my convictions and views to the same degree.' She asked her aunt to stay calm and not to manipulate Verena: 'She is in any case in a dreadful treadmill that will either break her or will make her grow stronger. I would have gladly desired a rosier youth for the dear creature.'[2] She signed the letter with her nickname 'Oceana', which seems here to symbolize the immense distance that divided her from her two old aunts.

Friedelind thus makes it clear that she had left her homeland for political reasons, not on account of her conflict with her mother or because of any mere desire for adventure. One of those who understood this was Wilhelm Furtwängler, who met her in Zurich in November when he was there to conduct a concert. She respected him greatly for his willingness to meet her, for she was now regarded by many in Germany as a traitor. 'Germans avoided me as if I were a leper!' she wrote. But Furtwängler ignored all that and invited her to dinner after his concert.[3]

At Christmas, Friedelind wrote a letter to her mother in which she said her farewells to Germany. She chose the most recent events to explain her stance. After Germany had invaded Poland's western border in September, the troops of the Soviet Union – as agreed in the Molotov-Ribbentrop Pact – had in turn invaded and occupied eastern Poland. Friedelind now situated herself in clear opposition to her family:

> Dear Mama, please accept my warmest Christmas wishes and greet-
> ings to all of you … I see no reason to cast myself into the arms of this
> nationalist-communist community and to greet it lovingly. Those that
> have betrayed Germany to Russia after playing a comedy of hatred for
> so many years have given a deathblow to Germany. And, sadly, the day
> is no longer so far away when all of you will have to pay for it. You have
> made all your sacrifices for nothing and will make all further sacrifices
> to no avail. But nothing should prevent you from continuing to do so for
> as long as you believe in it. However, this is not the case with me, and
> I cannot act against my conscience and support something that I must
> reject completely … I cannot make any compromises now – nor will I
> do so in future. But you will always be closest to my heart, whether you
> want it or not, since we simply belong together.[4]

By 'comedy of hatred' she referred to Nazi Germany's tirades against the 'Jewish-Bolshevist danger' of the Soviet Union, which had temporarily ceased since the signing of the Molotov-Ribbentrop Pact. And when she wrote that all her family's sacrifices would be for nothing, Friedelind was being remark-ably clear-sighted.

Wieland had a different view of things:

> Her craving for recognition has now led her to feel that she is a heroic
> emigrant … really, one has to feel sorry for her that she has gone so far

off the rails, because the extraordinary cleverness that people claim for her is hardly noticeable in her 'Credo'. The 'Jewishness in Music' from which she chooses her circle of friends may triumph now. Her spitefulness towards the Führer is not worthy of comment ... We have thus far followed our mother's desire to cover for Maus outwardly, but now we see no more reason for it. You will also surely understand this after her letter of 21.12. Sooner or later she will also come to her senses and realize where she belongs.[5]

And he wrote to Friedelind herself to say that he had been glad to receive her birthday telegram, 'since I still hoped that you would find your way home. Your Christmas letter taught me better, however. The influence of your Jewish "friends" was too strong to let you think clearly.'[6]

Daniela was of the same opinion as Wieland. She found her niece's letter to the family

quite shattering ... she has burnt all bridges between her and her family. But Friedelind cannot expect them to share or even merely listen to her political convictions, influenced as they are by the International. For quite apart from the politics and the party to which [her family] belongs, they are bound in deepest gratitude to the man who has taken them on and treats them like a second father![7]

All the same, she still came to the defence of her niece: '[Mausi] has been more or less "internationalized" through her long stay abroad ... but she is not the "traitor" that people want to make of her.'[8]

Wolfgang offered his own commentary to it all:

We have to wait and see what the 'poor child' intends to do in the coming time and what wise utterings about Germany and its leaders she sends by letter into the Reich (and which can thus be controlled). What's bad is that Mama and we don't have full knowledge of her epistolary stupidities. I gathered this from Frank, whom I recently saw at the opera and who knew everything about the matter.

'Frank' was Hans Frank, the Governor General of occupied Poland, later nicknamed the 'Butcher of Poland' and one of the worst criminals among the Nazi élite. Guilty of the murder of hundreds of thousands of Poles, responsible for setting up several death camps and a keen plunderer of art treasures to boot, he was close to the Wagner family. He knew Friedelind's letters and her views, for she was being watched carefully. 'Frank told me quite interesting things about Cracow. They are planning guest performances by the State Opera, which is to include a concert of works by Papa,' added Wolfgang.[9]

All the while, the brothers were busy dividing up the future family business between themselves. Heinz Tietjen was also once more at his intrigues, praising Wolfgang for his directing skills, and this prompted the latter to suggest a new division of labour to Wieland:

He thinks I'm more suited to directing than you are (which is also your opinion, as you once remarked to me). The matter could thus play out as follows: you take Mama's position, thus as manager of the festival, and you also take over the stage design, while I would take over Heinz's position, i.e. as artistic director and director … so you could stick to what you're gifted at, namely painting, and I could still pursue my other interests when the time arises.[10]

Friedelind now decided to invite her mother to Switzerland. Their relationship was beset by gossip and slander, and Friedelind hoped to be able to clear the air. But above all she wanted to assure Winifred that she did not want to damage Bayreuth. She was worried that the coming war might ruin the Festival and destroy the archives, memorabilia and valuables, and she hoped that everything might be transferred to Tribschen for safe-keeping instead.[11] So she now broke her own self-imposed silence. 'For I otherwise see no way to see you for God knows how long, since I'll first go to North America and then to South America … I would like to discuss so much with you.'[12] Winifred agreed to meet her, but not where her daughter was now staying. 'Under no circumstances can I go as a guest to Tribschen at present.' The powers-that-be would have taken a dim view of her visiting Lucerne, the place where Toscanini had conducted in the past two years and where numerous émigré musicians had already performed. So instead she suggested the Hotel Baur au Lac in Zurich.

There are, as you rightly say, connections of a deeper sort and I would like to ask that in the New Year you will at least treat these blood relations more lovingly than in the past year – you could thereby help me to get over much sorrow and much bitterness that your opinions have caused me … [please] preserve your relationship with us and let us have a little part in your personal life and wellbeing. You will get a letter of reply to every letter you send.[13]

But this was just what Friedelind could not do. By turning to the British 'enemy', a chasm had opened up that she knew was unbridgeable, and for that reason she had adopted silence as her preferred strategy.

Winifred arrived in Zurich on 9 February 1940 and she and Friedelind spent the night in the historic Hotel Baur au Lac. Here, 87 years earlier, Richard Wagner, while still a political refugee, had given public readings, over four evenings, of the libretti of his *Ring des Nibelungen*. And in 1856 in a spectacular soirée, Franz Liszt had accompanied him singing the roles of Hunding and Siegmund, in a concert performance of the first act of *Walküre* before an audience including Wagner's wife Minna, Otto Wesendonck and Otto's wife Mathilde, who had been the work's inspiration.

Winifred had received her special exit visa from SS Reichsführer Heinrich Himmler, who was hoping for the return of her renegade daughter. That naturally placed Winifred under extra pressure. Mother and daughter sat together to talk things out in the Veltlinerkeller, a restaurant in the Schlüsselgasse in the midst of Zurich's old city. 'Her face looked more English than ever, lively, distinguished, incorruptibly beautiful,' wrote Friedelind, and continued: 'We might have been strangers, polite strangers, for no warmth flowed between us.'[14] In her diary she wrote for 10 February: 'Big discussions. Stormy!' The tempestuousness was a result of two strong-willed women unwilling to give way to each other. Winifred suggested that Friedelind should visit Berlin for 24 hours and thus demonstrate solidarity with Germany. But Friedelind rejected this out of hand, since she wanted to make a public protest against Germany precisely by staying away.[15] Then Winifred suggested another solution, one she disliked but still saw as a possible compromise: Friedelind could stay out of Germany, but remain in a neutral country such as Switzerland. Friedelind, however, was not prepared to sit on the fence, but wanted to show how serious she was about rejecting National Socialism. She now had to listen to how she was in the service of the English intelligence apparatus and of 'international Jewry' (though the former charge, as it happens, was not wholly untrue, for she had made contact with Beverley Baxter while in Paris, who in turn had negotiated with the British authorities about her possible immigration. This was presumably already known to the German authorities).

Some of the words that Winifred is supposed to have used during this meeting were later denied by her, though they have often been quoted: namely that an order might come from on high that Friedelind would have to be 'eradicated and exterminated' if she did not return. But proof that Winifred did indeed issue such a warning is to be found in a letter that Friedelind wrote to Toscanini just after this meeting, for she would have had no reason to lie to him. Her sister Verena also claims that she heard these words from Himmler when she visited him, and that her mother had thus been quoting

him.[16] Verena's belief that the family was being protected by Hitler is proven
by a letter of Wolfgang's to Wieland: 'When we were recently with the Führer,
I immediately raised the matter so that he is properly informed. He says: as
long as she does nothing against Germany, it's not so bad, but if she did do
something then there would be no choice left but to deprive her of her citizenship ... as I already said, I told the Führer exactly of our opinion.'[17] Friedelind
had not yet published her articles ridiculing Hitler. It therefore seems that
Himmler treated the case more seriously than Hitler did.

Overall, the meeting with her mother went better than Friedelind had
expected. She wrote to Toscanini about it as follows (as always to him, in
English):

It was dramatic and pathetic in a way – but except one big discussion
we were peaceful and charming!! She got the permission to see me from
Himmler (of all people!! but otherwise it would have been impossible to
get away) – and this charming gentleman knew all my letters of the past
year by heart and recited them to her. And from him – and it seems
from Hitler too – I learnt the four ways I can chose [sic] between now:
1.   to come back to Germany at once
2.   to remain in neutral country and shut up and be a good Nazi
3.   to not shut up – then they would attempt to kidnap or kill me and
keep me shut-up somewhere during the war
4.   to go to enemy [sic] country, which means that I have to declare
that I am no more a German citizen – and that I have no more contact
with my family throughout my life etc.
No. 1 – of course – would be the most peaceful solution for any coward.
My mother offered me to live where I liked to and to do what I liked to
if I only came back.
  But I cannot! And I do not need to explain to you *why*!
No. 2 is impossible.
No. 3 does not scare me
No. 4 – which gives me full freedom – but at the same time stamps
me to a traitor – and which would make me loose [sic] my family and
everything inside Germany. Still – it is the only way I can go just now! I
may be a traitor to them – but I won't be a traitor to me – nor the entire
world. And I will never sign such a lousy paper and declare that I am no
more a German nor have anything to do with my family. I won't do that
– because I am a German. Because I am a German I am not in Germany
now – because this isn't Germany any more. And I am a Wagner – and
I love my family – even if it was little love that I received. I owe it to my

father – and the entire family – not only the one that lives now. And – I believe – once the war is over – my family will see clearer too.[18]

She then asked Toscanini for his opinion, which was more important to her than anything else. He replied to say that he agreed with her decision, and that he was ready to offer active help. This fact would soon assume great significance. In April 1940, Friedelind returned to her mother's threat in another letter to Toscanini:

> I am mightily sorry to have disappointed Herr Hitler so much and did not crawl back to his paradise to regain his favour after he had the wonderful idea of sending my mother to tell her own daughter that they would 'destroy and exterminate' me, if I did not behave as they did.[19]

We cannot assume that Friedelind mistook her mother's warnings. Decades later, Wieland's music teacher Kurt Overhoff interpreted them as a result of Winifred's fear of the possible consequences of her daughter's actions. 'A mother, scared to death, worrying about the fate of her child, was trying to prevent that child from taking a hugely dangerous step. If Friedelind had been captured back then, the dictator would not have let his veneration of Wagner's genius deter him from treating her as he did all his other enemies.'[20]

Although Winifred had achieved nothing, she still tried to maintain an otherwise friendly tone in dealing with her daughter. '11.2. Mama's departure. An emotional, warm farewell,' wrote Friedelind. On the way home from Zurich, during which the cheese she had bought in Switzerland was confiscated at the border, Winifred wrote to her:

> It would have been so lovely if we had made this journey together – we could be such good friends now and I would be happy about it – trials and tribulations occur in every life – but love can help us get over them and as I understand your point of view, so will you one day perhaps also understand your mother better! – Don't let Heinz stand between us – for my part I will make sure of that – but tolerate him next to me – I need him. – All my love and good wishes to you – and a hug from your Mama.[21]

Winifred had rarely displayed loving kindness towards her daughter, so the emotional tone of this letter is striking. Suddenly, Friedelind was no longer a 'child', but a fellow human being to be treated as an equal. Obviously the tensions regarding Winifred's relationship to Heinz Tietjen had played a role in their conversation. Apart from anything else, Friedelind could not get over his claim that she was somehow involved in the case of high treason against Baroness Gerta-Luise von Einem. The Baroness had been living in Paris, but had fled when it transpired that she was spying for the Nazis. In her absence she had been condemned to death by a military court on charges of espionage and bribery.

The overall friendly nature of their leave-taking might have been a conscious, strategic decision on Friedelind's part, because shortly after Winifred's departure she wrote her mother a letter whose calm and friendly tone seems in part intended to help her conceal her real travel plans:

> I was so pleased to have you visit me and am very grateful to you that you took the trouble to make the long journey. It was worth it, wasn't it? … I can't give you any precise decision yet. It is impossible to get out of contracts that have already been signed. I would not like to go but time will decide best of all. Who can know what will happen just a few weeks from today? I won't do anything ill-considered.[22]

She was not the only person who was deceiving her mother, for her brothers were doing the exact same thing. Wolfgang had written to Wieland just a few weeks before: 'It's important for Mama in human terms to have the impression that we haven't yet broken with her – because afterwards we have to draw a final line under everything and then we can do it!'[23] Friedelind was well aware that she was now beginning a new life, and she later wrote that 'It would perhaps be more accurate to say that I took another step forward; actually I had long been without a country.'[24] She had ordered her transit visa, but did not want to get her mother agitated before it was necessary. She also knew that her letters to Germany were being intercepted. All the same, the gossip about her continued in Germany: Gertrud Strobel heard from Frau Kittel that Friedelind was going to open a theatre in the USA together with Toscanini, and Friedelind heard again that she was regarded as an agent of British intelligence.[25]

We can only imagine how Friedelind would have reacted when Winifred told her the latest family tittle-tattle – how Hitler had visited Wolfgang in the Berlin Charité hospital where he was recovering from a war wound, and that after Hitler had left, 'Teddie' Goering had turned up to see him too. Wolfgang would soon be released from hospital, 'and it seems that Wolf wants to make sure he is kept out of the army and can begin his professional career.'[26] Wolfgang began his training at the Berlin State Opera a few months later and was also given lessons in harmony, counterpoint and musical analysis.

Friedelind can only have taken offence at the idea that her younger brother was quite naturally being prepared for a later role in the management of the Bayreuth Festival while she, despite her ambition, was now compelled to start a career from scratch in an unknown environment. Winifred also pretended that the shortage of goods in Germany was a mere trifle: 'Everything is fantastically well organized everywhere. We already know the rationing system from the World War and since the 100 point clothes ration card has been issued it means that there is no chance of any unfairness in distribution. So everyone is satisfied, because he knows exactly that he will get what he deserves, properly and promptly.'[27] Later, Winifred claimed that she had become completely 'estranged' from Hitler when Friedelind had left Germany. Be that as it may, the departure of her daughter might well have been a reason for the increasing rarity of her contact with him.[28]

Daniela wrote her last letter to Friedelind on 3 March 1940. She defended herself against attacks on her person (Friedelind had described her previous letter as variously 'Christian and humble', 'scolding and whingeing' and 'hysterical') and once more made clear the gap that had opened up between them: 'You are not a "black sheep" and we are certainly no "spotless little angels" – we don't want to change your political views either. You are standing, as you say, on an opposing river bank. In so many things we would surely understand each other, only in this one thing we don't, that I keep my firm faith in the Führer and remain loyal to him – and that truly has nothing to do with fanaticism.'[29]

The family 'tornado' had now finished with them all, and calm returned to Tribschen. Friedelind had warned Frau Beerli to let no one know where she was going. Bayreuth thus remained in the dark. Daniela wrote to Lucerne's city president, Jakob Zimmerli, to request more information: 'We are faced with an utter enigma. Frau Beerli, who is otherwise so effusive a correspondent, has not replied to a rather important letter that I wrote to her some three weeks ago. Our fear and worry regarding our niece has been intensified by this deplorable matter ...'[30] Zimmerli replied curtly: 'Fräulein Friedelind is going her own way. Nothing about it can be altered. Everyone has to accept the fact. She left Lucerne on 1 March. Her destination: America. We can do nothing but wish her the best from all our hearts and be patient.'[31] He informed Zinsstag about his letter to Frau Thode thus:

> I would not dream of having them "massage" me again in this matter. If her parent wants to undertake anything – as opposed to her extended family – then that is her problem alone and it does not concern us. My earlier unfavourable impression has long since changed. It seems to me

that the "Swiss air" has done the young lady good and has had a happy influence on her in every way. She will in later years remember this time with much gratitude and show it towards the city of Lucerne. It might take years, but that time will come.[32]

Zimmerli's words were well-nigh prophetic, for Friedelind did indeed choose Lucerne as the place of residence of her final years. She would also display her gratitude to the city by having Wagner's piano restored in the Tribschen villa.

Daniela was taken aback, as was Winifred when she heard the news. Now she, too, wrote to ask Zimmerli for information on the whereabouts of her daughter, for she had heard rumours that Friedelind had forbidden Frau Beerli from giving out any information. 'With all due respect to dear Frau Beerli – I would have thought that she had a duty to inform me as the mother of the child … you must understand that in these turbulent times it is unpleasant for me to be unaware of where the child is staying.'[33]

Someone else was also astonished at Friedelind's flight from Germany and could hardly believe that a child of Wahnfried would leave her homeland on political grounds: Franz Beidler, Friedelind's cousin, who had already left Germany in 1933 in protest at its politics. He felt far removed from Winifred and her family, so when Zinsstag wrote to him of Friedelind's departure from Germany, he replied acerbically:

> It is incomprehensible to me why she would not go back to the Reich: there cannot possibly be any political reasons. And what the personal reasons might be, there I have my own ideas that are not very complimentary, because I know the dubiously plebeian level – if not to express it more drastically – to which everything in Germany and also in Bayreuth has sunk. Just think if Madame Cosima had lived to see this!!! Your remark about the 'nature and behaviour of the lady' Friedelind says enough and seems clearly to prove that this granddaughter of Cosima has inherited very little of the nobility and the lifestyle of her grandmother.[34]

Friedelind was thus the recipient of both praise and criticism from all sides. But since little or none of it reached her ears, she was able to proceed unaffected. She had decided to choose her own path through life and was ready to 'take to my heart only as many things as can be packed into a suitcase.'[35] Leaving home meant that she lost her inheritance from her aunt Eva Chamberlain. She was originally supposed to inherit over 20 pieces of furniture, paintings by Stassen, jewellery and shawls. Verena was only supposed to get a silver tea and coffee service, an English silver jam dish and a series of smaller items that were in the drawers of the sideboard; Wieland was to get just a single oil painting by Edmund Steppes. Now everything shifted, since Eva did not want to reward her niece for leaving. On 3 July 1941 she added a final codicil to her last will and testament in which she left everything to Verena, should Friedelind at the time of her aunt's death 'not have returned to Germany or not stated her intention of doing so.'[36]

But the young émigré was not interested in furniture or knick-knacks. The long-awaited visa finally arrived, and now everything went swiftly. Gottfried von Einem visited her briefly and they chatted about an opera they wanted to write together, with Friedelind presumably responsible for the libretto. But it all came to nothing, as would so many projects in the course of her later life. On 1 March 1940 they had lunch together, after which she travelled to Basel and thence through the night, in a blacked-out train carriage, to Paris and on to Calais. She took the boat to Folkestone, arriving in London by train at ten in the morning. She was received by Beverley Baxter, who had promised her assistance in the fight 'for the real Germany and against Hitler'.[37] She assumed that being a German woman in England gave her a special status, and this was a mistake that would prove costly.

Furtwängler's former secretary Berta Geissmar had meanwhile been getting ready for her arrival in London. There was an apartment waiting for her in the same house where Geissmar was living: 25 Lyncroft Gardens, NW 6. It belonged to a Mrs Boliton-Biggs. Berta Geissmar had informed assorted friends of Friedelind in advance of her impending arrival, including the Wagner expert and music critic Ernest Newman and his wife, who now came to London to visit. Friedelind told them how she had been afraid that she might still be kidnapped and taken back to Germany while she was living in Switzerland.[38]

A whirlwind of activity now began. For her first few weeks she did the rounds and was out every evening, often accompanied by Geissmar. She met old friends, made new ones and lived an essentially untroubled life.[39] It was hardly a typical refugee existence. A Steinway grand piano was rented for her and she took singing lessons with Elena Gerhardt, who had just taken part in the National Gallery lunch concerts organized by Myra Hess. Friedelind later recalled her tuition with Gerhardt: 'I had to sing "Fü-Ja" constantly – she wasn't a good teacher – thought I was a soprano – but I'm a mezzo!'[40] A bank account was opened for her with over 10,000 Belgian francs,[41] presumably transferred by an admirer called Bracht. She had once spoken to Daniela in jest about her 'Belgian bridegroom' who was well-off and whom her aunt assumed to be a serious suitor (to which Friedelind reacted indignantly: 'He can be as rich and as nice as you want him to be, but if the Ogre doesn't love him, then the Ogre won't marry him!! ... Anyway, I don't think that Monsieur Bracht had the slightest intention regarding me, that was just an invention of Aunt Lulu's vivid imagination!'[42]).

Gottfried von Einem was the recipient of her first letter, which she wrote in English. 'You cannot imagine how lovely it is to be so far from all that dirt now – I feel like I'm in heaven – hell is so far away.'[43] She believed that it would be difficult to break the will of the German people, since they were still hypnotized by Hitler. But she also envisaged the time that would come 'afterwards', adding that 'I am not so optimistic as to believe that the Germans will all be angels once Hitler is dead and the whole lot with him.' Friedelind's inner circle in London soon included her old friend Isabella Valli, whom she had first met back in 1937 at a Toscanini rehearsal, and who later recalled having been unsettled by Friedelind's appearance when they met again: 'There, approaching us, we saw a rather large figure, dressed in a black cloak, walking slowly towards our door – "like a ship in full sail", as my brother said.'[44]

Friedelind attended rehearsals and performances of the London Philharmonic Orchestra whenever 'Tommy' Beecham was conducting, and on 4 March 1940 she and Isabella Valli went to what would prove Beecham's last concert in England until after the war. He conducted a programme of works by Sibelius in aid of the Finnish people, who were at the time fighting a war against the Soviet Union. Afterwards the orchestra gave a farewell dinner in honour of its conductor in 'Pagani', an Italian restaurant frequented by the musicians. Friedelind was presumably there with Berta Geissmar.[45] Toscanini had taken her there three years before (though on that occasion a barrel-organ player had tested his patience to breaking point and had only been induced to leave them alone after a donation of several shillings).[46] After the meal, Beecham left for the USA, from where he would not return until four years later.

Since Friedelind wanted to become active in the struggle against the Nazis, she placed herself at the disposal of the British press as someone who was both a granddaughter of Richard Wagner and a close acquaintance of Hitler. She wrote a series of articles for the *Daily Sketch* in which she described how she had at first been fascinated by Hitler, but how her feelings towards him had turned first to antipathy and then to hatred. She had drafted these articles already in Lucerne and they would later form the basis of her book. What she had sketched out in Switzerland was not yet suitable for publication, and Beverley Baxter helped her to develop her drafts. Since he had spent many years writing theatre reviews for the *Daily Express* and the *Evening Standard*, and since Friedelind had spent so much time in the theatre whenever she had visited London, they had probably bumped into each other in artists' dressing rooms several times before. Now they had to work closely together. On 26 March, for example, Friedelind sat with him for four-and-a-half hours while he edited her manuscripts. Later she would be angry that newspaper editors had felt free to cut out passages and to water things down. But for the moment she let them do as they wished.

Friedelind's articles about Hitler and Mussolini caused a minor scandal back in Germany. The Reich Chancellery rang up Winifred to enquire about her daughter's activities in England. She blamed the 'completely anti-National Socialist, anti-Hitler people' whose company Friedelind was keeping, and later claimed that 'If we weren't members of the Wagner family, we would all have been sent to a concentration camp there and then, of course! She was considered straight down the line as a traitor, so to speak.'[47] Friedelind devoted every article in the *Daily Sketch* to a different topic. It must have annoyed the political leadership in Germany that she often stressed the ridiculous side of Hitler: the way he would anticipate his big speeches by giving informal monologues in Bayreuth, the hysterical reactions of his acolytes, or his failed attempt to get the English king to understand *Lohengrin*.[48]

Later, Friedelind claimed that she had been practically sold off to the *Daily Sketch*.[49] Baxter had presumably arranged with its owner, the press magnate Viscount Kemsley, that her articles should be published in his newspaper, and Baxter for his part shortened her texts as it pleased him – when she later turned her articles into a single-volume autobiography she wrote that 'I can now publish the book in its real form – and not mutilated and in the cheap way Mr Beverley Baxter tried to force me into.'[50] A remark by a friend several years afterwards confirms that Friedelind and her backers were suffering from crossed lines: 'In 1940 a rather unscrupulous journalist obtained a visa to allow her to enter England for propaganda purposes. It was based on misunderstanding [*sic*] and proved disastrous.'[51] Baxter was the man in question, though he could hardly have realized the possible consequences of his offer at the time. Looking back, Friedelind felt cheated by him and was angry at the whole business.

The fact that Friedelind knew Hitler from close quarters and was planning a book naturally made her an interesting personality whom many people wanted to get to know. On 3 March 1940 Beverley Baxter organized a dinner party to which Friedelind and Berta Geissmar were invited. In these first weeks she primarily awakened the interest of those with their own political agenda, or who anticipated being able to market her on the basis of her contact to the 'Führer'. Thus she had conversations with Edmund Stinnes, the son of the German industrialist Hugo Stinnes, who was in favour of a quick peace with Hitler. Along with Edward Wood (the First Earl of Halifax) and other upper-class right-wingers, Stinnes belonged to the so-called Cliveden Set, named after their regular meeting place, the country seat of Lady Nancy Astor (who had incidentally been the first-ever woman MP in parliament). They were disillusioned by the Versailles Peace Accord, believed that Germany had been badly done by and, since they also saw it as a bulwark against the 'communist threat', they were keen to convince the British government of the continuing virtues of Chamberlain's policy of appeasement. Did they perhaps want to wean Friedelind away from her antagonism to Hitler? The English adherents of moderation towards the Nazis will surely have regarded her series of articles as a slap in the face. Friedelind knew of all these political machinations because on earlier visits to England she had often stayed with Lady Cholmondeley, who was close to Churchill, but whose brother Philip sympathized with Chamberlain.[52] We can safely assume that these political matters were debated in passionate detail at the time. Years later, Friedelind mentions 'Kemsley' documents that she had left behind in England.[53] These were presumably the drafts for her articles. Viscount Kemsley had wanted to smooth over relations between Germany and England and had even met and conversed with Hitler in Bayreuth in 1939. He had discussed an exchange of articles between German and English newspapers and had tried to convince the 'Führer' that Churchill was getting more attention that he warranted and that he, Kemsley, would welcome a meeting between Hitler and Chamberlain (whom he himself supported).[54] It is thus possible that Kemsley would have wanted to water down the negative depiction of Hitler in Friedelind's manuscripts. He seems not to have succeeded – except in one possible case where Friedelind might have let herself be influenced by the controversies raging around her. For one of her articles deals with Hitler's immense love of England, of which nothing can be found in her later book. Perhaps she was asked to stress this aspect of Hitler's personality in order to gain a certain sympathy for him in England. In any case, Friedelind chafed at the tutelage to which she was being subjected and cursed Baxter for years afterwards for having initiated everything.

Friedelind ate together with Hermann Rauschning on 8 March 1940, a former Nazi Party member and erstwhile President of the Danzig Senate who had distanced himself from Nazi policies and had fled to Great Britain in 1936. He had known Hitler personally, though his claim to have spoken with him over a hundred times up to the year 1934 was a lie. He published a book based on these spurious conversations, though its wealth of quotations was such that he could never have heard everything at first-hand, nor committed it all to paper with such precise recall. All the same, Rauschning succeeded in sketching a convincing portrait of the 'Führer' that in many cases is identical to the testimony of other contemporaries. His book became a best-seller and was published in several languages. Through him Friedelind came into contact with Emery Reves (1904–1981), a journalist and author of Hungarian extraction who had convinced Rauschning to commit his 'Hitler conversations' to paper in 1939 and had provided him with a generous advance.

Reves was now also interested in Friedelind's writing, and will surely have imagined similar prospects of success as with Rauschning. He had fled Germany, then founded a news agency in Paris and later gained dubious fame for publishing the book *I Paid Hitler*, which the industrialist Fritz Thyssen had dictated to him in the South of France. Reves published it in 1941 without Thyssen's knowledge or consent (Reves's own book, *Anatomy of Peace*, would in 1945 itself achieve great success and run to 27 editions; it called for an international federation to prevent future wars). Reves now declared himself ready and willing to edit Friedelind's manuscript. Later, when she was already living in the USA, he would present her with a bill of $320 for his work that she had to pay off in instalments.[55]

The banker Wilhelm Regendanz (1882–1955) also wanted to help Friedelind write her book about Hitler. He had been a good friend of the former German Chancellor Kurt von Schleicher, whom the Nazis had murdered on the 'Night of the Long Knives' in 1934. Schleicher's murder had drastically altered Regendanz's attitude towards the Nazis, and he had a keen interest in publishing Friedelind's reminiscences of Hitler and his cohorts. He paid her an advance of £200, with a further £600 promised upon finishing the manuscript. That was more than a best-selling author would have received and is proof of his great expectations for the book.[56] Friedelind wrote to him that her hitherto criticism of German policy had after the invasion of Poland turned into outright opposition, and she summed up her position in drastic words: 'As for Hitler – it's as if a certified madman were to set his asylum alight! An act of desperation! Except that this act is resulting in immeasurable, unforeseeable chaos ... with the pact against the Russians, Hitler dealt a death blow to his whole "ideology" and so-called "National Socialism" has no justification any more at all!'[57]

Friedelind met the popular author Dennis Wheatley (1897–1977), whose thrillers had a broad readership. She also got to know Elli Gundolf, the widow of the poet Friedrich Gundolf (1880–1931), who had emigrated to England in 1935. And she dined with yet another author, Sir Frederick McCormick – were there perhaps plans to make a novel from her material? Beverley Baxter also introduced her to Raymond Savage, who asked for the world rights of her as-yet unwritten book, presumably also in the hope of making money from it. Even the former Deputy Commissioner of Scotland Yard, Sir Trevor Bigham, was present at one of her meetings with Stinnes, as was Berta Geissmar it seems (named 'G.B.' in her diary). Friedelind further became friends with Marguerite Wolff, née Jolowicz (1883–1964), who had married the German lawyer Martin Wolff. Marguerite Wolff had been active at the Kaiser Wilhelm Institute in Berlin until she was sacked in 1933, after which she had returned to Great Britain (after the end of the War she would be the chief translator at the Nuremberg Trials).

Lady Domini Crosfield (1892–1963) also invited Friedelind to dine several times. A Greek millionairess who had married the rich industrialist and MP Sir Arthur Crosfield, she had run their home in Witanhurst alone since his death in 1938. It was situated between Highgate West Hill and Hampstead Heath and with its 65 rooms it was the largest private home in London (with the notable exception of Buckingham Palace). Lady Crosfield organized chamber music concerts and other events there, and when Yehudi Menuhin visited London he often lived in her house. It was through her that Friedelind also became acquainted with the Greek pianist Gina Bachauer.

All these contacts were with the upper stratum of British society, and although Friedelind could bring nothing with her except the Wagner name and her acquaintance with Hitler, she had rapidly become one of 'the' people whom one invited to dinner. After the war, too, she often lived with Lady Crosfield and enjoyed the pleasant life and the many parties that came with it all. Lady Crosfield's most famous parties were those held on the occasion of the annual tennis tournament in Wimbledon. But she was much more than merely a rich patroness dabbling in sports and music. She spoke six languages and on occasion became involved in politics too.

This easy-going, busy life now came to an end as quickly as it had begun. On 25 May 1940, Friedelind had spoken with her lawyer W. H. Woolley and dined with Berta Geissmar in a Chinese restaurant. She then watched two films: *Vigil in the night* and *Gone with the wind*. On 26 May a policeman knocked on her door and brought the news that she was to be interned on the 27th. She spent the rest of the day with Lady Crosfield, from whom she anticipated some protection from the law. She hoped for the same from Woolley, too. Both Crosfield and Woolley accompanied her to the West Hampstead Police Station on 27 May but could do nothing for her. Friedelind was taken into custody and brought to the Fulham Road Institution at 2.30 p.m. where she was searched and then sent to a reception centre in West London. She spent two days and nights imprisoned there – a distressing experience for a young woman who, after much inner turmoil, had decided to defect to her country's enemy.[58] Her aunts learnt of none of this, for Daniela had already died just a few weeks after Friedelind's arrival in England. Eva would die two years later.

Chapter 7

In England, behind barbed wire
1940 to 1941

WHY WERE GERMANS being interned, regardless of their political affiliation or opinions? In May 1940 Germany had opened up its western front, invading first the Benelux countries and then France, and this had put the British government on red alert. There was a fear that Nazi sympathizers might be lurking in Britain as a fifth column, waiting in anticipation of a German invasion and doing all they could in readiness for it. British intelligence was unprepared for the many tasks facing it at the outbreak of war. It had too few people in its ranks, and the reigning political uncertainty led to a rash turnover at the top. In May 1940 Winston Churchill fired the boss of MI5 and replaced him with Oswald Allen Harker, who was himself replaced by Sir David Petrie in April 1941. It was Petrie who reorganized the security services and was responsible for their many subsequent successes in the espionage war against the Nazis.

Great Britain had been accepting German refugees since 1933. There had been no doubt from the start that the Nazis wanted to erect a totalitarian, racist state, and by the end of 1933 already more than 37,000 people had left the country for reasons of politics or race. Some 2000 of these came to Great Britain. The situation worsened drastically in 1940 when Denmark, Norway, Holland, Belgium and France were overrun by the Germans and an invasion of Britain itself was feared by many. Most foreigners resident in Britain were opposed to German policies but, as their numbers increased, so did the fear and scepticism felt towards them by the general population. It was therefore decided to intern all those arriving in the country along with all resident Germans and Austrians. Whether Jewish refugees, active opponents of the Nazis, Nazi adherents or Germans who had long been assimilated – no distinction was made between them, for they were all regarded as figures of suspicion and potential enemy aliens.

In the first six months of the war, 64,000 citizens of Germany, Italy and Austria who were resident in Britain were made to undergo questioning by a tribunal to establish whether they were 'friendly aliens' or not. They were all divided into three categories: A, who were immediately interned; B, who were allowed to return to their homes but were forbidden from moving beyond a five-mile zone; and C, who were foreigners considered completely unsuspicious. Men belonging to the last group were interned all the same, though the women were generally left in peace. This complicated system was soon discarded altogether and it was decided to intern everyone. 'Defence Regulation 18B' allowed the authorities to take anyone into custody whom they thought might form a threat to the country. In early May 1940, the government announced its decision to intern all aliens on the Isle of Man in the middle of the Irish Sea. Friedelind will have assumed that she was somehow exempt, having been invited into the country by a member of parliament. But she was now classified as a suspicious person. This was hardly surprising, for however much she might protest her opposition to the Nazi cause, there was no denying her family's close proximity to Hitler himself.

On 27 May the first women were imprisoned and transported to the Isle of Man; they were aged between 16 and 60. Many Germans panicked in the belief that they were to be handed back to the Nazis in exchange for British prisoners of war, and Friedelind had no illusions as to what would befall her, were she to be deported back to Germany.

The journey to the island took more than a day. During the night the women were housed on the mainland in sports stadia where they were given the choice of sitting through the night or huddling in unhygienic changing booths. There were not enough washing facilities, and toilet doors had to remain open. Conditions were demeaning, the atmosphere was depressed, many of the women wept, and some of them began to panic. Friedelind was spared these overnight indignities because she arrived in Liverpool on the evening and was put onto her ship at 10pm. The internees were jeered at by bystanders on their way to the harbour. The boat was overloaded and the toilets soon became blocked. They landed at Douglas and were then taken by train to Port Erin, a pretty fishing village that had hitherto supported itself mostly from tourism. Since the island was a popular holiday destination it had many hotels and bed-and-breakfast establishments, and these were now appropriated by the state. The few remaining tourists on the island had to pack up and go home while whole districts were ringed with barbed wire and guards placed at the gates. The island was ill-prepared for this influx of people, and the women internees had to stand for hours in queues before being divided up between the different boarding houses and hotels.[1]

Friedelind reached the Rushen Internment Camp on the morning of 30 May 1940. It had been hurriedly set up for women internees in the southern part of the island, and she was one of the first to arrive. It comprised the two seaside resorts of Port Erin and Port St Mary and was intended to house 4000 women (of whom 3000 were quartered in Port Erin). The biggest hotel there was the Ballaqueeney, which had space for several hundred women. The locals were at first hostile, but soon realized that they could earn far more with the rent

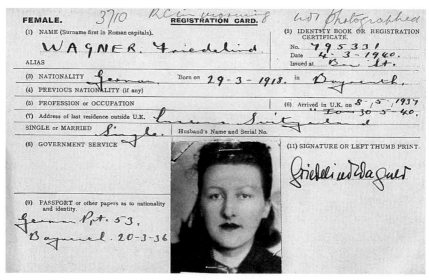

11 She chose freedom and got internment instead: Friedelind's registration card
from the Isle of Man, where she was sent in May 1940.

paid by the government than would otherwise be the case, for holiday-makers
were rare in wartime. During the harvest season, the local farmers would be
allowed to employ internees too.

Soon the island had two internees for every local. The women were scared
and suffered from having twice been uprooted; many had been driven out of
Germany, had created a new home for themselves in England, but had now
had this taken away from them too. Worse still, they were also separated from
their husbands. Others had fled from the occupied Netherlands and had to
suffer the indignity of being treated as the enemy. Nor could they know if
their roommates might in fact be convinced Nazis. Most internees had to
share a double bed, and there were cases of Nazi women refusing to share
with a Jewish refugee. All this was difficult to bear for people who had been
compelled to leave everything behind them to save their lives and who now
felt under attack all over again. They despaired because the English seemed
to hate them for being Germans, while many of the Germans looked down
on those who were Jewish.[2] Panic attacks, claustrophobia and screaming fits
were common. Wives worried for their husbands, and the emotional stress
was intense everywhere.

Whereas the men tried to improve their situation by organizing courses
for themselves in their internment camps, the women had to suffer a stricter
regime under their Commandant, Dame Joanna Cruickshank. However, conditions were gradually eased, making life more bearable and even pleasant.

Soon the women's camp, too, was offering various courses to pass the time. There was tuition in history and biology, and theatrical and musical groups were formed. 'Instruction on cosmetic practice' was offered, as were various handicrafts. An Austrian woman offered ju-jitsu courses in self-defence against potential Nazis.[3] A representative of the camp authorities by the name of Nora O'Connor organized fancy-dress dance evenings and card-playing competitions and also gave dancing lessons. Friedelind tried her luck at dancing, though she was not particularly gifted at it, for O'Connor later remembered the 'frustrating torment' of trying to teach her.[4] Whoever had money was able to go shopping, for the shops still had plenty of goods that had been intended for the tourists. The women were also allowed to visit a café, to sun themselves on the beach, to attend lectures and even to go to the cinema twice a week. Over time, everyone slipped into an everyday routine, with only the barbed wire a constant reminder that they were actually prisoners.[5]

Some women had the possibility of emigrating. But when the Andorra Star carrying 1500 internees to Canada was sunk by a German U-boat on 2 July 1940 with 800 dead, the shock in the internment camp was so great that many either postponed their plans to leave or abandoned them altogether.

Friedelind was assigned to the Hydro Hotel. She regularly went to the movies (she found Walt Disney's *Pinocchio* 'enchanting' and watched it twice; the other films she saw included *Ninotchka* with Greta Garbo). Soon she got to know the singer Jeanette Simon, a Jewish émigré from Germany who had been active in artistic circles in Berlin. She gave Friedelind singing lessons and they became friends. It was surprising that they had not met before, for Jeanette's own singing teacher, Marianne Mathy, had since early 1939 been living in the same house in London as Berta Geissmar. Jeanette was one of her best and most trusted pupils, and had early on smuggled her teacher's family jewellery into England, sewn into the lining of a fur coat.[6] Jeanette had performed for the Jewish Cultural Association and already had professional experience that proved useful to her now, for she gave lessons on the island and performed at church services. Friedelind attended her rehearsals and was thus able to partake of something akin to a music life, if on a very different level from before.

Being interned with a group of women of whom the majority were Jewish meant that Friedelind had the opportunity to listen to their life stories, besides telling her own. Mutual comfort and entertainment were the order of the day; one woman called Marja was able to amuse everyone else for months by speaking in a strong Saxon drawl[7] (to this day the Saxon dialect remains an object of fun to most other Germans). Perhaps precisely because of the seriousness of their situation, humour was frequent. One of them later recalled how Friedelind's faulty English led her to refer to the end slices of bread as 'the behind'. Friedelind also learnt Yiddish songs that a woman from Lviv taught her, and which to her was a welcome act of friendship.[8]

The young women were able to both divert and stimulate each other. Jeanette had a weekly solo performance in the Methodist church, whether of German lieder or opera arias or Christmas songs. Then there were the 'Friday night concerts' that Friedelind still recalled many years later.[9] According to the *Isle of Man Examiner*, Jeanette sang at a church service on 6 September, performing hymns and an aria from Puccini's *Madama Butterfly*. She also sang Elisabeth's Prayer from Wagner's *Tannhäuser* and the highly dramatic aria 'Suicidio!' from Amilcare Ponchielli's *La Gioconda* – which is surely testament to her experience and professionalism. Another singer by the name of Johanna Metzger sang an aria from Haydn's *Creation*. Such performances were organized regularly, and the church was full each time.[10] Music thus took on a therapeutic function in the camp. Jeanette's performance was rewarded with bouquets of chrysanthemums from the audience.[11] When the Bishop of Chichester, George Bell visited on 28 July 1940 and held a service in St Catherine's Church, Jeanette sang again. Bell was a constant campaigner for the rights of the émigrés and refugees living in Britain, so his visits had a special significance for them. 'Wonderful!' was Friedelind's comment in her diary. She now met Jeanette every day and, besides her singing lessons, they would go for long walks on the beach together, besides meetings in what she referred to as their 'cosy nook'. In these dangerous times when no one knew what the future would bring, a love grew between them that would bind them together for the rest of their lives.

Back in Bayreuth, the first wartime festival was being held. On 23 July 1940 Hitler arrived to attend the 'victory Festival' and watched a performance of *Götterdämmerung*. The Nazi organization 'Kraft durch Freude' had organized the distribution of tickets and invited the war wounded, soldiers from the front, nurses and others serving in the forces as 'guests of the Führer'. The SS division 'Leibstandarte Adolf Hitler' goose-stepped past the Festspielhaus. It was the last time that Hitler would visit Bayreuth. Wagner's construction supervisor for the Festspielhaus, Carl Runkwitz, was a guest of honour and one morning sat on a bench with Winifred, Wieland, Wolfgang and Verena, regaling them with his tales of Richard Wagner.[12] Frau Strobel became agitated about a performance of *Siegfried* in which Max Lorenz had in places sung with only half a voice, and the singer of Erda had done the same. Wotan had gone to Erda without his hat, and when he placed it on his head as Siegfried approached, he 'had fiddled with it long before it sat properly'. Fafner's voice could hardly be heard, and the audience itself was 'the worst ever', having come from the 'Ostmark', i.e. what had formerly been Austria. 'They always clap BEFORE the end of an act and many are asleep.' Frau Strobel saw Hitler in the garden of Wahnfried: 'On the right Frau Wagner and Wolf, to their left Verena and Wieland arm-in-arm; Stassen, Overhoff and Gertrud went in front ... when the Führer entered his box, everyone greeted him in silence with their arms raised in salute.' She found the performance 'terrible' once more, 'Lorenz quite impossible.'[13]

Did Hitler speak to Winifred again about her daughter who had 'defected to the enemy'? A letter from Wolfgang to Wieland at least confirms that Hitler did make his views known on various matters this summer in Bayreuth, including certain production aspects:

> You will have received a copy of the Führer's decision ... as the Führer himself told me, normal, peacetime conditions won't return for a year, i.e. all the current restrictions will still be in place ... I have already been asked several times whether there will ever be a Festival for the public again (the women are active in propaganda in this matter at the moment, it's also being said everywhere that we won't have to conform completely with the Aryan paragraph)[14] ... We can't do anything big without *Parsifal*. The Führer has also occupied himself with the work again, as he said to me, and came to the following realization: The only things that really are reminiscent of a church are the temple scenes and the church-like architecture of the hall (then of course there's the whole music and the action, as Heinz correctly points out), so we would have to reach a solution that takes us into the mystical, thus into the indefinable and the intangible. We'll be better able to reach a solution in scenic terms rather than in matters of pure direction, and these are just brief suggestions ... it was rather turbulent last night, but nothing more has happened. After looking out from the roof garden we realized that the flak and the other defences have been greatly improved.[15]

Wolfgang wrote to his mother as follows at the same time:

> Yesterday evening the Führer called me to him and I had ample opportunity of discussing Bayreuth matters with him alone. The following was the result of it: Everything should be prepared for *Tannhäuser* and for the big programme, but if the political or military position doesn't allow it (because for *Tannhäuser* etc. we would have to be at peace, he says), then he will take the consequences completely on himself and we will only be able to put on a Festival as in the year before this. Naturally,

straightaway I made him aware of all the difficulties that are caused by the current situation, and he also gave his full support to clear these out of our way. … I don't need to mention his agreement to give financial support etc. … he looked very well and made a very confident impression. Of course I have to greet everyone warmly. As always he asked after you all and how you are. Since I was alone with him for almost three quarters of an hour, and in between had a good meal with smoked salmon, I took my leave immediately and was at home at nine.[16]

On 6 June, her father's birthday, Friedelind's thoughts were very much with Tribschen and the *Siegfried Idyll* that Toscanini had conducted there. In late August her group baked plum and crumble cake to celebrate their quarter-year anniversary as internees – it seems they had the means of baking German cakes somewhere in the camp.

Journalism was an area where émigrés were exempt from the ban on work that had been imposed on them by the authorities,[17] so Friedelind was paid a fee of £150 for her articles in the *Daily Sketch*. However, the money was confiscated on the Isle of Man. (Incidentally, this same year saw the publication of the important book *Germany: Jekyll & Hyde* by the émigré Sebastian Haffner, who had been interned as an 'enemy alien' at the same time as Friedelind.) Friedelind's lawyer tried to get her money released so that she could begin to pay back some of the debts she had chalked up in England. He wrote to the authorities that it was difficult for her to pay these from where she was on the island. 'Many debtors are putting me under pressure to have their money repaid. But Fräulein Wagner can do nothing without any income; as far as I know, the only jewellery she has is of little value, and it is deposited with Lady Crosfield for reasons of security.'[18] Friedelind undoubtedly played down the value of the jewellery she had brought along from Baroness von Einem at the latter's request. This was the only way she could avoid having to pawn it.

Friedelind remained sure that Hitler would lose the war. 'I feel so certain that this terrible battle will bring doom to dictatorship. What a price to pay however, to rid the world from a lunatic – but at last there is hope again,' she had written in May 1940.[19] Meanwhile, Goebbels was furious about her: 'The small, fat Wagner girl is publishing revelations about the Führer in the London press. Such a little monster! That could become embarrassing … Wieland Wagner has been informed by the Führer about his shifty little sister. It is really a dreadful scandal that this stupid girl is stirring up.' Thus Hitler was very well informed about what Friedelind was doing and saying. A few days later, Goebbels wrote: 'The fat Wagner girl is publishing her first report against the Führer in the London press; a dirty business. Obviously trying to incite Italy against us. The Führer's views on Mussolini, calculated to put the Duce in a rage. An English propagandist has been collaborating with her. This fat wretch is committing out-and-out treason. She's been extremely badly brought up. Revolting!'[20] 'Small, fat' and 'stupid' – nothing else occurred to Goebbels to describe her. He had obviously underestimated her, but his reaction shows how much she was annoying him. The 'English propagandist' was presumably Baxter.

Friedelind tried to smuggle letters past the censor, but was found out and, as punishment, was forbidden from seeing friends. The British authorities doubted her opposition to the Nazis and began an extensive file that included comments from her former school friends in England. They testified to her having made pro-Nazi comments at the time (one of them mentioned that she had recommended a dictatorship for England back in early 1938). But on the other hand, the Nazi adherents on the Isle of Man regarded her as a traitor. And back home, Reichsminister Martin Bormann is supposed to have threatened that 'Friedelind must not come back to Germany; otherwise I will be obliged to take her before the People's Court.'[21]

In late August, the British authorities decided to set free those internees who were exceptional in the sciences or the arts, those who were clearly refugees from Nazi persecution and those who had fought in Germany or Spain against fascism. Friedelind's articles were now regarded as important to the war effort and so, after three months in captivity, she was allowed to leave the Isle of Man. She bade farewell to Jeanette in the Hydro Hotel, travelled back to Liverpool and from there took the train to London. There was already a bomb warning at Euston Station when she arrived.

What awaited her now was worse than the time before, because she was sent to an annex of Wandsworth Prison. The Royal Victoria Patriotic School in Wandsworth had the task during the war of investigating refugees if they did not possess a visa to travel onwards to another country. It was, however, a prison – inmates were not even allowed out for specific periods, and Friedelind now sat there along with many other women in a similar situation.

Friedelind had hardly arrived in London when massive bombing raids began – the 'Blitz' that lasted until 1941. From 7 September onwards there were bombings every night as the Nazis hoped to destroy the morale of the British population. Over 30,000 people were killed in the raids. Friedelind thus found herself in a prime target for German bombs. 'You are just expecting a bomb when suddenly the guns let fly with a resounding crack like the world blowing up. And all of us in the shelter stiffening suddenly in fright and then relaxing as suddenly, till the next volley,' wrote one woman who experienced the raids from close up.[22] In Germany, Joseph Goebbels noted with satisfaction in his diary: 'The reports from London are terrible. An inferno of unimaginable extent. The city is a hell. One can already detect signs of sinking morale. How long will this city of eight million people hold out? ... Question: Can London be forced to capitulate in this manner? I would like to think so. But we have to wait and attack, attack, attack ... one has to be overjoyed at this organizational masterpiece.'[23]

He was quite wrong, for there was no thought of giving up. Men, women and children slept in the tube stations on every piece of ground available. They even lay on the steps and escalators. Some were unable to change their clothes for weeks. The struggle to find a spot by the wall was great, and some people kept watch over their sleeping places round the clock. When the bombs fell and houses were destroyed, the homeless had to be found shelter, as one witness wrote:

> We had about 700 of the homeless poor crowding out the Feeding Centre this morning. I could have wept, as I put mugs of tea and slices of bread and butter into the trembling hands of old men dug out of the debris in their nightshirts, old women with blood on their white hair, little children covered with the dust of falling homes, fathers whose children are still beneath the ruins. It's their pathetic gratitude for the little we do that gets me by the throat.[24]

Once she was back in London, Friedelind immediately submitted a request for an exit visa. Toscanini had already been trying from a distance to procure one for her and felt responsible for her well-being. Friedelind was 22 years old, devoid of financial resources, and had never finished any tertiary education. Her artistic experiences had given her an irrepressible urge to find some field of activity, but instead she was stuck fast, unable to do anything. By 17 September 1940 she was filled with hope that she would soon be allowed to take a ship to Buenos Aires. Her lawyer Woolley was able to inform her that he had organized her journey with Toscanini's help, and that the conductor would pay all the necessary costs.[25] Sailing to South America was the only possibility of escaping her current inactivity, and she planned to use this as a springboard to enter the USA.

When Friedelind had to fill out her forms for Argentina she felt in ceremonial mood, for when the form asked for her career, she wrote: 'Stage director', and wrote proudly to tell Jeanette of it:

> HOW long I've been waiting to do that! I've longed for it just as I longed to reach adulthood!! But will I now become a good director? I already

have sleepless nights because in my thoughts I'm constantly directing. It makes me forget all the roaring outside in the world – or perhaps it would serve as stage thunder. After all, Grandfather was able to make a big noise too. My sweet, I really need you, otherwise I'll be a very bad director before the Lord!'[26]

On 27 September 1940 she at long last got her visa for Argentina and immediately felt better. She now reckoned on getting her exit permit within about two weeks, after which she could leave. 'Here everyone sleeps on their mattresses, hugging their visas. They keep their papers as close as they used to keep their lovers.' Berta Geissmar's house had recently had a partial hit from a German bomb, and she was now living in what had been Friedelind's room. So Friedelind planned to stay instead with Lady Crosfield after her release. She had taken singing lessons from Elena Gerhardt before, and now pondered returning to her again, once she was free. But the British authorities were still hesitating, and on 5 October 1940 Friedelind's application for an exit visa was rejected. She simply had not reckoned on this and was shocked. Baxter began writing assorted letters on her behalf to try and hurry matters on, but still nothing happened.

Soon afterwards, she and all the other inmates in Wandsworth had to move to the 'Residential School for Jewish Deaf & Blind Children' at 101 Nightingale Lane, five minutes away. The children had been evacuated to the countryside not long before, so the building was empty. Friedelind had not lost her sense of humour and wrote of her new home that 'it's very kosher and probably has very thin walls! Isn't that funny?? If our Wolf knew it – my fate would touch him. The prodigal daughter – in a home for the Jewish deaf and dumb … !!! I'm laughing constantly – everything is so hilarious, although it is really rather sad. But you have to at least keep a certain sense of gallows humour.' She was cooped up with 150 other women and slept in a hall on a mattress. The building was surrounded by barbed wire, making escape impossible. After a while, the barbed wire was removed and the women were at least allowed to go for walks in the garden – though all the while under the watchful eye of the guards. Contact with the outside world was forbidden. The inmates at first did not even have a radio, though the authorities later ordered one to be bought for them.[27] Despite her isolation, Friedelind will have learnt that the Germans were also carrying out so-called 'Baedeker' raids (nicknamed thus after the popular German tourist guides) in which they targeted culturally important cities for destruction. Coventry fell victim to one of these raids in November 1940 – it was cynically nicknamed 'Moonlight Sonata' by the Germans. Later, Bath and Norwich would be bombed too.

As on the Isle of Man, the women imprisoned in the former Jewish children's home had to be inventive in order to pass the time and not fall into depression. Here, too, they made music and read to each other. A violinist performed Grieg's Sonata. 'I read *Die Ideale* by Schiller out loud, which deeply moved me – wherever you go, you find parallels to our situation!' wrote Friedelind. She was a good reader, and afterwards some of her listeners were moved to tears. She planned an 'unsilly afternoon' when she wanted to demonstrate the tap dance she had learnt in Port Erin 'to make the others laugh'. She had also acquired a good grasp of Yiddish by now. 'The atmosphere is better than on the island, at least one knows with whom one is living. Here, where everyone is keen to get an exit visa, they are mostly Jews and the others are not suspicious.'[28] But she was not always able to remain cheerful. It pained her to have so little time to herself. During the day she slunk into a room on her own, even when it was very cold. But on evenings between 7pm and 11pm it was 'women's gossip time', which she could not escape.

Jeanette had had to stay on the Isle of Man, and Friedelind found the separation difficult. The letters she was allowed to write to her became an indispensable means of coping with the interminable waiting. Only a special, white, glossy paper in portrait format was allowed, and the ends had to be folded. This made it easier for the censors to open the letters, for there were no gummed edges. Some of Friedelind's letters bear a sticker with the remark 'Opened by Examiner 5264' or merely the stamp 'passed'. The two women thus had to weigh up carefully what they wanted to write to each other. And they corresponded often – in October, for example, Friedelind wrote at least eleven letters to Jeanette. If one reckons that each received a reply, the two women must have been in constant contact. Friedelind wrote to her as her 'sweet little girl', 'my loveliest one', 'darling angelface [*sic*]', and 'beloved rascal'. Time and again she rallied herself in order to cheer up both herself and her friend. She urged Jeanette to 'show strength and courage like Leonore' (the heroine of Beethoven's *Fidelio*) and not to fear the future:

> Soon the worst will have been overcome ... I miss you so terribly, my Darling – sometimes I feel pretty miserable at the thought of conquering the world so quite by myself. But we all have to follow our Bestimmung [vocation] – to be glad of it. There at last IS one! Keep your chin up, my Darling. Up to now, every sunset was followed by the dawn ... everything transient is only an allegory! If I have learnt nothing in all these months, then I have at least learnt to understand this phrase – in all its depth and significance. And I measure everything I experience against it so that I can see it in its correct proportions.[29]

But then her yearnings would surface again: 'I wish I were still with you, or rather, that you could come to me, to take care of you. I know how much you need a little pastoral worker … Lots of hugs and loving kisses without making you red! Ever your Mausi.' She felt protective of Jeanette and tried to boost her courage, though her own nerves were as frayed as could be. However much she wanted Jeanette to come to London, she found it better for her to stay on the island. There at least she was safe and far from all the bombings in London, where the Blitz was still raging.

Friedelind's days were thus spent cut off from almost everyone and without any knowledge of how her life might proceed. The waiting was agonising. Her release was still being delayed, supposedly because not all the prerequisites had been fulfilled (in fact, she was still being investigated to try and find out whether she was really an anti-Nazi or whether she was in fact a German agent). The authorities were swamped. They had too few personnel and their organization was completely outmoded. Incredibly long waiting times were the result. Those responsible were wholly aware of the situation, but things could not be changed so quickly. In November, Friedelind wrote that 'My case is proceeding at a snail's pace (can snails pace? I fear not!) and I seem to myself like an acrobat practising patience. My knitting is the only proof that time is moving forwards.' She read until her head was fit to burst, or she held conversations with herself. If there was no bomb alarm, she sang to the chestnut trees in the garden.

Woolley had hinted that Friedelind would indeed be allowed to travel on to New York after arriving in South America, though it remained unclear just how long she would have to stop over in Buenos Aires. So she began making plans and intended to procure an opportunity for Jeanette to sing Senta and Elisabeth in Argentina – she even asked her to start looking at the scores. She also asked her to learn Isolde's 'Liebestod' from *Tristan und Isolde*. Friedelind could hardly wait for the day when she could work as a director before an Argentinian or a North American audience. 'Everything will go well!' she wrote, as if to convince herself of it. Her feelings about her forthcoming journey were ambivalent, however: 'recently I was on the verge of howling with tears because I'm going to Buenos Aires. But then I told myself that I was stupid and very ungrateful. And yet I still feel like a package that someone has stuck a label on and simply sent off somewhere.' She could not forget the concerts during her internment in which Jeanette had so often sung: 'How I miss the Friday evenings! I almost wish others could not have them. But then I comfort myself – I know that when you sing you think now and then of your pupil – in between real thoughts.' She often pondered the friendships she had begun on the island. Now they were all lost, her friends had presumably all left, and she was 'sad at heart'. When acquaintances from the island arrived in Wandsworth, she told Jeanette of it: 'Ruth gave me a kiss from you, though I naturally would have preferred the original ...' On the one hand she wanted to get her exit visa quickly, but on the other hand she longed to see Jeanette again. But she would die 'a thousand deaths' if Jeanette were sent to Wandsworth after she had left for South America. She found it difficult to keep her letters short. 'If only I could write a proper Mausi letter – they never end. I can express myself so poorly in just a few words, I can't keep things concentrated if I'm writing to someone I particularly love! That's why everything is so chopped off. It would be loveliest of all if we didn't need to write to each other, but were together instead. I hug you most tenderly – and give every kiss back – sadly only by letter – as a copy – and I love you so much – always your Mausi ... I miss you quite terribly, my sweetest – I feel it more and more strongly, for I realize gradually that I have left my environment not just for a few days, but for ever.'³⁰

Friedelind's long-awaited release dragged on for weeks and weeks. In order to pass the time better, she read Goethe's *Iphigenie, Egmont* and *Tasso*, practised tenor roles and sang the 'Flower aria' from Bizet's *Carmen* and 'Celeste Aïda' with the necessary Italianate sobs. She sang the whole of *Tristan* to herself or went through the *Leonore* overtures in her mind. 'Is that a good mixture?' she asked. But her first love was Wagner. 'I have a dreadful yearning for the music of *Tristan*. And yet I feel that I could not listen to it at all without becoming at least a little crazy – it's all pure poison to our calcified brains. My sweet, what does an opera house look like? And a bed? I don't know either any more. And I long for both – although the train of thought seems somewhat confused.'

Friedelind's lawyer Woolley visited her in late December, but was still unable to give her any real hope. 'There is no prospect of a ship before the end of March, and then there is no promise that it will have space for me. No ships are travelling to the US at the moment and at present that is not at all strange. Since I was mentally prepared for it, the shock is not too great ... my whole life at present seems like an unending twilight, with no ray of light – but nor is it the dark of night.' She hoped that Jeanette would be able to travel after her. They would then be 'normal people, without 5000 jealous cats around us, and in an atmosphere that would be more artistic – oh, to be able to speak of opera and to bother no one by doing so!' She buried herself in the world of art in order to bear life as it was. 'The most depressing thing is the terrible fate of individuals – almost everyone has undergone unmentionable things. In comparison I seem to myself like a baby – everything is a reverie and in the right proportions. I think everything is well as long as one has people in the world whom one loves and who love one back. From this viewpoint, my sweet, we are still very rich. Aren't we??'

But the days simply refused to pass. She even read a French love novel. 'Since internment I have become incredibly educated … I'm waiting and waiting!' she sighed on 21 October. Yet her confidence never left her. Once she dreamt that Jeanette was on stage, singing Puccini's *Butterfly*, though she was also sitting in the audience – and there was no seat free next to her for Friedelind. In her daydreams she saw Jeanette's name together with her own on programmes – 'then we would have our springboard for New York!'[31] That city remained the goal she yearned for, and her optimism was irrepressible. 'I will try to get either *Tannhäuser* or *Holländer* done in Buenos Aires next summer. Kleiber would like to do both. We discussed the *Holländer* eighteen months ago when I last saw him in Paris. All three acts without a break, like in Bayreuth.' The Nazis had compelled Erich Kleiber to resign back in 1935 because he had conducted works that were contrary to their aesthetic (including works by Krenek, Milhaud and Alban Berg). He had emigrated first to Cuba, and then to Buenos Aires.

> How the months rush by. That is ONE good thing. Two years ago I was at a wonderful mass in Notre Dame – what must it look like today? One can't even think about it. Everything 'lost' seems in one's memory as if it were just yesterday – and thank God only the beautiful remains. If that were not the case, I would not want to think back on the past 10 years, which were a nightmare. But since only the bright spots shine out – it often helps a lot! When up in the sky there's buzzing and bangs, I start to go through a symphony in my head from A to Z – and compare the tempi of different conductors. You know of course that I hesitate with ONE conductor [Toscanini] because those impressions were far too strong and would make everything pale in comparison. But then I ask myself, of course, whether I shall ever experience such concerts again?[32]

In her imagination she directed operas time and again.

> So many things take on proper form and shape and are ready to be finished. Only the stage is missing – and the artists etc.! Will I ever get that far? Will we ever be able to perform Wagner again properly, after they have trampled over Bayreuth??! And will I really succeed in playing my part? It's all well and good to think that one is destined for something – but aren't we left at the mercy of chance today? … perhaps – when we have put all these, the most difficult of tests behind us in our

lives – we will see more clearly – and perhaps even understand that it had to be like this. Life forms us. And it becomes ever clearer who one is – whether we are chosen or whether we belong to the dull, vegetating masses. Everything one has learnt and that is false then falls away in situations like that and we appear either in all our greatness or in all our miserable puniness.[33]

Her shifting moods, swinging from emotional intimacy to a cool distance, are reminiscent of the experiences of the poet Elias Canetti who at this very time was in Hampstead Heath, not far from her, and watching the bombers fly past in the sky. 'The combination of excitement and dispassion during those hours are to me the most curious part of the memory.'[34]

It was Friedelind's biggest test in life thus far. Imprisoned with 150 other women who were all at their wits' ends, and then having to live with the uncertainty and the fear of her current situation. This was the worst she had ever experienced. 'I have been here for 10 weeks now – I should not wonder if they turned to 20, given the snail's pace that things are taking. It would be easier to bear if one did not always have the "terrible incertitude" of how things will end – and one then asks oneself: Why???' The British security services were still divided as to whether Friedelind might be an enemy agent. An author who was known for his opposition to the Nazis, but who is not named in the files, was given the task of interviewing her. He found it difficult to reach a conclusion, for he found her to be neither for nor against the Nazis: 'It is rather that she does not really possess a real understanding of today's political reality.' This is strange, for in her letters to Toscanini she had clearly positioned herself in opposition to German politics. Her interviewer presumably reached his conclusion because she told him that her main interest was not politics but directing operas, especially the works of Wagner. When he asked if she were not afraid for her family, who were all in enemy territory, she replied that they were out of danger because they had rejected her. The author concluded: 'I do not believe she is a Nazi agent.'[35]

Every evening she went walking around the grounds with her fellow internees. But when lights-out was announced, she alone remained outside while the others went back inside. Now even the nearby bomb craters were invisible; everything around was pitch black. Her thoughts were with the conductor she venerated so much, and the notes she made she kept to the end of her life:

I look up to the skies and await a small sign from heaven – something that is lovelier than all this misery on earth. I start a conversation with the Almighty ... but then suddenly I hear myself calling the Maestro. I never called God that, and I'm mixing them both up. Why am I begging him for strength from New York, and not from the invisible heavens, why am I sending him my confessions, why do I only want to carry on living in order to see him again?

She wept and then recognised a star – a small light in the darkness that comforted her.[36] Toscanini had stood by her when her father had died, and he had been there for her when she had attended school in England in 1937, letting her attend his rehearsals. Now she placed all her hopes in him, raising him up to be her one true friend and saviour. He fulfilled this role superbly, even taking on the responsibility for the everyday things in her life. Her lawyer's office asked Toscanini for £200 so that she could buy clothes and other items for her voyage; and he sent it.

Beverley Baxter remained understandably concerned about Friedelind's internment and tried to find a solution through his political channels. He turned for help to Sir Samuel Hoare in the Foreign Office and to Rab Butler, the then Under-Secretary of State for Foreign Affairs. Neither was of the opinion that he could assist, so they left the case to the Home Office. Baxter now raised the matter in the House of Commons, and a debate took place there about Friedelind on 3 December 1940. It appalled him that she should be treated like an enemy. In his argument in favour of her rapid release he stressed that she had earlier revered Hitler, but had then changed her opinion. He stated clearly that he and the Foreign Office had been responsible for helping her to come to England. He mentioned that Arturo Toscanini had offered her a post in Buenos Aires. Opposing him, Osbert Peake, Parliamentary Under-Secretary of State for the Home Office and also a Conservative, said that 'Fräulein Wagner was not a refugee from Nazi oppression but an ordinary pure-blooded German, and her case was exceptional.' He was nevertheless in favour of her being allowed to leave, though more to get rid of her than to help her.[37]

The uncertainty of the authorities was probably caused by the secret dossier that had been compiled about Friedelind. One document in it stated: 'Reports about her are contradictory. She seems to have a somewhat unstable disposition and could return to her earlier love, and support the Nazis again.'[38] Her sometime history teacher in Brighouse, Dorothy Stead, stressed that she had been 'very much for Hitler' back then, giving the Nazi salute everywhere. But the majority opinion was in the end that her ambition and aspirations were primarily musical in nature and neither political nor patriotic. In a newspaper article in her defence, Baxter called her 'stubborn, self-opinionated and tactless', but added that 'Richard Wagner was her grandfather and he also possessed these qualities'. He was thus able to counter the arguments against her

person, but there was nevertheless still no unanimity. The parliamentary discussion became news in Germany, for Winifred was informed on 3 December
for the first time that Friedelind had been interned.[39]

Later, after arriving in Buenos Aires, Friedelind learnt from Toscanini why
she had been kept so long in London without an exit permit: she had been
observed in Switzerland and Italy in the company of a person being shadowed
by the information services.[40] That person, of course, had been Baroness von
Einem, who after the War would cause many more problems for Friedelind.
But it had been Friedelind's transformation from a Nazi supporter and friend
of Hitler into a determined opponent that had caused all the confusion about
her. Whether or not the information about the baroness came from a reliable
source remains unclear, though there might have been other reasons for the
delay. The politician Osbert Peake had already uttered doubts in parliament
as to Friedelind's anti-Nazi ardour and wrote on 12 December 1940 in the
Daily Mail that, although Miss Wagner had stated her opposition to Hitler in
various newspaper articles, it was known that she had been friends with him,
and the reports about her from the British Consulate in Switzerland had not
been particularly positive.[41]

Thus days and weeks went by. Christmas was manna from heaven, for there
were three quiet days – three days without bombs – that let her think of
'the normal times, far, far away'. But behind the scenes things were happening
for her. Toscanini even drew the US Ambassador Joseph Kennedy (father of
JFK) into his efforts. Kennedy had already helped Toscanini once before, back
in 1939, when the conductor had been refused permission to leave Italy and
Kennedy had exerted pressure on Mussolini to give him his passport.[42]

On 8 February 1941 Friedelind's release was postponed yet again. She used
the time to knit Jeanette a bed jacket: 'Made with much love – every stitch is
a wish for you and a loving thought – and made all by myself!' A new arrival
had arrived from the island,

> like everyone she knows everything better and offers us old hands Etzes
> [good advice] or however you write that in Yiddish. I'm not at all inter-
> ested in her because she knows nothing of you, or at least she was never
> in the services [she presumably means when Jeanette sang in church].
> Wherever I shall be, you will always be very very close to me – and
> there is no such thing as distance. A thousand tender hugs – lots of
> loving kisses, always your Mausi ... 'man goes best in twos' you'll find in
> Wagner's Hans Sachs – and he's right.

Jeanette knew the second act of the *Meistersinger* as well as Friedelind. She closed with 'many many tender kisses and hugs – and thank you for so much love, warmth and understanding, always and always your Mausi'. Lady Crosfield visited Friedelind – she was touching in her concern for her – and there was 'a moving farewell. Everywhere you leave a little of your heart behind – scattered all over the world – and one feels ever lonelier ... but that is life! It is a terrible thing!'[43]

It was also in February 1941 that Friedelind learnt at last that Daniela had died. 'I heard of Daniela's death only just now – I don't know why nobody told me before. It was such an unexpected shock and I still cannot believe it,' she wrote to Toscanini. 'I am very, very sad because I loved her more than anyone else in the family. And I know what the loss must have meant to you, dearest Maestro. There are so few left now of our old Bayreuth – but as long as I have a breath I shan't let its soul die.' She mentioned that her aunts had nicknamed her 'Oceana', and was now confident that the ocean would bring her safely to Buenos Aires.[44]

For Friedelind, hungry for experience and always on the go, who had undertaken so many travels at home and abroad, always surrounded by people, her present circumstances were a severe test. Her closest relatives had spurned her, and even Frida Leider, who had suffered so much under the Nazis, had urgently warned her against leaving Germany. Now she was isolated. All she still had was Toscanini, who approved of what she had done and wanted to help. And she also had to deal with the sarcasm of the press. Thus the magazine *The Cavalcade* had mocked the sensation she was creating in its issue of 14 December 1940: 'To epitomise the adventure of Friedelind: Mr Baxter brought her to Britain; Mr Peake put her under lock and key; Mr Baxter wanted to get her out of Britain; Mr Peake is anxious to let her go; Mr Toscanini offers her a job in the Argentine. It only remains for someone to say "Auf Wiedersehen".'[45] For a young woman of just 22 who had travelled to England so full of hope, such derision cannot have been easy to bear.

Toscanini often sent her messages via Woolley, and that cheered her up. He remained her artistic idol, and she thought of him when she pondered the directing work that she wanted to carry out one day: 'If I did not have his shining example – who knows whether I would manage?' But his politics had influenced her too. Oddly, it was her anti-Semitic aunts whose idolization of Toscanini had encouraged her to get closer to him, and it was now he who was helping to open her eyes to what was really happening in Germany. 'How should I be able to thank him? What an angel he is to me. If I weren't sure of his friendship and affection, I don't know how I would have stood it for so many months.'

At last, permission for her departure came through. Friedelind later claimed that it had been thanks to the intervention of the wife of the publisher of the *Washington Post*, Agnes Meyer, who had apparently contacted Winston Churchill directly,[46] though presumably Toscanini's influence had tipped the balance. On 14 February 1941 she was allowed to quit internment in London and was brought to Glasgow, accompanied by an official, who one day later put her on board the *Andalucia Star*. Her suitcase with books, photos, papers and other material had been searched beforehand on official orders, though nothing suspicious had been found. Nevertheless, large portions of her book manuscript were left behind in England. She sent Toscanini a telegram from the ship to say that she was having a wonderful voyage, without any fuss, over a gentle sea.[47]

Information about her release and departure reached Bayreuth in meandering fashion. Eva Chamberlain wrote to Ellen Beerli on 25 February 1941: 'It was a great comfort that you were able to write to me reassuringly about our problem child, and it also had an effect in Wahnfried. Finally: no more rumours, but facts! May God give her life, so rich in adventure, a fruitful permanence!'[48]

Chapter 8

'My heart is overflowing'
From Buenos Aires to New York
1941 to 1943

THE EQUATOR was crossed on 1 March; on 5 March the Andalucia Star reached harbour in Rio de Janeiro in Brazil. Four days later it arrived in Montevideo and one day after that it reached its goal, Buenos Aires, the capital of Argentina. The journey had taken 23 days. The ship had come across just one submarine and had been able to outrun it. After her experiences in the Blitz in London, nothing could perturb Friedelind any more. She was met at the landing stage by Erich Engel and his wife, the soprano Editha Fleischer. Engel was an Austrian conductor who had lived in Buenos Aires for several years already and who ran the opera at the Teatro Colón, working closely with Fritz Busch and Erich Kleiber. Fleischer had sung at the New York Met more than 400 times between 1926 and 1936, and now taught in Argentina.

Engel surprised Friedelind with the good news that Toscanini would conduct in Buenos Aires just three months later. Although Toscanini had claimed to the British authorities that she would be employed as a theatre director in the city, the idea had long been dropped after Friedelind had herself expressed doubts:

> How could I possibly be efficient doing work on a stage I have never seen in my life – in a country where I have never been – facing artists and a chorus that are new to me and of whom I know nothing at all – finding myself in the midst of a season that is already in full swing – where I cannot change or propose anything according to my own wishes? I would have a few weeks' time to give a finishing touch to a performance that is someone else's – and all this should be signed with my name which of course would be a very nice advertisement for the opera, but never for me.[1]

Was it the burden of her famous name that made her hesitate, because she felt that something special would be expected of her? Whatever her reasons, she here refused the chance to start a career as a director on a modest level such as (for example) Hans Busch had done, the son of Fritz.

Buenos Aires boasted large parks and avenues, and its centre buzzed with big-city traffic, directed by policemen. There were lots of little buses, 'screeching trams, modern skyscrapers, cinemas, theatres, restaurants, pizzerias and lots

12 Buenos Aires at the time Friedelind travelled there.

of different shops'.[2] Argentina had strict entry requirements, but in comparison to other countries it accepted a large number of Jewish refugees. After the USA and Palestine, it was their most important destination outside Europe. In the years 1933 to 1945, some 40,000 German Jews fled to Argentina to escape Nazi oppression. However, as Friedelind noted with annoyance, there were also lots of German Nazi supporters there.[3] One could read German-language newspapers such as the liberal *Argentinisches Tagblatt,* which featured anti-Nazi cartoons, and there was a lively Jewish community with an upmarket Yiddish theatre. In the Ludwig-Tietz-Heim, a meeting place for émigrés, there were concerts with music by Beethoven and Haydn,[4] though we have no proof that Friedelind ever attended them. Ever critical in matters musical, it seems she preferred to wait for the arrival of her ersatz father, Toscanini. She learnt a little Spanish and was happy that no one laughed at her when she went shopping and asked for things in the local tongue. It was wonderful for her once more to walk about a city that was lit at night, where nothing was destroyed, where she could sleep in her own pyjamas (and not in her daytime clothes) and where she could even eat salads.

There was also plenty of entertainment around when compared to the barren life of London – though this was not what she hankered for. After months of internment, her journey across the sea had truly been like a departure to a new world. But she really wanted to go to the USA, and now her entry permit was being delayed. She wanted to get American citizenship, and Buenos Aires seemed to her a bothersome stopover. She was sure that New York would give her back the sense of security in life that her internment on the Isle of Man and her imprisonment in London had taken from her. Once more she stood as if before a wall; once more she had to wait without any hope for an end to it. These months would turn into one of the greatest crises she would ever endure, and she later wrote of it all to Jeanette:

> Sweetest, I would have loved to write to you a real Mausi-letter, full of courage and 'don't worries' – but how could I? Besides, until very recently I wasn't at all the Mausi you knew – but a person who had only one desire: not to live any more. It must have been the reaction to all the terrible experiences – the nerve-racking wasn't over once I was in Buenos Aires but started all over again.[5]

She set herself a deadline beyond which she would not wait any more, 'otherwise I would have put an end to it all'. It seemed to her worse to have to wait there than to be cooped up in an internment camp or living under the threat of bombing.

Friedelind's nerves were more than frayed after her experiences of the Blitz and her imprisonment. Later she described how difficult it had become for her to think in normal categories of time. 'When you face death at such close quarters, it is hard to think beyond the next five minutes – and you feel you must cramp everything right into those few minutes, because you may not be around any more after that. It took quite a few months for me to get re-adjusted.'[6] And yet she was more privileged than others – not just by being the granddaughter of a musical genius, but because her innumerable opera visits in London, Paris and not least in Bayreuth had acquainted her with so many artists. A majority of Jewish artists had managed to escape the dangers of Nazi Germany and several of them had either already settled in Buenos Aires or were visiting the city as guests.

The Engels brought Friedelind together with other musicians from the European élite. Thus she paid regular visits to Fritz Busch and his wife. She knew Busch's brother Adolf because he had led the ensemble that Toscanini had conducted in Tribschen in 1938. Fritz Busch (1890–1951) had been General Music Director in Stuttgart from 1918 to 1922, where he had established himself as a leading opera conductor. He had then moved on to Dresden to run the State Opera. He had also worked in Bayreuth for a season, though his proposals to engage better singers and to invite Toscanini had not gone down well with Siegfried Wagner at the time.[7] He had left Germany in 1933, after having been shouted down by a mob of Nazi storm troopers. 'It was a shame for the Nazis, who would have liked to keep him, and he was a decent chap. He gave up everything – the pretty title of "General Music Director" and his even prettier salary.'[8] Busch founded the Glyndebourne Festival in 1934 together with Carl Ebert, and it soon acquired an international reputation. By the time Friedelind arrived in Buenos Aires, Busch had already been running the German season of operas at the Teatro Colón for several years. Later, from 1945 to 1950, he would be the Artistic Director at the Met in New York.

Friedelind also met Josef Gielen, the Austrian actor, opera director and former director of the Burgtheater in Vienna, who had fled his homeland along with his wife Rosa, the sister of the pianist Eduard Steuermann. Being Jewish, she had not been safe in Germany, and marriages between Jews and non-Jews were in any case politically problematical (Tietjen had for that reason cancelled Gielen's contract prematurely in Berlin).[9] So the two of them had gone to Trieste in January 1940, and from there taken a boat to Argentina. Gielen had worked at the Teatro Colón before and was now given a contract there, renewable annually, so that he at least had a modest income (their son Michael, who travelled with them, was 13 at the time, and later achieved fame himself as a composer and conductor).

Friedelind also met Erich Kleiber again (1890–1956). He had been appointed as Leo Blech's successor at the Berlin State Opera in 1923, had remained there for twelve years and, as a conductor, had made a mark on German music life in a manner comparable only to Wilhelm Furtwängler and Richard Strauss. Besides being well known for his interpretations of Beethoven and Wagner, he had conducted the world première of Alban Berg's *Wozzeck* (1925) and given the German première of Janáček's *Jenůfa*. After settling in Buenos Aires in the 1930s, Kleiber gave the South American premières of assorted Classical and Romantic works and received the honorary citizenship of Argentina in 1938. In the year before Friedelind's arrival he had given a cycle of all of Beethoven's symphonies. She had written to him in September 1939 from Tribschen, and he had remarked on it as follows: 'Mausi Wagner is at Tribschen, near Lucerne, has spent a lot of time with Toscanini, and says that I'm the only living conductor of whom Toscanini says only nice things. None of the others has a hair left on his head when he's done with them. She's expecting a revolution in Germany. Her brothers are at the front and Mama is not quite so fond of Adolf as she used to be!'[10] Was this perhaps wishful thinking? Kleiber was incidentally a great admirer of Toscanini's art of conducting and always had a signed photo of his Italian colleague with him whenever he went on tour.

Engel was keen to bring the best singers to South America. One of them was the bass Alexander Kipnis (1891–1978), whom Friedelind had known since his stay in Bayreuth in 1927. In retrospect she thought she could remember seeing his son Igor (born in 1930) in his pram – an unusually pretty baby, she remarked of him (he would later become famous as a harpsichordist).[11] Kipnis had left Germany in 1935 because he was Jewish, and now often gave guest performances in the USA. Herbert and Erna Janssen had also moved to Buenos Aires; Friedelind had known them for years, and they were delighted to welcome her. Herbert Janssen (1892–1965) had sung the part of Wolfram in Bayreuth in 1930, then Amfortas in 1931, and as late as 1937 he had sung the Herald in *Lohengrin*, Gunther in *Götterdämmerung* and Kothner in *Meistersinger*. He had also been a member of Tietjen's ensemble in Berlin, and had given his first guest performances in Buenos Aires in 1938. Friedelind's diary lists many social events with them – jaunts in their car, lunches and dinners. She also became friends with the Chilean pianist Claudio Arrau (1903–1991), and they sat at the opera together on many an evening. He had studied in Germany, was married to the mezzo-soprano Ruth Schneider and had emigrated in 1940. His wife had followed him a few months later, after the birth of their child. In his memoirs he wrote of Friedelind as 'a wonderful person', though it bothered him that she paid little attention to her great-grandfather Franz Liszt and barely reacted when he praised Liszt's music.[12] When his memoirs were published in 1984, Friedelind disagreed with his recollection, though she oddly misread him and reacted as if his criticism were directed at her father, Siegfried: 'My father conducted Liszt in almost all of his concerts,' she retorted, 'I know only passionate veneration and love for him in my father's generation.'[13] (Proof that Arrau was right can perhaps be found in a remark that Friedelind made when planning to attend a performance of Liszt's *Faust Symphony* under Mitropoulos: 'Not that I am a great Liszt-fan.')[14]

Toscanini postponed his arrival in Buenos Aires. The Argentinian conductor Ferruccio Calusio, Toscanini's former assistant at La Scala Milan, was as desperate to see his former master as was the local public and he begged Friedelind to make him change his plans. Friedelind reported to Toscanini that she had met Calusio at a rehearsal. 'He looked more than ever as if he were wearing too tight shoes ... he begged me to telegraph you.'[15] And when the waiting became too much for her, she sent Toscanini a telegram: 'When are you coming very anxious dearest love Mausi.'[16]

Toscanini arrived on 9 June. He had had a dispute with his NBC Orchestra because its manager had invited a guest conductor whom he regarded as inadequate. Hot-tempered as he was, he then refused to work with the orchestra in the 1941–42 winter season. One year earlier he had gone on a South American tour with his musicians and had performed in Buenos Aires for the first time in 44 years. In fact, his connection to the city went back even further, to 1887, for as a 19-year-old he had stood in to conduct Verdi's *Aïda* at just a few hours' notice, and had been an immense success. Later, he conducted in the city for five seasons in a row, the last of them in the newly opened Teatro Colón in 1908. So his return in 1941 was something of a homecoming. He arrived now without an orchestra, ready to conduct the musicians of the Teatro Colón in Beethoven's Ninth Symphony and in Verdi's Requiem. It was largely thanks to Kleiber that the orchestra was employed throughout the year, for until not long before it had been dissolved at the end of every season.[17] In order to improve its quality, Toscanini brought along six brass players from Cleveland and the bassoonist of the NBC Symphony Orchestra.

At last, he was there. After months of imprisonment, the nights of bombing and all her fears for the future, the 74-year-old conductor came to Friedelind like a knight in shining armour, or perhaps a guardian angel. She broke down, wept uncontrollably and was ashamed of herself for doing so – but her nerves were too frail. 'Desperate weeping. Can hardly keep back tears when amongst people.'[18] A combination of effusive affection, expectant joy at the impending end of her odyssey over three continents (Europe, then South and North America) and gratitude for Toscanini's care and support – all these emotions overwhelmed her. She felt compelled to commit her feelings to paper:

I only want to live when I can be near him – ... Why vegetate? Why spend all the rest of my life going mad with longing to see him – counting every day that is lost – lost forever in which I didn't see him [*sic*] ... I am heartsick – I am sick for just a little warmth and affection. These last years were a little too much. I thought I could brave life alone – but I didn't count on this very life. It was all so well planned – well, one difficulty after the other came – until finally planning in years one can't even plan for the next day.[19]

She had always been so sure of herself, so independent of mind and spirit, but she had now reached her limits.

Friedelind was proud to find herself treated as an adult by the Maestro:

I had serious discussions about music with one of his friends in Buenos Aires. He sat next to us, listened to us and laughed, and when I finally said 'please tell him I'm right', he just smiled and said 'of course you're right, but don't stop'. Sometimes he acts as if he were angry with me and would keep it up if I fell into the trap – but I just ignore it and don't make a scene like many a stupid woman would. I just laugh and act as if I knew nothing, so he has to give up his posturing. The funny thing is that I then have a bad conscience and am afraid I could be cross with him. He tries to make up for his behaviour by being three times as nice. And at times I remind him of it: 'If you think that I have a tête de bois [wooden head] then you should know that mine is made of steel.' Then he says, like a little schoolboy: 'I know, cara, I know' – and looks very frightened.[20]

But despite all her sham superiority she was in these months very insecure, for her feelings towards Toscanini had outgrown the love one might feel for a paternal protector.

After he arrived, there followed six thrilling weeks. Friedelind had already decided in May to join the 160-strong choir for his concerts. She sang in all the many rehearsals and in the performances, and was blissfully happy. She had attended a performance of Beethoven's Ninth under Toscanini three years earlier, in London. Back then she had written:

I could have shouted it out to the world: 'Joy, lovely spark of the gods!' But instead, the whole world is getting crazier – 'be embraced, ye millions' is further away than ever, and instead one country invades another's borders, people shoot and murder their neighbours – holy art is the only bridge between us, and is international in the most ideal sense!'[21]

Toscanini conducted Verdi's Requiem three times and Beethoven's Ninth four times. As a member of the chorus Friedelind was given a contract as a 'Coristas extraordinarios' that brought her $4 per rehearsal and $15 per concert. Since she already knew the works very well, she had nothing to learn and could observe the Maestro all the while from her place in the chorus, directly opposite him. 'I had the best place in the world and felt as if I were in heaven.' She was happy to be a part of the instrument that he wielded. She held the piano score in her hands so that she did not stand out, thought she knew every note by heart and did not need it. Unaware of this, Toscanini asked her sternly in his dressing room whether she could not sing from memory. After all, he was used to conducting five-hour-long Wagner operas without a score in front of him. But she was able to reassure him.

With his performances of Beethoven's Ninth Symphony, one of the highpoints of the symphonic repertoire, Toscanini left his mark on the reception history of the work. With its closing setting of Schiller's Ode 'To Joy' and its message of the brotherhood of man, the Ninth encapsulated all the values that went counter to what was happening back in Europe where war was raging, and Toscanini's interpretation was understood as a call for a better world. He knew that the free world was looking to him. In those difficult war years – 1941 was one of the darkest – music was regarded as a harbinger of freedom. News was seeping through of the systematic murder of the Jews, and the military situation of the Allies was hardly encouraging. The émigrés in Buenos Aires were full of fear and worried about their friends and relatives back in Germany, whose existence was now so fragile. Toscanini's reputation in the Americas was in part a result of his political stance. He had turned his back on Bayreuth and Salzburg and had refused to conduct the fascist hymn in Italy. 'This threefold emigrant – who left Italy, Germany and Austria – is the greatest conductor of the present time,' wrote Erika and Klaus Mann in admiration. 'In the brilliance of his fame, his fearless, clear, knightly bearing makes of him a shining example.'[22]

Toscanini was able to draw on seasoned veterans whom Kleiber had engaged for the opera in Buenos Aires. There was the Mozart specialist Judith Hellwig (soprano), a former prima donna at the Berlin State Opera; Lydia Kindermann (contralto); the Belgian René Maison (tenor); and the Russian Alexander Kipnis (bass). Kipnis wrote of the event afterwards as follows: 'As for my impression of his performance, certainly it was different from others: it had more fire, more drive, more fanaticism; it was not what we used to call *sehr gemütlich*. And I remember the last section of the finale, which begins *Poco allegro* and which accelerates *sempre più allegro*: if it is too fast it is banal, but in the tempo in which Toscanini began it and accelerated it, it was extraordinary.'[23]

13 Friedelind in elegant evening dress: her resemblance to her grandfather,
Richard Wagner, had a big impact on her life.

'Be embraced, ye millions!' – in a world at war, this call had a shattering impact, and it echoed through the opera house. The first of the four performances took place on 20 June 1941. A recording was made of the last concert on 24 July, shortly before Friedelind was due to leave the city by plane with Toscanini and his wife. It conveys an intense, almost frightening eruptive power and is regarded as one of the most remarkable interpretations of the work that the conductor gave in his long career. The sopranos achieve the difficult high-lying passages with ease and follow the extreme tempo effortlessly. For Friedelind, who stood in the middle of it all, the performance was a deeply moving experience that she would not forget for the rest of her life. The first bars had hardly begun when she felt transported into a different world, one of which she had barely hoped to dream just a few months earlier. The Adagio seemed to her more heavenly than ever before: it made her think of Daniela, who had loved the Maestro so much. She tried to capture the overwhelming impact of the experience in words shortly afterwards:

> Why doesn't one die in such a moment – a moment of complete happiness – where the soul is already above this human misery and is reaching and touching the unknown heavens – that suddenly open their doors....
> I could not feel the presence of my body for the rest of the evening ... music is rejoicing in me – my heart is full – my soul is touched by his love and his music.[24]

Almost 50 years later she gave her friends a gift of the 1941 recording on cassette. She compared it with a recording conducted by Leonard Bernstein: 'A complete contrast – as valid as is each interpretation. Toscanini like an angry Zeus – he had every reason to be one at the time. The soloists were persecuted refugees – we had all been fair game for Messrs Hitler or Mussolini. It catches fire, it explodes – Lenny's version is then completely serene – Elysian – immaculate in its broad tempi.'[25]

After the last concert, the time was come for her to leave for the USA. Just as they were supposed to fly, bad weather delayed everything for yet one more day. Toscanini, his wife Carla and Friedelind flew with several stops along the way, so they were travelling for five days in all. Since they had left later than planned, it meant that they missed their connection in Rio. So they spent a day there, which Friedelind enjoyed to the full. Toscanini showed her everything, driving through the city and up into the hills with her. He was 'proud as a child' that he was able to show her the whole area.[26] There was a festive dinner in the Copacabana Hotel, and she felt enraptured: 'Gratitude, gratitude is all that comes to mind. Everything is like a dream,' she wrote in her diary.

The next day they crossed the equator in Belem, a town at the estuary of the Amazon, then spent a night in Trinidad. 'Long journey. I am very, very happy! I can see the northern skies again and could have wept for joy – I don't know why. Happy!'

The five days of the journey were wonderfully carefree – they were the calm before the storm. There must have been moments of great intimacy, for she was in such a euphoric mood and was convinced that she had never been so happy in all her life. She wrote to Jeanette that 'The higher up and the nearer our plane was to Heaven – the more wonderful I felt and the happier I was.' She wished for the plane to fall out of the sky, as she was so scared of what the future might bring. And she ended with the cryptic sentence: 'As there is one thing which I could and can never have alive – I thought it would be wonderful to have it dead.'[27] Was it her secret love for Toscanini that prompted these words? In any case, his paternal care touched her deeply – it was something that she had missed so much while imprisoned in London. She felt joy at Toscanini's presence, hope at the prospect of better times in New York and relief that she had finally left her European misery behind her. But she was also nervous, for in New York she would be just one of more than 100,000 German and Austrian refugees who had emigrated to the USA between 1933 and 1941.[28] She was quite prepared to use her name to help her make her way, but it was still clear to her that she would have to start her life all over again.

They reached American soil on 30 July 1941, landing in Miami. On the afternoon of the next day they touched down at La Guardia Airport: she was in New York at last. Eighteen years earlier, her parents had visited the continent and had been the guests of Henry Ford, the car manufacturer and virulent anti-Semite who had recently launched his notorious series of pamphlets entitled 'The International Jew', pillorying the supposedly pernicious influence of Jews throughout the world. Winifred later mentioned in an interview how Ford had supported Hitler financially through the sale of cars and lorries.[29] The Wagners could hardly have imagined that, many years later, their daughter would flee from their dear 'Führer'. 'Now you are at home,' said Toscanini after they landed. And she wrote: 'I am radiant with happiness. U.S.A. at last! The dream has come true. Walk in evening… Dear God – I know it is all over – but these days were the happiest ever. I am content.'[30] Toscanini reassured her and gave her hope for a new life, far away from bombs and war.

Friedelind needed a long time to get over both her harsh experiences as an internee in England and the subsequent, long wait in Buenos Aires. At Toscanini's suggestion she moved into the 'wedding-cake' building of the Ansonia Hotel on 73rd Street, just to the north of where the Lincoln Center would later be built. This massive building had opened in 1904 and had been intended for long-term guests. It originally had 2500 rooms and 340 suites over 17 floors. Musicians such as Caruso, Stravinsky, Rachmaninov, Mahler and others had stayed there because the rooms had good sound insulation. The Janssens, husband and wife, also lived there.

In New York there was no chorus of welcome for Friedelind, no reception with open arms. She alone was responsible for organizing her life, down to the smallest things. She possessed only her clothes, a few souvenirs from Germany and her written notes. Her thoughts returned again and again to Jeanette, for she was very lonely at first: 'The first months were terrible because of it.'[31]

After her arrival, however, Toscanini continued to support her financially. Carla was responsible for money matters, though she was not much better at it than her husband, who was quite helpless in such things.[32] After Friedelind had got her bearings in her new environment she went on a hunt for a publisher. She was hungry for success with her book describing her life up to the moment of emigration. She rapidly understood that in the USA advertising oneself was a basic requirement if you wanted to get on in life. But there were problems with the English authorities, for they did not want to send on her manuscript. She was worried that she had perhaps not adequately stressed her opposition to Hitler when she had begun working on the book, and feared that the authorities might have got the wrong impression: 'This book is about and against Hitler and there are many things which I would not publish but which are in the first sketch of the manuscript and which I think may be the reason why the authorities may have kept it. I want to help the Allied cause with this book.'[33] She was still angry about the manipulation of her texts by the *Daily Sketch* when, for the first time in her life, she had experienced first-hand how ruthlessly the representatives of the press were prepared to deal with the material she gave them.

While Friedelind was busy getting to know her new environment, a kind of trench warfare was being practised back in Bayreuth. Wieland was determined to direct operas and attacked his mentor Heinz Tietjen, who was still Winifred's confidant. For his part, Tietjen drafted a memorandum for Hitler, threatened to give it to him if Wieland continued his attacks, and also made his continued role in Bayreuth dependent on certain conditions. Wieland's intense resolve to get the directorship of the Festival gives us an inkling of the difficulties with which Friedelind would have been faced, had she stayed in Germany. Wieland pondered whether he should drive to the 'Führer' to explain to him in person the whole situation in Bayreuth, where the current 'armistice' between him and Tietjen only served to cement his own exclusion from directing operas.[34] This put Winifred in a highly delicate position, for as

Tietjen's lover and the mother of the designated Festival Director-to-be she was caught squarely between the conflicting interests of her men.

But Friedelind knew nothing of all this. Her first months acclimatizing to New York were marked by emotional turbulence. Her contact with Toscanini had become more intense during their stay in Buenos Airies and the five-day flight to the USA, and she could not help but notice that his interest in her was now also erotic in nature. It electrified her. For many years her love for him had resulted from their paternal relationship and from her admiration for his brilliance as a conductor. But now he interested her (and she him) in a quite different manner.

The good-looking Maestro was well known for his affairs. The eccentric actress Eleonora von Mendelssohn was often present at his evening soirées at home in Riverdale. She regularly drove by taxi to Toscanini's residence to stalk him, sometimes sitting on his lawn throughout the night – usually wearing a man's trousers, a jacket and a baseball cap in the hope of hiding her identity.[35] Eleonora already had affairs with Max Reinhardt and Gustav Gründgens to her name. She had also embarked on an affair with the writer Ruth Landshoff (the niece of the publisher Samuel Fischer), who was herself fond of appearing on public occasions dressed in a man's dinner suit. Eleonora's greatest love, however, was for Toscanini. Her brother Francesco was no less a subject of scandal and was similarly caught up in the sexual hurly-burly, for he had once had an affair with the pianist Vladimir Horowitz who, despite being gay in private, had since 1933 been the husband of Toscanini's youngest daughter Wanda. In 1935, Eleonora had invited Toscanini to her estate in Austria and in her exuberance had given him a painting by Guardi as a gift – and which Toscanini quickly put in the boot of his car before she could change her mind. Their acquaintance had turned into an affair and, after the cessation of their sexual relationship, that affair had once more turned back into adoring devotion on her part. She was just one of the conductor's many lovers, for his marriage to Carla had long since ceased to offer him erotic satisfaction. Carla seems to have taken these escapades in her stride, and in any case, divorce was not an option for either spouse because they had been married as Roman Catholics.

Friedelind was invited to the luxurious surroundings of Riverdale almost every day (though their suburb, incidentally, was not just for the wealthy; the family of the composer Jean Gilbert lived in relative poverty in rented accommodation nearby. Like many émigré artists, Gilbert had experienced great difficulty in finding his feet in the local music life).[36] Toscanini's imposing house was surrounded by large lawns and a garden that led to the rocks and reeds down by the banks of the Hudson River, of which the house offered a commanding view. On the opposite bank one could see the cliffs and forests of the New Jersey Palisades. Everything was on a generous scale. There were two grand pianos in the large living room (a third was to be found in Toscanini's studio in the first floor), and there was a record player with large loudspeakers in all four corners of the room. Shelves full of records lined one of the walls. These were not just Toscanini's own studio and radio recordings as the conductor of the NBC Orchestra, but also included various recordings by colleagues.[37]

In 1941, the conductor's life happened to be affair-free. He worked hard during the day, so it pleased him when he could at least invite women to dinner on an evening.[38] Friedelind was often among them and would sit with the other guests on the terrace, eating and admiring the moonlight.

Besides Eleonora von Mendelssohn, the pianist Ania Dorfman was often there too. She had been one of Toscanini's soloists. The writer Marcia Davenport was also in attendance – she was a daughter of the singer Alma Gluck and an enthusiastic admirer of the Maestro. Her book *Of Lena Geyer* – a novel about a female fan who idolized a woman singer – had been a bestseller upon its publication in 1936. Another frequent guest was Margherita de Vecchi, who had become acquainted with Toscanini on one of his earlier visits to New York and who since then had worked as a factotum for him and his family. She organized theatre tickets, sea voyages and kitchen staff, and Toscanini discussed many things with her – he loved gossip, and she provided him with ample offerings.[39] Friedelind had already corresponded with her from the Isle of Man and would now have frequent dealings with her. Toscanini liked to put on his own records after a meal, such as *Tristan*, *Götterdämmerung*, or works by Johann Strauss and César Franck. Another time, his interpretation of Beethoven's Ninth was compared with a recording by Leopold Stokowski.

'Lost and lonesome' – her feelings of loneliness and of being lost now applied less to Friedelind's situation as an émigré, and more to her feelings for the man whom she had hitherto seen as a father figure. 'I am happy – close to him,' she wrote – perhaps significantly, her diary entries about Toscanini are written consistently in English, which had long been their medium of communication. But she was aware that her love had no place here, and she enjoyed few moments of real intimacy. This merely made the situation all the more charged. 'Tense atmosphere. I go crazy. He tries so hard to hide his feelings and suffers agonies. So do I. I go mad if it goes on like that.... He looks at me that I think I go up in smoke – it burns so much.' The nocturnal telephone conversations began for which the conductor was notorious, since he himself needed very little sleep. 'Maestro sweet. Rings me after midnight "Your fault, your fault, your fault" – he says desperately'. Another time he avoided her gaze and looked away demonstratively: 'We are miserable, tortured'. But at other times he just stared at her, which she could not bear either. 'Maestro is unhappy. He looks – looks – looks. I go mad'. She wept at home, had fits of rage and suffered from sleeplessness. She decided to avoid him. But if she did not see him for two whole days, her suffering grew all the more. When she and Margherita were once the only guests, she acted as if everything were normal: 'He is not going to find out how I feel'. But there were happy evenings too. Once they sat outside until just before 11pm and enjoyed the gentle breeze. He called her 'la figlia' again and she was ecstatic. She was convinced that 'He still is crazy about me and tries hard to hide it'.

On 10 September 1941, three days late, they commemorated the anniversary of the bombing of London and Friedelind's imprisonment that had begun one year before. In the evening the Maestro and his wife went to a restaurant with Margherita, Eleonora and Friedelind and ate goulash, washed down with large quantities of champagne. 'Very nice party,' she wrote. Afterwards, Arturo and Carla brought her home. Often, her plans for the future were discussed: 'He is sweet and understanding.'[40] In late September, the tensions increased. Toscanini was now ringing her more often, sometimes several times during the day and also at night: 'Passionate love on the phone. He makes me sound so small. We are lovers – alas only on the phone'. Something special must have happened between them on the 29th of an unidentified month (perhaps in connection with her birthday on 29 March?). For she wrote: 'He blesses the 29th – I shall never – never in my life forget it. It has never happened to me before ... He rings me. We talk long long until day breaks: "The 29th is our day" he says'. One day later she went with Toscanini and his entourage to the première of the one-act play *The Human Voice* (*La voix humaine*) by Jean Cocteau, in which Eleonora von Mendelssohn played the woman having a telephone conversation with an ex-lover. The critic of the German-language emigrants' newspaper *Aufbau* was full of praise: 'The classical lines of her face and her body experience this tragic symphony of emotions ranging from love to hate, jealousy, disappointment, loneliness and the nearness of death.'[41] But the situation was also somewhat provocative, since Toscanini was given to ringing all his various girlfriends at night, not just Friedelind.[42]

The journalist Leo Lerman, who knew Eleonora, wondered afterwards whether Toscanini '... recognized that the heartrending words Cocteau gave to this poor character were in no wise different from words sometimes murmured by our Eleonora into the telephone from her own bed when talking to him, in the long, dark nights when she was alone – or almost alone'.[43] Friedelind did not enjoy the performance – everyone on this evening, includ-

14 Maestro Toscanini, renowned conductor and womanizer, 'To my most
beloved Mausi' in 1941, when Friedelind was still under his erotic spell.

ing Carla, was unpleasant to her. Did they perhaps see her as a troublemaker whose love for Toscanini was obvious to everyone? 'Afterwards an awful night – sit opposite him and at least under the table we enjoy being together. I ring him at 3.30, talk till 6.' The press, however, was delighted to see Eleonora and Friedelind in public together, and could not help from commenting on the friendship between 'Mendelssohn and Wagner'.[44]

Friedelind's combination of yearning and asceticism could not survive for long in its current intensity, and she gradually began to extract herself from her entanglement. She projected her frustration onto the conductor himself. She wrote:

> 'Royal court' – that is the only name I can give his Riverdale-residence, because it is a place full of intrigues, jealousies and gossip, of boot-licking and 'yes-men' – and poor me all in the midst of it, being persecuted with the jealousy of a hundred stupid women – all the time intrigues to make me a 'persona non grata' in his eyes. I follow the politics of just ignoring everything – which always turns out to be the wisest thing. It is disgusting at times – but I look upon it from the philosopher's viewpoint and smile to this comedy – most of the time it is opera buffa – but very often poisonous and I am sorry for him. It seems to be my fate always to run into a surrounding of jealousy [sic].

She could not understand this, for she was sure that she had never in her life been jealous herself – and at times she wished that she too could suffer from this strange affliction.

> Maestro is a wonderful friend – sometimes he tries to play the dictator with me too, but soon finds out that I am just as pig-headed as he is – and then he gives it up. I have a wonderful time when he tries his old tricks on me – finally he is very happy when I forgive him and just pretends that nothing has happened – then he calls me 'que tipo' and 'why are you so different from all the others' – and tries hard to make up for everything. I should have some experiences in handling dictators in just the manner they deserve it ...[45]

Toscanini remained her adored 'Maestro' throughout her life, and in 1944 she would dedicate her autobiography to 'my two fathers Siegfried Wagner and Arturo Toscanini', confirming her status to the world as 'figlia'. But inwardly she was setting herself free more and more, and when the conductor offended her a few years later she poured out her indignation into a letter to him:

Dear Once Upon a Time Father and Friend,

This may seem to be a rather strange anniversary letter – but nevertheless, I decided to follow in your worthy footsteps and let off a little steam, maybe I will feel a little better after it, in case your recipe works. If it doesn't – well, that's just too bad.

I think it is rather odd, to say the least, that you should see any necessity to find fault with my 'lack' of 'sex-life' and elaborate upon this great concern of yours with some of your newer acquaintances. I think it is bad taste to the highest degree, coming of all people, from YOU.

I believe that any woman with only an ounce of brain and self-respect would happily abstain from the indulgence of stolen kisses – after having experienced the humiliation, misery and loneliness, as well as the wonderful spectacle of the 'beloved man's' cowardice, that go with it. His worst enemy is treated kindlier by him, than the woman he supposedly loves. No thank you, I want none of it. If any man kisses me in the future, he will first have to go to the bother of taking out a licence and declare himself my legal husband. Until then, I am afraid, you will have to worry about my uninteresting conduct.

What kind of women you have met in your life, apart from everything else, I am beginning to wonder, too. According to my personal code, as well as my innermost sentiments, I would be incapable of having one man make love to me while I am in love with another. But seemingly you never encountered such odd people who feel that way. Too bad! It is too late now.

Thank you for continuing to destroy the thing that once upon a time was most precious to me in the whole World: The Myth that WAS Toscanini. I am glad you turned out to be only human, too.[46]

All her frustrations flowed out regarding his flirts with other women and his tactlessness. This letter upset Toscanini so much that he scribbled 'Wrong address' angrily across the envelope and sent it back. Nor was Friedelind the only woman whom Toscanini offended – Eleonora von Mendelssohn had to endure how the Maestro would gossip about her bedroom habits to his visitors.[47]

As a new arrival in the giant metropolis that was New York, Friedelind found it difficult to adjust. But friends and acquaintances from the Isle of Man and London helped her find her feet. They met for coffee and gossip, cooked for each other in their apartments, and discussed politics and the difficulties of starting a new life. 'My friends are a wonderful cross-section of every walk of life, every social step, colour, nationality, race, religion, profession.'[48]

They all found it problematic to begin their lives again. But talking with each other strengthened the sense of belonging that they had already developed in extremis. The women felt like a 'happy little family' that had no secrets from each other and told each other everything. Two of Friedelind's acquaintances worked as housemaids while two others were in a factory where the work was particularly hard. It was a matter of great satisfaction to the émigrés when the USA entered the War after the Japanese attack on Pearl Harbour. Friedelind commented with a mixture of irony and sincerity: 'We are all very happy ... we are all doing positive things – and we are all optimistic – and all eternally grateful to Hitler, who indirectly was the cause of our being here. We know only too well what our fate would have been, if we hadn't taken the plunge into the unknown in good time.'[49]

Friedelind never had to work in a factory, but her situation nevertheless demanded much flexibility. She had to negotiate with the authorities and find a career for herself, and she took on assorted jobs. Her lectures and articles did not provide enough to support her. She was not shy – quite the opposite was the case, as she was highly communicative – and she often went to the opera and to concerts, where the contacts that she had long cultivated with musicians helped her to meet other people and make new friends.

In America a distinction was made between the mass of 'immigrants' from all over the world to seek a better life and the 'émigrés' who had already made a name for themselves in their native lands and were highly educated.[50] Several German artists had already performed in the USA in the years before and were well known there – such as Artur Schnabel, Adolf Busch and the lat-ter's son-in-law, Rudolf Serkin. The violinist Adolf Busch had been a professor at the Berlin Music Academy since 1918 and his pupils had included Yehudi Menuhin. He had founded the world-famous Busch Quartet and had become acquainted with the pianist Rudolf Serkin. In New York, 'Rudi' lived together with the Busch family. But while Serkin succeeded in rapidly establishing a career for himself in the USA and was soon one of the country's most success-ful pianists, Busch had difficulty in settling down.[51] Busch and Serkin were at this time frequent visitors to Toscanini's home, where they also met Friedelind several times. Her circle of friends also included the Hungarian photographer, journalist and publisher Stefan Lorant (1901–1997), who had been imprisoned by the Nazis before being allowed to emigrate.

She also met the tenor Kurt Baum, who sang regularly at the Metropolitan Opera, and Konrad Wolff, a lawyer who had taken lessons from Artur Schna-bel in Italy and brought the traditions of the Leschetizky and Czerny school to the USA. He remained devoted to his teacher for the rest of his life, and celebrated him in a book entitled *Schnabel's Interpretation of Piano Music*. Ilse

Bing, his wife, achieved world fame as a photographic artist. They had endured traumatic times in France, where they had been interned after the German invasion, though they had managed to flee the country via Marseille. A turbulent journey ensued. Friedelind had earlier heard that they were stranded on the island of Trinidad, so she was now relieved to learn that they had succeeded in entering the USA. She also, on occasion, saw the Greek actress Katina Paxinou, whom she had met in London in 1939.

Friedelind celebrated her first American Christmas with the Janssens. Later, Lauritz and Maria 'Kleinchen' Melchior joined them. Herbert Janssen began giving Friedelind singing lessons (his later pupils would include Astrid Varnay).[52] He was now engaged permanently at the Metropolitan Opera and regularly sang in the Teatro Colón in Buenos Aires in the summer months. Friedelind always wanted the latest gossip: 'I'm keen to know how Mr Busch is doing. Is Kleiber really not conducting anything? How are all the new and the old directors?'

Finding her feet in New York also meant bumping into other exiled artists from outside the music profession. Monika Mann, the daughter of Thomas and Katia, met Friedelind as she was leaving a popcorn bar together with Kadidja Wedekind (the daughter of Frank).[53] Kadidja (1911–1994) was a writer, journalist, actress and graphic designer and, after her emigration to the USA, shared an apartment for several years with Monika. Kadidja met Friedelind several times and later wrote a laudatory article about her for a German illustrated magazine with the title 'She saved the honour of the Wagner family'. She described Friedelind as a lively person who 'even in America, and shortly after the War, had a disconcerting way of saying loud and clear what she was thinking'. Friedelind, so she continued, had tried after the War to convince the horrified Americans that the bestialities committed in the concentration camps could not be blamed on the whole German nation.[54]

When Klaus Mann attended a concert of Bruno Walter's in Carnegie Hall in 1942, he met Friedelind at tea afterwards. 'Why didn't you tell me that she looks so much like Pamela [Wedekind] and is in the process of becoming a proper Rubens figure?' he asked his sister Erika. 'Sometimes she says rather stupid, impertinent things, but of course there's something great, something charming about her. She likes me – her blue eyes made that clear'. The idea of a liaison between the famous families of Mann and Wagner would have caused a stir, but he abandoned the idea as soon as it came up: 'The notion of marrying her is self-evident: if only I had somewhat more of an interest in the fairer sex'.[55]

Money problems remained acute. Toscanini was still prepared to jump in and help where necessary, though it was clear to Friedelind that she had to see to her own future. Nevertheless, she began 1942 full of optimism. She was becoming better known in her new homeland. She wrote articles that had nothing to do with music, such as about Katina Paxinou, and continued working on her book – though dealing with the copy-editing was a burden. 'I did not go to Jones Beach because I am all wrapped up in work – having seen my boss as early as 11am today and approved another chapter. It is the first one that completely satisfied me – it was also one over which I had fought the biggest battles.'[56] She was constantly travelling to give lectures about Hitler. The destruction of Germany seemed to her to be the only way of freeing the German people from its Nazi convictions, and she told people of her own family's connections to Hitler. She claimed that she had hastened her departure after being told by friends in Germany that she was going to be declared mentally ill and placed in an institution.[57] To what extent she was exaggerating, we cannot know.

On 17 January 1942, Friedelind gave a talk on the radio in the interval of a performance of *Lohengrin* broadcast from the Met. The text was provided for her and presumably was not political; she had refused to do radio work in England, but had clearly abandoned her hesitation now.

A month later, Erika Mann succeeded in convincing Friedelind to give a radio talk to German-speaking listeners. Erika was a war reporter with the status of a US army officer and after the broadcast she wrote to her father that the 23-year-old granddaughter looked very much like Richard Wagner:

Nevertheless, barely had she reached adulthood when behind their backs she left Germany and fled to England, where they kept her interned for a year, brilliant though she is. 'Monstre' [Hitler] dandled her on his knee all through her childhood and idolized this ... half-English offspring of Wagner, although she was never anything but stubborn. Now she has got away and is full of new ideas and new melodies.[58]

On 14 February 1942, one day after the 59th anniversary of her grandfather's death, Friedelind broadcast a pugnacious text during a *Tannhäuser* in which three émigrés were singing, namely Lauritz Melchior, Herbert Janssen and Alexander Kipnis. Together with her agent she checked the script that Erika Mann had written for her, corrected a few things, and then read it in German to the audience in Europe:

German listeners! It might seem strange to you that I am commemorating the anniversary of my grandfather's death abroad, here among the supposed enemy, and am speaking to you from New York. But believe me, I did not leave Germany lightly, and only came away when the murderous intentions of the current German regime became clear. Even then, I asked myself how my grandfather Richard Wagner would have acted in my position. Would he have stayed, would he have placed himself at the disposal of the Nazis, would he have lent his name, which is also my name, to their crimes? There can be no doubt: Richard Wagner, who loved freedom and justice even more than he loved music, would have been unable to breathe in Hitler's Germany. Thus we commemorate a great German, though our country is at war with Germany.

The Allies were not fighting the spirit of Goethe, Beethoven or Wagner, she said, but 'the evils of Hitler and his hopes of world domination'. She was speaking in the spirit of her grandfather, she continued, when she prophesied that the hour of the Nazi's *Götterdämmerung* would soon come.[59]

Erika Mann presented the broadcast and was proud of her text ('I did a lovely piece') and was also impressed with Friedelind's performance: 'Her speech, however inaccurate, was nicer ['übscher', *sic*] than Shakespeare because it was straight from the mouth of this dear heir of Wagner (who around her neck wore her shawl and a bright scarf from Tribschen, made of the best material). It should thoroughly displease the animals. I was very pleased.'[60]

Did Friedelind believe that this broadcast would not reach the ears of the Nazis, or was she in fact happy for her family to hear of it? Four days after the broadcast, the 'displeasure' Erika Mann anticipated was confirmed when Winifred was questioned by SS Oberführer Alfred-Ingemar Berndt in Bayreuth, who sent her a summary of the talk. He asked what all this 'crass, anti-German' business meant. Winifred kept to her well-tried strategy of blaming everything on the evil influence the foreigners and Jews had on her daughter, for Berndt replied to her on 1 March, full of understanding:

I am sorry to have unintentionally touched a sore point in this manner. A young girl, especially from such an artistically gifted family, is undoubtedly particularly sensitive and very easily influenced. She does not need to be bad to the core for this to happen. I am also convinced that this is the case here. Even if we cannot anticipate it at the moment, nevertheless we can expect that your daughter will find her way home after this war and can be brought under German influence again.[61]

He added that the broadcast had not reached the German people and had thus caused no major damage. Winifred's good connections presumably saved her, for any 'normal' mother of a daughter whom the Nazis regarded as an evil traitor would not have got away with anything so easily. Friedelind seems not to have been aware of the danger to her family. But if she had read what Winifred wrote about her being incapable of independent thought, she would have been furious.

For her part, Winifred was engaged in advertising for the other side. In 1943, by which time the 'final victory' had already receded into the distance, she wrote in an accompanying book for Bayreuth's 'War Festival' that the *Meistersinger*'s Hans Sachs was the embodiment of the 'creative German man in his nationally conditioned creative will'. He was an inspiration to the German soldier in his battles and gave him 'the fanatical belief in the victory of our weapons' in this 'struggle of western culture with the destructive spirit of the plutocratic, bolshevist world conspiracy'.[62] In order that there could be no doubt that the text was hers, it was printed as a facsimile of her own handwriting. Wieland had created a conventional stage design for the production. Nike Wagner has explained it thus: had Wieland distanced himself too much from the ideas of Heinz Tietjen and Emil Preetorius, then he might have won the admiration of the conservative critics of both Tietjen and Winifred.[63] But Tietjen and Preetorius were far more experienced than he was and, together with Furtwängler, they had achieved exceptional things in the realm of Wagner interpretation. This triumvirate belonged to the best in the world in their craft. So Wieland had to manoeuvre carefully around them, even though in emotional terms a deep chasm had opened up between him and Tietjen.

In this same year, Winifred gave an interview to a German film crew in which she stressed several times that she herself was not active in artistic matters, but merely did her best to support the Director of the Festival. She repeatedly confirmed the role of the 'Führer', who 'with all his dedication and love for Richard Wagner and Bayreuth' had stood by her side to help set the 'War Festival' in motion. She felt herself to be a 'link' between her deceased husband and their sons. She said Wieland would be the one who would one day be responsible for artistic matters at the Festival, while Wolfgang would take over the organizational side of it. Friedelind was not mentioned at all.[64]

Friedelind heard nothing from Bayreuth. In 1942 Wieland visited Hitler several times, who expressed the desire to hear *Parsifal* once again. Verena suggested to Gertrud Strobel that they should perform only the 'erotically charged' second act, and when Wieland mentioned this to the 'Führer', he 'laughed terribly about it!'[65] Meanwhile, Otto Strobel published the first volume of his *Neue Wagner-Forschungen* ('New Wagner Research'). The garden room of the 'Siegfriedhaus' is pictured in it, with a large portrait of the 'Führer' prominent. In his preface, Strobel stressed that the research centre had been created at Hitler's command in 1938, on Richard Wagner's 125th birthday. Winifred opened up the family archives for this purpose, and the city of Bayreuth also placed its archives at the disposal of scholars. It seems that in Bayreuth, everyone still firmly believed that the 'Führer' would win the war.

Chapter 9

'Only you could still save our inheritance!'
1943 to 1945

F RIEDELIND WAS not without plans. On the contrary, she held a cor-
nucopia of them. Nor did she have a problem committing them to
paper. Besides giving lectures she also wrote for various journals such as the
German-language *Aufbau*. Founded in 1934 as the monthly newspaper of the
German-Jewish Association, it helped German Jews to stay in touch in the
USA, offered a venue for authors to write in their native German, and also
gave advice to émigrés on finding a place to live, finding work and generally
getting acclimatized. Friedelind had long cast off her early anti-Semitism and
her circle of friends already included many who were Jewish.

She got up late and used her mornings to write letters and articles on her
typewriter. Then she took a bath and, when the maid came at 2pm to tidy up,
she would leave for her various appointments. Attending concerts remained
her elixir of life. These included a series by the New York Philharmonic
under Toscanini. She was particularly looking forward to a charity concert in
late November 1942 when the Maestro was going to conduct only works by
Wagner: 'The young man is 75 now, but looking at his concert-schedule one
wouldn't expect it.'[1]

The concert culture of the USA was different from that of Europe in a
myriad of ways. Many a European pianist had to abandon his career hopes
because he had no idea of the customary repertoire in the States. Schumann's
Kreisleriana and his *Davidbündlertänze* were never well received, and to programme his Piano Concerto was regarded as 'suicide'.[2] When it came to opera,
it was less the choice of repertoire than the quality of the performances that
Friedelind disliked in her new homeland. Given to drastic judgements as she
was, she called the Metropolitan Opera a place whose abject quality could
prompt one to kill oneself without regret. But since the Met possessed considerable prestige, singers who wanted a career still had to try and sing there.
For Friedelind this was a matter of real annoyance. 'My grandfather would
have blown his brains out if he had seen a performance of his works there.
As a Wagner, I ought to have shot myself too, but I'm more determined than
ever to organize festivals here in New York. As soon as the war is over, I hope
to pursue my plan properly.'[3] The reasons for the current plight of opera lay
largely in money problems. The costs of the war, the restrictions on public
transport and the rationing of petrol all kept the public away from the opera

house. Furthermore, many boxes in the opera house had been bought privately by sponsors and had been passed down the generations, with the latest inheritors often showing little enthusiasm for maintaining their family tradition of sponsorship and instead merely blocking lots of seats. Not until 1944 did the Met's finances emerge into the black again. Friedelind thus experienced a phase of experimentation in which the management was engaging young, cheap, native singers instead of expensive European stars, and this often led to disappointment. One music critic in 1942, for example, described a certain Marie Wilkins as having 'A career that began with headlines and dwindled to a foot-note ... her singing was close to a disaster at several points', while one Stella Roman, who sang Elisabeth in *Tannhäuser*, 'was another instance of clutching at vocal straws'.[4]

Back in Bayreuth, Friedelind had experienced an opera house stocked with talent, while in the Berlin State Opera under Tietjen she had observed a well-subsidized house at close quarters. She knew every bar of Wagner's music and had an extensive knowledge of stage design, costumes and technical matters. The Met was unable to match the level of Wagner productions seen in Germany, and in her damning assessment Friedelind paid no attention to the mitigating circumstances. But New York still offered cultural highpoints: *Don Giovanni* under Bruno Walter in March 1942 featured Ezio Pinza, Jarmila Novotna, Rose Bampton and Alexander Kipnis, and has remained the stuff of legend. But on the whole, Friedelind was disappointed with what was on offer.

In 1942 she began a series of lectures in which her topics centred on Nazi Germany, Wagner and opera. To speak in public meant either to sink or to swim, she wrote to a friend.[5] In her lectures she repeated how important it was to keep pace with the music of the twentieth century, and she argued in favour of modernizing the concert repertoire. She did not hesitate to criticize the opera companies of the USA and included the audiences in her critique, for they were, to her mind, too conservative. She much preferred to talk about Wagnerian topics than politics, though the latter could not be avoided since the political machinations of Bayreuth were a matter of continuing interest to the Americans. Friedelind would gladly have worked for the radio as did Eleonora von Mendelssohn, who was an announcer for the Office of War Information (OWI) from August 1942 onwards, reading the news in German for the 'Voice of America'. Friedelind hoped that she might find a home in this government organization for war information and propaganda, for they paid $225 a month and this would have put her on a firm financial footing. But she failed to get a permanent appointment.

Time and again she was overcome with yearning for Jeanette, back in England. 'Do write to me soon, Darling, tell me lots and lots about yourself, what are you doing, who are your friends – any "boyfriends" as we say here – in the picture?' She still hoped that Jeanette would be able to move to the States and advised her to keep a concert programme ready. Numbers such as Salome's final monologue from the opera by Richard Strauss made a good impact, she said, but she should also specialize in lieder such as Lotte Lehmann and Maggie Teyte did, for then she would have plenty of opportunities to give concerts. Friedelind said Fred Gaisberg, who was in England at the time, should bring records of her with him.

Jeanette had returned to London from the Isle of Man – exactly a year after Friedelind had left her behind in Port Erin. Friedelind had been able to take one recording of Jeanette along with her, but this merely served to intensify her homesickness for her friend and teacher. She longed to resume the singing lessons that Jeanette had given her, for no one in New York had a method which suited her. 'I have been thinking of you so much – and have forgotten you for not a single second – but life is a 24-hour battle. Trying to start a career is no fun, neither here nor anywhere else.'[6]

Despite her financial bottlenecks, Friedelind still dreamed of setting up her own opera company. She earned her money as a waitress, a saleswoman and an office worker, took singing lessons and at the same time worked on her book *Heritage of Fire* that was to include her reminiscences of Bayreuth as well as her criticism of the Nazis. Her real goal, to direct operas, was the most difficult to realize. She attended classes in acting, pantomime, elocution and stage technology at the Brenda Matthews Theater of Columbia University. She had sat in on rehearsals in Bayreuth but had never studied or directed herself, and the 'tuition' she had been given by Tietjen was little more than intermittent instruction. She knew a great deal, but it was all self-acquired.

In 1943 an official from the State Department interviewed Friedelind several times in depth about her knowledge of Adolf Hitler. It seems that the authorities hoped she might help them to get a clearer profile of the dictator. The same man interviewed Ernst ('Putzi') Hanfstaengl, the sometime foreign press spokesman of the Nazi Party who had fled to Great Britain in 1937 and had from there made his way to the USA. He sent his best wishes to Friedelind.[7] The US authorities were keeping a close eye on her because she had known Hitler since early childhood and, by her own admittance, she had met members of the 'Cliveden Set' in England – those known appeasers who had been ready to make concessions to Hitler out of fear of the supposed communist threat. She was called in to give reports several times; the authorities presumably wanted information about possible Nazi sympathizers. For a while they were particularly interested in Edmund H. Stinnes, one of the sons of the legendary German industrialist and a man who was already engaging with questions of the post-War order in Germany.[8] He had at first been in agreement with Nazi policies. But when Hitler offered him a ministerial position on condition that he separate from his Jewish wife and children, he had decided enough was enough and left Germany instead. According to Friedelind he had tried to make contact with her several times. It seems that he did not want her planned book to be as critical as she clearly intended. He would have preferred her to avoid criticizing Hitler and Germany, and instead stress the importance of German culture in an effort to improve Germany's reputation in the USA. He maintained that Wolfgang Stresemann, the later Intendant of the Berlin Philharmonic, the conductor Bruno Walter and Hermann Rauschning all shared his opinion. He also claimed to have tried to convince the politician Heinrich Brüning, who had emigrated in 1934, to take his side.[9]

In late 1943, Toscanini received a telegram from Friedelind: 'Harpers bought book – very good contract signed and sealed. Happy Mausi'. *Heritage of Fire* had just been taken on by a publisher, and she was over the moon. The book begins with her childhood, treats the 1930s with broad brushstrokes and reaches up to Winifred's visit to Zurich in 1940. Friedelind describes Adolf Hitler as a psychologically disturbed *petit bourgeois* – a view that was, of course, directly contrary to that of her mother, who remained faithful to him to the end of her life. Later, Friedelind criticized her co-author Page Cooper, who had been engaged at the insistence of the publisher: 'Since the publisher preferred a Cinderella story to a report about the Nazi era, she squeezed the missing parts out of me. Furthermore, she cut down my comprehensive manuscript by at least half if not more. But every word in the book is the truth, nothing but the truth, and it was all mine'.

The British publisher chose to title the book 'Royal Family of Bayreuth'. Memories of the German bombers, with their very real 'fire' over England, were still raw. Friedelind's reaction to this new title was: 'Over my dead body'. But 'since authors in any case are just dead bodies once they've signed their contracts, I was of course ignored'.[10]

Besides her writing and her lectures, Friedelind began to practise directing on a small scale. In early 1944 she also took on a small acting role: 'I'm supposed to be a born actress!' Contact with other artists were important to her. She remained close to Erna and Herbert Janssen, with whom she had spent so much time in Buenos Aires. He was singing at the Met, where he would remain until 1951. She also maintained her friendships with Lauritz Melchior and his wife. And since Lotte Lehmann had rented a house in the Riverdale district where both Toscanini and the singer Elisabeth Rethberg lived, Friedelind will surely have met her on occasion too. Lotte's husband Otto had died recently and she was living together with a university lecturer named Frances

Holden who had given up her post at the New York University in order to be with her. Shortly after arriving in New York, Friedelind met Lehmann's agent Constance Hope. She was the daughter of the concert pianist Eugene Bernstein and knew all the tricks of the publicity trade. She was even so unscrupulous as to invent stories about Lehmann just to get her name in the media.[11] Friedelind's meeting with her was presumably with a view to a collaboration of some kind, though nothing came of it.

While Friedelind was enjoying good relations with the male members of New York's artistic fraternity and their wives, she had little contact with female émigré musicians, of whom there were many trying to establish themselves. There was the pianist Grete Sultan, who had for several years performed for the Jewish Cultural Federation in Germany and had survived a hellish train journey from Berlin to Portugal in a locked cattle car. Her beginnings in the USA were difficult, but she soon got more and more engagements. Then there was the pianist Frida Kahn who taught for several years at Princeton University. The famous harpsichordist Wanda Landowska had lost her irreplaceable collection of harpsichords and music to the Nazis, who had confiscated everything in Paris. She rented the New York Town Hall of her own accord and enjoyed much success with her concerts.[12] And Ursula Mamlok had left Germany as a young girl in 1939 and in the ensuing years studied composition with Roger Sessions. She became an adherent of twelve-tone music and later taught at conservatories and universities in New York. Vally Weigl was really a composer, but became a pioneer of dance therapy, while the pianist Pia Gilbert composed for dance; thus women artists who moved to the USA were creating new areas in which they could succeed.[13]

The piano teachers had the best time of it, for they usually had excellent qualifications from Europe and a wealth of teaching ability and experience. They also generally found it difficult to restart their career in a new country, but the smaller towns in particular could offer a regular source of income. Friedelind had no such training behind her, and wanted to become an opera director without any practical experience. So it was far more difficult for her to find a way into her chosen profession. But at least she had her name – and her typically Wagnerian profile – and these opened up many doors to her. And with her lectures and her book she was making a name for herself with the broader public.

In 1944 Friedelind was once again asked if she would make a German-language radio broadcast. She agreed, and in it urged the citizens of the USA to buy war bonds. 'Don't you think the boys on the fronts should have the very best and the utmost in equipment?'[14] Such a statement, which implicitly accepted the death of German soldiers as a given, was bound to provoke controversy among German immigrants, and Friedelind was made to feel it. But her appeal in its own way mirrored her mother's public assertions back home of the German soldier's fanatical belief in their final victory.

Often her despair about the War broke through. The news from Europe pointed clearly to an imminent German defeat, and she was worried about friends and family. She heard that 'our darling Frida' (Leider) had given a song recital in the Singakademie in Berlin, and that the hall had been destroyed by bombs one day later.[15] While Friedelind was giving her lectures, people back home were struggling with the problems of everyday life, with the consequences of the Allied bombing raids on the civilian population and the vast destruction that they were wreaking. Yet in Bayreuth, Gertrud Strobel had been told by Winifred about a 'charming report' from Hitler's doctor, Dr Brandt: The 'Führer' would sit for hours in his bunker with his cat in his lap, feeding it confectionery.[16] What would Friedelind have thought of her mother's capacity for ignoring reality?

Meanwhile Verena had married – her husband Bodo Lafferentz was the head of the 'Kraft durch Freude' ('Strength through Joy') organization. That would hardly have pleased Friedelind either. But she would have been happy to hear that Verena and her husband had called their first daughter after her, as a token of affection: 'Amélie-Friedelind'.

In September 1944 Goebbels closed all the theatres in Germany. As a result, Wieland was due to be drafted into either the Wehrmacht or the Volkssturm militia. But his brother-in-law Lafferentz came to his aid and employed him instead as a civilian in a satellite of the concentration camp Flossenbürg, where military research was being carried out. It was set up in the summer of 1944 in a former Bayreuth cotton mill and completely destroyed in May 1945. Its prisoners later related that their conditions were bearable in comparison to those at other camps. It is believed that Wieland spent his months at the camp working on stage sets, but he never spoke about it in later life and it remains a stain on his reputation. He even succeeded in keeping it secret from his daughter Nike, who in 1998 was still writing about his having been employed at a 'place for secret military research', not a concentration camp.[17] If Friedelind had suspected the truth about her brother's employment, their reunion several years later would not have been as harmonious. When questioned by the Allies after the war, Bodo Lafferentz also remained silent about his role in the institution and its employment of concentration camp inmates.[18] If one considers the lifelong public condemnation endured by Leni Riefenstahl who had 'borrowed' concentration camp inmates for unpaid work in one of her films, then one cannot but wonder at the speed of Wieland's later rehabilitation.

The last performance of the Bayreuth 'war festivals' was of *Die Meistersinger*, and was performed with sets designed by Wieland. In the third act, members of the Hitler Youth, the Bund Deutscher Mädel and the men of the SS division 'Wiking' joined the Festival Chorus on stage. Of all this, Friedelind naturally heard nothing, nor of Wieland's vain attempts to get Hitler's blessing to take over the management of the Festival.[19] In September 1944 Wieland wrote about the current political situation to Kurt Overhoff: 'There's still no reason to believe that all is lost and to draw any consequences from that. For the moment, this would only be a sign of individual weakness. There is still hope that the Grail will shine again. Don't say that this is flippant optimism – that was never my style. Our present work has to be carried through.'[20] Friedelind had seen the inevitable end years before, but Wieland was still blanking it out.

Winifred was as determined as ever to get the best possible training for her two sons. There was no room for daughters in this scheme of things. In 1944 she wrote to Heinz Drewes, the head of the Music Department at the Propaganda Ministry: 'On 7 June I will have the pleasure of hearing *Bruder Lustig* in Berlin, which will be the first independent opera production by my younger son Wolfgang. For me that is a great source of satisfaction – it lets one hope that both sons will one day fulfil their duty.'[21] A year before Germany capitulated, Wieland was given the task of directing Wagner's *Ring* in Vienna in a production conducted by Karl Böhm, though the political and military situation made it impossible to carry through. According to Verena Lafferentz, Hitler congratulated her on her birthday on 2 December 1944 by telephone and she was invited to a meal on 7 December along with Wieland and Gertrud. 'When we moved from the dining room to the lounge he was helped by an adjutant who carefully placed a cushion at his back. We did not speak about the Festival, but instead wallowed in memories. Towards five in the morning we were brought home (Wieland, Gertrud, Bodo, Verena).'[22] Hitler ate nothing and seemed agitated; one of his hands trembled a lot and he constantly stroked his Alsatian dog with the other. All the same, Gertrud wrote: 'We left him with very positive feelings, and that did us good.'[23]

Did he still exude charisma? Those 'positive feelings' would in any case not last long, given the present scale of destruction. Since the Allied landing in Normandy and the Russian Army's advance from one victory to the next, it was obvious that the war was lost. The cities of Germany were being turned to rubble, the enemy armies were at the borders of the Reich and the end was near. And yet as late as January 1945 – before the abortive Ardennes offensive in which many Germans placed their last best hope of victory – Hitler was informing Winifred of his hope that Wieland would direct *Walküre* in Bayreuth. 'He wants it to remain secret for the moment – the final decision has to be made in early March – but if the war situation hasn't eased by then, I think it will be impossible,' she wrote. She was doing everything to get Wieland directing experience. She also called on Kurt Overhoff to put in a good word for him in Vienna. Whether any production could be realized was doubtful, she admitted, 'for they need all remaining material as clothing for the Wehrmacht and the Volkssturm. And there are innumerable hundreds of thousands who have lost their homes in the bombings. But our youth, thank God, is not as weighed down as we are and thinks instinctively more egotistically,' she wrote.[24] Despite all those homeless people, and despite the misery across the land, she was still able to contemplate putting on an opera for the 'Führer'. As late as 1945 Wieland was trying to reach Hitler in Berlin in order to get his blessing for his transformation 'from crown prince to big boss', but he could not get through to him.[25]

For us today, this all seems like a different world. How was it possible that a former postcard painter was able to run a modern industrial state according to his own whims, with the servants of the state dependent on the banalities of his everyday existence? A man who made the night into day, who at times simply suspended the workings of government, whose notions of world politics were those of a dilettante and whose decisions as head of both state and military were improvised from one moment to the next?[26] Did the Wagner family believe that they were linked directly to the fate of Germany – rather like Richard Wagner's relationship with Ludwig II of Bavaria? By late 1944, if not before, it was obvious to everyone else that the war was lost. But the Wagners still placed their faith in the trembling, sick man who sat in his bunker, stroking his dog and rambling on to Winifred about future festivals.

However, Winifred was of a practical nature when it came to her family. When the bombing increased she decided that Bayreuth was no place for expectant mothers. So she sent Gertrud and Verena – both of them pregnant at the same time – to her house in Nussdorf on Lake Constance, along with little Amélie. Wolfgang's wife Ellen was also pregnant and was with Wolfgang and Winifred in the cellar of the Siegfried Wagner House when an American bomb fell on Wahnfried on 5 April 1945. One wing of the house was badly damaged. In the last days of the War, heavy bombing raids meant that Bayreuth lost a third of its housing. Up to that point, many people in the town had seriously imagined that Friedelind was in the USA ensuring that nothing would happen to her home city.[27]

The war now finally came to an end, to the relief of all. On 18 May 1945, in celebration of the German capitulation, Toscanini conducted Beethoven's Fifth Symphony, which was also broadcast on the radio. The Americans marched into Bayreuth and confiscated the Festspielhaus, the bombed-out family house and the undamaged Siegfried House next to it in which Hitler had always stayed. The Festspielhaus and all family assets were placed under trusteeship, while the Festspielhaus itself was used for entertainment shows for the occupying US troops. The orchestra pit was covered over for the purpose, a proscenium constructed and a warm-air heating system installed.

Several members of the Wagner clan escaped from the town before the occupiers arrived. Wieland, his pregnant wife and their two children were joined by Verena and Bodo Lafferentz. Shortly before French soldiers arrived at Lake Constance they set off for Switzerland, taking several scores as capital with them. But their plan backfired, as they were turned away at the border. Their proximity to the Nazis was well known, and the Swiss authorities thought it too risky to admit them. It was naturally a humiliation, given the privileged position that the family had enjoyed until now. 'How do you think it was for your loved ones to wake up? Are they all fully aware now? I hope they will learn something from all that has happened,' wrote Ellen Beerli from Lucerne.

> I know that your Mama told an American Colonel in an interview that she never listened to foreign radio stations and so had no idea of anything that was happening. Would you have been so obedient? It's tough for your mother, of course, to live through these times and to have to hear about everything that this 'god' – or rather, 'idol' – and his followers have left as their legacy to the German people.[28]

Information gradually filtered through to Friedelind, and in August 1945 she told the Janssens that she had seen pictures of Bayreuth in the *Sunday Times* in which workers were clearing away rubble from Wahnfried.

> The whole family is apparently living in Oberwarmensteinach. Straightaway I tried to find out where my sister is – perhaps a soldier can find her, for I doubt she is living with her husband and the rest of the family, as her relationship to my mother was not so rosy either – and she did everything to get away from home. I'll make no effort to get in touch with the rest of the family – not after that damned interview that my mother gave! If she wants anything from me, she knows where she can find me again.[29]

She meant an interview that Winifred had given to Klaus Mann, who was now a US soldier working for the magazine *Stars and Stripes*. Friedelind was shocked that her mother continued to admire Hitler. She had hoped that

Winifred would offer an admission of guilt and show regret about having entangled Bayreuth in the Nazi cause. There was none forthcoming. Friedelind even had to admit that she felt a tinge of admiration for her: 'At least she's not wriggling out of it like all the other Germans who now claim they were always opposed to the Nazis.' But overall she was deeply disappointed that her family could ignore Hitler's crimes, and she already suspected that this would place a burden on her future relationship with them.

> If they were convinced of all the crimes Hitler has committed, they couldn't possibly admire him to this day – and as far as our future relationship is concerned, it seems like zero for all time to come. I guess I was a little hopeful of a day when they all would say to me: you were right, even though my cold logic told me that such a day would never dawn – now I can't see any basis of ever meeting again – it would be as futile and unproductive and unpleasant as our pre-war relationship.[30]

She even asked Wieland if he could not exercise any influence on Winifred to get her to be silent.[31]

Friedelind was able to find out Winifred's strategy for the coming years thanks to a document her mother sent in August 1945 to Colonel Fiori, the US commander of the troops stationed in Bayreuth. A copy of it reached Friedelind in America. Winifred rejected his criticism that she had paid her artists badly throughout the Festival, as she also rejected his accusation that she had enriched herself personally. As for her political role, she stated that she had never had any political ambitions, had never given up her membership of the church, had never been a member of the Reichstheaterkammer (the Nazi's theatre organization) and had always helped people in need. Her invitation to Hitler to attend the Bayreuth Festival was, she insisted, no different from all the other invitations sent out to heads of state across the world:

> I believe that if Bayreuth was an American community, the town authorities would stand up for a family to whom the town owes its worldwide fame and prosperity, instead of looking on and doing nothing to prevent all the Wagner souvenirs, traditional furniture etc. to go to pieces because there is no safe storage room left to the family in which to keep these treasures – not talking about the facts, that after 'Wahnfried' was destroyed by bombs, Wagner's grandchildren do not have even the most modest home in the town which he gave its fame and celebrity![32]

This text was also the basis for her later defence at her court proceedings.

Winifred once more stressed that she had kept her distance from the Party, and spoke of the supposedly private ties of friendship that had led her to invite Hitler to the Festival. Without his protection, said Winifred, the Festival could not have survived these years. But in her 1944 memoir, Friedelind had already written of the political aspect of all these connections. Her current silence towards her mother was perhaps a result of what Winifred wrote here (another reason might have been her impending naturalization in the USA; she did not want to be seen as someone who was in contact with former Nazis). Although Winifred sent her first letter to Friedelind on 7 April 1946, her daughter took a year to answer it.

Winifred's statements omitted to mention her admiration for the 'Führer' and her hatred of 'nagods', as she called them, namely her Jewish fellow citizens. She had more than once got Hitler's support for her decisions regarding the fate of Bayreuth and had expressed her enthusiastic confidence in the imminent victory of Germany in the War. The 'Führer' had indeed meddled in matters pertaining to Bayreuth. He had refused the appeal made by Daniela and Eva regarding the changes to the production of *Parsifal*; he had ordered the Festival to appoint Alfred Roller as its stage designer; he had repeatedly given financial subsidies; and he was even planning a new building to house the Festival. The explanations that Winifred offered now were merely a foretaste of the defence strategy that would be practised by many former Nazis. Friedelind was appropriately sceptical regarding Germany's supposed renewal and its purging of the past. Instead she remained convinced that traces of the Nazi mindset would survive. She was justified in this, too, for if one considers that the roots of anti-Semitism and Nazi ideology stretched back to the nineteenth century, then it seems obvious that even the revelation of the horrors committed by the Nazis would be insufficient to extinguish their ideas altogether. It was not like simply turning off a light. Ulrich Drüner has suggested that the retention of the existing ideological convictions, not least in the worlds of music and culture, was possible because

> ... there was too little cultural openness after the War, while the highly questionable process of 'Vergangenheitsbewältigung' – coming to terms with the past – sometimes gave a higher priority to protecting perpetrators, beneficiaries and followers of the regime than to displaying any interest in their victims ... if one looks at the sources, one sees that the cultural epoch moulded by fascism needed far more than half a century to develop and to die away again. The actual duration of the Nazi dictatorship was so brief that many were all too ready to regard its concomitant cultural circumstances as an 'accident' and simply to draw a line

under it. If we wish for justice for the victims of the 'Third Reich', then we must oppose this categorically.[33]

Others were of a similar opinion. Friedelind's cousin Franz Wilhelm Beidler, who as mentioned above had also fled from the Nazis, wrote before the end of the War to Thomas Mann that they must assume 'that Europe will be lost for a considerable time and is doomed to a spiritual death by suffocation'.[34] And in 1945, Mann wrote his essay 'Why I am not returning to Germany' in which he insisted that the previous years could not simply be wiped away. He had been subjected to such a smear campaign in Munich that any possibility of return had been 'cut off' for him.[35] The scriptwriter Salka Viertel, who had also fled to the USA, did not want to live under the 'ex-Nazis' in Vienna who had made Hitler and the Holocaust possible.[36] The composer Robert Stolz (1880–1975), who was living in New York, said at the end of the War: 'Inasmuch as composers are still celebrated and active among you who wrote hymns for the former murderers, the time is … not yet ripe!'[37] And the musicologist Alfred Einstein, who had been fired as the editor of the *Zeitschrift für Musikwissenschaft* in 1933 and had chosen exile in the USA, was even more radical: 'Out of this bestial Germany, a human Germany can never emerge. Whoever identified with it has lost the right even to speak out loud the names of Mozart, Beethoven, Goethe and Schiller.' He was grateful for his new home in the USA and regarded post-War Germany as the 'Fourth Reich'. He refused to return to his country of origin and turned his back on everything that could associate him with German musicology.[38] Such a rejection of any kind of reconciliation reflects the degree of trauma that Einstein must have endured.

Material want was widespread in Germany after all the bombings and plunderings. Wieland and Gertrud, Wolfgang and Ellen, as well as Bodo and Verena all had children to feed. Germany lay in ruins and, even if one had money, it was barely possible to buy anything. Illnesses such as diphtheria, polio and whooping cough were widespread and a serious danger to children, not least since neither penicillin nor inoculations were available. Friedelind now began helping out her family by sending packets with food and clothes to Tribschen in Switzerland, which the custodian Ellen Beerli then forwarded on to them. On one occasion she sent several kilos of coffee for her mother to sell, as she could get a lot of money for it. Her willingness to help knew no boundaries, for it was in her nature to help to excess when she was convinced that others were in need.

But Friedelind had her own money problems. In February 1945 she wrote to Toscanini's assistant Margherita de Vecchi and admitted that she had not even been able to pay the rent for January. She also said that she had to give the pawnbroker money for Baroness von Einem's jewels, given to her for safe-keeping back in 1940. She had arranged with Toscanini in autumn 1944 that he would continue to support her until she got her debts in order. He wanted her to look for work, which she did willingly. But her budget remained tight, and he was now supporting her for the fifth year of her emigration. She at least managed to keep the jewels for another year, as her calls for help had prompted a good friend to pay the pawnbroker's fees for her.

In exchange for paintings that Wieland was producing, Friedelind organized care packets. For his part, he offered to copy portraits of Richard Wagner to sell them and thereby make a contribution to the family finances. How Friedelind financed her parcels remains a mystery, given her own pecuniary circumstances: 'Things are not getting better and they are asking for more and more and more – there is no end to it.' Her brother-in-law Bodo was arrested and put in an internment camp where he was not allowed to write letters and was only permitted to speak with outsiders every three months. Friedelind's sympathies were with Verena, who simply could not cope with the situation.

'Now a second war has come upon the earth that has left huge swathes of Germany in rubble. The modest red house on the Festival hill has been left untouched. Will the spirit of Richard Wagner be able to live there once again?' asked the conductor Fritz Busch, who had been perturbed by the many swastikas around Wahnfried as early as 1930.[39] He was not alone. Friedelind, too, was concerned about the future of the Festival. Many émigrés thought it impossible that the cultural life of Germany could recover rapidly. But in time they had to realize that the people who had freed themselves from the Nazi yoke and gone into exile were not particularly welcome in Germany after 1945. Most of them were not asked to return home after the War. This was what Ralph Giordano has called the 'second guilt' that the German population brought upon itself – probably because it was impossible for it to come to terms with the horrors committed in its name, now gradually being brought to light. Exiled musicians would be invited here and there to give concerts or to take part in summer schools, but there was no concerted effort to deal with the issue of exile – or else it was regarded as an accident for which others were responsible. 'People closed their eyes with a shocking insensitivity to the criminal expulsion [of the exiles].' Even scholars found it difficult to write of 'expulsion' or 'banishment', preferring in their reference works to write of acts of 'relocation'.[40]

Friedelind's first letter after the end of the War was sent to Ellen Beerli in Tribschen, not to her family. She had learnt of the death of her aunts Eva and Daniela through the US press and wanted to know if they had continued to live their illusions to the end, or whether 'they ever thought or wrote that

Mausi was right after all?'[41] She refrained from asking about her mother, for she was too angry at Winifred's intransigence. Disappointed that her family was refusing to deal with its past, she remained sceptical of Germany:

> I have no illusions about my family ... all of Germany is supposed to be more fond of the Nazis than ever – and the occupation has sadly done nothing to alter this because they haven't understood the problem at all. And now the people are getting cheekier every day because they know that they won't be strung up any more if they open their mouths. But instead of criticizing Hitler's regime, they only criticize their former enemies because it's easier and relieves them of their feelings of guilt.[42]

She felt sympathy to be inappropriate, because

> there are millions who deserve it 100%, but not our former countrymen and women. It's no wonder that the Germans – individually and *en masse* – haven't yet said a word in sympathy for their former victims and instead cry indignantly: look what you're doing to us – for if you read the papers here you could almost believe that they are the only victims of the war – and of course they're innocent on top of it.[43]

From what perspective should one regard this lost war? Hedwig Pringsheim, Katia Mann's mother, was heartbroken at the thought of all the young German men who had been sent so senselessly to their deaths. Golo Mann, on the other hand, felt they deserved their fate.[44] Katia Mann situated herself uncompromisingly on the side of the Allies, as did Erika Mann, who wanted no reconciliation with Germany. For Friedelind, too, it was clear that the Germans had begun the war and were responsible for the millions of people killed and murdered in it. Like the Mann family, she detested the German patriots in the USA, and she was disgusted by any and every sign of 'emigrant nationalism' among the Germans there who had sympathized with Hitler.

For Winifred, however, it was clear that she would never be able to abandon her feelings of friendship for 'Wolf'. Unwilling to admit that she had refused to acknowledge the facts for too long, she put the blame on those around him and, in all seriousness, insisted that she had never spoken of politics with him. Instead she gave extensive descriptions of what had been destroyed in the bombing of Bayreuth by the Americans and the English, as if they were to blame for everything.

In their attitude to the War, insurmountable differences remained between Friedelind and Winifred. So Friedelind continued to maintain a stoic silence in the face of the many letters that her mother sent her. After the War, 'USA' became for Winifred a defiant acronym for 'Unser Seliger Adolf' ('Our Blessed Adolf'), denoting her continuing affection for the mass murderer. But for Friedelind, 'USA' meant freedom: a country in which she felt she could become what she wanted, and where she now took on citizenship. These two poles – America as a land of freedom, one first dreamed about and then turned into a reality, and 'Our Blessed Adolf' as a stubborn adherence to a sham existence – can serve to sum up the rupture that had taken place between mother and daughter and that would continue to dominate their relationship.

> In order to pay the doctor's bills for the diphtheria treatment, Wieland and his wife have sold their dining room set (the lovely one in green from Berlin). They only got 800 marks for it. I sold a fur coat and got 900 marks – but it's naturally only a drop in the ocean, for a pair of shoes now costs 70–120 marks, for example. We are living more than modestly – but nothing can keep us down and we're planning and will achieve something again – as long as the Russians don't come.[45]

Winifred displayed her will to live in every situation, and she did all she could to help her grandchildren. Her transformation from the friend of the highest-ranking German to a berry-picking housewife seems to have been mastered effortlessly. She had a Danish cousin send her knitting needles and wool, and spent her time knitting clothes for her now numerous grandchildren. Lemons, meat extract, jam, writing paper, electric light bulbs, toilet paper, safety pins, coffee and more were sent to them from abroad and were 'a huge help' in relieving their needs. Since their rations proved insufficient, she carted potatoes up the hill to Oberwarmensteinach in a wheelbarrow and went gathering wood and pine cones in the forest. Preserving fruit was now part of her daily routine. The journey to Bayreuth cost four marks so, to get the money, she sold blueberries for 40 pfennigs a pound. '"Hunger, poverty and dirt" was the last line of an English poem that I learnt as a child – and sometimes I'm afraid of it,' she wrote to her cousin.[46] But she would not be defeated. On the contrary, it is almost as if her strength increased in times of crisis.

Friedelind was now regarded as the 'rich aunt in America', whom one could ask for anything. Wieland wrote to her:

> I would like to ask you, shamelessly, for some wool for me – it doesn't weigh much and probably won't be too expensive for you. We could knit the panties that the children urgently need and I can't deny that a hand-knitted sweater to warm my earthly form would do my immortal soul

good. If there is an empty corner in the parcel you could fill it up with tea or delicious Ness coffee [*sic*].

He was delighted with the 'shoe parcel' for the children that Friedelind had sent to them via Frau Beerli.

It was in Billy Wilder's film *A foreign affair* with Marlene Dietrich that many émigrés got their first view of Berlin after the bombing, and they were horrified at the extent of the destruction. But now, after the War, Friedelind's brothers back home had to exercise a complete volte-face in their thoughts and action. Just recently they had been friends with the mightiest man in the land. But now he was dead and their mother stood accused because of her relationship with him. The military government formed a 'main committee' as a forerunner to the first post-war Bayreuth city council, and staffed it with opponents of the Nazi regime – such as Dr Konrad Pöhner, who would later play a significant role in the renewal of the Bayreuth Festival. Their prime concern was clearing away rubble and providing basic supplies to the population. Culture would have to wait. In 1948, three years after the end of the War, operagoers in Berlin were still 'paying' for their tickets with briquettes. It was so cold that you could see the singers' breath, and there was almost no infrastructure.[47] But Friedelind's brothers were less concerned with material problems. They considered taking over the Festival straight after the War, but were afraid that Friedelind, who was politically 'clean', would pre-empt them and demand the job for herself. And they were also naturally aware that Bayreuth's close connection to Hitler and the support it had received from the Nazi regime was a heavy burden. Friedelind tried to get Wieland to state his opinion of those who had stayed in Germany under Hitler, but in vain.

In July 1945 Friedelind learnt from American friends that the Festspielhaus was being used for variety shows for the occupiers. 'My poor grandfather must be turning in his grave! Sinatra is no doubt whizzing around in the Rhinemaidens' machines and singing: "Don't fence me in." I naturally have no direct news from the family – nor do I expect any, since they are as faithful as ever to their Führer.'[48] She had not reckoned on contrite confessions of remorse, but her sarcasm is a sign of both her dismay at the humiliating 'desecration' of the Festspielhaus, and at her unreconstructed mother.

While Wolfgang was helping to clear Wahnfried of rubble, Wieland wrote from Nussdorf that he was without any news from home but hoped that all was going well. He was sure that the Festival would take place again in the next year.[49] In fact, no one knew what was going to happen, if anything. There was even talk of the Festspielhaus being taken over by the state.[50] In contrast to Wolfgang, who was against continuing the Festival, Wieland tried right from the start to re-establish it at any cost. 'I wrote respectfully to Toscanini in September 1945 to tell him that he was the only man who could succeed in continuing the Festival.' Remarkably he adopted the grand, religiously tinged vocabulary of Daniela and Eva. He recounted how the Festspielhaus was being used as a variety theatre and that Wahnfried had been confiscated:

> I cannot believe that *Parsifal*, in which Richard Wagner announced a religion of compassion to the world, that the *Ring*, in which he warned prophetically and with terrible clarity of the results of an egotistic striving for power, and that *Tannhäuser* and *Tristan* will no longer be heard in 'their essential home' by all those who, after years of chaotic horrors, devoid of culture, now seek the pinnacle of experience and inward contemplation on the 'Hill' ... may the 'secret' that the Master hid away in the foundations of his house no longer be revealed to the world?

He continued to write of the 'tragic circumstances' that had forced Toscanini to avoid the Festspielhaus.[51] It is notable that Wieland avoids mentioning Adolf Hitler.

Wieland sent a copy of his letter to Friedelind and wrote to her that 'you will see – reading between the lines of this sober account – that you have a mission – the existence of the Festival is in danger – please ask the Maestro for his help and his support – without him, *Parsifal* will surely long remain unheard in Bayreuth ... only you could still save our inheritance!'[52] It is the cry for help of someone who is completely disillusioned, who for far too long had held fast to the man who had promised power and influence, but whose value had now collapsed.

The conductor did not reply. But Friedelind felt called upon to do so and in November sent a letter that was warm in tone, yet displayed a sense of calling that was bound to irritate Wieland.

> I knew eight years ago when I left you all, just as I know today, what my mission would be one day. I know that today the continued existence of the Festival can only be saved through me, although we must acknowledge that it will probably still take years. The Maestro will always stand as a friend and advisor at my side, and he knows the steps that I have already undertaken.

She wanted to know if any attempts were being made to confiscate the Festspielhaus, and to what extent the family was affected by the directives of the occupying authority. Did her mother still have the status of prior and sole heir during her lifetime, or could her children, now that they were of age, be counted as provisional heirs? 'You must understand that no one will lift a finger to preserve our inheritance for as long as Mama is at the head of it all.' As for using the Festspielhaus as a variety theatre, she wrote: 'The Wagner in me reacted just the same when I first heard of it. But my practical side said: first of all, war is war, and "Kraft durch Freude" was no better, for God's sake. The true Festival and the Wagnerian shrine must rise up anew, completely – and then the last twelve years will be buried and forgotten!'[53]

In March 1946 Wieland wrote to his mentor Overhoff: 'It seems that Bayreuth will remain in future a matter for – women. For with regard to my sister's plans I have no illusions – nor does Mama, it seems.' He added that he did not want to 'give up the struggle [*Kampf*]'[54] – a phrase that is highly indicative. The brothers were torn between resignation, anger and hope. 'For the future of Bayreuth, my sister – as an émigré and anti-fascist – had the least cause for concern, for she clearly – as her book makes clear – had all possible qualities necessary to take over the management of the Festival,' wrote her brother Wolfgang in his autobiography many years later, only to continue that Friedelind had lied in promoting her abilities as an opera director and as the possible future manager of the Festival: she simply did not possess the talent for it.[55] Was the very woman who had caused so much political grief to those back home now set to return as the victor?

Chapter 10

After the War is over
1946 to 1950

A GERMAN-LANGUAGE edition of Friedelind's autobiography was published in Switzerland in 1945, and in February 1946 the first extensive
reviews began to appear in the German newspapers. It contained 'many a
spicy matter', they wrote, and headlines were made by Winifred's threat that
'You will be eradicated and exterminated.'[1] Winifred denied having uttered
it, and blamed Friedelind's co-author Page Cooper for all the book's 'lies'.
'[Friedelind's] whole behaviour is still a mystery to me, because she is sending
money to Lucerne for them to forward lovely food parcels every month to the
head of the family!'[2] The news of the book's publication shocked the whole
family, for they anticipated the worst and feared personal attacks. Wieland
wrote to their mother that the book 'will be its own downfall among decent
people' and did not change his opinion once he had actually read it. The family
wrote it off as 'trivial and mediocre'.[3] Wolfgang wrote to Wieland: 'The whole
thing is a strange product and many a matter is psychologically puzzling to
me.'[4] Gertrud Strobel aptly summed up the family's disgust with Friedelind –
and at the same time their willingness to accept her food parcels: 'Spoke of
the book by Maus. The Swiss earnings are used to finance the care packets …
The Wagner family is thus living off its own shame!'[5] A Swiss social democratic
newspaper commented triumphantly: 'Future generations will have to decide
whether Bayreuth can have a reason to exist after all the horrors of National
Socialism. But if Bayreuth ever blossoms forth again, then Friedelind will at
that joyful time stand in the spotlight. Her highly developed sense of national
honour and the untouched purity of human dignity have saved Bayreuth!'[6]
Such an opinion will not have pleased her family, nor was it shared by most
people across the border in Germany.

In April 1946, when postal communications were once more allowed with
foreign countries, Winifred had written immediately to Friedelind. She seems
to have been able to disguise her feelings, for, although she had read the book
by now, she shows not a hint of anger about it. On three closely written pages
she tells her 'beloved child' where their relatives and mutual friends are, and
about the destruction that had taken place. After Wahnfried was bombed,
Wolfgang had searched through the rubble, one shovel at a time: 'But much
could not be saved and the house is now gradually falling apart, since I have
not yet received permission to rebuild it … 250 fire bombs were extinguished

over the whole property.'[7] In October she wrote to Friedelind that her part of the inheritance was secure in any case. 'If I should no longer be in a position to keep you informed, then Wolfgang will take on the task. I have to antici-pate being sent to a labour camp – thus deprived of my liberty – since people seem unwilling to recognize my many proven acts of assistance for people persecuted during the Third Reich.'[8] One looks in vain for any mention of Friedelind's book.

So what was Friedelind thinking when, just a few months later, she allowed the magazine *Neue Auslese* to publish the chapter from her book that contains her mother's threat, at the very same time that the courts were dealing with Winifred's guilt under the Nazis?[9] To be sure, Friedelind delighted in provoca-tion, though in this case the fate of her own mother was at stake. The Bayreuth stage designer Emil Preetorius (1883–1973) described her book as 'backstairs trash in which 90% is completely invented'.[10] That was hardly surprising, given the attacks in it on his colleague Heinz Tietjen. The latter did not like the way he was portrayed and protested to the publisher of the German edition: 'I maintain that where some things correspond to the truth, much has been distorted and is even based on absolute lies. I regard this as considerably dam-aging to my international reputation and to my standing as an artist and as a man, and it could also cause me professional difficulties, including here at home in Germany. I am hereby informing you of my protest and would like to know whether and how the publisher would be ready to publish the correc-tions that I can send.'[11] Friedelind had wrongly accused him of having helped the Nazis to interrogate English spies.

Winifred asked her to take out this comment in the German edition. She told her that Tietjen had a heart condition and tried to soften her towards him. 'I am completely convinced that you never wanted to damage people for the rest of their lives when you wrote the book in the early 1940s and that you could have no idea of the possible consequences.' Friedelind did not take back the statement. Why not? Was her hatred towards her mother and her lover so all-consuming? Winifred added: 'You've been bad to some other people too – Bockelmann, for example, and Frau von Manowarda – Bockelmann is singing again in Hamburg and Frau von Manowarda is probably in an Austrian camp, for in contrast to me she was an "activist"!'[12] Friedelind had written that the singer Rudolf Bockelmann had become a 'raging Nazi', while of Mrs Manowarda and her husband she wrote that 'they roared enthusiastically in their Austrian dialect that Austria would at last now become a Nazi state'.

In one case she was, however, forced to alter a passage in the Swiss edition. In the English original of 1945 she had written that Richard Strauss had offered to conduct a concert in Berlin as a replacement for Bruno Walter. That was untrue. Furthermore, in the English edition she called Strauss 'a weather-vane, veering with every political wind. Monarchist, Social Democrat, a little pink, a little brown, he got along with all regimes.' This sentence was later omitted completely, for Strauss had threatened legal action after being informed about the book by Willi Schuh. Friedelind might have taken her information on Strauss from the book *Escape to Life. German Culture in Exile* published by Erika and Klaus Mann in 1939, six years before the publication of *Heritage of Fire*. In it, they write how Walter had been forced to cancel a concert in Leipzig because he was Jewish, and that Strauss had taken his place. The German version of Friedelind's book merely stated that Strauss had never been involved in politics, and that his desire to have his works performed had prompted his 'nonchalant attitude towards political change'.

Winifred was the only member of her family who stood accused of complicity under the Nazis and her court case took place in the years 1947 and 1948. First she was classed as a major offender (Class I), but after her first hearing she was assigned to Class II, 'incriminated'. August Roesener, the husband of Winifred's best friend Helene, wrote to Friedelind in advance of the proceedings to ask for her help. He had written a text in Winifred's defence in which he stressed her past artistic and organizational achievements at a time 'when politics threatened to swamp everything'. He wanted Friedelind to make his arguments more widely known and hoped that the family would stick together during the hearings. 'Everywhere people are clear that you will have a special, decisive role to play in the way things are done in future.' It was important, he insisted, to 'draw a line' under the past, 'whose victims we have all become'.[13] In other words: he was using the prospect of working in the Festival as bait to try and get her to help defend her mother. Friedelind refused to have any part in it. She was still too hurt about the interview that Winifred had given to Klaus Mann for *Stars and Stripes* that had clearly demonstrated her intransigence. How could she now defend her mother, she who had left Germany out of her own conviction and had been interned and imprisoned in Britain on account of it? Did her family now expect her to denounce her own book as fiction?

In the first round of the denazification process on 25 July 1947 it was determined that the accused had been a member of the Nazi party since 1926, had been awarded the gold party badge, had been an enthusiastic supporter of Hitler and – thus the bill of indictment – 'went so far in her fanaticism that she placed the inheritance of Wagner at the disposal of National Socialist ideology'. It was assumed that Friedelind's book would play a major role in the case. Indeed, it would have done her mother harm if the numerous descriptions of their meetings with Hitler had been quoted in court, along with that of their meeting in Zurich in January 1940 when Winifred had threatened her with 'extermination'. It is often stated in the literature that Friedelind had sent a telegram to Winifred's defence lawyer to forbid the use of her book in court.[14] But the telegram in question reads as follows: 'Bill of indictment against Winifred Wagner of 14 May in my possession. After speaking with influential people in Washington and New York I request that the proceedings be postponed until I arrive in Bayreuth. As a legal representative of the Wagnerian inheritance and as a US citizen I must insist that my testimony be heard.'[15] Friedelind thus wanted an invitation to attend as a witness so that she could stand before her mother and 'save' her – a psychologically revealing scenario.

But the prosecution placed no importance on having her there. 'The prosecution will use neither Friedelind Wagner nor her book as proof.'[16] There is nothing in the files to suggest that Friedelind herself had forbidden the use of her book. We must assume that Wolfgang, who repeated this rumour, had wanted the world to believe that Friedelind had prevented its use as an implicit admission that it was full of untruths. Winifred had also been working in advance in order to discredit Friedelind's autobiography, for she wrote to her as follows: 'Your book is playing a big role, but since I can use your own letters to correct a lot of mistakes, I hope that it won't have so much weight.'[17]

Although the book was not used as evidence it still played a background role, for a witness by the name of Elisabeth Schäfer mentioned Winifred's threat of 'extermination'. But Winifred immediately denied having said any such thing, and her lawyer stressed that the court had already rejected the idea of using her daughter's claims as evidence against the mother.[18] So mother and daughter managed to scrape out of a situation that could have irreparably damaged their relationship, had Friedelind's book been used in court. Given that Friedelind was famously blunt in conversation, she would hardly have been willing to deny the veracity of anything in her book had she actually taken the witness stand – that would have been tantamount to a public declaration that she was untrustworthy. Nevertheless, it troubled her that her mother had to appear in court like this. She wrote to her brother: 'Janssens have just sent off a 22-pound packet to Mama. Everyone is concerned and highly indignant.'[19]

Besides noting Winifred's enthusiasm for Hitler, the court found her guilty of having purchased looted property in Prague in the official car of the Nazi Mayor Fritz Kempfler, and of having engaged in propaganda for the Nazis. Sixty per cent of her assets were to be seized, she was to be ineligible for a pension and would not be allowed to vote. For her heirs, the idea of losing her assets – their assets – was something they could not ignore, for it would have made it impossible to open the Festival in the near future, if indeed ever again. Wieland wrote to Friedelind, horrified: 'I ask you: where is the difference between all this and the notorious "family liability" and "revenge against the family" practised by the SS state under Himmler...?' He found it unjust to take something from the family that 'for more than 75 years has been managed and led – to the fame of Germany and the honour of its art – by a family who in this time has maintained its commitment to humanity and its artistic sense of responsibility under all prevailing circumstances, and that today, besides its completely apolitical members, even has in you a confessed, active "anti-fascist" in its ranks.'[20] He thus now performed a volte-face and acknowledged Friedelind's break with Bayreuth as a praiseworthy act – whereas up to now he and the family had only despised her for it.

Could one really speak of 'apolitical' family members, as Wieland did here? After the end of the War, Heinz Tietjen styled himself a 'resistance fighter' (though that remains impossible to verify[21]) and in his own defence described the extent of the political conversations that had gone on in Bayreuth. Since 1933, he claimed, Bayreuth had offered him a 'treasure trove of highly important political information.' The burning of the Reichstag had been discussed, as had the judicial murders during the so-called Röhm Putsch. These were, according to Tietjen,

> major cornerstones in [my] opposition to Hitler. The Nuremberg 'cultural speeches' and the armaments programme were discussed openly in Bayreuth during the building of the 'strategically' important Autobahn, which left no more doubt as to what was being planned. What I heard indirectly (I was never present in person at the family evenings with Hitler) made me politically vigilant on two prominent occasions: I mean Hitler's personal provocation of Czechoslovakia in 1938 and Hitler's rejection of the English ambassador in 1939.[22]

According to Friedelind, there was also open talk about the bombing of Spain, the invasion of Poland and the murder of Chancellor Dollfuss of Austria.

During the hearing, most witnesses were on Winifred's side. But there was also evidence against her. Especially tragic was the case of the Jewish widow of Max Baron von Waldberg, who had been due to be deported to the east in 1942. Max von Waldberg had edited Cosima's letters to Daniela and his wife had been chairwoman of the Richard Wagner Association of German Women. Daniela had known her and had already intervened to prevent her deportation to Gurs in the Pyrenees. After Daniela's death, a certain Frau Brandner had tried to get Winifred to help too, but for various spurious reasons had been repeatedly turned away from Wahnfried. Had Winifred's earlier conflict with Daniela wounded her so much that she now chose not to intervene for the friend of her sister-in-law? Whatever the reasons, Frau von Waldberg took her own life shortly before she was to be deported.[23]

Winifred had succeeded several times in saving individual Jews when she felt it was necessary. This had required both an independent mind and a degree of courage, too. Like many anti-Semites she was ready to argue for specific people if she had a personal connection to them. The feeling of having helped someone was a psychological reward that briefly overcame her prejudice. However, the prosecution wrote the following in this regard:

> Here the accused truly descends to the level of the minor block and cell leaders, and the other officials of Class II, who almost all insist that they greeted Jews, bought goods from Jewish shops and even spoke nicely to Jews. The accused should remember that as a party member from early on she played no small role in helping to construct the National Socialist regime that exterminated millions of Jews. Does she really regard herself as so innocent in all this?[24]

The measures of atonement decided upon by the court were never imposed, because Winifred appealed. She took everything laconically and showed not a trace of regret.

> We old ones are not so important any more – we've done our work and my only concern is the next generation and how they survive. On the one hand I always fear that I'm a millstone around your neck – but I have neither the noose nor the courage to hang myself, and my curiosity as to how we'll get out of this mess once again will keep me alive, even if I have to go to a work camp for several years![25]

In December 1948 her conviction was as good as annulled by the appeals court in Ansbach. She was now officially regarded as 'mildly incriminated' and was given no punishment. However, she was excluded from the management of the Festival in future. This mild judgement was the norm with the courts that sat in judgement of Nazi crimes. At times they themselves even resorted to Nazi vocabulary, speaking of 'Volksgenossen' ('citizens of the national community') and coming to the defence of the accused. Mitigating circumstances were often submitted and often also accepted.[26] Furthermore, Winifred was fortunate to have numerous witnesses for the defence. She was classed as a 'Mitläufer' or 'collaborator', Class 4. And this meant there was no more talk of any seizure of assets. One observer ascribed the refusal to assign guilt to circumstances in Bayreuth. 'Mrs Wagner has been set free, so to speak … the public were unanimously in favour of the Wagners, who are the princely house of Bayreuth. They have the hearts of their subjects, these Wagners. And Mrs Wagner behind barbed wire would be the same as putting Bayreuth behind barbed wire.'[27]

Winifred wrote long letters to her daughter about further hearings that friends had to undergo, about their being taken prisoner and put in camps, and about people's apartments being occupied by refugees. She complained in general about the post-war state of things:

> The French aren't getting their denazification done very quickly and it's in Wieland's interest to wait for as long as possible for that. But as long as he isn't given a classification he can't be employed ... it is all so counterproductive and you would really think it would be better if an atom bomb would simply dissolve this crazy earth into all its constituent pieces ... nevertheless I hope to be able to write to you again soon, for homo sapiens is a tenacious species and so is your mother!'[28]

The Mayor of Bayreuth had given permission to rebuild Wahnfried, 'but at the same time declared that there could be no thought of assigning us building materials – so we stand exactly where we were before!'[29] The currency reform was described by her as 'the plain bankruptcy of everyone', and she mistrusted the way things were developing after the War. And she pondered political questions – though not in a manner that Friedelind would have wished: 'Will we be able to keep Bolshevism back at all? – The proletarianizing of the masses is simply leading us towards it – especially when what was at the bottom rises to the top, like here! – With 1 dollar in the month you can live nicely – but we don't have it!!! The black market price for 200 American cigarettes is 1000 mark ... while the real price of 2000 American cigarettes is 80 cents!!' At the same time, she displayed her indomitable strength of spirit: 'If despair threatened on account of things lost for good, or because of humiliating experiences or of the daily misery, then I fled into nature, which always helped me – and which comforted me by making me aware again of all the intransient things of value.'[30]

In the meantime, Friedelind was dreaming of directing *Tristan und Isolde* and taking it on a big tour across the USA. She particularly loved this work and since, out of all Wagner's mature operas, it needed the smallest orchestra (in relative terms), it seemed to her suited to just such a project. In the firm belief that it would still take years before the Bayreuth Festival could open its doors again, in 1946 she officially founded the 'Friedelind Wagner Opera Company', planning to direct a different opera every season. She succeeded in getting various cities interested in the project, and they made undertakings that encouraged her. Wieland was asked to draft the stage sets – a gesture of solidarity that was later not reciprocated when Wieland and Wolfgang went about organizing the Bayreuth Festival without her. Friedelind wanted to finance the whole project like a Broadway show by offering small investors shares of $100 and upwards.

Was she aware of the financial and artistic risk that she was taking on? In 1937, a planned US tour with the play *The eternal road*, directed by the world-famous Max Reinhardt, had been cancelled because of legal challenges and unpaid royalties.[31] But Friedelind was never wanting for courage. She threw herself into the project, checked applicants for the roles and made costume calculations. Since she assumed that they would give five to six performances per week, she needed three Tristans and Isoldes, two Kurwenals and Brangänes, plus two conductors and assistants and a chorus of 10 men. She would then need three sets of 45 costumes, 30 pairs of shoes, 28 wigs, six spears, twelve daggers and much more.

In the meantime, she took on a directing job for a dance theatre (*Jacob's Pillow*) in Lee, Massachusetts, and went about her work with enthusiasm. She committed herself to directing a ballet to melodies from Schubert, excerpts from Verdi's *Aïda* and Act 1, Scenes 1 and 2 from *Tannhäuser* plus Scenes 1 and 2 from the first act of *Lohengrin* – not an overly demanding programme, but a lot of work all the same. In the programme books she is also mentioned as the director of Mozart's *Entführung aus dem Serail*. In July, *The Berkshire Eagle* announced: 'Wagner's Granddaughter Directs Opera', and published a photo of her. The singer Rosamond Chapin, who ran the opera and ballet department, was delighted at Friedelind's arrival.[32] Here Friedelind could gather important experience. On some days she rehearsed from 8.30am to 1am the following day. But when Chapin announced cuts just before the première of the *Entführung*, Friedelind was upset and wrote to a friend afterwards that the performance had been a 'fiasco'.[33]

In early 1947 her agent, H. N. Gump, became restless. He asked her to get her *Tristan* tour underway soon because gossip was circulating in New York that her high-flying plans would come to nothing. He urged her to conclude agreements with the unions, to finalize contracts with the artists and organize the stage sets and costumes. That would be the best way to pre-empt gossip, he told her.[34] But Friedelind wouldn't let herself be rushed. The first rehearsals were set for December 1947, with the first tour of eight to twelve weeks due to embark in early January 1948. A second tour of similar length was planned for the following autumn. By late August Friedelind had 45 dates set up, though her aim was to organize 100 performances. Her plans always tended to the monumental. But it was in her character less to bother with practical solutions for manageable goals and instead to let her ideas and dreams escalate. She no longer wanted to conquer just the United States, but the whole world. Europe, South Africa and even Australia now came into her sights for possible further tours. 'I am completely convinced that it will be a huge success if the people are properly prepared without any sloppiness. And I won't allow sloppiness – nor will my staff, so the danger does not exist. The most hard-nosed business-men have said to me that the whole thing is economically completely sound, from whatever angle you look at it – so nothing risky is going to happen.'[35]

In the summer of 1947 it was clear that the schedule could not be kept, so she postponed everything until autumn 1948. In March 1948 she received a number of paintings that Wieland had made in order to earn some money and she planned to organize an exhibition of them in Chicago. After that, she wanted to take the pictures with her on her opera tour, of which she now wrote to Wieland. It was intended to take in at least 50 cities:

> The technical preparations are such that it wasn't possible earlier. I have to negotiate with some 20 workers' unions who all have different laws and prices in the 48 states. So I have to deal with every state separately and draw up contracts. Getting the theatres is the second feat, for they are usually rented out for years and finally a tour has to be arranged so that you have the smallest distances to travel, not from NY to Los Angeles and then back to Philadelphia.[36]

In January 1948 she announced that 'My *Tristan* is for the moment not yet up and running.' She would know more in late January when she was visiting Chicago and Detroit, she said. 'Until everything is smoothed over, no plans are possible.' With his broad experience, Toscanini could see that such a massive project could not be organized by a single person, quite apart from the logisti-cal and financial problems. She rang him on his 81st birthday – it was half-past one in the morning, New York time:

> ... he was so sleepy that he could not even scold me for the fact that I was still travelling, but only croaked 'Come home soon'. I preferred this by far, for he is very much opposed to my operatic ambitions and we have already argued twice about it so that I refuse to say anything more about it to him. Since then, of course, his curiosity is nagging him and he bombards me with questions. But he doesn't get any answers.[37]

In 1949 Friedelind's financial problems were greater than ever for, in order to print publicity material for the tour, she had taken money from the pot

intended to pay the wages of her singers. Her lawyer and friend George Brickbauer saved her this time, it seems, but her problems just increased. Some
singing coaches waited in vain for the fees promised them. A singer by the
name of Köhler gave her particular problems. He had borrowed money from
his friends for her, and now he started ringing her own friends to tell them of
it. He even rang Toscanini, who was furious and refused to speak with Friedelind afterwards. She was already paying back a bank loan and now had to meet
Köhler's demands too. Several sources suggest that some refusals were due to
a negative attitude to German art in general. All of this, besides the conflicts
with unions in assorted states, made it ever less likely that the tour would
happen at all. She blamed her education for some of her problems:

> I notice every day in my profession that American children have a better
> understanding of business than I do, and that I will never learn certain
> things. (I leave business matters completely to my lawyers and manag-
> ers – though I very often have to manage the 'contacts' and the first
> negotiations.) But the decisions then depend on me. Back home ... I
> never got a look at the business world – nor did I have anything to do
> with such people. Thank God! Or 'tant pis' – perhaps it would have been
> a good experience. But the highbrow arrogance of the circles we moved
> in would never have allowed any such contact at all ...[38]

Perhaps America itself was also partly to blame. As the granddaughter of
Richard Wagner and a former 'close acquaintance' of one of the biggest dicta-
tors of world history, Friedelind had been a welcome guest. But in her role as a
theatre manager, no one showed any interest in her. Everything that had been
exotic about her now fell away and she became simply another émigré who
had to work as hard as all the others just to survive.

Since Friedelind sent her no information, Winifred was dependent on other
sources for news of her daughter. She met Furtwängler in Munich, from whom
she learnt that 'Maus has gone broke with her *Tristan*, she is now giving lectures again and has written a new book' – this was the version of events that
Gertrud Strobel passed on to all and sundry.[39] Wieland now spoke only of
the 'skint mouse'.[40] Wolfgang had already expressed his concerns in advance:
'What we've got to do first and foremost is defend ourselves against Friedelind's claims; she has already announced quite officially in her prospectus for
Tristan that with this tour she plans to "conquer Bayreuth from the outside".'[41]
There is no proof that Friedelind ever said or wrote any such thing. But her
apparent failure pleased Winifred too: it was 'a hard, but a very good lesson
for M[ausi]s conceit that she just needs to turn up in order to win. And for her

later relationship with her brothers every defeat that she endures over there is an advantage.'[42]

Friedelind had written her first post-war letter to her mother in April 1947. It was her first in seven years. The letter has not survived, but it was intended to ensure that her rights to her share of Wahnfried and the Festspielhaus were protected. She seems to have warned against selling them, to which her mother replied that inheritance duty would be 50% and that they might in any case lose ownership rights to their house, for the Festival had for the moment been placed under the custodianship of the occupying authorities. The court proceedings about her proximity to the Nazi bosses was intended to clarify matters of ownership and thus also the future of the Festival. As far as her children were concerned, no hearings about their collaboration were expected. The criteria did not apply to Wolfgang, Verena was covered by the youth amnesty and Wieland would at best be classified as a 'collaborator', since he had only joined the Nazi Party in September 1938 – in general, only those who had joined before 1937 were compelled to answer for themselves.[43]

'Zero hour' brought problems not just for the Germans who had stayed in the Reich, but also for those who had been forced to leave their homeland. The former were prone to stress their supposedly 'silent' resistance to Nazi politics whereas they had in fact simply accepted what was happening. The émigrés, on the other hand, often saw themselves as the legitimate successors of the 'old' Germany that had given the world so much culture. They cast doubt on the 'inner emigration' of those who had stayed, because they had had, on the whole, little impact. But those who had stayed found it unfair that their countrymen abroad, whom they saw as having enjoyed the benefits of security and democracy, now looked askance at them.

Friedelind was not prepared to declare herself unequivocally for either side. But she did intensify her efforts in defence of Wilhelm Furtwängler, who had stayed in Hitler's Germany and was now under serious attack in the US press. She had already written an article in 1942 for the magazine *Opera News* in which she had defended him. She wrote to the editor of the *Musical Courier*, saying that Furtwängler's tragedy was that he was regarded within Germany as an opponent of Hitler, but outside the country was unjustly regarded as a Nazi.[44] In order to support him she now joined a group of émigrés that included Fritz Zweig, Gilbert Back and Hugo Kolberg (the former concert master of the Berlin Philharmonic), Alicia Ehlers, Ernst Gottlieb, Louis P. Lochner (a Berlin correspondent of the pre-War years) and others. They contacted other émigrés whom Furtwängler had helped to escape Germany or Austria under Nazi rule. Dr Hugo Strelitzer wrote a report in his favour – he had been let out of prison in 1933 thanks to Furtwängler's intervention – and so did Prof.

Robert Hernried. Zweig wrote to *Life* magazine to explain how his nephew had managed to free him from a concentration camp in 1938 with Furtwängler's help. Friedelind sent the State Department ten declarations from émigrés, all signed under oath.[45] Her article in defence of Furtwängler, published in the *Musical Courier* in March 1946, was a courageous riposte to the Allies' refusal to employ him once more as conductor of the Berlin Philharmonic,[46] and shows that she was surprisingly capable of weighing things up diplomatically:

> Let us sit back for a few minutes, forget all personal dislikes, and behave not like Nazis, but the fair and civilized people we profess to be. Since none of us is perfect, we should not cast the proverbial stone. The least thing we can do is to hear both sides – and find out what motivated the other person's actions.[47]

She further described how the conductor had succeeded in avoiding getting caught in the grip of the Nazis (a fact that was long afterwards confirmed in several biographies).[48]

Despite her efforts, the conflict around Furtwängler flared up again in 1948 when it was proposed that he should conduct the Chicago Symphony Orchestra. Artists such as the pianist Vladimir Horowitz, the singer Lily Pons, the conductor André Kostelanetz, the violinists Jascha Heifetz and Nathan Milstein and the cellist Gregor Piatigorski all declared that they would not perform with the orchestra, if Furtwängler were to arrive as planned in 1949.[49] The pianist Artur Rubinstein declared that if he had been a good democrat, Furtwängler would have turned his back on Germany in protest like Thomas Mann.[50] Others, such as Yehudi Menuhin, took up an opposing stance and refused to perform with the Chicago Symphony Orchestra for as long as Furtwängler was not allowed to conduct there.[51]

Meanwhile, Wieland was still planning how to continue with the Festival. First he thought he might be able to join up with Friedelind's tour. Then he wrote a paper in which he declared that the family was unanimous in wishing to found a new family business to perform Richard Wagner Festivals abroad. 'We should endeavour to build up these festivals on an independent financial and business footing, such as was the case in Bayreuth. Investments might need to be secured to achieve this.' And then he drew a clear line with regard to any possible claims to dominance from Friedelind. 'Should the family or family members be able to take up the running of the Festspielhaus in Bayreuth once again, the new foreign operations will be continued in harmony with the interests of Bayreuth … independent of any division of tasks, the individual members of the family will participate in the refounding of Bayreuth in equal parts.'[52] Since Friedelind wanted to engage Wieland for the sets of her *Tristan* tour, he was planning to create for himself an equal position at her side in order to prevent any possibility of his sister taking over the running of Bayreuth herself.

The brothers' nervousness was well founded, for in 1946 Friedelind was visited by the then military governor of Bayreuth, Colonel Caroll J. Reilly, who told her that there were plans to install her as director of the Festival. The occupying forces wanted to exclude former Nazi Party members from the world of culture and were seeking suitable people who were both profession-ally qualified and at the same time politically acceptable. But Friedelind did nothing about it, so when Reilly's stint in Bayreuth came to an end, the Mayor of Bayreuth, Oskar Meyer, wrote to her in the same vein. He said it was the greatest desire of people in her home town that she should take on the cultural inheritance of her grandfather.

> Sadly, week after week has gone by without hearing from you. In the meantime, however, so many pressing questions have arisen with regard to the Festspielhaus that I regard it as a matter of great urgency – before fundamental decisions are made – to hear first the views of those who bear the name of Wagner, and who according to German opinion still have a right to participate in the work of Bayreuth.[53]

Friedelind had thus moved into prime position among the Wagner heirs for, according to US law, anyone who had been prominent in promoting or sup-porting National Socialism would have their assets confiscated. The current housing shortage also meant that it would be impossible to cope with visitors to the Festival from outside. 'But this must not mean that we want to sit back and just wait for better times. On the contrary, we have to show the world that Bayreuth still lives, despite everything, and that the old Bayreuth spirit is still alive.'

He explained that the question of financing remained unresolved. It was uncertain whether the Wagner family assets and the Wagner foundations – which had also been seized – would be released. He was putting his hopes in donations and in a new management. He put forward the idea of a board of trustees of qualified people and suggested several names: Dr Karl Siegmund Benedikt from Munich, who had managed the Women's Wagner Associa-tion and the Scholarship Endowment Fund, plus the musicologist Carl Engel. 'Prof. Dr Weiss, Charlottenburg, the well-known musicologist and Wagner researcher from Berlin, has assured me of his readiness to participate, as have others.' But he did not want to decide anything before hearing Friedelind's opinion, and he closed with a lofty appeal that must surely have touched Friedelind:

> Together with all friends of Bayreuth I must hope that you are aware of the significance of the task that history places before you. We strongly believe that the management of the Bayreuth legacy would be in the best possible hands, were you to accept it. Your attitude towards National Socialism makes you the most secure guarantee that the spiritual estrangement and aberration that the Bayreuth tradition suffered under Winifred Wagner's direction, and that was so disastrous for Wagner's cause, will remain an episode that we can leave behind us.[54]

Meyer drew up a report – presumably intended for the US administration in Germany – in which he gave his reasons for his appeal to Friedelind:

> I am not of the opinion that the heirs of Wagner should *categorically* be excluded from any influence on Bayreuth, but those members of the family who submitted unconditionally to Adolf Hitler and his charitable friendship – whether as party members or not – are unworthy of their inheritance. Now, with the possibility of a change of ownership, they are full of self-praise as keepers of the Grail. Nevertheless they allowed the unknowing to be deceived, by falsifying Wagner's thoughts and words about the German spirit for party political purposes (e.g. 'The works of Wagner comprise everything to which National Socialism aspires') and misused them to spark off unthinking class and racial hatred. They took Wagner – a fighter for freedom – and boxed him into a petty nationalism. Coupled with a venal, mercenary expertise and undiscriminating amateurism they claimed that he was the prophet of a 1000-year Reich. Both my letter to Friedelind Wagner, and a letter that I had handed over to her, remained without any success.[55]

Why did Friedelind not grasp the chance that was offered to her? Several factors held her back from travelling straight back to Germany. For one thing, she believed that the destruction of the Bayreuth infrastructure meant that she would be able to delay her decision. Furthermore, she had applied for US citizenship, had been invited to a hearing in August 1946 and was now waiting for the decisive papers. A journey abroad would have meant interrupting that process. She was delighted at the prospect of becoming an American citizen.[56] But she also still hoped to achieve confirmation and renown as an artist through her *Tristan* tour. If the press was good, it would give her the political and, above all, the artistic legitimacy to claim the director-ship of Bayreuth. At this point she was still convinced that her tour plan was viable. In Bayreuth, on the other hand, there were as yet no means of financ-ing the Festival. And there she would have had to work with a committee that included former Nazis – unless she were to protest immediately and energeti-cally. The Wagner associations had always backed Winifred. Friedelind could well imagine that beginning the Festival anew would become extraordinarily complicated. To whom would the Festspielhaus belong in future? Would the family get it back, or would it be taken over by the state? And, finally, there were her brothers to consider, who had been trained for years to take over the Festival. Despite all her criticism of their collaboration with the Nazis, she did not want to exclude them.

The US press was now treating her as a Bayreuth heir-in-waiting. On 6 March 1947, the *New York Times* wrote: 'Wanted: A Wagner.' They reported that Bayreuth was looking for a new director, and the last sentence ran: 'The only member of the family bearing the name of Wagner who was not incrimi-nated is Friedelind, a daughter of Siegfried who lives in the US and according to the *Courier* music critic shows no desire to return to Germany.'

Friedelind did not offer a consistent answer when asked about the director-ship of the Festival, which shows that the decision was not an easy one for her. Decades later she was tempted to do a spot of myth-building. She claimed that

> I never answered the then Mayor of Bayreuth because I hotly resented and rejected (and still do and will to my dying day) the implication that the directorship of the Festival is a political appointment, whether ten-dered by Nazis, anti Nazis, opportunists or neutres – and I made it quite clear in regard to my family that I would never kick anybody who is down – that I fight with equals only – and that I would not take what isn't mine or only partly mine (25%).

In 1947 she assumed that everyone would wait for her. She was very much aware of her special status as an 'unsoiled' émigré, and wrote to Jeanette: 'I have to help look after a family of 16 on the side, and the battle for Bayreuth has only just begun! I have drawn it out as long as I can – but I had to step into the ring now in order to save and preserve everything.'[57] In an interview that she gave to the *Fränkische Presse* and was published on 20 May 1947, she stated at the outset that the Festival could only open its doors again in ten years' time, at the earliest, and mentioned her own operatic plans with her US tour.[58] She had also mentioned both matters recently to a US newspaper. People still had too many false ideas about the connections between Wagner and the Nazis, she said, and they had to be expunged. And she made it quite clear that the inheritance belonged not to her mother, but to the four children, and that nothing could be sold or divided up as long as they were alive.[59] And in an article for the journal *Aufbau*, she portrayed herself as the only member of the Wagner family who had the moral legitimacy to start up the Festival again.[60]

Friedelind repeatedly expressed doubts about the process of political cleansing that her native country was undergoing. She wanted to return as someone who had turned her back on evil at the right time, not as a traitor, and under present circumstances this seemed impossible to her.

> God knows I don't feel drawn back to Germany. Not because of the post-War circumstances, but because I can't discern any difference from Nazi Germany. Spiritually nothing has changed, or at least that's how it seems from afar. The same little people are sitting in all their big jobs again and are quite openly mourning Herr Hitler. One could at least have hoped that the liberal elements would have won through, but sadly the occupying powers had other ideas – if they had any ideas at all, which seems very doubtful. The bickering between East and West has naturally only helped the third party to go out laughing – and that third party was the wrong one again, alas.[61]

As late as 1948 she was still telling the press that she would probably never want to return to Germany.[62] Did she want to do everything from a distance? In an undated statement in her archives that has to be from the year 1947, she writes: 'My ultimate goal would be to try to buy my brothers and sister out of the Wagner estate, but for the time being I suppose to claim it – and be the nominal head, probably is all I could achieve.'[63] Modesty was not her natural mode; but her brothers would never dream of giving an inch.

In Bayreuth the alarm bells began to ring when Franz Wilhelm Beidler turned into another 'competitor'. Just like Wieland, Friedelind, Wolfgang and Verena he was a direct grandchild of Richard Wagner. He had worked for five years in Berlin alongside Leo Kestenberg, the reforming socialist head of music education in Prussia, before leaving Nazi Germany in 1933 and taking up residence in Zurich. In 1947, the Mayor of Bayreuth wrote to ask him to draft a concept for the renewal of the Festival. Beidler took up the challenge and proposed forming a board of trustees that would have the necessary intellectual firepower to reinvent the Festival. He put forward Thomas Mann as the honorary president. The Wagners were not mentioned in his draft, but he had no qualms about involving them; Friedelind received confirmation of this in a letter from Konrad Pöhner,[64] a Bayreuth industrialist and city councillor who according to Winifred was 'a member of the old guard'.[65]

Not surprisingly, this idea was anathema to the family. With a keen awareness of their own power, they had steered the Festival ship through all the perils of wartime. They had been supported financially by the 'Führer' and had been protected year after year. Was this all to be taken from them now? That would have been more than an act of disempowerment: it would have been a humiliation without parallel. Winifred wrote to Friedelind:

> In the meantime you will have been notified of the concoction that W.B. has brewed up for us – I am trusting in your healthy common sense and your healthy attitude to these things. Pöhner is behaving in an exemplary, tactful manner ... he naturally sees things differently from the many 'new citizens' who know nothing of the past and little of art and culture. Compare this poison brew with Papa's will – and you will see the way forward clearly. At Easter, these people want to come back to Schilda [= Bayreuth]. Personally, we have nothing to do with each other, and I also told Wolfi that. Frau Beerli calls it: ambition and a false mania for rehabilitation.[66]

Wieland wrote to his sister as follows:

> With his memorandum, our dear cousin Willi has made an approach to Mr Edwards via the latter's close friend Karl Amadeus Hartmann, whom he mentions is a hopeful Wagnerian. He is an ultramodern composer with communist sympathies and plays a major role in Munich. Beidler's plan fell on fertile ground with Edwards – with phrases such as 'there has to be a breath of fresh air in Bayreuth' and 'it became a mausoleum under Cosima'. He is in love with the idea of making Bayreuth into an international opera theatre in which important contemporary composers can be performed, and he thinks he has found the right man for it in Beidler. But no decisions of any kind have been made and it would surely interest him to get an idea of the reaction from a 'representative of the opposition'. You have seen how things are meant to be run in that singular document by Munich's cultural expert. It couldn't get any clumsier. Dr Stenzel (a Jew), slaughterhouse director Meyer, Mr Hartmann, Mr Beidler and Mr E[ngel], who is pretty well soaped up but by no means completely lost as yet – that is the interest group from the south with whom we will have to deal in future. I do not know who belongs to the Berlin commission mentioned in the papers that intends to put on *Parsi-*

fal with due reverence in 1948. Is our old friend H.T. going to get himself installed again in this manner?[67]

Wieland here cleverly played on Friedelind's horror of the scheming Heinz Tietjen, from whom she had long since distanced herself inwardly.

Wieland's description of Stenzel as 'a Jew' shows that his anti-Semitism had continued unabated. Winifred wrote in the same tone about a board of trustees 'with Thomas Mann at its head and only Jews in the committee'.[68] The war had ended two years earlier. But it was still unnecessary to denounce anyone, for just calling them a 'Jew' sufficed to conjure up all the old, insidious Nazi stereotypes. Neither Wieland nor Winifred asked themselves whether such prejudices would have any impact on Friedelind – they simply took it as a given. When it was a matter of expressing horror at 'communist', 'ultramodern' composers they proved how the old terminology of the Nazi era remained very much alive. Only the word 'degenerate' was missing from their vocabulary, though it was in any case implied. Hartmann had refused to participate in the Nazi state music apparatus, and Wieland still regarded him as an opponent. The horrific notion that Bayreuth might become a Mecca of the Modern dredged up all kinds of fears, and the director of the local slaughterhouse was mocked simply by being denoted by his profession. Wieland tried to get his sister into the same boat with him:

> The memorandum of our cousin … is to our mind a clumsy attempt to achieve a dictatorship over the Festival under the pretext of a large international organization. For the members of this board of trustees are so carefully spread out over the whole world that in practice all responsibility and management duties would be in the hands of the secretary – which post he modestly reserves for himself … I think that the simplest and best way of bringing down this noble plan would be if you contacted Thomas Mann. We think it is hardly probable that he would give his name to such a dubious business for which there is neither moral nor legal justification. A refusal would automatically thwart the whole plan, for as Beidler writes, it is all built on the use of Mann's name. I am writing this to you in the conviction that you are of the same opinion as us. Should we really put up with this insolence on the part of our cousin, who knows the art of expropriation so well – he's a real Nazi superman in this … I really think it would be possible for you to get Th. M[ann] to agree with you!.[69]

Wolfgang added to this tirade by writing to her of 'our cousin, whose mind is geared towards ruining Wahnfried under any circumstances and with all means at his disposal.' He continued: 'I assume that you will know how to work against that.'[70]

Did Friedelind know that Thomas Mann had written in an article in 1939 that Wagner had prepared the way for the Nazis?[71] Probably not. In any case, she agreed with her brothers and visited Mann in May 1947 in order to convince him not to support Beidler's plan. In retrospect, she felt that Mann had played a dubious role in the business, assuring her that he would decline the honorary presidency of the board, while at the same time confirming to the US cultural representative in Bavaria that he would be willing to take on the office.[72] She also visited General Lucius D. Clay, the commander in chief of the US Forces in Europe and military governor of the American zone in Germany, to warn him that Beidler was a socialist.[73] Her denunciation of Beidler seems all the more repugnant, given that it was at this very time that the dreaded House Committee on Un-American Activities (HUAC) began its persecution of communists both real and supposed. Nor did she stop there. She went on the hunt for other reasons for Beidler to be excluded, siding clearly with her brothers while quite unaware that she was doing herself no favours in the process. She asked Wolfgang to look for documents

> ... that would prove without a doubt that Herr Beidler was a communist and that this is why he left Germany. As much as I recall from before, it was always claimed that he was an active communist. Was he perhaps even a member of the party? And what was his role in Munich in the early 20s during all the political upheavals and the revolutions?? I seem to recall various stories and claims. What I really want is for someone who knows about him to send me as complete a CV of him as possible, for I can't make any claims that I can't prove. After my lawyer warned him several weeks ago about the consequences if he publishes excerpts from Grandmama's diary, because it would contravene copyright – by the way, he hasn't answered that yet – I can imagine that he would dearly love to threaten me with a libel case. That's why I have to have in my hands as many documents as possible about him, in order to back up my assertions.[74]

Winifred praised her: 'with regard to ... F.W.B. ... you've hit on a brilliant idea to knock him out!' According to Verena Lafferentz, Friedelind's message to Clay had the desired effect.[75] In June 1948, the US authorities were given a memorandum on the Bayreuth Festival that said: 'The important thing is to present an evaluation of the subject in fairly simple terms, letting General Clay decide what would be preferable.'[76]

These panic attacks on the part of the Wagner family seem astonishing when one considers that Beidler had hardly seized the initiative himself, let alone out of any hunger for power; he had merely been given a brief to draw up possibilities for the future of the Festival. Wieland's claim that Beidler had 'made advances' to the Mayor has a negative connotation that merely indicates his own fear of losing power. Beidler was immediately cast in the role of an enemy, and Friedelind let herself be drawn into the game. She did not include their cousin in the family tree that she had printed in her book (Beidler is still missing in the later German-language edition of 1994, though it includes Cosima's children by von Bülow who were not even related to Wagner). Nor did Beidler think much of Friedelind at the time, either. 'You can't take her seriously,' he wrote of her to his former colleague Annemarie Landau.[77] Ellen Beerli in Tribschen, however, was wholly on the side of Siegfried's children and praised Friedelind: 'Thank God they've taken up a fighting attitude, for one can't allow such an inheritance to go to strangers, nor allow B[eidler] to snoop around in the archives and in Cosima's diaries, all in aid of his "rehabilitation book"!'[78]

This vehement reaction was also founded in part on Beidler's reputation in the family for, since leaving Germany in 1933, he had been regarded as an apostate. Back in 1938 Daniela had written to Adolf Zinsstag: 'As for the son of my poor, unhappy, great, highly talented but sadly bewildered sister ... already in early childhood he was known as a "raw socialist", and he and his wife are supposed to have mixed with communists in Berlin and in Paris, which is why they were expelled etc. (please keep this between us).'[79] Communist, dispossessor, concoctor of a 'poison brew' – the list of accusations reveals the intense fear that was conjured up by the prospect of losing power in Bayreuth, and the vocabulary also shows the continuing influence of Nazi ideology. Cousin Beidler had so much in common with Friedelind: he was an opponent of the Nazis and an émigré, he spent his life burdened by money worries, and he too had been compelled to leave the country of his birth. But now he was cast in the role of a great enemy. Weren't Friedelind's real 'enemies' back in Bayreuth? By the time she realized this, it was too late.

Decades later, Friedelind was still claiming that she had saved the Festival for the family. 'With the aid of the most distinguished firm of international lawyers I prevented its being gobbled up by the Bayreuth-hungry State of Bavaria, and thwarted the attempt of our cousin Beidler, who was backed by a group headed by Thomas Mann, to disown the family and gain control of the Festival.'[80] She was referring to her message sent to Clay's office, where Clay's lawyer confirmed that, in any case of dispossession, ownership of all property and belongings would return to Siegfried's heirs after Winifred's death.[81]

Wolfgang informed Friedelind in March 1948 that, after having surmounted so many difficulties, they were now hoping to rebuild Bayreuth again. He complained about 'people who had been a complete failure in the past and 13 bitter years later now believe they can start up where they left off!'[82] To whom was he referring among those who had been excluded 'for 13 years'? To 'the communists', 'the socialists' or 'the Jews'? To Friedelind's ears this did not smack of shame or an admission of guilt. Wolfgang hoped that the denazification of their mother would soon be over and he believed that 'the return of our Swiss cousin, which has been suggested could happen this summer, will then have no more impact'.[83] He was busy drawing up draft contracts with Wieland and Winifred in which the management of the Festival would be entrusted to both sons.[84] Wieland was hardly able to earn anything, wrote Winifred: 'With his four children and the impossibility [of finding a job] before his denazification, which for understandable reasons he doesn't want to push forward himself – it will soon all fall away – he perhaps leads a more difficult life than any of us.'[85] But soon, without any hearing and in his absence, Wieland was declared a mere 'collaborator' by the denazification court, so he had nothing more to fear.[86]

Developments in Bayreuth were proceeding much quicker than Friedelind could ever have imagined, and it was all happening over her head. In April 1948 the State Secretary for the Arts in the Bavarian State Ministry for Education and Culture, Dieter Sattler, visited Winifred and indicated to her that the state of Bavaria was willing to become involved in supporting the Festival. His condition was that the trustees would have to comprise representatives from the city, the state and 'international friends' – which was in fact very close to the plan put forward by Beidler. Winifred refused and suggested that she would be ready to pass on possession of everything to her two sons. This was something that the state was not prepared to accept, and it was hardly a matter of chance that several weeks later the Bavarian Culture Minister, Alois Hundhammer, gave a speech in Bayreuth on Wagner's 135th birthday in which he stressed the important role of the state of Bavaria in financing and maintaining the Festival. He also mentioned the 'shadow' that still hung over Wagner's music. In July 1948, Sattler tried to change Winifred's mind once again, but she insisted that she could only contemplate accepting state help if her sons took on the management of the Festival. She warned Sattler not to underestimate her determination.[87]

Shortly before Winifred's appeal hearing in December 1948, the family's possessions were handed back to them. Winifred informed Friedelind that her brothers wanted to invite her to a family conference, since the financial situation had become untenable 'and we would much prefer not to take any steps that aren't agreed upon by all four children.'[88] But Friedelind wouldn't budge: she preferred to remain in the USA. She had been brimming with self-confidence in this year: 'I don't believe that I am any better loved by my family, but I naturally have the strategically stronger position – and they recognize it, even if it annoys them all the more that the black sheep was right about everything.'[89] She had always thought that she sat firmly in the saddle, for all four children had equal rights as Siegfried's heirs. She had also played her part in booting out their émigré cousin. But Friedelind could hardly have been more wrong in her assessment, for now she would be the victim. According to Gertrud Wagner, the two brothers had a secret motto: 'After Cosima and Winifred, we'll put an end to the dictates of women!' To which Wolfgang had added: 'Die Weiber lassn mr draussen' – 'We'll leave the womenfolk out of it.'[90]

Wieland and Wolfgang had been compelled to fight major battles with their mother before she would agree to give up the management of the Festival, for she had truly believed that she would be allowed to take up the reins and start things afresh after the collapse of Germany. Her obstinacy found a supporter in Tietjen, who swore to maintain her rights once her probationary period was over, 'in the interests of Bayreuth.'[91] Only when the appeals court decided to forbid her from managing the Festival did she act. The next step taken by the family was one negotiated by the brothers and their mother that would serve to exclude Friedelind altogether.

On 19 January 1949, Winifred, Wieland, Verena and Wolfgang signed an agreement that authorised the two brothers to act independently. In other words: to speak in the name of the family.[92] Winifred renounced all claim to her inheritance rights with regard to the continuance of the Festival, assigning these instead to her sons. On 21 January 1949 she then declared in writing that she would refrain from any activities and that she 'would give [her sons] the corresponding power of attorney'. In the meantime a new Mayor of Bayreuth had been elected, and the city's cultural officer, Karl Würzburger, made it clear that Siegfried's will made it impossible to consider either a takeover of the Festival by Friedelind or the foundation proposed by Franz Beidler. 'The will is so unambiguous,' he wrote, 'that I do not understand how Dr Meyer could so wish to meddle with the Festival.'[93] The brothers were happy. Wolfgang admitted in his autobiography that each one of the children possessed equal status as a reversionary heir, but added: 'According to my opinion then and now, this would inevitably also have meant the end of the business as run by members of the family.'[94]

Friedelind's mother flooded her with information about her grandchildren, her sons, and the planned rebuilding work on the west wing of Wahnfried. In 1949 Wieland had portions of the stucco work taken away and floors and walls in Wahnfried were removed in order to create living quarters to his own taste. Old furniture was broken up, which Winifred herself understood as an attempt to dispose of the past.[95] She carefully avoided any mention of things gone by in her letters, just as she was silent about her displeasure at Friedelind's book. But she was indignant at her treatment in post-War Germany: 'I am old and have been pushed aside, which is hardly surprising when you think how they boss me – us – around!'[96] Friedelind will have read such lines with mixed feelings, for there was little to suggest that her family had undergone any kind of catharsis regarding the past. Not long before, Wieland had written to her to say 'how wonderful were the years 1917–1920 compared to what is happening now in poor Germany.'[97]

It took a long while before German émigrés could convince themselves that the new democratic structures in western Germany were functioning. In September 1948 a parliamentary council of 70 members had met in Bonn under the chairmanship of Konrad Adenauer in order to draft a new constitution. The three western occupied zones came together as the Federal Republic of Germany (i.e. West Germany). Bonn was declared the seat of government in May 1949, the western military governors approved the new constitution and the first elections took place in August 1949.

It was more than mere coincidence that 1949 also saw the formation of the 'Society of Friends of Bayreuth' whose aim was to gather donations to enable the Festival to begin again. Emergent West German businesses were keen to help the Festival, for it had formerly been of international importance and could now help the country to re-establish its reputation. The first president of this society of private sponsors – which still exists today – was Dr Moritz Klönne. He had joined the Nazi Party and the SS in 1940, though he had many contacts with the resistance in the Germany military. Like innumerable others he had adapted to the regime to get by. His right hand in the Society was Konrad Pöhner, already mentioned above. They were joined by various other big businessmen, such as Dr Hans Bahlsen of the Hanover bakery company; Martin Schwab of Telefunken; and Berthold Beitz, General Manager of the Iduna Germania insurance company in Hamburg. By 1950 they had already collected DM 400,000, most of it donated by representatives of industry. The speed of their work was surprising, for much of the country had been destroyed in the war and most people still had difficulty in coping with everyday life. It was acknowledged that reopening the Festival would be unrealistic in 1950, so the brothers decided on 1951. They organized an opening concert with Beethoven's Ninth Symphony, conducted by Wilhelm Furtwängler, to be followed by five performances each of *Parsifal* and *Meistersinger* and two complete *Ring* cycles.

In the meantime, Friedelind was keeping her head above water financially by giving lectures, taking part in radio discussions and writing articles. She hardly heard anything about the plans for the Festival. She attended whenever Toscanini conducted in New York. On one occasion she rushed from an afternoon performance of *Die Meistersinger* at the Met to hear him conduct in the concert hall of the NBC.[98] She was once again making big plans, and tried to convince Jeanette to give a debut song recital in the New York Town Hall. But Jeanette, in the end, felt inadequate to the challenge and called off her visit, at which Friedelind decided to keep the booking and use the venue for a lecture of her own. It was an ambitious plan: the Town Hall, situated in midtown Manhattan, held up to 1500 people, and was filled to capacity when world-class artists like Wanda Landowska and Yehudi Menuhin performed there. Friedelind wanted to speak about Germany, 'the problems there, which at the same time are the problems of the whole world today' – which was surely far too ambitious for a young émigré who had not seen her homeland for eight years. Despite advertising, the hoped-for hordes failed to turn up.[99]

Friedelind had more success when she received an invitation to give a lecture, as in Chicago, where she travelled in December accompanied by the Janssens and the soprano Irene Jessner, who was to sing *Elektra* under Artur Rodzinski.[100] In March 1948 Friedelind also went to the symphony concerts in Chicago, where she heard the pianists Rubinstein and Casadesus and a song recital given by Lotte Lehmann: 'She was wonderful and thrilling, even if her voice is no longer the biggest or youngest, she still is the best Lieder-singer in the world today.'[101] But Friedelind also had unpleasant experiences there, for she was boycotted by Americans of German extraction who had read her book and been offended by its criticism of Hitler, German politics and Bayreuth. She took this as a compliment, but was also shocked by it. She stayed in a hotel that belonged to Germans and 'with every course you got a propaganda speech that made you lose your appetite straightaway'. The singer Claire Dux (1880–1967) had lived in Chicago since 1921 and had taken on numerous roles at the local opera house; but she refused even to receive Friedelind, 'because she was so shocked by my book and my behaviour'. Friedelind had to listen to how the Allies were the biggest criminals because they had dared to bomb Germany; by contrast, the crimes of the Nazis were glossed over. 'It makes you sick; and then people expect those Germans who remained in Germany to be better!'[102]

Chapter 11

Friedelind returns
1950 to 1955

F RIEDELIND SPENT Christmas 1949 with William Suida (1877–1959) and
his family. He was an important Austrian art historian who specialized
in the Italian Renaissance and was a nephew of Daniela's divorced husband,
Henry Thode. After the annexation of Austria by the Nazis he had lost his
professorship in Graz and had fled via England to the USA. Since 1947 he had
been working as the head of art historical research at the Samuel H. Kress
Foundation in New York.

When Friedelind saw Gian Carlo Menotti's opera *The Consul* in New York
in spring 1950 it moved her deeply, since it gave expression to something she
knew all too well – the oppressive, helpless feeling of someone whose life
depends on inhumane bureaucrats. She had experienced something similar
in London, waiting for her exit visa. The American soprano Patricia Neway
sang at the world première in Philadelphia on 1 March 1950 and also in the
New York run two weeks later. Friedelind had intended for Neway to sing
Brangäne in her abortive tour of *Tristan* and she was a good choice, for Neway
went on to enjoy a major career in the years thereafter, remaining in demand
as a singer until the 1970s. After *The Consul* performance, Friedelind went to
Neway's dressing room and was moved by how the singer had changed. 'The
success makes her look like the proverbial million dollars ... it is finally the
long-deserved recognition.'[1]

In early 1950 Friedelind was still working in an office, but hoped to get a
three-year contract for lectures through an agency: 'That would then be my
last day as a secretary.'[2] She had numerous projects of her own in mind and
was planning trips to India and Israel. She wanted to concentrate wholly on
writing and was convinced that she would need little money for her big trips
because she could 'live everywhere with friends and friends of friends'. She
now felt at home on the US cultural scene, though she had no desire to give
up her own heritage. 'My friends are all surprised at my swift "Americaniza-
tion," but, believe me, it was a 24-hour-per-day job to get all the best things out
of America ... and yet I'm a European through and through, as far as "savoir
vivre" is concerned – customs, likes and dislikes. But the mixture of the old
and new worlds is very good – and often very amusing.'[3] As for her relationship to her mother, she admitted to Jeanette that 'I have really nothing to say to
her, because if you're spiritually completely estranged, is anything left at all?'[4]

15 Attending Gian Carlo Menotti's opera *The Consul* in 1950
together with the composer.

Her scepticism remained regarding the reopening of the Bayreuth Festival.[5] 'I still think that it is too soon, since I can see nothing of the spirit there that would justify a reopening. A "true work of peace", "dedicated to all music lovers of the whole world", "in the spirit of international brotherhood" etc.: these words sound pretty hollow.' Presumably these were phrases that she had come across in Bayreuth's own marketing. 'The incredible speed with which Germany is being re-Nazified casts a shadow over the future of Bayreuth.' She found it wrong of the Bavarian government to subsidize the Festival, because it awakened memories of the Nazis who had similarly funded it. 'We would have been better placed without that kiss of death.' She also rejected plans to make the Festival into a tourist attraction: 'We always avoided every trace of commercialism.' The fact that the Festival was negotiating with Furtwängler was something that surprised her, given his mixed experiences in Bayreuth: 'Whether he is disposed to come, after his shameful treatment by my mother, Heinz Tietjen and the Nazis, is something I don't know' (she was here referring to the dispute between Tietjen and Furtwängler in which Winifred, supported by Hitler, had decided in favour of the former).[6] She felt that reopening the Festival too soon could be fatal for its spirit as well as its finances. But no one was listening to her.

Did she believe that with such provocative, sweeping criticism she would be able to put a spoke in the wheels of Bayreuth, or even prevent the Festival from going ahead? Whatever her reasons, her criticism now became more intense. She announced that she could not be expected to participate actively in the revived Festival, 'since attempts to cooperate with my family still seem to end in permanent disharmony – and a life in a re-Nazified Germany is just as impossible for me as was life in the old Nazi Germany.'[7] The reason for this statement was a newspaper article that claimed her mother and siblings were planning to sell autographs of Richard Wagner in order to finance the reopening of the Festival.[8] Now there was no stopping her, and she protested immediately to her family, emphasizing that any sale without her permission was not allowed. She added fiercely: 'There are many possibilities for financing the Festival that you don't seem to have thought of, without destroying the only true possessions we still have, and whose value is eternal. In a few years this would bring about a complete bankruptcy from which there would be no hope of rescue.'[9] She sent copies of this letter to the Bavarian president and the Bavarian High Commissioner, and in November 1950 she wrote to Verena and Bodo Lafferentz. She said that it would be pointless to sell off manuscripts in the USA – apart from the fact that it would mean selling their heritage – because the money would immediately be confiscated by the government. Only she as an American citizen would get her portion transferred to her.[10]

She described herself as being 'in the midst of a battle with my family', but exempted Verena from this, as she was being treated just as badly.[11]

But Friedelind had reacted to a report that was simply inaccurate, and her brothers immediately demanded a public denial: 'It would be a matter of extraordinary regret to us if you forced us to accuse you in public of being a liar (though after your book this is hardly necessary).'[12] This poisoned the atmosphere, for the family disliked pursuing their conflicts in public – something that Friedelind, with greater experience of the media, was happy to engage in. The brothers made it clear to her that, as the so-called 'preliminary heir', their mother had the perfect right to sell manuscripts. In any case, the autograph scores that Hitler had been given as a gift on his 50th birthday had not come from her, but from industrialists who had bought them from the estate of King Ludwig II.

Friedelind's quarrels with her family were compounded by her disappointment over their lack of willingness to deal openly with political matters. She had long hesitated in getting involved in the planning of the Festival, and now realized that she was being excluded, with her brothers preferring to take the credit for any success themselves. 'I gave you one-and-a-half years to send me reports about the future of the Festival – in vain. Don't think that a *fait accompli* will take me by surprise. I would in any case have placed no obstacles in your way, regardless of how much I am against such an early reopening. To finance the Festival later would have been much easier, because it would have been possible on an international basis. But this way you are compelled to rely on Nazi friends or the politically indifferent, which once again only damages the reputation of Bayreuth', she wrote to her brothers.[13]

If she was expecting confessions of remorse, then she was much mistaken. Germany had been blasted by bombs and thoroughly humiliated, but there was a hunger for culture and for a return as quickly as possible to some kind of ordered everyday life. She felt that the sense of right and wrong that state and society had lost during the Nazi era had still not returned, several years after the end of the War.

> The mental, moral, intellectual, emotional desert that Hitler left behind is devastating – and much more shocking than any ruins ... What can you do with shrivelled souls, immature minds, bent and corrupted thinking, emotional hunchbacks – whose guilt ridden consciences force them to be eternally on the defensive ... 'You had it great' I hear again and again, 'you did not suffer'.[14]

Her scepticism regarding the efficacy of denazification in Germany was not without justification, for the young Federal Republic was making use of numerous politicians, lawyers and academics who had done more than merely collaborate, but had enjoyed active success under the old regime. Everyone had known back then that Jews were being expelled, that opponents of the Nazis were disappearing and that the Gestapo was making arbitrary arrests. And yet many had played along. Even if they had not been actively involved, then they had at least accommodated themselves to circumstances. Some 8.5 million Germans had been members of the Nazi Party, but many now insisted that they had been given no choice in the matter. Although the Allies employed strict principles when they began to weed out active Nazi adherents, these were soon allowed to work again. One of the men who had written commentaries to Hitler's race laws, Hans Maria Globke, even managed to become a State Secretary in the Chancellery. He served as Konrad Adenauer's right hand and succeeded in getting influential positions for former Nazi diplomats. Such activities could only inflame those who had fled into exile.

When Thomas Mann was invited to give a lecture in Bayreuth in 1953, he was prevented from doing so by the Society of the Friends of Bayreuth. A little later, the president of this enthusiastic band, Franz Hilger, commissioned a martial bust of Wagner from none other than Arno Breker, Hitler's former favourite sculptor. It was made of marble, and when it was becoming ravaged by the weather, the city of Bayreuth in 1986 ordered a copy of it to be cast in bronze that can still be seen today in the park in front of the Festspielhaus. Such gestures made evident the links between Wagner and the Nazi era, as well as the fact that some preferred to whitewash bygone times instead of emphasizing the historical break that had actually occurred in 1945.

Friedelind did not tire of denouncing such attempts at continuity, of which her mother was a prime representative. Winifred had no intention of giving up her old Nazi contacts or of removing her Nazi literature from her bookshelves. Her daughter, on the other hand, was subject to malign attacks for her stance. Jens Malte Fischer has described the conflict as follows: 'The émigrés were a living, walking reproach to those who had stayed – for which reason they were by no means met with remorse or confessions of guilt, but rather with arrogance, self-righteousness and even aggression.'[15]

It was not just the resurfacing of old Nazis that enraged Friedelind but the inability of many – including her brothers – to come clean about their former role. Hitler had been in charge, and whatever he had wanted had been done immediately. Thus Tietjen had written in 1934: 'The decision to make a new production of *Parsifal* ... was made by the Führer himself, so it is beyond reproach.'[16] Not only had Wagner been the favourite of those responsible for Nazi aesthetics, but the Nazi leaders themselves had been granted free access to the Festival as it pleased them; and of course, there was Hitler's own close relationship with Winifred. All of this continued to be a source of scandal after the war. Had the brothers admitted to these entanglements with a press release in 1951, such a gesture would have been clearly registered across the world. After all, there had been no other artistic institution that had been visited so often by the dictator and his entourage or that had received so much financial support from them. The cult erected around Wagner during the Third Reich was something that no other composer had enjoyed. Wieland had photographed Hitler several times, and the postcards that he made of the prints were distributed by the 'Imperial Conference' of the Nazi teaching association and elsewhere. The photos of Hitler in the festival programme books of 1934, 1936 and 1939 were all taken by Wieland. He had even tried to get 'Wolf' to support him in his takeover bid for the Festival.

Whereas other institutions confessed to complicity in the crimes of National Socialism – such as the evangelical church with its 'Stuttgart confession' of 1945 – Winifred continued to confirm her allegiance to Hitler while the rest of her family preferred to suppress and forget everything. Wieland came to terms with the past in his own way by developing a new aesthetic as a director, which at least was symbolic of a new beginning.

Heinz Tietjen was enraged when he heard that Wieland wanted to take over the Festival and to start directing operas. He wrote to Emil Preetorius:

> Incidentally, the Bavarian government seems to have gone with heads bowed to the Wagner family, promising to grant them every wish that they desire. They're right: it indeed seems that you have to have been a favourite of Hitler to make a career in today's Bavaria, because otherwise this incredible fact, this moral foul-up, this artistic idiocy now being imposed on the Festival Hill would all be unthinkable. And it's being done with the neighbourly love and protection of Hundhammer and – sadly – Sattler too. And according to the newspaper articles that you sent me, which have not been contradicted, Mr Wieland Wagner appears, in his world of co-believers, to be the only one possible. When will anyone take a stand against this wretchedness?![17]

And he added, mockingly, that 'Granny – is once more all melting motherly devotion; unfortunately, Wolfi is also under his spell, and from abroad Mausi completes the farce'.[18]

Friedelind wrote to her sister that she had a plan that would guarantee the future finances of the Festival. And she had more to say, too: 'They have to be aware over there that I can take legal steps to block everything that is undertaken, up to a point where no one would have any room for manoeuvre at all.' She had received an 'outrageous' letter from Wieland in the summer of 1950, she claimed.[19] Wieland had presumably had enough of all her advice and her attempts to delay the opening of the Festival while he and Wolfgang were successfully gathering donations to make it possible. She mistakenly believed that her position as a politically unblemished émigré had placed the reins firmly in her hands. But Winifred had already engaged a lawyer to make a contract with her sons. 'It is very hard to create a settlement for myself while also doing justice to my two daughters as co-heirs,' she wrote to a friend.[20] She wanted to find a way to exclude Friedelind from the management of the Festival, but without ignoring Siegfried's will and testament.

Friedelind at first heard nothing of all this. Instead, Winifred told her of the continuing preparations for the Festival: they had engaged Knappertsbusch to conduct *Parsifal* and Karajan for the *Ring*,[21] while Wieland had organized a big reception in Wahnfried for Christmas: 'All the prominent people and friends', young and old, had attended. 'The boys are hard at work preparing for the Festival and have achieved everything they wanted: subsidies from the state, subsidies from the radio – favourable conditions from the radio and record companies, and what was missing has been provided by the "Friends of Bayreuth". Advance bookings are doing surprisingly well … For my part I have now been notified of the conclusion of my denazification and they have definitively classed me as "complicit".[22] Thus Friedelind learnt in compressed form that star conductors had been secured, tickets sales were optimistically good, various forces in society were ready to help with the finances, and her mother had been rehabilitated politically. Friedelind's gloomy predictions had proven quite inaccurate. Being in the USA she was literally detached from it all and had no more say in anything. Wolfgang later admitted: 'Above all, it had to be made completely clear to the public without any doubt that my brother and I alone – not the Wagner family – were the managers responsible for the Festival.[23] His emphasis on what had now supposedly been fixed ('above all', 'without any doubt', 'completely clear') shows how important it was to him to exclude his insubordinate sister from everything.

Friedelind had not a suspicion of the thunderbolt that Wieland would unleash with his production of *Parsifal*. She would gladly have visited Europe and written articles for newspapers about the state of things in post-War Germany, but she could not find the funds to do it. To be sure, she retained a presence in the media – and indirectly in Bayreuth too. As the *New York Times* wrote, her name was on the lips of many in the cafés of Bayreuth.[24]

It was a considerable achievement that Wolfgang and Wieland were able to get to grips with all the complexities of Festival management. They had

16 Friedelind never forgave her brother Wolfgang for rejecting the younger generation as successors to the directorship of the Festival.

to cope with the artistic, organizational and legal factors as much as with the sheer technical side of things. If they were not to fail right at the start, everything had to begin at the highest artistic level. There were critics already waiting in the wings such as Emil Preetorius, who wrote with a mixture of maliciousness and envy that 'there's a big run on tickets ... at some point the bomb will blow up, inflated as it is by impotence, arrogance and dishonesty.'[25]

Wieland had had several years to wrestle with issues of opera direction. He wanted to make a clean break, to cast off the shackles of tradition and at the same time forget his own role in the recent past. His teacher of many years standing, Kurt Overhoff, told the magazine *Der Spiegel* that he possessed three files full of letters from his former pupil that proved his intense involvement with the Nazis.[26] But that was all forgotten now. Wieland had studied Wagner's works in detail and during his years in Nussdorf had gone through the scores time and again, usually together with his wife Gertrud. The soprano Anja Silja, who knew his productions in great detail, wrote:

> For him, the only contemporary theatre was a symmetrical theatre of archetypes. The ideas that he realized in it were revolutionary in their time, and modern music theatre is today unthinkable without them. He needed a severity of form, an 'empty space' for his art of direction. Before the New Bayreuth, the style of the scenery had constrained the visual imagination of the director and had led to an ossification of the movements that the singers wanted or were able to make.[27]

There had already been attempts during the war years to un-clutter the scenery at Bayreuth, but Wieland now succeeded in putting something truly new on stage, in particular with the aid of many light effects and by reducing the stage sets to a minimum. Heroic pathos, pomp, thoughtlessly naturalistic scenic depictions – all this was absent from his production of *Parsifal*, as were its former Romantic elements. The rocky and woodland landscapes of previous productions were now a thing of the past, as were the temple, the swan and the doves. The sets utilized to the full the immense depth of the Bayreuth stage and imparted an almost magical atmosphere to the scenes with the Grail. Eleven years later, Wieland put into words what he had done: 'Just as it is time to adapt the whole musical interpretation to our twentieth-century attitudes to life – tempi, agogics, dynamics (thus Wagner must not be celebrated any more in an exhibitionist, ponderous, brass-laden, bombastic fashion!), so everything concerned with the visual and dramatic aspects must continually be formulated anew.'[28] He thus bade farewell to the monumental-heroic, Faustian, sublime qualities that had been so important to the Nazis and that they

had exploited to their own ends. When one considers Wieland's earlier identification with National Socialism, this revolution in staging must surely have
also reflected a personal desire for a fresh beginning.

The audiences were divided in their opinion. Many were enthusiastic, for
they saw in the new production an engagement with deeper levels of meaning
that were inherent in the work. Others were horrified. *Die Meistersinger*, conducted by Herbert von Karajan and directed by Rudolf Otto Hartmann, met
on the other hand with great approval. The brothers' motto: 'Hier gilt's der
Kunst' ('Here art is our objective') was a quotation from the second act of the
Meistersinger, sung by Eva. 'The innocent and virginal Eva was thus appropriated in order to cleanse a tarnished Bayreuth and, by extension, Richard
Wagner,' writes Nicholas Vaszonyi, and he adds: 'However, this arguably dis-
ingenuous and rather hypocritical attempt at depoliticization represented only
the first of many phases of *Vergangenheitsbewältigung* (overcoming the past),
or, more accurately, the absence of it.'[29] In general, however, the reopening of
the Festival was regarded as 'an auspicious sign of recovery', commented Wolfgang Stresemann.[30] It was noted with satisfaction that foreigners had shown no
qualms about coming to the Festival: 753 cars from 22 countries were counted
by one traffic policeman. Every visitor helped a little more to forget the shame
of the Nazi past – and that is presumably how the Bayreuth population also
felt, for they were all too aware of the important political role that their town
had played until recently. The Bavarian President was in attendance, as was
the President of the Bavarian Parliament, and when Wolfgang Wagner gave
his thanks for their financial support, 120 journalists from all over the world
were ready to record the event. Bayreuth's Mayor (who wasn't the same man
who had once invited Franz Beidler and Friedelind to run the Festival) 'gave a
warm declaration of support from the city to the house of Wahnfried and its
"young masters".'[31]

After the Festival, the Society of Friends brought out a commemorative
booklet where every page outlines a desire for normality and recognition.
While the women of the bombed-out cities were still clearing rubble and
stacking bricks – the so-called 'Trümmerfrauen' – the photos of the Festival show the glitterati of the day with their evening dresses, their fur wraps
and their dinner jackets, sitting around a banquet table. The critics praised
the brothers for 'creating a Wagner from the inside' and for their 'increased
spiritualization' and 'spiritual consolidation'. 'The miracle of the Grail in 1951'
was one epithet given to the *Parsifal* production. 'However important it is to
rebuild bombed-out cities, it is more important to rebuild the soul and the
spirit, to reflect on the great values of the past, and to recognize their true
meaning for the present and the future.'[32] The relief is almost tangible that

everyone was at last able to put the past behind them. In all these hymns of praise there is not a word about the loss of credibility brought about by the abandonment of all values under the Nazis – and this in a country that had hitherto been so convinced of its own cultural and moral superiority. There was nothing said about the former dominance of the Nazi ideology, nothing to suggest how degrading it was to their victims that a line should simply be drawn under all that had been done. Richard Wagner's work was held up as the embodiment of a humanist, western culture that had to be maintained without moral blemish. In order to do this, a façade was now erected that was all but impenetrable.

In this same year, Franz Wilhelm Beidler published a 'critical view' of the reopening of the Festival in the weekly journal *Das literarische Deutschland*.[33] He complained that those involved were acting as if the unprecedented material and moral collapse of Germany had never happened. He recalled Bayreuth's unhappy past, and stated that Cosima's 'great world, that fatal amalgam of feudal aristocracy and the industrial upper middle classes' had begun a shoddy tradition that had been continued with Chamberlain's writings. He denied that Hitler had been the first to politicize the Festival, and recalled 1924, when the Festival had been reopened after the First World War, and 'all the factions from the Kaiser's collapsed empire came together against the "Jewish republic", with Ludendorff demonstratively at their head'. By no means had Germany been purged of the Nazi spirit; he held the same views as Thomas Mann, the writer he admired so much. There was an immediate counterattack in the journal of the Friends of Bayreuth, which complained that 'the negating tendencies' of Beidler's article was clearly 'the result of personal resentment'. 'Beidler does not seem to know that the jubilee Festival of 1951 concluded with a closed performance for the unions that was sold out,' wrote Karl Würzburger, conveniently forgetting that there had been performances for the unions before 1933 and for ordinary soldiers in Hitler's day.[34] Beidler's primary concern – his criticism that no one had properly come to terms with the Festival's catastrophic past – remained unmentioned. The reference to 'personal resentment' was malicious, for Beidler had displayed particular fairness in all his dealings with the Bayreuth Wagner family when it seemed that they would be dispossessed, as the Mayor of Bayreuth had wanted at the time.

Abroad, too, the seamless transition from the old Bayreuth to the 'New' was criticized. The American music journalist Ross Parmenter noticed that no one spoke of the Hitler years. 'There were ghosts at that press conference, but they were scarcely acknowledged ... The buergermeister referred delicately and gallantly to Frau Winifred's sacrificial gesture in giving up her connection with the Festspiele.'[35]

Friedelind could only look on, powerless, as Bayreuth swiftly made the new arrangements permanent, with Wagner's two grandsons prominent in the public eye as his natural successors. This dual construction could hardly last for ever, but for the moment it was opportune. Winifred had found a means to exclude Friedelind by perfectly legal means, using her own status as preliminary heir to conclude a rental contract with her two sons on all that the family owned. They thus leased from her the Festspielhaus and Wahnfried along with all its subsidiary buildings and their contents. The annual rent was at first DM 33,000 and was to be renegotiated every year according to the Festival's income. Although she was at first only allowed to spend DM 200 per month, it guaranteed her a secure income for the future.[36]

By separating the financial and organizational aspects of the Festspielhaus from the management of the Festival, both daughters were effectively excluded, though Siegfried's will had clearly stated that they were to be treated equally with the boys. Verena was horrified and complained to her mother: 'What Maus has had to say to you in such bitter words is something that I have felt already for a long time: that no one is taking any notice of us and has not considered in the slightest that we also have rights – besides our love for what Bayreuth stands for – and that it is your duty to defend them.' By installing her brothers as the directors of the Festival, she felt that Winifred had 'sown the seeds of discord within the family'.[37] Winifred told her friend of this:

> Verena – who is also representing Maus – takes the stance that I should not renounce everything in favour of the two sons who, naturally, in my opinion, should continue to run the Festival – the inexperience of the two of them worries the daughters, who think that they will lose their Festival inheritance, and they want me to retain supervision of everything. That's not what the sons want, who want to be independent and Meyer should tell me tomorrow what I can give to the boys and what I can't, so that all parties are treated fairly.[38]

Bodo Lafferentz requested a clarification of everything and had to be content to learn that Winifred as the so-called 'free preliminary heir' was thoroughly entitled to sign a lease contract such as the one now in force.[39] As for Friedelind's dissatisfaction with the contract, her mother wrote:

> Because of all the pending questions I hope that you can get all the explanations you need here on the spot. You can be sure that your rights as reversionary heir have been maintained scrupulously as have those of your siblings, and that Verena gave her permission in your name for both of you in the agreements that were made. That is how it was arranged.

This is indubitably cryptic. She continued thus:

> Of course the contrast between my legal status before and after the denazification seems completely confusing and hard to understand from afar. BEFORE the denazification I was completely without rights – because everything was confiscated and incompetent trustees had been appointed who were able to manage everything here with omnipotence … at the appeals court I was classified as less guilty. The possibility of having everything confiscated thus receded and in the meantime I have advanced to class 4 (complicit) that makes any sanctions against me impossible and gives me back all my rights.[40]

Winifred's arguments regarding the lease contract are subtle, and she is eager to insist that Friedelind will suffer no financial disadvantage. In reality, however, all she wanted was to give power to her sons and thus promote them to the directorship of the Festival in a manner that was unimpeachable. Winifred wrote to her cousin as follows:

> The past year has given me the satisfaction of seeing that my sons are undoubtedly capable of carrying on with the Festival in the spirit of the family's mission and that the whole world took part – with perhaps 80% approval and 20% disapproval – but those who disapproved belong to the stubborn members of all generations who insist on holding to the past and on principle reject any new paths.[41]

Her sons, she continued, 'have arrived at a stroke at the epicentre of artistic interest' and had already received invitations to direct operas elsewhere.

Since the end of the War, Friedelind had increasingly been concerned that she would be outsmarted by her brothers and mother. She was aware that her family owned something of real value and wanted to ensure that her portion of it was maintained, with nothing of it sold off without legal permission. Her lawyer was Robert Kempner, who had been active at the Nuremberg War Trials. On 13 May 1953 he wrote to Winifred to insist on Friedelind's rights in Bayreuth. An extrajudicial settlement was now mooted. The lawyer for the other side, Gottfried Breit, rejected any suggestion that Friedelind was being disadvantaged. The new settlement was 'unassailable, especially because of its new legal status arranged by the preliminary heir Winifred Wagner'.[42] According-ing to Breit, the two daughters had no prospect of successful action during Winifred's lifetime. However, after the death of their mother they could insist that Wahnfried be auctioned off. For this reason, it would be best to find a

17 They planned to help one another, but the fight for power intervened:
Friedelind and Wieland.

peaceful, just solution now. Winifred proposed that the daughters should be assigned all the income from the rental of the opera house after her death – though this was not acted upon in the end.

'Wieland wanted to avoid everything that could lead to Friedelind having a direct role in the Festival (or rather: interfere in it) or intervene in the running of it', wrote Wolfgang many years later with astonishing candour.[43] In fact, this was what both brothers wanted. The negative connotations of 'interfere' and 'intervene' in the same sentence make evident their opinion of her. Both were at one with their mother, as Nike Wagner has remarked: 'With a snap of her fingers, Winifred excluded her adult daughters from any access to supposedly "masculine" self-realization. Like a jealous old goddess of fate, she unceremoniously severed the thread of life that bound them to Bayreuth.'[44]

Did Friedelind recognize the risks that the contract contained? Did she understand that she would in future be dependent on the goodwill of her brothers if – for example – she wanted to live in rooms at Wahnfried, or wanted tickets for the Festival for herself and friends, or even wanted to participate actively in the Festival? (She would later realize just how dependent she was when she set up her master classes; see Chapters 12 and 13.) As the holders of the lease to the Festspielhaus, the brothers had an instrument of power in their hands that would enable them to exclude their refractory, capricious sister for the coming decades. And this was wholly in line with the wishes of their mother. Friedelind had sent them food packages in 1945 after the collapse of Germany, and had done so at times under the most difficult of circumstances; she had supported Wieland and tried to sell stage designs and portraits on his behalf, even if the money in the end had never reached him.[45] But since Wolfgang repeatedly spoke of Friedelind as a 'traitor',[46] her exclusion suggests that it was an act of revenge. By going into exile she had compromised the family during the Nazi era. Her book and her newspaper articles had rubbed salt into their wounds. And now they could pay her back.

Verena and Bodo refused to accept the conditions of the contract and considered how Friedelind might yet become involved in the Festival. Her idea of training American students and musicians in Bayreuth in the summer was ahead of its time. But Friedelind had already taken matters into her own hands and offered a trip through various European festival cities with visits to operas and concerts. Advertising leaflets were quickly printed, though her ideas were – as so often – on an impossibly grand scale. The trip was intended to last from July through to September and to take in Bayreuth, Edinburgh, Florence, Lucerne, Munich, Naples, Paris, Rome, Salzburg and Venice. Winifred was impressed: 'An American travel company has ordered tickets for the first cycle for 21 people "under the guidance of Friedelind Wagner"!! ... I'm now rather looking forward to seeing her again!!'[47] The travel agency that had put together the project had assumed that Friedelind's circle of friends would immediately gather round and join the trip. But when she explained that most of her friends were either professional musicians who wanted nothing to do with music in their free time, or people who couldn't afford the trip, all the plans for the tour were shelved.[48] Once again she was thwarted by a lack of proper preparation. But she remained philosophical and tried to get commissions from magazines and newspapers who might be prepared to pay her to write articles for them from Europe.

The money for her coming visit to the 1953 Festival was earned on an hourly basis by working as a secretary for two psychoanalysts, 'which is roaring fun for me – as you can imagine – because they are always more googy [sic] than any of their patients'. She had in the years up to now already worked as a typist, a waitress, a telephone operator, receptionist, payroll clerk and bookkeeper.[49]

Friedelind's mother sensed that her first visit after 15 years could prove explosive and so planned everything carefully. She was afraid that the press might react swiftly to any hint of scandal and so asked 'Maus' to spend her first night with her in Oberwarmensteinach, 'because you will perhaps understand that I don't want our first meeting after all the difficult past years to take place in the public eye.' She suggested that Friedelind should ring her soon after leaving Nuremberg. 'You drive 45 minutes more or less to the motorway exit "Bayreuth south" – and I'll drive at the same time from here to your motorway exit ... once you've joined us we would then accompany your friends to where they're staying and would drive straight here.'

Friedelind had written to complain about the slander to which she was being subjected, but her mother rebutted it:

> The fact that you did your best at the most difficult times is something that neither I nor any family member has ever denied, and no one over here has ever dared to suggest that you 'let us go hungry' or 'sent us to the gallows.' Those are claims spread by irresponsible people who take pleasure in driving families completely apart. I hope with all my heart that our reunion will create the circumstances necessary to let the past be the past, and that in future we will be united before the outside world. In the meantime you have all become independent and stand alone, and I can respect that best by having withdrawn from things and am here for you all only if you want me. But my heart and my home stand open to you, and with this in mind I am expecting you here with the warmest of feelings! Why you seem to be afraid that 'the existence of the Festival is being put at risk once again, without anyone stopping it', is incomprehensible to me. When you are here you will be able to convince yourself of the opposite![50]

These lines convey caution mixed with scepticism. The mother knew her daughter well and knew too that she would not mince her words if she was convinced of something. So she chose a tactic of embracing Friedelind in order to avoid any confrontation, while at the same time protecting her and her sons by asking her to avoid speaking about the past.

After a radio appearance with the actress Eva Gabor (1919–1995), the sister of the more famous Zsa Zsa Gabor, Friedelind travelled to Europe. Ahead of her journey she gave an interview to the *Arbeiter-Zeitung*, in which she announced that she planned writing a book about Richard and Cosima Wagner and about Franz Liszt, all in order that she could prevent any prejudice and distortions of the truth. She referred to herself as having been an 'assistant director' under Heinz Tietjen, she mentioned her study of acting and singing and also her work as the director of *Jacob's Pillow*. This was a clear indication that she felt she had a claim to direct at Bayreuth in the future. We can see how little she knew of Wieland's ideas of stage direction in that she argued in favour of naturalistic scenery, for an atmospheric depiction of nature on stage and for staying close to Richard Wagner's own stage directions – all things that her brother had abandoned in his productions. She concluded her interview with a complaint about her family who were preventing her from performing the works of her father Siegfried in shortened versions.[51] In this she was dependent on Winifred's goodwill, for the rights lay with her.

On 19 July 1953 Friedelind flew to Paris, a city that she had last seen in 1937. It had lived through a world war since then, but it still captivated her. She stayed with a family by the name of Moreau and two days later set off for Bayreuth in Monsieur Moreau's chauffeur-driven Bentley, stopping off in Strasbourg where she did some sight-seeing in the Cathedral. Once she arrived in Nuremberg she contacted her mother and the reunion went off as planned. Her arrival at the Festspielhaus the day after was carefully stage-managed, and *Der Spiegel* offered a correspondingly populistic account of it:

> The super-heavy limousine took the road to the Festspielhaus a little too quickly. It did not wholly fail to stop at the right place, but it could not be denied that the incident was something of a mis-hit. For a moment the black driver showed his teeth, the tyres groaned and the chrome-plated limo swayed. Then the miracle occurred. The dark-skinned master of the horsepower opened the door deftly like a butler and lace wafted out, a head of blond hair, perhaps slightly too blond, appeared above finely drawn eyebrows and that unmistakably bold, curved nose. There was a quiet murmur among the awestruck bystanders in the face of what had been believed to be impossible. Friedelind, the lost daughter, had returned home. It might all sound like a scene from a novel by Hedwig Courths-Mahler, but the facts are true … Friedelind's return at 35 years of age, the return of the 'rebel', as she has called herself, proved the opening night sensation of this year's festival.[52]

It was important to her to be seen in person, and she planned her appearance meticulously. She had left Germany as an ugly duckling, a girl who wore badly fitting clothes and coats too big for her – all of which served to make her overweight torso seem all the more unattractive. Now she had arrived back in Europe 'undulating and Americanized',[53] wearing tasteful cosmetics, dressed elegantly and thoroughly blonde. Reporters and photographers thronged around her. Their photos show her with wavy hair, looking exquisite in a floral evening dress, thin from dieting and radiant. She stands next to her mother, and one might imagine at first glance that their relationship was back

18 Friedelind with her mother in 1953.

on track. Friedelind's photo became the best-selling postcard at the Festival. She played her role as if the world were perfect again – when reporters asked if she had been reconciled to her family, she answered in the affirmative.

Winifred told her that she would find everyone in the family box, and so she went there as asked.

> We entered the pitch-dark box, someone kissed my hand – it turned out to be my brother-in-law – and then six tiny heads turned – and a whisper started from one to the other: 'it's Maus – it's Maus – it's Maus'. They all tried to see something in the darkness – but had to wait for the light. I finally made out three pony-tails and grabbed the nearest to me and asked her who she was. Iris, Wieland's oldest. Then I made out Amélie, my sister's oldest, next to Iris. Finally the lights turned on – and the looking-over of the aunt started. Wolfgang's children are always hidden away by their parents and I had to sneak to their country-home to finally get to see them, too.[54]

She now had the ground of Bayreuth under her feet for the first time since the War. Fifteen years had passed altogether, during which she and her siblings had grown older, more mature and more experienced. The performances at the Festival were broadcast by the radio across all five continents, with a potential audience of 200 million – which was an immense responsibility borne by those involved. They managed to cope with the media spectacle and put on a happy-family act. 'The legal questions still hover unsolved, but personally it has all been most pleasant and agreeable, because I decided to make it so. I never had any hard feelings about the family except about their politics and some of their gangster-friends.'[55] Despite the stridence of many of her opinions, Friedelind had a big heart and could still be generous.

Six-year-old Gottfried found his aunt to be a likeable woman, dressed exotically and tomboyish in manner. Straightaway she told him about the North American Indians and won his heart with her tales: 'She was the only one in the family who asked about what interested me and treated me like a boy my age.' But his father forbade him from having any more contact with her.[56] She was sad when she wasn't with her nephews and nieces:

> I am all out of a job as far as being an aunt is concerned – no children around – and sitting in the box without holding two kids in my arms – and being in bed without four of them – and the tub without at least two – is a very lonesome life. Unfortunately, only too quickly, one gets spoiled by and used to so much love and adoration – and all the squeezing, hugging and kissing is being sorely missed.[57]

She was a real aunt to the children, one who could listen, who always had a story ready and who would fool about with them. Her niece Nike later wrote that:

> The person most damaged by the family was the one with the most positive family spirit. And the one who had no children was always tirelessly ready for action with the children and their children in turn, full of imagination, funny and unconventional – like an archetypal aunt who was 'different' from the common or garden adults.[58]

Perhaps Friedelind remembered her own childless aunts Daniela and Eva, who had so often protected her, given her presents and who had exerted such a positive influence on her.

In Bayreuth Friedelind saw *Tristan*, the *Ring* and *Parsifal* in Wieland's productions, plus Wolfgang's production of *Lohengrin* with the magnificent Astrid Varnay as Ortrud. Ramón Vinay, who sang the role of Parsifal, already knew Friedelind from New York, as did Varnay and Eleanor Steber (who sang Elsa). And she was also already known to numerous other artists. Above all, having attended innumerable productions in the USA and in Europe, she recognized the potential of Wieland's work, and she was truly enthusiastic about his innovations. For Wieland, it was the people on the stage who were at the heart of the plot, not the sets, which were thereby reduced in significance. No 'historical' stage sets were to be seen, just the theatrical space with abstract, basic forms. Colour and light did the rest.

'Bayreuth was a wonderful surprise. The performances are magnificent and I am completely in favor of the "new style". One has to see them to believe them, because the colors are everything and a black and white photo just does not convey any idea at all'.[59] Her scepticism about the reopening of the Festival, the exclusion she had suffered on the part of her brothers – all that was as if swept aside. She had little problem in acknowledging without envy an exceptional achievement, even if it meant revising her own earlier opinions. And she was happy at the Festival's international success.

She refrained from asking unpleasant questions about the past. Perhaps she sensed that it would be pointless to wrest back into the spotlight those things that had been buried away; or perhaps she just wanted to enjoy the reunion. Wieland was in any case devoid of any sense of guilt, just like many other artists who had composed, made music or directed under the Third Reich – such as Orff, Egk, Karajan, Krauss and those who 'believed that they and their art were victims of Nazi oppression: they … were proud of having preserved their integrity'.[60] In an interview with the *Abendzeitung*, she rejected any form of collective judgment of the Germans. And here, too, she praised the productions that she had seen in Bayreuth. 'I think that after them, you can't bear any other kind of Wagner. But to copy them at another theatre, you would have to be as talented as Wieland. I am delighted for Wolfgang at his success with *Lohengrin* … I was very surprised when I saw how the distinguished Festival audience suddenly broke out in jubilation'.[61] Friedelind was perfectly capable of offering opinions quite removed from her often biting criticism. Besides honest praise, she even showed a degree of tact by refraining from criticizing Wolfgang's production and instead praising the audience.

On 24 August, mother and daughter set off by car to visit Switzerland and Italy – a courageous attempt on the part of both women to stitch up their difficult relationship. They visited Tribschen and attended a Furtwängler concert. 'Fu' promised Winifred that he would conduct the next year in Bayreuth. They left Lucerne and drove through the Gotthard to Pallanza on the Lago Maggiore where Toscanini now lived. Friedelind wanted to visit the Maestro with her mother – despite all her lapses in the Nazi era he had generally spoken positively of her. But they were turned away – Toscanini's daughter Wanda was there and refused to receive them, though not on Winifred's account. She had never forgiven Friedelind for falling in love with her father.[62] Although

Friedelind later always played down this affront on the part of the daughter, it must have hurt her deeply, for the conductor had always remained one of the most important people in her life.

While Winifred spent a few days with the Wille family in Mariafeld outside Zurich, Friedelind stayed in Tribschen – and Winifred commented upon this in her own fashion: 'She enjoyed the company only of her funny émigré friends who were there at the time.'[63] Friedelind then flew from Munich to the Berlin Festival, which she had been commissioned to write about for the USA. There she was astonished at the differences between east and west. She saw Frida Leider for the first time in years and was delighted that both she and her husband had been given professorships in Berlin. She ignored Tietjen, walking straight past him; their relationship was now irreparable. Always keen to hear new things, she went to hear works by Paul Hindemith and Karl Amadeus Hartmann. Back in Munich she went to a performance of *Götterdämmerung* under Knappertsbusch that impressed her greatly. 'I felt like weeping that my brothers let such a man leave Bayreuth. There is just no one like him around any more. This was really great conducting, with all the nobility, sweep, feeling, grandeur, fire and sensitivity that you expect – but find so rarely.'[64] She then went to Cornwall in England, where she visited Ernest and Vera Newman, who were both astonished at how pretty she had become.[65] Newman's four-volume Wagner biography had established him as a leading Wagner expert and he had showered Wieland's productions with praise after the reopening of Bayreuth.

Friedelind spent six months in England, though she went back to Wahnfried for Christmas 1953 and spent New Year with Verena. Winifred commented:

> Maus spent the whole time with Nickel in Nussdorf … after all these long years she is really enjoying the family and family life! … She is still a problem for us all – because somehow or other she would like to work with her brothers staging the Festivals – but on the other hand she never learnt enough to be able to do so and then she has become so American: publicity, publicity seems to be her prayer by day and by night and we just hate the intruding press! … She never mentioned her book and so I did not either!!!![66]

Friedelind returned to New York in late January 1954, where she attended one of Toscanini's last concerts. He was aware that his memory was deteriorating and the realization that he would soon have to retire from the podium depressed him. His fiery temperament had not abandoned him, however, and Friedelind witnessed a moment in a rehearsal when his fury reached such a pitch that he cast his heavy score into the auditorium where it landed in the tenth row.[67]

Winifred found it difficult to come to terms with her loss of power. She sat through the winter in Oberwarmensteinach, knitted pullovers, made lampshades and wrote letters, including some to Mausi, who thereby learnt that her mother was keeping in contact with her former partner and lover: 'My few days in Milan were a nice change for me, and since Tietjen paid for the journey and for my stay, I have no qualms of conscience!' He had taken her there in his car and visited Bellagio and Lake Como with her.[68]

Over the course of time, Wieland and Wolfgang had become hostile to each other, for the competition between them was intensifying. Wolfgang had begun directing operas himself in 1953, but Wieland had nothing but scorn for them. For his part, Wolfgang made fun of Wieland's supposed genius as a director. As far as the outside world was concerned, their collaboration continued to run smoothly. Wieland was responsible for the artistic side of the Festival, Wolfgang for its organization. But Wolfgang was expected to be subordinate to his elder brother. Thus there arose two groups in the Festspielhaus, constantly feuding with each other.[69] The brothers remained united, however, in their continuing endeavours to exclude Friedelind as much as possible. Verena and her husband, on the other hand, were trying to think of ways in which Friedelind might be bound closer to the Bayreuth project. Their aim was to provide financial support for her, for back in New York she was continually having money problems. When she offered to advertise for Bayreuth in the USA in return for a fixed sum her brothers refused, finding it pointless. The percentage of visitors from the USA was minimal, and the marketing that they enjoyed through travel agencies was cheaper. When Verena and Bodo insisted that something had to be done to provide Mausi with a livelihood, the brothers expressed further reservations. 'This conversation was brought to an end by a rather unmotivated, violent outburst from Wolf,' wrote Verena.[70] Their unwillingness to help is all the less comprehensible when one considers that Wolfgang had written a confidential letter to the Bayreuth council in 1952 in which he asked 'for help through person-to-person marketing and such activities', because so many tickets were being returned from abroad and he and his brother were afraid that there might be lots of empty seats in the auditorium.[71] Friedelind wanted to have a part in things – if not in the productions themselves or in artistic decisions, then at least a part of the profit made by the Festival. And with her good contacts in the USA she was convinced that she would be able to recruit visitors to the Festival there. So her brothers agreed to pay her DM 3000 for her to fly to Europe to attend the next Festival, and she in return would undertake promotional work.

But there was yet more trouble with the family when Friedelind announced to the press in 1954 that she was going to publish a 'new' picture of Wagner, without realizing that it had already been reproduced in Zdenko von Kraft's Wagner biography of the year before. It was the second drawing that Paul von Joukowsky had made, just one day before Wagner's death. His first drawing had already been published everywhere. Friedelind had found the sketch in the so-called 'red notebook' while looking through Cosima's papers in Bayreuth in 1953; Cosima had used the notebook in question to record her appointments. Without asking her mother about the copyright, Friedelind had the music journalist Howard Taubman write a story 'around the picture' and was insistent that publishing it would be a 'sensational success' for Bayreuth.[72] She did not bother unduly about the rights to the picture, nor was scholarly accuracy of overriding importance to her: she wanted advertising impact. Her family was appropriately indignant. The *Bayerisches Tagblatt* wrote mockingly: 'Shame, shame! In the atlas of Richard Wagner's life there is no blank spot any more that any discoverer could clean up, so it had to be sullied secretly for the purpose.'[73]

Friedelind could not know that the Festival was meanwhile on a sound financial footing, that visitors were desperate to get tickets, and that advertising was in fact almost superfluous. She continued to try and build up her network of contacts, visiting the TV station of the Ford Foundation to ask if they might be interested in recordings from Bayreuth, and even going to London Records (i.e. Decca) to see if they would combine advertising for their new *Lohengrin* recording with advertising for Bayreuth. She gave out brochures to travel agencies, recommended that they advertise, and suggested to Wolfgang that someone should be appointed in Bayreuth to collect ticket orders for the following year.[74] All this had little impact, and so she was unable to do enough to earn the fee that she had managed after much difficulty to negotiate with her brothers. She was now barely able to pay her rent. This also made it difficult for her to keep her promise to the BBC in London to give a lecture about three productions of the *Ring of the Nibelung* (in the New York Met, at Covent Garden and in Bayreuth), for she was dependent on the DM 3000 promised for her flight. She had arranged with Wolfgang earlier in the year that she would be given a round ticket for her trip to Europe instead of having her travel costs paid in retrospect. But Wolfgang now wrote that he would be holding back the money. She was furious. 'This is a complete disgrace etc., well, there's no point at being surprised or even angry. Of course I sit here without a penny. After getting word from Bayreuth that I could definitely reckon on the money transfer I completely plunged into work for Bayreuth.'[75] Now she was stuck in New York, for she had run up many debts that had to be

19 Friedelind with the composer Gottfried von Einem, who claimed to have
had an affair with her – an allegation she denied.

paid off before she could borrow more money. Lady Crosfield in England was
perplexed and wrote to ask why Friedelind had neither come nor notified her
that she would be staying away. Friedelind replied that she could not tell the
radio station the truth, nor did she want to lie: 'There was also another reason:
my family has a phobia about seeing my name in print. They want me to work
for them as an anonymous astralbody.' She also intimated that by staying away
she felt she would be able to teach her family a lesson.[76] If she really believed
that she could anger her brothers and mother in this fashion, then it is merely
proof of how far removed she had become from the reality of Bayreuth.

The real reason for Wolfgang's refusal to pay for her flight lay in a scandal
that had been brewing for a while but now threatened to blow up in their faces.
Baroness Gerta von Einem was insisting on having her jewellery returned that
Friedelind had taken to America with her for safe keeping. After arriving in
New York she had been compelled to pawn it all for $1700 – some 25% of the
actual value – and for this the pawn shop had demanded 5% interest, which
Friedelind however had difficulty in paying, as her letters of the time make
evident. Her hopes of being able to pay the interest with the income from lectures in June 1949 proved in vain, so she had asked a friend to help ensure that
the jewellery would not be lost. It was at a time when she had to leave the city
to speak to a sponsor about her planned tour of *Tristan*. She did not want to

lose the jewellery because of the mere $300 she owed, for it was worth much more. 'The tiniest amount of money to keep myself going at present is of the utmost importance. Since I am in trouble as usual with my hotel and the bank (Oh Tristan – you trouble child!!) – I could just keep my head above water until everything is set up, if you could agree to this arrangement.'[77]

Her request was heeded, and the jewellery was saved for another year. But her money troubles in the end compelled her to sell it. She still possessed a copy of a valuation made in 1941, when it was valued at £422.[78] After the War she had used 'every penny that I could scrape together to help feed my family and save Bayreuth. That meant I had to miss the payments and the jewel-lery was put up for auction.'[79] Wieland had written to his sister back in 1950 that Gottfried von Einem was expecting an explanation of where his mother's jewellery had ended up, and that if Friedelind did not contact them, then the von Einems would be compelled to take appropriate action.[80] Friedelind had replied in writing to guarantee a payment of $4500. But then she went silent, and the Baroness had now decided to start legal proceedings. It was on Christ-mas Eve 1953 that Friedelind received written notice of it.

Baroness Gerta von Einem had led a shady life. The Gestapo had arrested her on suspicion of spying in 1938, but in the end she was convicted instead of a severe breach of exchange controls. In 1940 a French military court had then convicted her in absentia of bribery and espionage and sentenced her to death. She was finally arrested in France in 1946 and spent two years in prison before being tried – at which she was promptly declared innocent and set free.[81] It was never clarified for whom she had supposedly engaged in espio-nage, nor about what. She had inveigled herself into the acquaintance of many prominent men, ranging from musicians such as Wilhelm Furtwängler and Bruno Walter to politicians such as Winston Churchill, and her friends also included assorted Nazi bigwigs. After the War she surfaced in Bayreuth and with her contacts to the members of the up-and-coming business élite she helped Wolfgang Wagner to gather sponsors for the Festival. Wolfgang asked her to use her connections to the Federal Government to get financial support from them – despite the fact that cultural matters were devolved to the indi-vidual states of the federacy. She also helped to organize business advertise-ments in the Festival programme books. It was she who procured the lighting equipment that was urgently needed and in 1953 she helped organize a special subsidy that served to cover all the Festival's obligations to their banks.[82] As a result of all this, Wolfgang tended to sympathize with the baroness rather than with his own sister.

The newspapers now shocked the cultural world with headlines that cast a dubious light on Friedelind: 'Lawsuit over pawned family jewels' – 'Legal action against Richard Wagner's granddaughter' – 'Pawning the jewels of others' – 'Jewels worth DM 300,000 pawned for $5000' – 'Two tenacious female litigants – the jewellery affairs of Friedelind Wagner' – 'Anguish in Bayreuth'. The topic was seized upon everywhere, from the *Bamberger Volksblatt* to the *Alfelder Zeitung*, and the background to the 'scandal' (as the press inevitably called it) was reported in all its lurid detail. In March 1954 an agreement was reached that the accused party had to pay a sum of $5000 and £80, plus interest, from April 1954 onwards.[83] Friedelind accepted this. But there was a postlude to the story, for the Baroness's lawyer, Dr Karl von Raser, suddenly claimed that Friedelind possessed assets in Bayreuth from the estate of Eva Chamberlain. However, since Eva had altered her will in favour of Verena, the Baroness was unable to profit from any of it (in fact, Verena later gave most of these effects back to Friedelind).

Wolfgang now wanted Friedelind to agree to stay away from the Festival that summer. 'The jewellery became a "weapon" for my brothers to ward off any claims Friedelind might have had in Bayreuth,' wrote Verena Lafferentz.[84] Indeed, the negative press to which Friedelind was now subjected could only be useful to them. And it was this lack of solidarity on the part of her brothers that hurt Friedelind the most. She could not escape the feeling – almost certainly justified – 'that Wolf and the Baroness are in it together,'[85] and she wrote to Frida Leider that

> the family is playing a really sad role – except Nickel and her husband, who from the start didn't believe a word of it – but it was just what my brothers and my mother were waiting for in order to exclude me from Bayreuth – and that old bag would never have dared to go to court if she had not been supported and encouraged to the full, at least by Wolf … of course it's all up to him to sort out the von Einem matter in a decent fashion.[86]

She could not even access the necessary documents at first. She was living in the residential Hotel Ansonia but was behind with her rent, so the Hotel had confiscated all her luggage, and that was where the papers in question were stored. When she finally managed to procure them and take them to Bayreuth, 'there was an awkward silence among the family – they had assumed that I would never be able to prove anything. Thank God I have always kept every scrap of paper, and it was a stroke of luck here.'[87]

Friedelind had no intention of staying away from Bayreuth in 1954 as Wolfgang wanted. When she arrived in Nuremberg on her way to the Festival, a Volkswagen bus stood waiting for her. Its driver gave her a letter from Wolfgang in which he announced that he wanted to have nothing more to do with her. She had refused to accept his ban on her coming to Bayreuth, and so she must refrain from 'compromising' him 'at official receptions'.[88] As usual, Friedelind hid her feelings and offered resistance instead. After two days and nights with her mother, she moved into the Hotel Post where her brother-in-law Bodo had rented a room for guests arriving at short notice. She could live there free of charge. 'With all the houses we have, it is rather strange to be homeless'.[89] Before going to Bayreuth she had taken a trip to Salzburg with Max Lorenz in his car, where she saw an 'abysmal' *Freischütz* of which she claimed that Furtwängler 'dragged it to death'.[90]

Wolfgang seems to have utilized all his connections to ensure that Friedelind received no invitations in Bayreuth.

> And the people who greet me in a friendly fashion the one day are immediately given 'instructions' so that the next day they don't know me any more … I naturally breeze through all these intrigues with a radiant smile as if I knew nothing – every day I do myself up nicely, which also often prompts a poisonous reaction! – and I only curse wildly about everything inside the family – you have to do that, I've learnt that from Bodo, otherwise they just don't get it – they misunderstand every friendly gesture as weakness. Amidst all this luxury I go about without a penny to my name, it's a truly charming situation.[91]

For the moment she was able to sign off her bills in the Festspielhaus restaurant, but every day she expected Wolfgang to find out and put an immediate stop to it.

How was she able to bear this rejection – not just on Wolfgang's part, but also on the part of all the friends and acquaintances whom he was manipulating? There was still a small group of people who were faithful to her. They included her sister and her husband Bodo, who had even considered staying away from the Festival out of protest. Then there was Jeanette Simon (who in the meantime had married and was now Jeanette Eisex), who also never lost faith in her. Jeanette thought that the two brothers were acting like 'little Hitlers'. 'Mausi, don't forget that you also have to live, not just exist … and that you haven't yet sworn a vow of complete poverty.'[92]

A year after the judgment on the jewellery, Friedelind appealed against it – but it brought her nothing, for she did not appear in person. Her lawyer abandoned his brief, explaining to the court that Friedelind had 'grandiloquently announced [the initiation of appeal proceedings] but thereafter had not shown the slightest interest in the legal proceedings and had not replied to any letter sent to her.'[93] She was ignoring all post that she received in New York because she simply did not want to be troubled by unpleasant things. Three years after the legal proceedings had begun, they were concluded in March 1957. Since she could not pay her debts, Wolfgang and Wieland paid them – with the sum in question to be deducted from her future inheritance.

Chapter 12

The master classes begin
1956 to 1960

NOW THAT the Festival had reopened and, despite Friedelind's gloomy predictions, was running successfully, she wanted to be part of it. As if to prove her determination to herself, she now moved back to Europe for three years. She would stay variously in England, France, East Germany and the Netherlands and would attend more than 300 opera performances and innumerable rehearsals before returning to the US in November 1957. Even Winifred – ever the energetic, go-ahead type – was sometimes exhausted when her daughter came to stay in Bayreuth. 'Maus is coming more often than I'd like! – but she means well!'[1] She came regularly to the Festival now and earned her living from journalism, writing reports and articles, mostly about the Festival productions. The music journalist Irving Kolodin received long letters from her in which reports on European opera houses were mingled with flirtatious comments – thus she expressed regret that she couldn't come in person to get her 'annual kiss' and announced that she would let it gather interest.[2]

From 1955 onwards Friedelind lived in the gardener's house next to Wahnfried, where she had four small rooms and a makeshift kitchen. She dubbed it 'Haus Wahnfriedelind'. Since she would often be up till three in the morning, washing up after visits from friends (in German 'abspülen'), she also called it her 'Festspülhaus'. On one occasion, male visitors wandered into her bedroom by mistake, which she found hilarious. In 1955 the celebrated French writer Geneviève Tabouis came to Bayreuth. She had correctly predicted in advance many events of the Second World War, and her English-language memoirs, published in 1942, bore the title *They called me Cassandra*. 'She has an inexhaustible store of arguments and examples and her gentle but penetrating voice never tires of telling France, Europe and the world of the calamity that the totalitarian states are preparing,' said Klaus and Erika Mann of her in 1939.[3]

Friedelind spent Christmas with Verena and Bodo at their home by Lake Constance, cleaning children's noses, reading fairy tales, fixing roller skates and bathing babies. When she watched Verena stuffing a goose and a duck Friedelind insisted that she was a well-trained Yiddish housewife and 'we New York Jews call that the stuffed derma'.[4] She needed quite a few glasses of schnapps to help her digest the meal. Her waistline was no longer thin, and she was banking on a forthcoming journey behind the Iron Curtain to lose some weight.

The following summer she was back in Bayreuth. When the Wagner scholar Robert Gutman was pottering around the local antiquarian bookshops he was told by one dealer that all the German-language versions of her autobiography had been bought up 'by one and the same source'. Friedelind saw the ironic side of it: 'I ought to get the publisher to have big print-run, it seems to be a sure-fire seller!'[5]

The performances in Bayreuth were broadcast by some 100 radio stations all over the world. The Festival was once again firmly established on the society and cultural calendars. But there were strident protests and boos for Wieland's production of the *Meistersinger*. The conservatively minded visitors and press were offended that his stage sets abandoned all depictions of old Nuremberg. As Wieland himself said, he had 'de-sentimentalized' Hans Sachs, 'divesting him of his role as a kind of Reich Governor'.[6] The head of the Friends of Bayreuth, Moritz Klönne, pointed out to Wieland that 'Bayreuth is a sacred German shrine and *Die Meistersinger* is Wagner's most German work', while the Bavarian State Secretary Kurt Eilles declared that he would leave the Society, explaining that 'a healthy old Bavarian' could 'only describe [the production] as a spasm'[7] – though all this left Wieland unmoved.

The lease of the Festspielhaus to the brothers was now no longer enough for them. In 1956 new contracts were agreed, to Friedelind's chagrin:

> First they put a pistol to our heads, Nickel and me, saying we had to sign away our rights to the Festspielhaus. You can imagine the rage we felt and that we naturally opposed it. In the meantime they have been trying the same game, only with different words and they think we'll fall for it. We're constantly running to legal advisors and to the courts to dig out old documents etc. – and then there's this wild rage against all these unreasonable demands and everything that goes along with them.[8]

The reason for this lay in her brothers' desire to separate the ownership of the property from the management of the events held in it. For this would deprive the family council of any access to the Festival itself. While the real estate and the valuable archives still belonged to the whole family, the Festival was run by a private company with the two brothers in charge of it.[9] Winifred insisted that Wieland and Wolfgang should have the same rights, in order to avoid any serious disputes from the start. But Verena and Friedelind had nothing to say in the matter – just as hitherto. Thus the two sisters could only look on as Wieland and Wolfgang continued to hone their artistic skills, rehearsing endlessly, trying out experiments with lighting, engaging people as they saw fit to make the sets, costumes and masks, and taking administrative and organizational decisions as they went along. Friedelind thus remained far behind her brothers in matters of experience. For although she had seen hundreds of Wagner performances and knew all the ins and outs of what went on behind and on the stage, she had next to no experience as a director. Even Wieland's wife Gertrud was allowed to have a creative role – she was a dancer and helped with the choreography. She would later complain that she had never insisted in having her name mentioned in the programme books, but at least she was allowed some artistic responsibility up to the death of her husband. Friedelind was never asked to direct an opera in Bayreuth – and had the foresight never to try and insist on it, for she would never have been allowed anyway.

Since she had settled in for a long European stay, Friedelind decided in 1956 that she would at last like to visit East Germany, i.e. the communist German Democratic Republic (GDR). She wanted to see as many opera houses, concert halls and theatres as possible, to write about them and sell her articles to magazines in the USA. She undertook a mammoth trip with some 70 opera, concert and theatrical performances in East Berlin, Karl-Marx-Stadt (today Chemnitz), Weimar, Erfurt, Leipzig, Dresden, Halle and Dessau. It is astonishing how, with a minimum of financial means, she succeeded in getting access everywhere in the GDR – a country brimming with regulations restricting the movement of people. But she was helped both by her existing media contacts and also by her physical resemblance to her grandfather. She met many artists in the East and visited Leipzig University, the Liszt Conservatory in Weimar and the Academy for Fine and Applied Arts in Halle that was primarily responsible for the high quality of arts and crafts in the GDR. She walked up the hill to the Wartburg in Eisenach, where Wagner had set the action of his *Tannhäuser*, and she went to the Zwinger Gallery in Dresden to admire the paintings that had been confiscated by the Soviets after the War and had just been given back. She attended a church service on Reformation Day in the Thomaskirche in Leipzig, and the city appealed to her so much that she already began planning to return for the reopening of the Leipzig Opera House in autumn 1960 (which she indeed did). Its revolving stage with platforms that could be lowered and raised was designed by Kurt Hemmerling and remains to this day one of the most remarkable in Germany. She 'met all the Communist big-wigs and had a delightful time', she wrote,[10] and she had no fear of reaching out to others. She had long been hoping to organize master classes in Bayreuth and there was now a real prospect of their coming to fruition; so she sounded out Hemmerling about engaging him as a lecturer and also about the possibility of bringing students from her master classes on a visit to Leipzig.

One of Friedelind's most important encounters in the East was with Joachim Herz, who from 1953 to 1957 was Walter Felsenstein's assistant at the Komische Oper in Berlin. He and Friedelind got on well, not least because she liked an innovative, creative approach to opera direction. Since hardly anyone from the west made an effort to attend performances in Leipzig, they were to all intents and purposes closed off to the outside world. As an exception to the rule, Friedelind succeeded in making friends for herself in the GDR.

This trip proved to be just the beginning of a long relationship with the GDR and its music scene. It seems to have appealed to Friedelind's oppositional spirit that the country was at odds with the West – and in the GDR the authorities liked to stress that they had given no quarter to old Nazis, but would prosecute them wherever they found them. Did Friedelind not learn that the same Academy in Halle that she visited was subject to attacks by the state in the late 1950s, and that many of its teachers emigrated to West Germany? In her letters at least there is no hint of criticism of the GDR, except on occasion when she complains of the drab state of the cities in the East.

When Friedelind saw Walter Felsenstein's production of Janáček's *Cunning Little Vixen* at the Komische Oper in Berlin, she immediately recognized it as an extraordinary achievement and went to see it several times. It was first given in May 1956, and would stay in the repertoire for nine years. Friedelind's enthusiasm grew each time she saw it. Felsenstein rejected the notion of 'interpreting' operas and endeavoured to create what was called 'realistic music theatre'. The action of this opera stresses the necessity of reconciling with Nature. This was clearly thematized in the rehearsals and staged as something expressive and thoroughly real. Felsenstein insisted that the acting had to adapt itself exactly to the music. His aesthetic ideas were in many respects diametrically opposed to those of Wieland, yet Friedelind admired the artistic potential of each of them. She soon got to know all the staff at the Komische Oper. After returning to Bayreuth she spoke with the secretary of the Komische Oper for one-and-a-half hours on one occasion, and she hoped 'that I won't be in Bayreuth any more when the bill arrives! – although it will all be taken off my inheritance, like everything else!!'

Back in West Germany, her hectic life continued. She corresponded with agencies, journalists and artists, and in order to maintain her income she sent reports to various magazine editors. After hearing David Oistrakh play with the Leningrad Orchestra in June 1956, for example, she went to London the next day in order to attend one of the renowned garden parties held by her old pre-War friend Lady Crosfield – all in the hope of writing an article about it for the German newspapers that were desperate for gossip about aristocratic circles. She mixed with the British upper classes as easily as she did with famous musicians. But things were not always pleasant. In late October the Friends of Bayreuth and the Wagner Society organized a boycott of a lecture she was giving in Düsseldorf, 'with threats, anonymous letters etc. against me and the organizer. I feel highly honoured that these old Nazis still hate me.'[11] Many an old Wagnerian still regarded her as a 'traitor'. Her mother had meanwhile moved back into the Siegfried Wagner House in 1956, which she defiantly called the 'Führerbau' (the 'Führer building'); the annex at the front she called her 'SS-Esszimmer' ('SS dining room'), which she had decked out 'very austerely in the style of the Führer', in memory of the times when Hitler had lived there and had received guests.[12]

Friedelind's efforts to be paid a fee for marketing the Festival in the USA at long last bore fruit. The contract was in Wolfgang's hand and was criticized by her because her fee would be deducted from her inheritance if she failed to meet its expectations. She thought that this was 'pure extortion for the future'.[13] But Bodo and Verena advised her to sign it, since otherwise no money would be forthcoming at all. In family matters, Bodo usually sided with his sister-in-law, not least in order to protect his wife who had as little to say in Bayreuth as Friedelind. In the end Friedelind signed the contract that bound her to act as a mediator for donations and advertising contracts for Bayreuth of which the proceeds would be for the maintenance of the Festival. The contract was full of snags, for while Friedelind would be given DM 600 per month, this was intended as an advance for a fee that was to comprise 30% of all the monies that she procured. If she did not succeed in procuring any money, then she would have to pay back her monthly sums, at the latest when her inheritance finally came in. In order to secure the deal, she gave her brothers a right of lien on her inheritance (even though Baroness von Einem already possessed such a lien on account of the jewellery affair).[14] Wolfgang's shrewdness had secured him another victory. Gertrud Wagner – probably with good reason – saw the whole business as 'a kind of act of deportation. When Wolfgang sent his brother the draft contract in October 1957, he made his intentions perfectly clear. Their common interest, he wrote, lay in getting rid of Friedelind as soon as possible. Keeping "the women folk" out had long been an elemental component of the male domination of the Green Hill.'[15] Bringing Friedelind's future inheritance into play was a harsh step to take if one considers how many packages she had sent from the USA to Nussdorf and Bayreuth after the War, and how she had gone into debt to finance her assistance to the family. Would it really have been unthinkable to employ her as a member of the staff with a small, basic fee?

In order for Bayreuth to maintain a worldwide presence it was necessary to treat representatives of the press favourably. Here, Friedelind could bring

20 Friedelind with the singer Jeanette Eisex, née Simon (centre), close friends since their internment on the Isle of Man, and the Greek millionaire Lady Crosfield.

her network of contacts into play. First she dealt with Howard Taubman, who wrote music reviews for the *New York Times*. Wieland did not like him because he had expressed a critical opinion of the Bayreuth orchestra in his biography of Toscanini.[16] But since Friedelind knew of Taubman's importance in the US press she did her best to make his stay in Bayreuth as pleasant as possible, despite a certain antipathy on his part. Thus she regretted that he wanted to come to the opening ceremony, because 'the pompous Nazis will be there'.[17] Besides her media work, however, she had enough time to attend many concerts and operas. Her diary for 1958 offers proof of her hectic activity. She went to concerts under Leonard Bernstein and Dimitri Mitropoulos with Emil Gilels and Glenn Gould respectively as the piano soloists, she ate with Daniel Barenboim and had numerous meetings with her friend Robert ('Bob') Gutman, the later Wagner biographer. She saw Maria Callas as Tosca and Leonie Rysanek as Lady Macbeth. And so it went on.

> When people first meet Friedelind Wagner, granddaughter of the composer, they expect to see either a quavering, lace-shawled old lady; or an equally ancient but formidable matriarch. The reality is an extremely pleasant surprise. She turns out to be gay and strikingly good-looking in a blonde, Teutonic style that would do credit to one of the streamlined productions currently staged at the Wagner festival in Bayreuth by her brother, Wieland Wagner.

Thus wrote the *Washington Post* of 17 January 1958. In her lectures her use of radical turns of phrase and her witty, often provocative arguments kept her audiences enthralled. Back in the 1940s she had had to speak repeatedly about her experiences with Hitler, but now she could concentrate more on Richard Wagner. In the 1960s she would devote herself more to the topic of Bayreuth and used slides to help explain how operatic productions had changed in post-War Germany. Other topics about which she spoke were the philosophy of Wagner's music dramas, opera productions in Europe in general and cultural developments in the GDR. She had also given much thought to the matter of broadcasting opera on TV. Her restless travels during which she visited the opera houses of Europe now proved their worth, for she could base her lectures on a wealth of first-hand knowledge. Her easy command of English was also in her favour. She usually spoke at universities, colleges, high schools and music academies. Ever humorous and entertaining, her talks were popular and formed the basis of her livelihood. In order to be able to lecture in greater depth about Wieland's productions, she took advice from a psychoanalyst who explained to her the difference between Freud and Jung and recommended books to read. 'Thank God I now have several lectures that are well paid. On 2 April I'm at Lincoln University, Delaware, that's on the way to Washington, a black university. On 22.3. I'm here in White Plains N.Y. and on 8.4. I'm in a women's convent in Washington, talking every time about Bayreuth and showing slides of the productions.'[18]

In Europe she was drawn back to the Komische Oper in Berlin time and again, for her enthusiasm for Felsenstein's art of direction remained undimmed. In January 1959 she saw *Turandot* and *Tales from Hoffmann* there, and said it would have been worth swimming the Atlantic to see them.[19] A concert given by the then near-unknown Wolfgang Sawallisch intrigued her, for it was difficult for her not to make unfavourable comparisons with Toscanini. She knew it was unfair to measure the young conductor by the achievements of the Maestro. 'But how does one ever get it out of one's system? It seems engraved and part of oneself forever.'[20]

She went via Munich to Lake Constance and from there to Zurich where she met Otto Klemperer and dined with him and his daughter Lotte. Being Jewish, Klemperer had fled from the Nazis early in the Third Reich and had emigrated to the USA like Friedelind. He could be gruff to the point of impoliteness – Katia Mann had once described him as a combination of sovereign precision and reckless flamboyance – but his rough edges did not bother Friedelind.[21] He had been living in Switzerland since 1954, and since his wife had heart problems and did not want to travel with him any more, Lotte had jumped in and dedicated herself to assisting her father.[22] Friedelind was distressed to learn that he had suffered severe burns while smoking his pipe in bed – he had set his woollen pyjamas on fire and in order to quench the flames had mistakenly reached for a bottle that contained alcohol, not water.

Friedelind was not wildly successful with her advertising efforts for the Festival, and so she now looked around for another possible sphere of activity. In October 1958 she discussed with her brothers her plans to set up a training opportunity in Bayreuth, and they allowed her to organize courses shortly before and after the Festival. Their agreement read as follows: 'The proposals laid out by Miss Friedelind Wagner in a paper of 13.10.1958 to hold master classes during the Bayreuth Festival for young conductors, singers, directors, set, costume and mask designers, répétiteurs, theatre architects, lighting technicians and other young theatre professionals are of particular interest to the Bayreuth Festival management. Once the necessary organization and the required finances for the project are secured, everything will be done to allow these courses to be held during the Bayreuth Festival.'

Once her master classes were legally registered as an association ('Festspielmeisterklassen e.V.'), 'I was greatly relieved, because in Bayreuth I never

21 Those who knew her loved her sense of humour,
her sharp wit and her charm.

know what kind of intrigues might still be brewed up at the last minute.'[23] Wolfgang stressed once more that the Festival management would offer moral support to the project and its ideals, but that it would be financially and organizationally separate from the Festival itself. It was confirmed that, 'according to what is operationally possible', rooms in the Festspielhaus would be placed at her disposal free of charge. 'The course participants will also be allowed to attend rehearsals free of charge', he wrote.[24] That was as far as they were prepared to go.

The Society of the Friends of Bayreuth protested against it, because they wrongly assumed that Friedelind would be profiting from the monies destined for the Festival. 'The dear Freunde felt that Bayreuth cannot afford to lose more money. Well, if Wolfgang will not straighten them out on it, I certainly will', she wrote. She was convinced that her brothers would stand up for the project and would not renege on their commitment, even though a certain resistance was evident on their part. Their mistrust of her remained: in no way could she be allowed to get a foot in the door as far as directing in Bayreuth was concerned.[25]

Friedelind found it a mistake to keep the different disciplines apart in opera houses, for it prevented those involved from gaining comprehensive access to the work whose performance they were all preparing. She was convinced that everyone should possess a broad basic knowledge. Thus she conceived the idea of getting representatives from different fields together in Bayreuth for several weeks, during which they would observe the final rehearsals for the Festival and take part in courses, exercises, discussions and lectures in their own specialized topics. This was all reminiscent of her own grandfather's ideas, for he himself had wanted to set up a 'stylistic school'. Cosima had in fact founded just such a training centre in 1892 that had at first functioned well, but which had failed in 1897 because she had taken on beginners. Another attempt was made in 1913 and 1914, when Siegfried and Cosima set up a singing school for 60 children to be trained to sing in the chorus of *Parsifal*. But the outbreak of war in 1914 had put an end to it all. Friedelind's concept was thus part of an existing tradition.

The classes were attended by students whom she chose personally. The courses were grouped around rehearsals and performances and were intended to encompass all aspects of opera production. In order to avoid the mistakes that Cosima had made, the students had to have either begun their professional career or be on the cusp of it; but they were to be young and talented. Anyone older would only be allowed to participate in exceptional circumstances. The concept gradually took on concrete shape. 'As soon as we have our planned 30 students in the bag, I'll come across,'[26] she wrote to her mother. She profited from being already known in the music world. She asked foundations for money and was supported by the Fulbright and Rockefeller Foundations. She also hunted for well-known experts who could offer lectures and exercises.

Friedelind was determined to have Walter Felsenstein on board and invited him to attend a production by Wieland. She was prepared to

> ... meet you at any railway station or airport in the world, and if the moon rockets were up and running I'd fetch you from the moon. I cannot tell you enough what prestige your name carries here – and my master classes would immediately become 'top class' if you would be involved in them.[27]

She managed to engage him every year, and he unintentionally became the centre point of her courses.

Four months before the first master classes were to begin, Friedelind set about selecting exceptional students. She travelled all over the USA to get to know them and to examine them. There were some 100 applications, almost all of them worthy, and while she listened to many singers she was also glad that there were candidates from other fields too.

When it came to the final selection, she was under pressure: 'We can only take on 30 in the first year and naturally we must only choose first-class material, so my brothers can't complain about the "rubbish she's bringing with her".[28] Her fear of negative criticism from Wolfgang and Wieland surfaces repeatedly, for the competition between them was considerable. And there were distressing moments while she was gathering sponsorship funds. Some Germans she met insisted on making jokes about President Roosevelt, calling him 'Rosenfeld' and mocking him for having supposedly been Jewish. 'And you have to sit there and be a lady and not spit in their faces – damn it all, it is a strain to be a lady!!!! And I was being told by a drunk again and again what a terrible thing I did by going against the Nazis and so on ... Is a scholarship worth that much? I believe: no.'[29]

At the core of her concept remained the interdisciplinary idea. The Wagnerian tradition was to be the focus of many of the lectures and discussions, but not exclusively so, and his music would feature only where it suited the schedule of the master classes. She chose proven experts as her lecturers, because she knew from her own experience how important matters of presentation were for the success of her endeavour. She would have liked to win over the critic Irving Kolodin as her expert in music history, for her admiration of him had turned into something far more intense. 'My private life has made some astonishing progress,' she wrote, and her letters of these months exude a positive, cheerful spirit.[30] But her feelings were not reciprocated, and his rejection was a bitter blow to her.

In her negotiations with Felsenstein, Friedelind offered him DM 1000 per lecture, plus expenses – which at the time was more than a director's monthly salary. She also invited him to give more lectures (in 1963 he received DM 8000 plus expenses for several lectures; since she offered other lecturers only DM 200, this confirms her keen interest in securing his participation). She was all too aware that success would depend on the quality of what she could offer. Felsenstein was one of the most significant theatre directors in Germany, and she could be justifiably proud of having won him over. She also invited the opera director Herbert Graf (1903–1973).

Ilse Laux ran a drama workshop in the Margravial Opera House (Bayreuth's old Baroque theatre). She had previously taught at the Max Reinhardt School in Berlin, and Friedelind had got to know her through Felsenstein. She was assisted by Rudolf Heinrich, who was responsible for the sets of all the important productions at the Komische Oper in Berlin in the 1950s. Laux took particular pleasure in using movement exercises to get the participants to lose their inhibitions. Bayreuth artists were also intended to give lessons and demonstrations of everything that went into an operatic production. Karl Schmitt-Walter, the Beckmesser in the Bayreuth *Meistersinger*, worked with the group on text expression for singers. The lecturers also included A. M. Nagler from Yale and the psychoanalyst Max Friedlander, who spoke about the *Ring* and *Parsifal*.

Friedelind enjoyed juggling 'big' names. 'Since Orff doesn't want to teach – which I'm very pleased about! – I want to invite Martinu now. He lives in Basel so he's easily accessible. I like him terribly much and have him in high regard as a composer. Menotti wants to come if he can spare the time. Perhaps I'll still invite K. A. Hartmann or Henze, or both, because I like them and believe in their talents. Orff is too Nazi for my taste, in style and mindset – my invitation to him was a gesture for Wieland's sake – and I laughed delightedly that he turned us down.'[31]

Hans Werner Henze met her in Munich. He was willing to take part in the classes, though it never came to anything concrete. The 30 minutes that she planned for her meeting with him turned into several hours. She had recommended his *König Hirsch* in the USA and tried to get tapes of it. Henze was very keen to have his opera performed in Washington and also wanted to co-direct it with someone – and perhaps even conduct it too.

> He would love to come to the States, but is worried about not knowing anybody and so on. I told him that he should only come when ASKED – and that one should always start at the top and never at the bottom. He is writing an opera on 'Prinz von Homburg', but demilitarized, with love as the theme: to love someone with his weaknesses, or because of them will be his central theme. It will be world premiered in Hamburg next spring. He wants Visconti to stage 'Homburg'. He is a very nice and interesting young man, very straightforward, who lives in Italy because he cannot stomach much about the Vaterland. He grew up looking from his class room onto a destroyed and desecrated Jewish cemetery which was left to look like that for 'educational purposes'.[32]

The master classes began their introductory year with a welcome bang on the publicity drum. Friedelind's friend Howard Taubman, the music journalist, placed a report about the planned classes in the *Sunday Times* in February 1959.[33] Some two years later, she recalled that 'The article was worth more than a million dollars in the bank – since then, they've only written good things about us, and we're still profiting from the article which began it all.'[34] Taubman referred to the earlier attempts by Cosima and Richard to set up a training institution in Bayreuth, and stressed that the new master classes had a professional aspect that should ensure them the success that had been denied to their predecessors. Friedelind printed the article in her programme book.

The summer approached slowly. Work piled up. Friends, acquaintances – everyone bombarded her, and she didn't like to say no. In May, Lotte Lehmann got in touch. She was going to attend the Festival and wanted to exchange her current tickets for better ones. 'Mausi' was expected to organize it. Lehmann had announced her retirement from the concert podium in 1951 and in that year set up a master class at the Music Academy of the West. She only taught for two months in the year and was well paid. She liked the work, and she presumably told Friedelind of her experiences. Like Friedelind, Lotte dreamed of putting on a full-scale opera production with students, but while she would indeed achieve her goal,[35] Friedelind would never find the time to do it.

The classes started in mid-June. Participants with the necessary artistic and academic qualifications thronged the green hill. Since there was as yet neither chorus nor orchestra, the first days were spent doing lighting rehearsals and other such matters. Felsenstein's lectures were a special highpoint of the classes, for his realistic approach to the stage contrasted with Wieland's more aesthetic ideas. On one occasion he held a six-hour discussion with the participants, and they only stopped because the *Meistersinger* was about to begin.[36] Every year Friedelind travelled with her group to selected productions in East and West Germany. They also went to Berlin in order to see Walter Felsenstein's productions at the Komische Oper and productions in the western half of the city. Friedelind expected a high quality of performance in Berlin on account of the competition between the two halves of the city, the one communist, the other capitalist. She also attended exceptional theatre performances with her students: in the Schiller Theatre in the West, at the Volksbühne and the Brecht Ensemble in the East. Their travel plans were organized according to where the best quality was – and in assessing such matters, Friedelind was able to rely on her decades of experience.

To her delight, Friedelind was given an office in the Festspielhaus. Now she would be able to smuggle her students into performances. Such behaviour brought her into conflict with her brothers, but she did not care. Yet when it seemed necessary to her, she showed them deference. The group was given its own box for the rehearsals so that they could follow their scores with pocket lamps without Wieland noticing while he was busy directing the singers. Every evening he decided on his rehearsal schedule, and Friedelind had to wait until then to draw up the next day's timetable. Almost every Sunday, the class participants played chamber music in the Siegfried Wagner House, with Winifred placing her music and garden rooms at their disposal.

After the close of the master classes in 1959, Friedelind attended Felsenstein's rehearsals for *Otello* in the Komische Oper, which she adjudged 'the most exciting and thrilling experience in all my operatic life.'[37] Wieland went

22 The master classes existed from 1959 to 1966 and often took place in a meadow
when no rooms were available in the Festspielhaus.

to the opening night with her, and joined her too for Janáček's *Cunning Little
Vixen* a few days later – though Gertrud reported that he couldn't understand
it. This was in contrast to his sister, who had already seen it 18 times and
whose enthusiasm knew no bounds.[38] When Friedelind went to visit Verena
in Nussdorf in October, she had spent her last money on petrol and had just
30 pfennigs in her handbag. Verena was used to her arriving in penury.[39] It
sprang in part from her insouciance regarding herself, but this time it was different, because she was now also in charge of her master class students. When
one applicant was accepted but had to withdraw, Friedelind sensed that things
would be hard. 'What this does to our budget is quite another matter. I hope
I can get through the season somehow.'[40]

It was originally planned that Bayreuth should receive a specific sum per
student. Friedelind thereby wanted to buy her brothers' goodwill. But soon it
proved impossible to fulfil. Long before the courses had finished, unpaid bills
were landing on Friedelind's desk. Since she wanted to be independent of state
influence she seems to have refused to ask for money from either the city of
Bayreuth, the State of Bavaria or the federal government.

In the USA Friedelind had a prominent lawyer at her side, Jeremiah ('Jerry')
Gutman (1924–2004), who was willing to help her out in financial matters.

A lifelong advocate of civil rights and free speech, he was the brother of Bob Gutman, the Wagner scholar. Along with Alexander ('Sascha') Merovitch, he helped to look after the finances of the master classes. Sascha was horrified at how Friedelind dealt with money and chided her for not having paid bills – including one from her travel agent: 'I think that, when one cannot pay one's debts and is over 15 years old, one should either say so to the person one owes money to, or write a few words about it.'[41] She replied that her brothers had sent her less than expected and that she at present owned not a single cent. She saw no alternative than to pay the bill from her lecturing fees in November, if a miracle didn't happen in the meantime. 'How I survive the next eight days – the last day of Masterclasses, at the moment is the biggest question-mark and my biggest concern.' Since two participants had withdrawn in the end, the courses brought in $1550 less than expected and left her in a difficult situation.[42]

Jerry urged her to try and find sponsors in Europe, too, and recommended that she speak with her brothers about it: 'I think your brothers ought to be willing to forego all or a substantial portion of the fee for the first year because they have parted with nothing and have expended no money and very little effort and suffered barely any inconvenience, and Master Classes will be a bonanza for them once it gets going.'[43] But he could not have been more mistaken. To her brothers, the master classes were just another troublesome attempt on Friedelind's part to inveigle herself into the management of the Festival. And that was something to be avoided at all costs.

Jerry and Sascha also warned Friedelind not to act as driver, city guide and advertiser all at the same time when she ran the classes.[44] The two men made pertinent suggestions, but Friedelind would alter nothing: she could not and would not delegate any responsibility. There was also an epilogue in Germany, for Martin Hirsch, a socialist member of the Federal Parliament who would later be appointed as a judge of the German Constitutional Court, urged Friedelind several times to attend the newly founded society for the promotion of the master classes. According to its statutes, a formal general meeting had to take place. Furthermore, an annual financial statement had to be drawn up and presented to an auditor.[45] These were unpleasant tasks that Friedelind preferred to ignore. These matters dragged on over the years, even after the actual end of the master classes themselves. As late as 1969 Hirsch was advising her to pay back DM 300 per month to the Bavarian State Bank and to do everything 'so that at least there is a sign of goodwill'.[46]

Friedelind's overriding goal remained to promote the careers of her students and to find jobs for them. In this she spared neither trouble nor expense. In her first year she was able straightaway to place some of them on their career paths, including the singer Frances Martin, who was given a Bayreuth contract as one of the Valkyries. In her delight Friedelind even informed the press, and Wolfgang allowed her to have photos taken of the signing of the contract for her to use for publicity purposes in the USA. After this, Frances Martin was engaged in Darmstadt. Thanks to Friedelind's support, the African-American singer Ella Lee was given engagements in Germany, including with Felsenstein in East Berlin. She helped the pianist Bruce Hungerford to get engagements by writing to the conductor Franz Konwitschny and arranging an audition for him in Berlin. She thought he would have a good chance to make a splash in both East and West Germany with one of the top orchestras, and she organized a concert for him as soloist in the Margravial Opera House in Bayreuth. The singer Mary MacKenzie also made an impression in Bayreuth, and Friedelind did her best to find money for her to travel to Vienna to sing for the conductor Lovro von Matačić. She was successful: Matačić offered to perform with her in several European cities. One year after the master classes, MacKenzie was given a contract at the New York Met.

'Of course it's great fun to see that one's work and trouble have such lovely results – it has gone on long enough until I could carry out this dream plan,'[47] she wrote. 'Even many enemies are awed by its success – and especially by the financial backing we have been getting ... this is a dream come true and brings me great happiness every day, I guess only very few people realize.'[48] And she wrote to Jeanette: 'It was a great success, and I have every reason to be satisfied. The whole Festspielhaus took to them and the group has made an excellent name and reputation for itself with everyone. I feel quite mauled and need a breather before I plunge into the preparations for next year.'[49]

Bob Gutman wrote to her in irony that the enthusiasm for the project on the part of the 'Holy Family' was astonishing (this was a reference to Joukowsky, who had thus immortalized the Wagner family in an oil painting). 'The worst that we feared, that is active opposition from Valhalla, did not materialize and for this the candles should be lit in all Bavarian synagogues.'[50] He and Friedelind had obviously expected much more opposition.

In early 1959, Friedelind was asked to direct the world première of the *Odyssee*, an opera by Rudolf von Oertzen, in Shreveport, L.A. It was a great opportunity for her. She had been corresponding with the composer for some time and was well aware that the press would take careful note of how she managed, for she would be labelled the 'third Wagner heir' and it would be assumed she was encouraging comparisons with her brothers.[51] But internal strife ensured that things never got that far. Friedelind wanted longer rehearsals, she wanted to work closely with the set designer and she wanted to choose the artists herself; she also made it clear that she would tolerate no cuts at all.

Such guarantees were impossible for the organizers. They insisted on hiring local singers, which she in turn could not accept. So she abandoned the project. She tried to convince von Oertzen to withdraw the worldwide rights to perform his opera. She wrote to Alfhild Brickbauer that 'this again is one of the instances when you get a reputation of being "difficult", just because they can't step all over you and because you would rather do nothing than cheapen yourself. [...] I am sure that the Oertzens will understand and approve of my decision and back me up on it.'[52]

Friedelind's success with her master classes in Bayreuth was perhaps what prompted her election as 'Mistress of Ceremonies' by the Guild of the Metropolitan Opera in December 1959. She had to compère the Guild's event in the large ballroom of the Waldorf Astoria Hotel and decided to present unknown Wagner songs. Those present were not disappointed: 'You were absolutely superb as mistress of ceremonies at our Luncheon yesterday. Just the right mixture of interesting information, humor and reminiscence.'[53] Also present were Erich Leinsdorf, Birgit Nilsson – who was preparing for the role of Isolde at the Met – and Ramón Vinay. Friedelind used the opportunity to convince Lang van Norden, the longstanding President of the Guild, to sponsor a singer to attend her master classes. She decided to have the Wagner songs recorded and have the proceeds flow into the master classes. She would gladly have used two of her students for the recording, for they could have benefitted from the royalties. 'I am not ever going to exploit my children in any way or manner and this will be straight business.'[54] Her concern for them was sincere.

To her surprise, Friedelind was now offered the position of Intendant of the Berlin Radio Symphony Orchestra under Ferenc Fricsay, though they were not personally acquainted. She would have been the successor to Wolfgang Stresemann, who was moving to the Berlin Philharmonic. Fricsay felt that she would easily be able to combine her work for the master classes with her work for the orchestra, but she had no desire to become involved with the cultural politics of Berlin. And the notion of a permanent position back in Germany gave her 'an acute attack of claustrophobia'. She wanted to remain independent at any price. But the offer flattered her, and 'I dropped it casually into "familiar" ears, because it would be good for them to know, for various reasons....! I am not even using it for publicity, the more quiet I keep personally at the moment, the better for us at the Festspielhaus. The grapevine takes care of such things, anyhow!'[55] Shortly afterwards, she offered to act as Felsenstein's assistant producer in Hamburg. 'It would be irrelevant to me whether I get a fee or not. I would almost be happier without one.'[56] This came to nothing, for the Hamburg Intendant Rolf Liebermann did not allow outside assistants or trainees,[57] though the episode demonstrates how little money and financial security meant to her compared to gaining artistic experience. In this she was not unlike her famous grandfather, who had a similarly easygoing approach to debt and still managed to live his life.

Chapter 13

Heyday of the master classes and their end
1960 to 1966

FINANCING THE master classes remained a matter of urgency. Neverthe-less, Friedelind doubled the number of participants in 1960, inviting 23 young Americans to Bayreuth: set designers, future conductors, singers, répé-titeurs, and six architects – among them Walfredo Toscanini, the grandson of the conductor.[1] Convinced that her classes should include a study of how opera houses are built, she also increased the number of courses on offer. They would take a two-week trip to view famous theatres, see operas and discuss the results of an architectural competition. In June the group went first to Malmö in Sweden in order to visit the city theatre, then to Stockholm to the Congress Centre and the royal theatre at Drottningholm, and then they moved on to Copenhagen to see the Tivoli Concert Hall and the Radio House. In Berlin they visited Hans Scharoun (1893–1972), who was busy building the Philharmonie (it would be finished in 1963). There followed trips to the opera houses of Düsseldorf, Gelsenkirchen, Cologne, Hamburg and Münster. They went to the new theatre in Lünen, which was equipped for special lighting effects, and to the local Geschwister Scholl High School that Scharoun had designed. There followed the Beethoven Hall in Bonn, the Mannheim National Theatre, the Schwetzingen Court Theatre, the Frankfurt Opera House, the Liederhalle and Kleines Schauspielhaus in Stuttgart and finally the Festspiel-haus in Salzburg.

It remains a mystery as to how Friedelind managed to organize, finance and realize such a mammoth programme – one can only imagine the sheer logistics of it. But the enthusiasm of the participants was great, as one of them confirmed afterwards: 'This was an immensely valuable excursion and a very stimulating one. From this tour I developed definite ideas about an "ideal" theatre. Without this experience much of the force of the architects' pro-gramme would not have existed.'[2] Back in Bayreuth they were joined by Sven Gottfrid Markelius (1889–1972), one of the most important Swedish architects and one of the planners of Stockholm after the Second World War, and the Danish architect Jørn Utzon (1918–2008). Friedelind was especially fond of Utzon, and she stood up for his Opera House in Sydney: 'It has caught the imagination of an entire nation, who had no interest whatsoever in opera.'[3] She engaged Thomas Münter to lecture in theatre architecture in Bayreuth and Dr Werner Gabler to give classes in acoustics. The participants were encouraged to create a model of an opera house themselves. Sadly, the architecture course was only offered for this one year – presumably it proved just too complicated to repeat.

'The summer ended this time truly on a highly harmonious and happy note, and we are already drawing up firm plans for next year,' Friedelind wrote in August to Walter Felsenstein with a sense of contentment. 'Many will come again, and I am flooded with applications. So I hope we will once more be able to get a good selection. The highpoint for everyone remained your visit – as well as the visit to Berlin.'[4] One observer wrote to her to say that 'I found it incredibly interesting and highly rewarding to be there. With your master classes you have brought a child into the world which I only hope will grow, blossom and flourish ... it's inherited all it needs for that from you.'[5]

Over the course of the nine years in which the master classes ran, the studies they offered included musical interpretation, opera history and aesthetics, theatre architecture and opera direction. In 1961 the musicologist Edward Downes gave public lectures in German and English on every day of the performances. He had been visiting the Festival for decades, which made him an authority on the history of its productions. But he also offered general lectures in music history. His contributions received an excellent response, unlike those of the psychologist Max Friedlander (not to be confused with the musicologist Friedländer), who proffered obscure interpretations of Wagner's works.[6] Friedelind engaged the singers Astrid Varnay, Hanne-Lore Kuhse, Kurt Winter and Willi Lose to give classes; Pierre Boulez and Gian Carlo Menotti also agreed to come, though in the end a contract was signed with neither of them. Wieland and Wolfgang were prepared to help as well.

The lack of space in Bayreuth meant that the classes took place variously in school classrooms, in a police station, in a tiny theatre and in any rehearsal rooms that happened to be free. Wolfgang had made it clear right from the start that the classes were a private event for which no rooms could be made permanently available. When the pianist Bruce Hungerford arrived, Friedelind immediately recognized his exceptional talent and spontaneously organized piano classes under his direction. She was able to get matinée performances for the particularly gifted participants and the results were often superb. In 1962 the master classes gave a public concert in the Margravial Opera House, with Hungerford at the piano, with the violinist Isidor Lateiner, Lawrence Foster conducting and the three pianists Howard Wells, Peggy Donovan and Patricia Sage. At a Sunday matinée in the Siegfried Wagner House, Isidor Lateiner and his wife Edith played works by Beethoven. Among the many Festival visitors who came along to listen was the authoress Agatha Christie.[7]

The New Zealand journalist and musicologist John Mansfield Thomson (1926–1999) committed his experiences of Bayreuth to paper.[8] As was so often the case, his selection as one of the students for the master classes happened rather by chance. He knew the photographer Helmut Gernsheim (1913–1995), who had been a German refugee interned on the Isle of Man. Friedelind had presumably become acquainted with Gernsheim's wife Alison in the women's camp. She was a photographer like her husband, and together they were among the pioneers of photography. Helmut Gernsheim suggested to Thomson that he should look in on Friedelind when he was in New York. 'It was amazing to see that classic Wagnerian profile for the first time, with those intense blue eyes and her concentrated energy,' he wrote. They played through arrangements of Wagner's music for two pianos and Emmanuel Chabrier's *Souvenirs de Munich* for piano duet, and she took him to a party at Eric Salzman's, the music critic of the *New York Times*. Just as spontaneously as she had invited him into her home she now invited him to take part in her master classes in 1962, even promising him a scholarship. One might perceive a certain recklessness in such swift decisions – but there is no denying that Thomson later became one of the most prominent musicologists of his native New Zealand; he co-founded the renowned journal *Early Music*, wrote a ground-breaking work on the history of music in his country (*The Oxford History of New Zealand Music*) and became a well-loved teacher. Friedelind instinctively recognized his great gifts and charisma.

After arriving in Bayreuth, Thomson was taken straightaway to the Festspielhaus where Wieland was running a lighting rehearsal. After that, Wilhelm Pitz rehearsed the Pilgrims' Chorus from *Tannhäuser*. On their tour of assorted other opera houses, the group travelled to Leipzig to see productions of *Rienzi* and Prokofiev's *War and Peace* – a work that was barely known in the West at the time. In Munich they saw Schoenberg's *Moses und Aron* and Strauss's *Schweigsame Frau*. Operas were at the time being staged in the Prinzregententheater, for the main opera house had been destroyed in the war and would only reopen a year later.

Friedelind was undaunted by the Wall that went up in 1961 between the German Democratic Republic in the East and the Federal Republic of Germany in the West. She still went to East Berlin all the same. At the border she behaved as if it were a well-rehearsed theatrical performance. When a policeman from the East took on dictatorial airs she waved him aside: 'Young man, I had to cope with the Gestapo so you don't impress me.'[9] In the Theater am Schiffbauerdamm in East Berlin they saw Brecht's *Threepenny Opera*, then a day later in the Deutsche Oper in West Berlin they were at rehearsals for Pfitzner's *Palestrina* – their programme could hardly have been more

23 The Austrian opera director Walter Felsenstein was the most prominent
lecturer at the Bayreuth master classes. He and Wieland Wagner both had a major
impact on post-war aesthetic practice in Europe's opera houses.

contrasted. They studied technical developments in theatrical lighting at the company Reiche und Vogel, which had been advising the Festspielhaus in Bayreuth for many years. The visit to the Komische Oper in East Berlin was a particular highpoint. Walter Felsenstein's production of Verdi's *Otello* was utterly compelling, as was a performance of Britten's *Midsummer Night's Dream*, which the group found especially moving. Thanks to Friedelind's good offices, Ella Lee had been given the role of Titania. Felsenstein remained the outstanding lecturer at the master classes, and the discussions that he led left a lasting impression – not least because Friedelind was able to translate the rapid-fire questions and answers back and forth in accent-free English. Thomson went home to New Zealand immensely enriched by the experience and remained grateful to Friedelind for the rest of his life.

Some of Felsenstein's classes have survived on tape, as for example a discussion held on 2 August 1962, which we shall summarize here. The group was astonished at the large number of rehearsals that he insisted upon for his productions, and questioned him about it. For him, a theatre had no right to exist if it only produced repertoire performances – and for this reason he called himself 'anti-state opera' ('Staatsoper-feindlich'), which prompted laughter. As performances went on, meticulous care could help them to attain even higher standards – also because one would thereby recognize new aspects that had not been noticed before. He was unhappy with the repeat performances of his productions of *Traviata* and *Rigoletto* that were running at the time in Hamburg, and was considering having his name withdrawn from them. They had slackened – not outwardly, but inwardly. When asked about the type of audience he had, he said it was difficult to differentiate between a true theatre audience and the 'acoustic audience'. The latter would accept even the worst performances as long as the high notes were right. He could not understand it when people said that this or that production was only 'musically excellent', for he believed that opera only had a single content; an opera was to him 'comprised exclusively of programme music'.

When asked how he chose which operas to direct, he replied that the question of the cast was paramount, but also whether the opera could suit his music-theatrical requirements. By that he meant that he would prefer a work that had been written on account of its real content and not for purely musical motives. Rossini's *Barber of Seville*, for example, was more subtle and more accomplished than the opera by Giovanni Paisiello based on the same Beaumarchais play. For him, it was worth directing a work if he could commit to it in terms of its human content. If you were to perform just for your own pleasure, then you would fail to fulfil the purpose of theatre. Every performance is for the general public, not just for experts in music and theatre. He neither wanted to make concessions to the taste of the masses, nor did he want to 'educate' the public.

How did he find things in the score that other directors missed? There was no particular technique involved, he said. 'If someone is ready and willing to read the work then he will get to know it. But most opera experts are not prepared to do so. They think they know the work. Above all, you need a little humility.' The difficulties begin, he said, when you have to convey to other people what you have learnt from a work. It's not enough just to explain things in words to the singers. You have to have different methods of communicating, for only in the rarest cases is a singer prepared to do so much research and ask questions until he has understood something. It's thus the task of the director to get what's missed by the 'yea-sayer' who just nods his head to all suggestions. 'If a singer only imitates what the director tells him, he's not fit to sing the role. The director can only get out of him what the singer himself doesn't know. Obedience is forbidden.'

Time and again the participants raised the fact that the Komische Oper was in the GDR. Felsenstein said:

> If you derive the word 'political' from 'polis', you can't confuse it with politics. If you understand it as meaning that which concerns the public, then theatre is one of the most political endeavours of them all. It fulfils this political function by offering a means of ethical and moral ennoblement and improvement. It is both dangerous and comfortable to claim that theatre has nothing to do with politics. Theatre has a lot to do with it. Is there a work that is more political than *Otello* or *The Magic Flute*? At the same time, a work of theatre must entertain. It's embarrassing for the public when it's being instructed or has the feeling that it's being told what to think. The public should not just listen, it must be drawn in. I don't mean that you should 'identify' with it, but that you should participate – just as when two people argue and I'm interested in what they're arguing about, then in spirit I'm arguing too.[10]

Such highpoints in the classes could not compensate for Friedelind's immense volume of work, which occasionally led to tension and a tendency on her part to adopt a peremptory tone that others found unpleasant. She was proud of her success. 'But while I was chauffeur, secretary, nurse-maid and what-not to master classes, I had no time to think about someone called Friedelind, who at times is a lecturer and assorted other things. There was not time; I was taken up by a million little things, in order to keep the wheels turning.'[11] She saw that she was doing too much, but was unable to do anything about it. She liked to mediate between different artists wherever she could. Thus on one occasion she conveyed a message from Benjamin Britten to Felsenstein: 'He prefers the original version with 14 instruments, but will happily allow the number to be doubled at those German theatres that perform *Albert Herring*. He simply insists that all the instruments be doubled.'[12]

Friedelind was as little bothered by political sensibilities as her mother. When the Intendant of the Berlin State Opera, Hans Pischner, came to Bayreuth with a delegation from the GDR to lay a wreath at Wagner's grave on his birthday, it caused a commotion. His reputation was that of an excellent musician and someone who was courageous in political/cultural issues, for he maintained the repertoire of his theatre despite opposition from the state. But this did not make Wolfgang or the Mayor of Bayreuth any happier about the 'Delegation from the Eastern Zone', even despite the support that Winifred herself gave the visitors. 'All in vain – neither of them wanted anything to do with the gentlemen.' So Winifred proceeded independently, invited the group to the 'Golden Anchor' restaurant and had to make them understand that 'laying a wreath together with West Germans was not desired' but that they would be allowed to turn up an hour later than the representatives of the city of Bayreuth. 'It's quite impossible!!! People talk constantly of reunification but when feelers are put out a little they pull back like cowards!'[13] Winifred at least did not lack courage, and it was a trait she shared with her daughter.

On 22 May 2009 the magazine supplement of the *Süddeutsche Zeitung* brought an interview with a male couple who had lived together for many decades. Friedelind's name came up in it: 'I spent the summer in Bayreuth, but Friedelind left us stranded in the middle of the night and took the monies that the students had given her for their room rent.'[14] The man speaking was Alfred Kaine, who had attended the master classes in 1961 and had later worked as a pianist with the choreographer John Cranko, at the time the head of ballet at the Württemberg State Opera in Stuttgart. His story is well worth telling, because it was a 'classical' dispute of Friedelind's.

Kaine had been invited to the master classes as a trained pianist. The harpsichordist Igor Kipnis (son of the bass Alexander) had given him the idea, along with the journalist Martin Bernheimer. Friedelind was a friend of Bernheimer, and Kipnis too had known her since his childhood. Friedelind asked Kaine to bring records with him from the USA. In order to transport them he bought a suitcase and paid DM 100 for it. Friedelind could not pay him back straightaway, and afterwards did instead what she always did: she ignored all reminders. Kaine wrote her three letters, and then she could stand it no more. She pointed out that money was tight for her, and reminded him that he had been given a scholarship worth $1250. She could only pay back the money after having paid off her debts and felt he was being ungrateful. 'I have managed to raise DM 18,500 so far in bank loans, which have to be repaid, but am still short of the other DM 21,500 with people closing in from all sides to collect their bills.'[15] From her point of view, her student's request was unethical and impertinent – but for the young pianist, who desperately needed the money, she seemed merely unreliable. Kaine was a penniless student who had been overjoyed to get promises that a job could be found for him – but now Friedelind had brought him rudely back to earth. For her part she had invested all her energies in order to offer something worthwhile to her students and was offended that one of them was now complaining. She used to write to her former students once they had found jobs in order to ask them for donations for the master classes, and Kaine, too, received a begging letter three years later. He took his revenge by putting himself down for DM 100 – the very amount that she had never paid him back and that he had thus already 'donated'.[16] The result was a rift between the two of them that was never mended. In later years they would pass by each other in Bayreuth without exchanging any greeting.

This case typifies the fundamental problem that faced the enterprise. Its director had brilliant ideas but was unable to implement them all properly: first because she insisted on being responsible for everything, and secondly because the whole endeavour right from the start was devoid of any firm financial footing. Friedelind relied on her own intuition and on her many years of experience of dealing with artists. But this meant that she often took decisions based on whims, which in turn created informal hierarchies in her groups of students. When disputes arose she was often unable to deal with them properly. The composer and music theorist Leo Stein – the author in 1950 of the book *The racial thinking of Richard Wagner* – had such a bitter quarrel with her in 1961 that it ruined their relationship for good. The highly intellectual Stein found himself faced with someone emotionally complex and given to vigorous reactions; it was impossible to achieve any conciliation with her. He wrote of her that 'The empathy for understanding another person's point of view or feelings was not developed.'[17] Tom Lipton was a photographer friend of Friedelind's who observed her at close quarters, who was sympathetic to her and who willingly granted that she had in many ways exerted a positive influence on his life. All the same, he summed her up thus: 'Friedelind dropped people immediately in the moment that she felt her leading position or "exclusivity" brought her no more advantages, or when she felt her influence on them was diminishing.'[18] There could be a whole list of psychological reasons for this: her 'naturally' dominant nature, already evident in her childhood, and the constant battle to be loved and accepted by her mother; her lack of a clear career path that might have resulted in a greater desire for recognition; her feeling that as Wagner's granddaughter she *a priori* stood out among others; her years of relative isolation as an émigré, and much more. If one compares Lipton's view with the statements of two of her students, we can get an idea of the sheer scope of her personality: 'In 1961 I thought I had landed in paradise' and 'all of us chosen by her for those Master Classes owe her personal and career debts of a lifetime'.[19] She had the courage to engage the very best in their fields and she remained true to her pursuit of the highest quality. In return she had to deal with endless money squabbles in which, however, her own personal benefit was never involved.

Friedelind's strength was the selfless dedication that she showed in trying to further the careers of her protégés. She fought like a lioness for many of them, and the fact that some of them later enjoyed prominent careers points to her talent for identifying potentially gifted applicants. One of them was the art historian and stage set designer John Dew, born in Cuba in 1944 and resident in New York. He came to Bayreuth in 1966 and later worked as a director's assistant at several German theatres. In 1967 Liselotte Heuberger – Friedelind's friend of many years and the 'chauffeur' for the master classes – helped him to get a position working as Felsenstein's assistant at the Komische Oper in Berlin. He designed sets for a *Magic Flute* in Durban in South Africa and soon after began directing operas himself in Ulm. He then became senior director in Bielefeld, Generalintendant in Dortmund and is currently Intendant at the State Theatre in Darmstadt. 'She wrote to me that someone crazy enough to hitchhike from Oxford to Paris without being sure of actually meeting her there would be just the kind of person who would suit her master class', recalls Dew. The master classes were for him an important factor in his career, with their visits to rehearsals proving the most beneficial aspect.[20] Other participants, such as Jonathan Dudley, were convinced that the master classes showed them the way forward as artists. Dudley grew up in a small North American town, studied conducting and was advised to apply for a place in the master classes. Friedelind invited him to go and see her, and they spoke about everything except music. She accepted him – presumably because she found him likeable and relied on her intuition. Nor did it fail her this time. For Dudley, as with Dew, it was less the tuition than the chance to observe the Bayreuth Festival that was the most important aspect of the classes. In 1961 he attended all the general rehearsals and all the actual performances too, either in the orchestra pit, from behind the stage or in the family box. These experiences remained unforgettable.[21]

The list of artists who attended the master classes and who later rose to success is a long one. Pamela Rosenberg became Intendant of the Berlin Philharmonic. The Hungarian-American conductor Peter Erös was born in 1932, fled his native land during the 1956 Uprising and later worked with the Concertgebouw Orchestra in Amsterdam and as Otto Klemperer's assistant at the Holland Festival. In 1960–61 he was Hans Knappertsbusch's assistant in Bayreuth. Abe Polakoff was an engineer by profession but also studied singing and performed in an amateur operatic society in New York simply because he loved to sing. Friends of Friedelind recommended him to audition for her. 'I never thought that such an opportunity would have such an impact on my later career'. He drove to the Ansonia Hotel; since many musicians used to stay there it happened to have a rehearsal room, and there he sang several arias to Friedelind. She invited him to the master classes on the spot, but since she could not find him a scholarship he was unable to go. Shortly afterwards he won a prestigious singing competition (there were only 5 winners out of 1000 participants), and his prize was an engagement in Milan. Friedelind suggested that he should audition for her brothers in Bayreuth.

> It was clearly an unequivocal boost to my singing career at a very critical period. Now I had to choose between the safe field of steady employment as an engineer and the perilously irregular aspect of the operatic stage. Later, I learned that such encouragement was typical of Friedelind. When she believed in an artist, she reacted like a devoted mother, with total support, never hedging in a commitment.[22]

A year later he managed to get a scholarship to her master classes, and in his later career he sang leading roles at the opera houses of Berlin, Hamburg, Munich, New York and elsewhere. The singer and pianist Patricia Sage took part in 1962 and 1963. She had come to Friedelind's attention thanks to her debut as Grimgerde in the newly established Lyric Opera in Chicago. The master classes gave her so many ideas that she ended up founding a training institution herself. Her theatre project *The American Center for Musical Arts Wagner Theater Project* (ACMA) introduces talented singers to the operatic repertoire, with a focus on the works of Wagner. Singers from minority groups and disadvantaged districts of New York are given preference – the theatre itself is situated in Harlem.

> I am trying with all my heart, passion and commitment to follow in Friedelind's footsteps and give back a little of the incredible gifts she gave to me and to all of us!! I hope this has filled out a few more moments of those wonderful summers in Bayreuth, and the subsequent years when she continued to assist all of us in any way she could – a phenomenal human being, a great artist, a compassionate woman and a wonderful

friend – my memories of her are as colourful as she was, and I owe her a debt that can only be repaid in kind, by continuing to reach out to others in love and sharing of talents!

The conductor Lawrence Foster took part in the master classes in 1961 and 1962. In the late 1960s he worked as a guest conductor with the Royal Philharmonic Orchestra and since then has conducted all the major British and American orchestras. He conducted the world première of Paul McCartney's oratorio *Standing Stone* and is currently the Music Director of the Marseille Opera. The set designer John Conklin enjoyed success on Broadway and became internationally known. The American opera director Siegfried Schoenbohm was given a scholarship for Bayreuth in 1962. From 1966 he worked as Felsenstein's assistant and later directed in Kassel, Freiburg and Heidelberg; he has also directed Wagner's *Ring* in Bonn. Ella Lee, already mentioned above, was honoured as 'Woman of the Year' in California in 1965 and subsequently sang in leading houses in the USA and Europe. Another graduate of Friedelind's was the singer John Moulson, who studied in Atlanta, got to know Felsenstein through the master classes and was engaged by him at the Komische Oper in 1961, where he remained for over 30 years. In 1966 he sang Don Ottavio in Felsenstein's TV production of *Don Giovanni*.

Gretta Harden got an engagement in Flensburg, Patricia Sage in Münster and then in Munich (she owed both engagements to Friedelind's help), Emily McKnight was invited to Lucerne, Betsy Davidson to Heidelberg, Frances Martin to Darmstadt, Coburg and Münster. Isidor Lateiner later played with orchestras such as the Berlin Philharmonic and the Concertgebouw in Amsterdam, and taught at the Conservatory of The Hague.

The director Lotfi Mansouri also profited from his participation in the master classes. He had studied with Lotte Lehmann and others and was recommended to Friedelind when she was looking for someone in Los Angeles to help her deal with applications. She then offered him a scholarship to take part himself, and he gladly seized the chance to observe Wieland's work at close hand. He recalled that 'My time in Bayreuth would prove exhilarating and stimulating – but also frustrating as hell.'[23] As a budding director he was interested primarily in the rehearsals and performances and found himself swept off his feet by the sound of the chorus and orchestra in *Parsifal*. The lectures and seminars interested him less; he disliked having to join the group in a pilgrimage to Wagner's grave and to Winifred (whom the students nicknamed the 'dragon woman'). Nor did he like the lectures by Bob Gutman, whom he felt made Wagner's life into a soap opera. If students skipped the classes, they were punished by being deprived of their tickets to the dress rehearsals – though Mansouri managed to smuggle himself in several times nonetheless.

According to one of her students, it was Friedelind's dream to discover a real, world-class talent among them.[24] She finally succeeded in Michael Tilson Thomas, who went on to enjoy a major career as a conductor. He liked Friedelind a lot, which was probably because he found her just as 'passionately eccentric' as he was himself. In Bayreuth he was asked to jump in as a répétiteur at the last minute. He helped Pierre Boulez with his production of *Parsifal* and was soon taken on permanently, which was a great honour for such a young musician. It was thus in Bayreuth that he got to know the Wagner repertoire. Friedelind engaged him to give a piano recital in Wahnfried devoted exclusively to modern music (Ives, Copland and others), for which he had to 'practise like mad.'[25] In 1971, when Tilson Thomas was just 26, the *New York Times* published a long, euphoric report about his meteoric career.

Friedelind promoted the careers of her lecturers, too, whenever she could. In 1966 she arranged a guest engagement in the USA for Hanne-Lore Kuhse and asked her friends to distribute publicity material about her 'strategically' in the Philadelphia area. When Kuhse gave a song recital in Bayreuth, Friedelind decided to have it recorded as an LP.

In January 1961 Friedelind found that she had until May to find $25,000. She did not want to go begging to the big foundations any more, but preferred to remain independent. 'The more I think about it, the less I want Ford money,' she said.[26] Was this perhaps to cover herself for fear of rejection? Later on she revised her opinion. 'I got myself into a nice hole – by being too proud to apply for funds from foundations... I certainly shall never be quite so proud and independent again, I have learnt my lesson!'[27] But for the moment her stubbornness proved disastrous, for the deficit only grew. Wolfgang was planning to deduct her expenditure from her inheritance, for she was continually leaving bills unpaid that then found their way onto his desk. Since Wolfgang was pragmatic by nature, her erratic behaviour was torture to him. In order to drum up money, her 'pianist in residence' Bruce Hungerford recorded Wagner's piano works on two LPs that were sold to the master class support association at $25.[28] But the production of the LPs proved so costly that Friedelind only ended 'up to my neck in debts.'[29] So she borrowed money from Winifred and sent the proceeds from the sales back to her as they came in.[30]

In her nonchalant fashion she often just had her bills in the Festival restaurant chalked up – but then disappeared at the end of the season without paying them.[31] Since she had a gift for handling the media and had good relations with the music journalists at the *Times*, *New York Herald Tribune*, *Opera News* and *Saturday Review*, she hoped that their support would get her better known and that sponsorship money would then flow all the more easily. Somehow she was able to keep her master classes afloat; but they simply lacked any kind of professional management. Why did she have to organize the students' accommodation herself? Why did she travel with them to East Berlin instead of delegating the task to someone else now and then? Why did she correspond with every individual applicant? It was not because her brothers were unwilling to help, but because she wanted to keep control of everything and was simply unable to delegate. Financing her project was important to her, but money considerations never overwhelmed her artistic ideals. On the contrary, money remained for her a means to an end; she never hoarded it or allowed herself personal luxury. This should have been explained to Alfred Kaine, just as Friedelind should have learnt not to use others, especially when they were themselves dependent on every dollar they could get. Such instances of a mutual lack of insight were responsible for many emotional scars.

If one takes stock of these master class years overall, their impact was highly positive. In 1965, for example, the students were able to hear and see world-class singers such as Birgit Nilsson, Wolfgang Windgassen, Leonie Rysanek, Hans Hotter and Jess Thomas under the baton of Karl Böhm and André Cluytens. They had discussions with Walter Felsenstein after attending performances that he directed in the Komische Oper in Berlin, and they saw the rehearsals of Wieland's now legendary *Tristan* with its superb lighting direction and sets inspired by the sculptor Henry Moore. Wieland's 18-year-old nephew Gottfried was deeply impressed, though he recalls becoming almost painfully aware of the chasm that lay between Wieland's artistic achievements as a director and his own father's efforts. Where else in the world did young, up-and-coming artists have the opportunity to experience at first hand an efficiently organized musical institution with a worldwide reputation, and at such close quarters? Here they were able to devote themselves to an intensive study of Wagner's work, and many of them realized that his music is central for an understanding of western music as a whole.

In these years Friedelind lived only for her master classes. She was often in the USA and continued to advertise them there. In May 1963, for example, she travelled to Vancouver, Los Angeles, San Francisco and Chicago, giving 15 lectures, eight radio talks and two TV interviews alongside auditioning applicants.[32] Wieland was planning a trip to the USA since he intended to direct there, and Friedelind had already organized a banquet for the 'Friends of the Master Classes' so that they could have a discussion with him.[33] But he took ill and had to be hospitalized. He was able to leave his Munich clinic in the autumn and go back to Wahnfried, but he soon had to return to hospital.

Friedelind had been oblivious as to the seriousness of his illness and visited him in Munich just days before his death – she was the only family member to see him before the end except for his wife Gertrud, who was there on the day he passed away. 'I saw how hopeless his state is, but was the only one among his family and friends who did. I lied heroically and with success!' It was a huge shock to everyone to realize that Wieland was incurably sick.

The summer of 1966, while Wieland lay dying, was a challenging time for Friedelind. 'No one from the master classes knew about it – only once in this time did she let her guard down, otherwise she had her private feelings completely under control,' wrote one of her students.[34] Wieland died of lung cancer on 17 October 1966. His marriage had long since disintegrated, though he was not yet divorced, and after the official funeral ceremony Friedelind demonstratively went to his partner, the singer Anja Silja. She had been shunned by the children of Wieland and Gertrud – understandably – and later recalled that 'I was not allowed to accompany him on the way to the graveyard. I went later, together with Friedelind Wagner, who had of her own accord come back from the private funeral to fetch me and take me to the grave. A few townspeople from Bayreuth were still there, as well as a photographer who was lying in wait for me.'[35]

At Christmas Friedelind invited Silja to join her at Nussdorf, where she sought and found comfort among Verena and her family. Such behaviour was typical of Friedelind, who retained a lifelong fondness for non-conformists and for those who lived against the grain. Her friendship with Anja Silja remained until she died. At this time Friedelind gave an interview to the *Times*, in which she described her brother's productions as 'trend-setting' and that there was no going back from them. But she also remained critical and rejected any notion of 'canonising' his work, or of standardizing his ideas in any way. She was convinced that he still wanted to expand his style, and so no one could regard what he left behind as in anyway definitive. 'The essence of Wieland's work is that he was trying to get to the core of everything he produced. He asks the questions we weren't ever allowed to ask ourselves in the past, and our human problems remain the same.' She detected a deep sense of pessimism in his work, and quoted him thus: 'My generation had no reason to be optimistic.'[36] The two siblings had experienced the Second World War from different perspectives, but had reached similar conclusions. The press once more praised his courage in breaking with traditional Wagnerian aesthetics and in committing himself to a new beginning in 1951. The weekly newspaper *Die Zeit* wrote that so-called modern opera interpretation since 1950 had manifested itself at home and abroad 'between Walter Felsenstein's realistic and Wieland Wagner's visionary-psychological epic music theatre.'[37] Both were placed on the same pedestal, and they each had a similar impact on the opera aesthetic of these years.

For Friedelind, Wieland's death was as sudden a shock as it was for the whole music world. She felt a painful void after Wieland's death. 'It sounds terrible but I really don't know what I can or should write to Mama. The distance between us seems greater and more unbridgeable than ever – and the farewell was truly eerie, with Wolf in the Festspielhaus, Gertrud in Wahnfried, Mama in her house – to leave this group of three behind was downright intimidating.' She had also learnt that Winifred would contemplate no one but Wolfgang as Wieland's successor: 'Mama thinks that he is the only one who is competent and she is already looking forward to a new, golden, Tietjen era.'[38]

The master classes continued for one more year after Wieland's death, until Wolfgang acquired sole control of Bayreuth. 'In 1967 there were so many debts and I had taken on so many private guarantees for Friedelind that the master class project ended without a murmur in the midst of a complete financial and organizational disaster,' he wrote.[39] The master classes were indeed weighed down by money worries. By 1966, Friedelind had to admit that her credit with the banks was exhausted. She lost some of her lecturers because they had to wait too long for their money. She had even been served with a default summons for the rental and transport costs for two grand pianos in 1965 after having simply ignored the bill for two years.[40] Wolfgang's abrupt cancellation of the classes made it easy for her to put all the blame on him, though she bore responsibility on account of her financial negligence. Wolfgang also accused her of grandiosely declaring that the master classes had ceased to be of interest after Wieland's death. In his autobiography *Lebens-Akte* he wrote with some annoyance that 'This tone and interpretation were just like those used by other members of my family whenever something happened in and around Bayreuth that did not go according to their own wishes.'[41]

At the same time, Friedelind had to stand by and watch how her mother sold her house in Oberwarmensteinach and gave the profit to Bodo Lafferentz (DM 100,000). Shortly before this, Winifred had bequeathed her house in Nussdorf to Verena. Friedelind went empty-handed. However, there is no hint anywhere that it angered her – she simply took it all in her stride.

Back in the USA, Friedelind watched with fascination how a whole generation of singers was being overtaken, slowly but surely, by younger performers such as Marilyn Horne and Joan Sutherland. In 1966 the Metropolitan Opera decided to move its home to the Lincoln Center. Before the old building was torn down there was a gala evening. The festivities began with dinner in the opera house at 6 p.m. and finished at 2 a.m. after the last numbers were sung.

Friedelind was a guest of honour with a free ticket – at $200 a head she would otherwise never have been able to afford to go.

> On Saturday we buried the old Met. It was an indescribable circus – 60 old stars and 60 current ones. The old ones marched in to the jubilation and delight of the roaring public, one after the other, alphabetically. They started with Marian Anderson, then Lotte Lehmann, Elisabeth Rethberg and others. Then came the parade of singing primadonnas and primesignori – and each primadonna naturally tried to outdo the others in matters of wardrobe and jewellery. It was wonderfully comic! Almost all of them were like circus horses.[42]

Friedelind's relationship with Lotte Lehmann was still complicated. Perhaps there was an element of competition between them, for Lehmann was also organizing her own master classes. Lehmann lived in Santa Barbara, and when Friedelind once stayed not far away in California, she wrote 'Since she is always only unfriendly to me I didn't visit her. She's more or less the queen there – but what do I care!'[43]

In the vacuum that existed for several months after Wieland's unexpected death, it was unclear whether Wolfgang would actually take over the whole Festival himself. Friedelind was convinced that there were enough highly qualified, talented individuals in the next generation of Wagners. She described them all as musical and interested in stage design and directing, and was of the opinion that they could jump in at any time.[44]

Her brother-in-law Bodo also wrote to Wolfgang with a suggestion for the Bayreuth succession. 'Verena would like the female family members to be considered too, not just the male members, insofar as they possess the necessary talent and are suited for this difficult office.' Verena repeatedly tried to help her sister, but Wolfgang blocked everything. At long last he wanted to exercise sole control over all the possibilities that the Festival offered. He was of the opinion that his sisters should have no say at all in managing the Festival, and he felt the same way towards his own children and those of Wieland.

Wolfgang finally decided to consider neither Wolf Siegfried, Nike, Eva nor Gottfried for the succession – and certainly not his sister Friedelind – but to go it alone. At a press conference he referred to the memorandum of association that he and Wieland had agreed upon in 1962. If one of the brothers were to die, the other would manage the Festival alone and pay a monthly pension to support the dependents of the other. Wolfgang was thus able to use his responsibilities towards the Wieland clan to justify his position. It was his chance to emerge from out of the shadow cast by his exceptionally talented brother, and develop his own ideas. Wolfgang announced that he would be giving more space to outside directors and mentioned that he was negotiating with August Everding and Giorgio Strehler. He also hinted darkly at the unpalatable possibility – which he had to prevent – that the Wagner estate could be split up after the death of his mother, who was the sole prior heir and owner of the Festival.

As for the master classes, Friedelind didn't doubt for a moment that they would continue. Still in Bayreuth, she organized interviews with applicants in New York and announcements in the press. She was delighted to read an article in the *Times* that praised her classes, and used it in her programme brochure. She hoped for further income from allowing interested tourists to attend the classes as observers. And her recording of Wagner's piano works was now selling rather well.[45] But the gap between income and expenditure remained vast and unchanged. Now was the time to deal with it. A newspaper in northern Germany wrote:

> As for the opinion uttered by Friedelind Wagner that she had made a significant contribution, both politically and financially, to the fact that the Festival was able to take place again after the war, Wolfgang said that he had no desire to diminish his sister's missionary zeal. But the facts did not necessarily speak in her favour. Since Friedelind set up her Festival master classes, they had provided DM 5000 for the Festival. 'That is less than 0.08% of what our real sponsors from the Society of Friends of Bayreuth have gathered over the same period.'[46]

That blow hit home. The Festival Director now insisted on a 'review of the contractual relationships and the loyalty of the so-called master classes with regard to the Festival.' This was a kiss of death, for in his insistence on solidarity Wolfgang was banking on Friedelind's inability to keep her opinions to herself. It was well known that her strong points did not include demonstrations of tact or of consideration to others. The end of the master classes was a heavy blow to her, for she had invested heart and soul in them. She also became bitter because Wolfgang had supposedly done everything 'to ruin us financially. Thus in the last two years I had to buy tickets to the value of DM 22,000 because my students would otherwise have been unable to see any performances. In the early years we were always given free tickets for seats on the steps into the stalls or up by the lighting platforms.'[47] Quite apart from the painful loss of her mission in life, she also had to endure having her younger brother show her quite clearly who was now the lord of the manor.

Chapter 14

Sibling conflict
1967 to 1970

IT WAS ALL OVER. In 1967 the master classes took place for the last time, after which Friedelind was once more an outsider, just as she had been in New York in 1941. She did not belong, was without a real home and yet again had to build a new life for herself. To make matters worse, the 'Nationaldemokratische Partei Deutschlands' (NPD), a new far-right party founded in Germany in late 1964, had managed to achieve a respectable 13.6% of the vote in Bayreuth. It offered a home to numerous ex-Nazis, and Winifred was delighted: 'Well – the result of the elections was a real surprise – let's hope that the representatives of the NPD now prove themselves too. It's really time to muck things out!'[1]

What's more, a former prominent Nazi called Hans Severus Ziegler was busy giving a series of lectures at the Bayreuth adult education centre (the 'Volkshochschule'). He had organized the infamous Nazi exhibition of 'Degenerate music' in 1938 and had, in 1964, published his anecdotal book *Hitler aus dem Erleben*, in which the 'Führer' is portrayed as a cultured, intellectually interested man. After the book's publication the city of Bayreuth banned Ziegler from giving any more lectures, so Winifred invited him instead along with 80 other interested parties.[2] Her daughter was annoyed to see how Winifred continued her old friendships with Nazi enthusiasts and made no secret of it. Edda Goering, Ilse Hess, Gerdy Troost (the wife of the Nazi architect Paul Ludwig Troost and herself an architect) all called on her regularly. Her other guests included the controversial film director Leni Riefenstahl, who had glorified the Nazi Party gatherings in Nuremberg, the British fascist leader Oswald Mosley, and the current NPD leader Adolf von Thadden. Ziegler also belonged to her inner circle. She also met Ernst Röchling, whose father, the industrialist Hermann Röchling, had been close to Hitler and had joined the armaments advisory committee of the Army Ministry. Both father and son had been arrested after the war on account of their Nazi affiliations, but were soon set free again.

While Winifred did not hesitate to make her convictions known, Friedelind was naturally just as vociferous in her politics, which were diametrically opposed to those of her mother. In September 1965 there was an anti-Grass demonstration in Bayreuth. The writer Günter Grass had become politically involved with the German socialist party, the SPD, and the party leader Willy

Brandt had been challenged by hecklers at a political meeting to 'withdraw his confidence from the noisy, politicking poet'. Brandt had no such intention and instead appeared at the demonstration along with Grass and other illustrious guests including Hans Werner Henze, Fritz Kortner, Ingeborg Bachmann, Bernard Wicki and Friedelind; together they turned the event into 'a real media spectacle'.[3]

Winifred was also a firm supporter of her surviving son. During the Festival she shooed her daughter out of the family box – Friedelind had yet again invited too many friends and had herself taken a seat reserved for someone else. In June 1967 Winifred had written to Verena to complain about a conversation that Friedelind had had with the Mayor of the city. She had wanted to thank him for her German driving licence, and according to Winifred she had then 'claimed that her brother was now giving free rein to his hatred of Wieland! The Mayor rightly felt that this remark was directed against the responsible director of the Festival, a remark that if expressed in public could only do damage. So he immediately informed Wolfgang.' She felt that they should refrain from any public statements of opinion for tactical reasons, because the financial well-being of Wieland's family depended on Wolfgang running the Festival. Winifred's lease contract would also lapse if the Festival were not run by a family member. She would never contemplate the idea that Friedelind might take over the post. 'Anything that makes Wolfgang's work more difficult – which could even perhaps lead to the ruin of the Festival business – would be sawing off the branch on which we're sitting.' Wieland had endeavoured to exclude Wolfgang from all artistic work in Bayreuth, she wrote, 'and for a while the Mayor and many members of the Friends of Bayreuth made themselves into his mouthpiece – and in this regard were quite outspoken to me too'. Now these gentlemen had understood that the equal treatment of the two brothers, as determined by the contract, had been sensible. She suspected that Anja Silja had influenced Friedelind. Silja had left Bayreuth, she said, because while Wolfgang had offered her the roles she had hitherto sung, he had not offered her that of Eva in the *Meistersinger*. Friedelind – according to Winifred – had interpreted this as an expression of Wolfgang's hatred of Wieland. And she finished her letter with what was most important to her: 'at least during the Festival itself we must maintain our solidarity in the face of the OUTSIDE WORLD'.[4] Winifred filled five pages with her concerns, and sent a copy of the letter to Friedelind.

The atmosphere could hardly have been worse between Friedelind on the one side and her mother and brother on the other. Friedelind now claimed that in 1938 her mother had wanted to give Hitler all the family's Wagner autographs. There is no proof of this, and her brother-in-law Bodo Lafferentz, who tried to mediate, asked her to drop the accusation. 'It would have been a completely senseless gift and would have *de facto* ended in a nationalization of the archive. A detour through Hitler back then would have been pointless and unnecessary, for Hitler could only have given everything to the state ... So if you don't have concrete proof, desist from the accusation.'[5] Friedelind could not offer any proof, but continued to insist that she had heard it all herself. She had even, she said, asked her British friend Lady Cholmondeley to provide a good lawyer in order to take appropriate action against it.

Friedelind also requested a precise catalogue of the holdings in the family archive. The rough list that existed at the time was insufficiently precise for her. She will have been pleased at one particular success in official Wagner research: 30 years after the attempt to set up a Wagner centre under the auspices of Bayreuth (primarily directed against 'the Jews' who were supposedly working systematically to undermine the composer[6]), the Volkswagenwerk Foundation appointed the renowned musicologist Carl Dahlhaus to set up a historical, critical, complete edition of Wagner's works.

1968 was a notable year for Friedelind because she was invited for the first-ever time to direct an opera in Germany. The niece of the General Music Director Bernhard Conz had proposed inviting her to direct in Bielefeld. Since Conz had engaged Patricia McGee, who had participated in Friedelind's master classes, he wrote that 'as I also have good personal relations to the house of Wahnfried, I could imagine getting Friedelind Wagner to direct *Lohengrin*. Even if it brings with it a certain artistic risk – which would not be great, since I would be involved myself – I think that we could achieve a sensation with it in the best sense of the word.'[7] When the contract was drawn up, Friedelind made two conditions: she wanted to work with the singers of the house ensemble, not with stars drafted in for the occasion, and she wanted two whole months for rehearsals. Her fee was DM 3500 plus expenses. It was her first opportunity to direct an opera on German soil, if only in a city of 200,000 inhabitants. She prepared the sets with her assistants, rehearsed with the singers and worked out all details of the production.

Friedelind utilized the media to organize a flood of advance notices. Back in 1946 she had criticized, in print, the American productions of *Lohengrin*. The opera's historical context was just as important to her as its dramaturgical logic. Ortrud was often depicted as a 'Gypsy' instead of the noble daughter of a king, and Telramund was mostly a gloomy older man with a black wig and black beard. But Friedelind insisted that he was no villain, rather the innocent victim of a power-hungry woman. 'Telramund is weak, but not evil.' She was also annoyed when Elsa was dressed differently from the chorus. The miracle, she felt, was that Lohengrin immediately knew who she was in the first act, without being able to recognize her by her costume. She also noted that the action took place in Antwerp in the tenth century, 'and not in the land of a thousand-and-one nights'.[8]

Back in the USA in the 1940s it had seemed strange to her just how little opera directors had understood of the work. She, on the other hand, knew Wagner's articles, letters and stage directions quite precisely. She was annoyed that many opera houses used old, shabby sets time and again. She often found the costumes inappropriate, as well as the appearance of the singers themselves. She felt equally indebted to Wagner's work and to Wieland's style.[9] 'I am trying to present the timelessness of a Jungian interpretation – that is what appeals to me most. Of course Wieland is my great role model. I want to continue in his line of thought and hope that I don't stand still, but move onward.'[10] She often expressed the opinion that one cannot 'freeze' operas as the old guard used to play them, though at the same time she insisted that the tendency to sweep everything away was not in the spirit of Wagner. So, true to this dual conviction, she tried to find a middle road. In a lecture she described herself and all members of the Wagner family as typical mavericks, non-conformists who served art and art alone. In her work, she said, she had the same goal as her brother Wieland: she wanted a deep psychological approach to the fate of Wagner's characters. She offered examples from Wieland's productions, using colour slides. Besides the spiritual and religious content, it was the human beings and the gods with their earthly prejudices that were important to her. She would close by emphasizing her eagerness for her grandfather's work to live on – not just bound to tradition, but as something that pointed beyond its own time.[11]

Friedelind continued her running battles with Wolfgang in an article in the *Spiegel* that was published shortly before her opening night. She chatted openly as was her wont, claiming that Wolfgang's production at the recent Festival had made of *Lohengrin* an amusing *Singspiel* and that his work had been 'without any clear concept'. The *Spiegel* quoted her as saying that her Telramund would have to act 'as power-hungry and as weak as my brother Wolfgang', and it continued that 'this director [i.e. Friedelind] loves barbed comments and delights in satirical slogans against the family piety, and took her mother Winifred as her model for the heathen schemer Ortrud'.[12] That was her answer to Wolfgang having cancelled her master classes with their mother's sanction.

Since her sets and costumes were not allowed to exceed the financial and technical restraints of the Bielefeld stage, the Deutsche Oper in Berlin allowed her to buy 100 chorus costumes that barely needed to be altered, at a knock-down price. What Bielefeld could not offer, she procured herself, such as light-

ing fixtures – 'There weren't enough of them. So I ran up debts' – or money for
the production itself. 'I think DM 6500 were budgeted, but that's a joke. The
local society of friends of the theatre and concert jumped in with DM 2000. I
scraped the rest together myself.'[13] She would probably even have been ready
to invest her own money to achieve the results she wanted in her production
– if she had possessed any money.

Bernhard Conz was delighted with the sets.

> I have no doubts at all: this design and no other must be realized with
> all possible means. You either love these sets straightaway or hate them.
> Thank God I loved them from the first moment. You, dear Frau Wagner,
> have already achieved something that I believe is fundamental: Wieland
> Wagner's ideas and his concept are here not imitated or rehashed, but
> taken forward in a consistent manner. You have succeeded in remaining
> 'modern' in the best sense of the word, and I don't mean 'trendy', but
> a concept that has grown from out of our life and our relation to our
> time.[14]

The *Spiegel* wrote: 'This *Lohengrin*, says Bielefeld's General Music Director
Bernhard Conz, "will bring a fresh breeze to our opera". With this fresh breeze,
hopes Friedelind Wagner, "other directing jobs will follow. For I never wanted
to do anything other than direct".'[15]

Friedelind had observed the canonization of Wieland's work with scepticism, for she believed that he was still developing and deepening his style and
had died too soon. 'It is difficult for men to grow up in the shadow of so colos-
sal a grandfather as hers and to be musicians. In a sense, she believes Richard
Wagner is the enemy of his brilliant grandsons, and resentment of his over-
powering stature, she feels, was at the heart of many of Wieland's scathing
references to Bayreuth in the past.'[16] Perhaps she was herself also grappling with
matters from the past and wanted to distance herself from Tietjen's old *Lohengrin* production back in Bayreuth in 1936. He had endeavoured to achieve a
heroic telling of the tale in which it was not Elsa's fate that was central, but 'the
might of the whole German empire in its struggle against the enemy in the east',
as a reviewer of the time wrote.[17] The heroic was far from what she wanted. She
altered Elsa's role inasmuch as she asked her beloved the famous question out
of fear for him, not out of curiosity. To Friedelind, it was Elsa's tragedy that she
was constantly afraid for him, and it was this fear that brought her down. She
avoided pathologising Telramund; he was not drawn unsympathetically. There
was little movement in her production. The chorus was intended to comment
on the action and walked ceremoniously across the stage (oddly, Friedelind

24 Friedelind directed *Lohengrin* in Bielefeld in 1968, receiving praise
from the audience but condemnation from the critics.
It remained her only production in Germany.

had once complained about a *Rienzi* production that Wieland had directed in
Stuttgart, saying that the chorus had 'once more had to stand there like a herd
of sheep, uniform in its costumes and in its movements').[18]

The opening night on 1 January 1968 was hotly anticipated. The record
producer Isabella Wallich, Friedelind's friend from her youth, travelled across
from England to be there. She knew how important it was to Mausi to fulfil at
last her deeply felt calling and direct an opera. '[Friedelind] was fully aware that
it was unlikely that her brother Wolfgang would ever give her this opportunity
in Bayreuth. The portals there were tightly closed and, in any case, Mausi was
persona non grata there because of her anti-Nazi activities during the war,'
wrote Wallich.[19] She was aware of Friedelind's nervous anxiety and that she
could barely keep her excitement in check; she also felt that the tension was a
result of her isolation. The conductor Wyn Morris came across from England,
as did many other friends. Her sister Verena was also in attendance. Isabella
Wallich found the production truly beautiful. She was struck by the warm
colours that suggested a gentler side of Wagner. The costumes and sets were
simple; the colours were pastel, and they suited the overall concept.

The sets were designed by the young artist Dacre Punt and comprised
several long plastic tubes that formed two large concave strips and suggested
the curves of a swan. Later, they rose up to form the cathedral and the bridal

chamber too. The chorus represented the people and was static, like a Greek chorus. The swan itself did not appear, but was a light projection.[20] The opening night prompted stormy applause at the close that lasted a long time. There was a large-scale party afterwards. The relief felt by Friedelind's friends turned to enthusiasm at her success.

It is hardly possible to judge a production when one only has reviews to go on, not least because in this case Bayreuth had spread its tentacles far into the media world. Everyone who knew Wolfgang was aware that he would not allow his sister any success. His broad network among journalists seems to have worked. 'You can't underestimate the influence of Bayreuth in the opera scene,' said one man who knew it all too well.[21] When asked about Bayreuth's influence, Verena Lafferentz said: 'It's always nasty to have to say how extensive my brother's influence was with the press. But since my father Siegfried also often got a bad press despite his great success, Friedelind was used to it.'[22] Besides this supposedly malign influence, there was also the usual malice often shown towards women in management positions at the time. Horst Koegler wrote a biting criticism of the direction by this 'dearest *enfant terrible* of the Wagner family'. The choreography, he said, was 'recognizably an illegitimate daughter of Isadora Duncan and Gertrud Wagner', and as for the direction, 'the lady has capitulated'. As if this were not enough, he mentions having heard, amidst the cheers and applause, the cry 'Friedelind, go home!' (in English), and he closed by remarking that 'like Elsa I cannot guarantee whether I really heard it or not'. Had the critic not taken the trouble to consider what 'go home' meant to a former émigré, who after her departure from her native land was truly at home neither there, nor in her chosen country of residence?

Almost all the critics were unanimous in finding the singers outstanding – which was surely also thanks to Friedelind's intensive rehearsals – and praised Bernhard Conz for the masterly efforts of the orchestra. Heinz Joachim wrote a laudatory review in *Die Welt*: 'Her readiness to take risks is to be admired no less than the courage shown by this theatre in engaging in an experiment that demanded the very utmost of everyone involved.'[23]

Wolfgang had stayed away from the production, but was convinced that it was bad. 'The woman has directed her first opera at the age my brother was when he died, at 48 and three-quarters. If she waits to direct her second opera until she is 99 and a half, then it will be well. But she should cease claiming that I, her brother, produce only shit.'[24] The critic of *Die Zeit*, Heinz Josef Herbort, criticized Friedelind for having copied Wolfgang's ideas – and the very ideas she had herself criticized often enough:

Without the New Bayreuth of her brothers Wieland and Wolfgang, Friedelind Wagner would not cope. She takes on Wolfgang's almost oratorio-like statuesque quality, the crippling symmetry, the measured steps of the men (the whole cast seems glum, for they're po-faced all the time) and of the ladies of the castle (who are obviously very religious as they're always folding their hands). She follows last year's efforts by her brother at times even in the way her figures are positioned, often in their gestures. But Frau Wagner also goes her own way – albeit a strange way. Ortrud, the heathen woman, now and then waves beseechingly and threateningly with a staff covered in runes, thus compensating for the monotony of the gestures.

The critic of the *Abendzeitung* in Munich wrote that Friedelind organized her characters like marionettes: 'The scene remains almost bourgeois,' he wrote, 'a cabinet of Brabantine waxworks.' Far removed from the green hill of Bayreuth, she had been tested and found wanting; her direction had proven to be 'gauche, devoid of inspiration, almost amateurish.'

Since Lohengrin appeared to Elsa only as a dream figure and the love between the two was an illusion, Herbort commented that 'after all this, Friedelind Wagner's own dreams of directing in Bayreuth are presumably at best an illusion too.'[25] The critic of the *Rheinische Post* wrote of a 'mish-mash of designs that don't fit together – "light organ effects" and "op art effects".' The chorus 'stood and stared into nothingness,' while Ortrud 'behaved like an opera student at an audition.' One can only imagine Wolfgang's delight and the degree of hurt that Friedelind must have felt in the face of such mockery. The 'publicity hungry *enfant terrible* from the USA' was truly hauled over the coals. The sets of her student and assistant Dacre Punt were subjected to biting irony by just about everyone,[26] which is difficult to fathom, given the high degree of praise they had enjoyed from the director of the opera house itself.

Friedelind's old friend Frida Leider had read a positive review somewhere and sent her heartfelt congratulations: 'I was truly happy to read of your big success with *Lohengrin* and hope that you will be able to expand on it. Do you really want to tear yourself apart again for Bayreuth? Forgive my butting in, but it would be cleverer if you would continue your magnificent, fruitful work. I can only sigh! I love you as much as ever.'[27]

Had Friedelind taken on too much with her directing ambitions? The predominantly negative response to her first and only directing job in Germany might have been unjust and even a result of pressure exerted from Bayreuth, but there is no doubt that she also lacked experience. A comparison with Wieland's training demonstrates the chasm that separated them. Wieland was

able to start experimenting with sets for *Parsifal* in 1937. In 1940 he decided
to engage the conductor Kurt Overhoff as his mentor and worked through all
of Richard Wagner's works with him. They analysed the scores bar by bar until
the student knew their musical syntax inside out. He could hardly have chosen
a better teacher: Overhoff's music theory books were among the prime literature for conductors, musicologists and theatre professionals,[28] and he will
have explained every detail to Wieland. To be sure, Overhoff tends to stress
the mythical aspect of everything and ignores the societal factors that moti-
vated Wagner, but he does offer deep musical insights into the music dramas.
Wieland was thrust into the real world of the theatre in 1943 when Goebbels helped him to get a post as a director in the Landestheater in Altenburg.
Goebbels even gave an extra 120,000 reichsmarks so that Wieland could direct
a production of the *Ring des Nibelungen*.[29] Wagner's grandson could hardly
have enjoyed more ideal conditions for his apprenticeship. If we count the
operas that he directed in Nuremberg, then, altogether in 1943 and 1944, he
directed nine operas for which he was also responsible for the set designs. He
was thus able to move into the professional world of opera direction and draw
on both his extensive observation of everything in Bayreuth and on his own
gifts as a painter. While Wolfgang had to be satisfied with assisting rehearsals
and learning stage organization at the Berlin State Opera, his older brother
was already trying everything out in practice on his own.

Wieland continued his work after the end of the war, devouring all the
books he could. In Nussdorf, where he stayed after the cessation of hostilities,
he studied Wagner's works with a view to their dramaturgical aspects and
discussed his ideas with his wife Gertrud and his sister Verena. He often sat
with Gertrud on the floor in Nussdorf and drew Verena and Bodo into discussions of the psychology of the characters in Wagner's dramas, though they
mostly discussed how that psychology might be translated into movement and
gesture. Gertrud played a far more significant role than is usually recognized,
and with her training in choreography she was able to demonstrate different
possibilities. Wieland would also at times ask Verena how a particular scene
had been played on the Bayreuth theatre, since her memory proved more
reliable than his.[30]

It is in Wieland's light experiments that we can observe the fruits of these
years of engaging directly with the material. He was meticulous in devising
these, and they helped to ensure his international fame. His stage depictions
were intended to probe psychological depths and were so far removed from
all realism that they almost led to a dissolution of all scenic contours. Wieland
prompted many objections but also earned the highest possible praise.
Although he called himself an 'autodidactic enthusiast', he utilized light and

colour in an ingenious manner to give form and atmosphere to the music and the drama. 'Clouds mustn't just appear and disappear; they must form out of haze and dissolve into mist. The colour of a costume is as important as the sound of a violin. A false shade is as painful to me as a sour note is to a conductor.'[31] The lighting system was installed after the war. Bayreuth now possessed a new cyclorama: above the stage there was a huge apparatus that could produce hundreds of light effects, and then there were 40 film projectors and floodlights for particularly intensive lighting that Wolfgang was able to manage thanks to his technical expertise.

Bielefeld was far removed from all this. Friedelind had to make do with the simplest of equipment and auxiliary constructions. The only experience she had to draw on was of having directed individual acts of works back in the USA. She had attended innumerable performances, but while Wieland was studying with Overhoff she had been interned in Britain or was eking out a living in the USA with secretarial jobs. If she had been allowed a testing ground for her own directing ideas after the war, then she would have grown into the profession. But she had overreached herself with her *Tristan* project, in which her attempt to do everything at once – the planning, the direction, the touring and the overall organization – had simply failed. One could accuse her of having bitten off far more than anyone could chew when planning her *Tristan*. But there is no denying that the fiasco in which it had ended had allowed her brothers to overtake her in matters of experience, up to a point where she could never hope to catch up.

In 1968 a legal dispute between Winifred and the State of Bavaria went to the appeal court in which the Wagner family would lose the case. They had protested against involving Bayreuth in the 'law to protect German cultural artefacts' that prohibited the export of important cultural goods. The family presumably wanted to sell individual items from their archives in order to make some quick money. There were long and difficult negotiations in which it transpired that the family would barely be able to demand any income from the Festspielhaus because the public authorities had already invested so much in it. Nor would a sale of Wahnfried bring much money either, because renovations would soon be necessary to it. The only item of real value was the comprehensive Wagner Archive, which was worth an estimated DM 7.5 million.

Money – or, rather, the lack of it – was thus the reason for a family conference that was held in January 1968 just after the run of Friedelind's *Lohengrin* ended. The problems were no longer Friedelind's alone, for Gertrud now needed money, and so did even Verena and Bodo, whose businesses were not doing well. Winifred, too, was running short. One year earlier she had stipulated in her will that the family archives should be entrusted to a foundation in order to prevent individual family members taking out specific items and selling them – it was a clever decision on her part that ensured the future of the archival holdings. But the family members were far from unanimous. Friedelind was at first against her mother's plan to transfer all the family assets into a foundation (Wahnfried, the Festspielhaus etc.). She and Verena did not want to give up their interest in the Festival in exchange for money, but wanted to remain involved in matters as direct heirs and to find a way in which the younger generation could one day take over the whole inheritance.[32] This was bound to lead to a dispute with Wolfgang. 'The whole meeting (on 6 January 1968) climaxed in a gigantic row, with Wolfgang going into a rage and leaving the room when he was corrected. Mother spat hatred towards me just like she did in the worst of the early days.'[33] According to press reports Friedelind even called her mother 'the evil spirit of this family. There will be no peace while she's alive!'[34] They were incapable of reaching any agreement. Although Friedelind still spent three months back in Bayreuth after this, for the moment she ceased all contact with her mother. When another meeting was called six weeks later, she sent her lawyer. The heirs would have to wait even longer to be paid out, for the negotiations in the end lasted until the 1970s.

When Friedelind was asked to take part in a TV programme for the BBC in February 1968, she left the studio after the very first interview when the young journalist in question told her that he admired her mother for keeping faith with Hitler. She could not bear such gaucheness; it seemed to her to trivialize her emigration and her long separation from all she loved. But things were to get worse. A Dr Erich Hoffmann wrote to her from Vienna:

> I have long held a suspicion that has now been completely proven: you are mentally ill. There is no other way to describe your behaviour, which is devoid of character and loathsome to the highest degree. You fear the growth of a new 'brown plague' in Bayreuth, but you are yourself the most malodorous plague pustule among the descendants of Richard Wagner. I can only give you one good piece of advice: Never show yourself in a German country ever again – if you do, my friends and I will ensure that you are placed in a mental home as swiftly as possible.[35]

This was a perfect example of the primitive Nazi ideology of hatred that Friedelind knew only too well from before – the compulsion to take people who refused to be pigeon-holed, to classify them as unworthy and shunt them off. Little remained for her except sarcasm. She wrote to Jeanette in April 1968:

> As someone recently observed, 'Wieland died at the right moment.' During the 15 years that he was active, Germany had to act as if it were

open to the world, liberal, international and avant-garde. Now that is over and they can be openly nationalistic, intolerant, small-minded, reactionary and fascist. Wolfgang moved up into the boss's chair at just the right moment.[36]

In the weeks after the family meeting, Friedelind's public comments were the source of many a scandal. On 2 March 1968 the German national TV company ARD broadcast a programme entitled 'Hand aufs Herz' ('Cross your heart') in which Friedelind was interviewed by three journalists: Günter Bendig, Lovis H. Lorenz and Bernd Wessling. Years later, Wessling said of this programme that 'I have always admired Frau Wagner's candour, her critical faculties, her common sense and her positive contradictoriness.' But he also recalled that the programme caused much irritation and that 'it stirred up tremendous trouble, the result of which was that Wolfgang Wagner is upset with me to the present day. Ah well.'[37] When she was asked about the possibility of a resurgence of Nazism, Friedelind said that Bayreuth was in danger from the far-right party NPD: 'In East Germany it's major news that the NPD is so strong in Bayreuth.' The Neo-Nazis had won three of 42 seats on the city council in 1966, and this had stirred deep-seated anxieties in Friedelind. She also repeated claims that a book burning had taken place in Bayreuth. The report in question had been immediately denounced as a lie by the city council, though Friedelind remained somehow unaware of this fact.

Friedelind's remarks were met with indignant attacks on her in the press, including one from the Bayreuth Mayor, Hans Walter Wild. He wrote her an open letter in which he said that 'Your declaration on German TV was made despite knowing better. The damage that you have done to your native city is incalculable. After all, you contradicted the denial by the city of Bayreuth and did so before a large, possibly international TV audience. You also effectively allied yourself with the organs of the press of the GDR, which as a whole had used the incorrect report for political purposes against the Federal Republic and against Bayreuth, while taking no notice of the rectification issued by the city.' Wild further quoted the note that her brothers had pinned to the notice board of the Festspielhaus in 1951: 'No politics. It's only art that matters!' and added 'the depoliticization of the Festival remains a guiding principle of what happens on the Green Hill today.'[38] To be sure, he did not mention that the two brothers had always refused to engage in any way with the Nazi history of the Festival. The fact that Friedelind was accused of being 'on the side' of the press in the GDR shows that she was regarded once more as a traitor. (And the fact that art and politics are most definitely intertwined in Bayreuth down to the present day is proven by the intervention of the city authorities in the election of the two current Festival directors.)[39] The opera director August Everding now blamed Friedelind for the fact that the GDR was supposedly no longer letting its artists travel to the West, which enraged her. 'I don't know if I can just ignore this renewed witchhunt against me,' she wrote to her lawyer.[40]

The TV programme had given Winifred and Wolfgang more ammunition against Friedelind. Winifred wrote bluntly to a friend:

> You really could have written that Friedelind deserves to have her bottom properly smacked … she was always an *enfant terrible* and, over time, she is becoming a plague for us here in Bayreuth. I think that if she wanted to write a book entitled 'Pardon my return' then I would have to write one called 'Friedelind go home' (after all, she has become an American!).[41]

The child whose bottom ought to have been smacked had recently turned 50 years of age.

Another thunderbolt was a report in the tabloid magazine *Quick* of 19 June 1968 in which Friedelind expressed her views openly on assorted matters and in which other family members also said their piece. She had claimed that Konrad Pöhner, Bavaria's Finance Minister, 'gives out with one hand what he sticks in his pocket with the other as the Bayreuth building contractor who for years has been carrying out reconstruction work at the Festspielhaus'. Pöhner was beside himself with rage and wrote to the family lawyer of 'unqualified statements made by Friedelind and Wolf Siegfried Wagner'. In future, he said, he would refuse to communicate with anyone from the family except Wolfgang and Winifred. 'I am not prepared to continue the Bavarian State Government's negotiations about setting up a foundation. In view of the notions that certain family members have, such negotiations are in any case pointless. A quite different solution would have to be found, or the Festival can pass away. It's impossible to say whether infamy or stupidity has the upper hand in the family.'[42] Wolfgang thereupon forbade his sister from entering the premises of the Festspielhaus:

> I had repeatedly asked you to refrain from all public statements that are detrimental to the family and the Festival. For example, the illustrated magazine *Quick* recently published statements by you that have not just damaged the family and the Festival, but which are objectively untrue. This is something that I can explain only if you are either unaware of the actual state of things, or are making claims against your better judgement. The consequences are already being felt. Thus, for example, Dr

Pöhner has already declared that he is not prepared to be slandered by members of our family. Under these circumstances, out of due regard for the representatives of the public authorities, for many members of the Society of Friends and for the artists involved in the Festival, I cannot be expected to meet you during the Festival. I therefore request that you refrain from entering the premises of the Festspielhaus until further notice.[43]

Wolfgang also wrote to Friedelind's lawyer, referring to her statements in a regional interview with the WDR radio station in December 1967, in the *Spiegel* (which she had at no point corrected, despite Bodo Lafferentz's having asked her to do so) and in *Quick*.

These statements have caused me to take this step now. In the family meeting of 6 January 1968, my sister said she believed that, by engaging an important assistant, I had ruined my brother's *Ring* production that is currently running. She thereby does not just question my artistic sense of responsibility, but is maligning my attitude towards my deceased brother. This is not just a matter of the slander directed at the State Minister Dr Pöhner of the Bavarian Finance Ministry, but above and beyond this of maligning our private sponsors in the Society of Friends of Bayreuth … In the year 1958, thus eight years before the death of my brother, Friedelind took it upon herself to gather donations for the Festival. The result of her endeavours was only DM 5000; on the other hand, she has taken on loans from the Festival to the sum of DM 80,000 as an advance, as it were, for her failed financial activities. Above and beyond this we have resolved my sister's earlier debts which arose from the sale of jewellery belonging to a third party. This situation was embarrassing to us all and was cleared up by me in 1958. Finally, I took on a personal guarantee for her with a bank in order to help her with the financial difficulties that arose while organizing her master classes. This guarantee has in the meantime been settled. Wherever I was able to help her, I helped her. She is presumably unaware that these considerable financial submissions were greatly criticized by the public subsidy-givers. The General Accounting Office of Bavaria has once more requested that the debts taken up by my sister should be repaid. Under these circumstances I could surely expect her to avoid everything that could be to the disadvantage of the Festival, to my work and to those offices that subsidize the Festival.[44]

Friedelind thereupon got her lawyer Servatius involved who, on her behalf, assured Wolfgang that his client would make no more damaging statements in the media. But after this concession, Servatius remained insistent: Friedelind would still have to get her free tickets. Winifred's comment was:

> Maus won't put up with her ban on attending the Festival and her Hamburg lawyer has filed a protest – though even he seems to be unable to find anything other than inadequate reasons against it. Wieland's children will certainly be coming to the first cycle – they'd been asked only to come to the second – but they won't do that – So the problems are building up for the first week of the Festival! Neither the state government nor the Friends of Bayreuth nor Wolfgang want these family whiners at the receptions – but if they're not invited there's a row, and if they're invited there's a row! It's enough to make you want to throw up – but we'll get over this as well![45]

When Friedelind arrived on the evening before the official Festival opening on 24 July 1968, several people whom she saw in the city refused to greet her any more. Letters sent to her at the Festival address were sent back unopened with the remark 'address unknown', presumably on Wolfgang's orders. But someone – either at the city post office or at the Festspielhaus – was kind enough to forward the letters to Bielefeld. Verena decided not to go to the Festival at all under these circumstances. She was afraid that something might happen to Friedelind, and her fears were not without foundation. On the fourth evening, when Friedelind wanted to meet friends in the restaurant of the 'Reichsadler' Hotel, the owner asked her to leave because his guests were apparently bothered by her presence. 'My family had used this hotel for years, but Wolfgang now instructed its owner that that they should prevent my sister from entering,' said Verena.[46] Since it was cold, Friedelind asked if she might wait in the anteroom until her guests arrived, but this too was forbidden to her. So in her thin evening dress she went out to the square by the railway station. It was a new experience to her to be thrown out of a posh restaurant.

> I wasn't a bit upset, but quite cheered, for I at last understood how it had been for the Jews under Hitler ... here, in my home town, something had happened to me that I had never expected! I was not just able to sympathize with the Jews and the blacks, but I could also identify with them. Despite everything, I kept my sense of humour when I realized how funny it was that Wagner's granddaughter had been thrown out of a hotel in Bayreuth of all places, by members of the 'Friends of Bayreuth' of all people![47]

But Friedelind took ill from standing so long in the cold without a scarf or a coat, and it was so serious that she had to be taken to hospital to get antibiotics. Verena drove there to help look after her. Friedelind found out that an anonymous bouquet had been sent by their mother, and asked herself: 'What would Freud have made of that?'[48] Verena was still allowed to go in and out of the Festspielhaus, unlike Friedelind. After she left the hospital, Friedelind went to two performances as a member of the public, with two tickets she had bought. She saw the *Walküre* but cried all the way through the *Meistersinger* because it pained her so much to realize that Wieland was dead and that his Bayreuth had died with him.

The shock at the humiliation she had suffered did not abate quickly. She saw how Wolfgang was supported by the city, the Bavarian government and the Society of Friends. These three institutions were his most important supporters and ensured that he was undisputed as the director of the Festival. After the hurly-burly of this year's Festival was over, Friedelind refrained from making any comments in the press for a while, though she did not believe that there would be any artistic improvements: 'Wieland's Bayreuth has been successfully and wilfully killed in two short seasons and as one paper put it: "It is as if Wieland Wagner had never lived." Thank God I closed down the classes last summer. We hope to reopen on an all-year basis within the year, but naturally in another location.'[49] But if Wolfgang had thought he could permanently silence his sister in her urge to speak openly to the media, then he was mistaken. Later in 1968 she gave a TV interview in England about how she had been thrown out of a Bayreuth restaurant, and she made it clear that she regarded her brother as partly responsible.[50]

Friedelind's lawyer, Servatius, wanted at least to ensure that she would have no problems getting Festival tickets in future. In a letter to Wolfgang, he proved a clever tactician. 'Your sister's unequivocal behaviour during the Festival, her refusal to give any interviews and the declarations of the undersigned before the press will have convinced you that our client is serious about what we wrote to you on 16 July of this year.' He now assumed, he wrote, that at future Festivals Friedelind would 'not be hindered from again taking the places to which she has a hereditary right.'[51] Servatius did, however, urge her to be careful in giving interviews and closed his letter to her with humour: at their meeting, Wolfgang had piled up files of 'Friedelind's past sins' behind his chair, and Dr Pöhner had tripped over them.[52]

In the meantime, Friedelind was travelling around Germany to try and find a new venue for her master classes. The valley of the Rhine seemed ideal to her, but she could not find anything definitive. At the same time she was trying to help out Anja Silja, Wieland's former partner who had been cut off by his family. She took Silja to the beer festival at Kulmbach, which Wieland used to say was the best thing about the Bayreuth Festival; and they went together to the Eule, the Bayreuth pub that was a favourite of the artists. When Friedelind had directed *Lohengrin* in Bielefeld, Anja had arranged to visit the house at the same time, singing the title role in Strauss's *Salome*. 'I always liked being with her. She had helped me so much in the year before, and furthermore she was a part of Wieland,' wrote Silja. When she had to travel to Hanover to catch a flight home after Bielefeld, there was a thick fog, so Friedelind drove her to Frankfurt. 'That's how she was, always ready to help at the drop of a hat.'[53]

But Friedelind was also a fighter, and never demure when she got angry. And she was indeed angry now: Wolfgang's death blow to her master classes had hurt her deeper than she was prepared to admit, and the injury she suffered might well have increased her tendency to criticize him. She was still giving as many lectures as possible, often in Great Britain, and they centred on four main topics: 'The Bayreuth Story' was about the history of her family and the Festival. 'My grandfather Richard Wagner' gave an overview of his life and work; another lecture dealt with the New Bayreuth, in which she discussed the productions by her two brothers Wieland and Wolfgang; and 'Modern Opera Production in Europe' was based on her broad knowledge of European opera productions. There were times when travelling to her lecture venues could be nightmarish – if the weather was bad, if there were no luggage porters at the stations, or if the organizers simply forgot to organize anything at all, leaving her stranded somewhere instead.

Friedelind's admiration for Felsenstein continued unabated, and she admired him not just as a great artist but as a human being. She was worried when he had to undergo an operation and so travelled to Berlin 'to hold his hand'. She enjoyed occasional successes in getting engagements for artists; thus in 1967 the singer Hanne-Lore Kuhse from the GDR was engaged in Philadelphia to sing Isolde alongside Ernst Gruber as Tristan and Ramón Vinay as Kurwenal. But Friedelind was unhappy with her current situation. She pondered where she could set up her master classes again, she studied Wagner's early operas and spoke of her desire to direct Wagner's *Ring* one day. 'My grandfather painted a terrible picture of this particular world, but at least he glorified Brünnhilde and Sieglinde and makes the women human – which they are not in the original sagas. Then there is his topic of "redemption", which was also unknown among the predecessors of his characters. In my *Ring*, Wotan would be the baddie!'

Back in the USA, she took Lotte Lehmann's place as guest of honour at a 'Viennese ball' in Hollywood, which she regretted. But she kept her sense of humour, and wrote to her lawyers. 'In any case I followed your advice to keep my mouth shut so well that I promptly lost my voice.'[54] She was offered the chance to direct *Tristan* in St Paul and *Tosca* in Portland, Oregon, though neither came about. Plans to direct a Wagner opera in Pasadena also fell through. A new international university had been established in San Diego, and Friedelind visited the 'canyon' where an open-air theatre was to be built. She was highly enthusiastic about the idea. It was to be built alongside a theatre with a roof, where the stage would be set on different levels. This was just what she had dreamt of – along with an open theatre, and all situated in a sunny climate. But her natural insouciance went too far, as was so often the case: she complained to the management about their architect, tried to get involved in the planning of the venture and proposed employing Werner Ruhnau, an architect who was completely unknown in San Diego. Again, it all came to nothing.

Friedelind had also suffered a severe bout of ill health that prevented her from getting down to work properly. As for Bayreuth, she wrote that 'I have no connection with the Festival whatsoever any more since 1967, as I do not see eye to eye with its present administration and their artistic and political leanings.'[55] Her Bielefeld production had not led to any other offers, and she ascribed it to the fact that she had no manager in Europe: 'Knowing all the German agents, I know that they are not only nudniks [show-offs], but cowards, and would not touch me because of Bayreuth pressure. So it had to be somebody outside of Germany, as my work will be outside of Germany, as long as the present Bayreuth administration is so powerful politically.'[56] But Friedelind still wanted to return to Europe, for she had 'been sitting around for too long'. She took less pleasure in giving her lectures than had previously been the case, and she claimed that she would rather go back to Schrafft's restaurant where she had worked in the 1940s, because there she could at least earn an honest living as a waitress.

The situation in Bayreuth continued to occupy her thoughts. She wrote to her lawyer:

> You will be pleased to learn that I am supposed to be directing the *Hol-
> länder* in Johannesburg and Pretoria in July. I'm to make a trip there in
> late January to get preliminary information. Please make no mention
> of this at the family meeting, because otherwise my mother will organ-
> ize all the Nazis who emigrated to South Africa so that they torpedo
> my contract. Verena's family knows about it, but it's better if Wieland's
> family isn't told anything for the moment.[57]

But this plan, too, evaporated. Her projects and plans fell apart like houses of cards, almost always because she refused to make what she regarded as compromises.

Richard Wagner was a means to promote her own name, but she could only make use of it under certain conditions; it was rather like having a mortgage. Her emigration had not just cut her bonds with Bayreuth and ruined any chance she might have had of making an impact there, but had also impeded her chances of re-establishing herself. But her lack of practical directing experience meant it was difficult to make a name in the profession. Only rarely did she manage to set projects in motion and bring them to a successful conclusion. Thus it is impossible to determine conclusively whether it was biographical circumstances or personal limitations that were responsible for her failures. But in any case, it is clear that, right from the start, her mother and brother did what they could to ensure her exclusion from the business.

Friedelind once more began travelling the length and breadth of the USA, as if again consumed by restlessness. She gave lectures, spoke on the radio, and everywhere she was dogged by money problems. 'I had to beg, borrow and steal to get here and survive here until I was able to cash a cheque yesterday.'[58] But old friendships helped to keep her going. On one of her travels she heard the former *heldentenor* Lauritz Melchior sing in his 'glass palace' in Hollywood. He was now almost eighty, but 'his voice had all its old brilliance and glow, and its power too – (it was during dinner – we had antelope ragout, shot by him, don't ask me where) – he kept taking his hearing aid out of his ear and started monologuing.'[59]

Chapter 15

Schemes and setbacks
The 1970s

F OR FRIEDELIND 1970 was not a good year. She still had not paid off her
debts from her master classes, and Wolfgang was the only person who
could help her with them. She was back in Europe, and wrote to her lawyer
Servatius in the autumn that she could not return to the USA before the
debts were paid. 'Twelve months have passed since my arrival in Europe and
we have had nothing but empty talk.'[1] She was given no information about
what was being concocted in Bayreuth. She learnt from the TV that there was
progress in the plans to turn the Festival into a foundation, but that it could
take a long time before any money was paid out to the heirs.[2] And she was
for the moment without any clear goal in life. She was still smarting from the
death of her master classes.

Friedelind spent the summer partly by Lake Constance, but also in Salzburg, Zurich, Lucerne and elsewhere. She avoided Bayreuth. When she was
staying with Verena in Nussdorf, she left a few hours before her mother was
due to arrive – she did not want to see her. Instead she maintained contact
with good friends, meeting Otto Klemperer and his daughter Lotte in October
in Zurich, as well as Tilly and Fritz Zweig. The Zweigs remained her friends
till the end. 'They are fabulous artists, teachers and friends, both had splendid
careers of their own up to Hitler,' she wrote of them.[3] Fritz Zweig (1893–1984)
had been a private student of Arnold Schoenberg and had worked as a répétiteur and conductor at assorted opera houses including the Kroll Opera in
Berlin. In 1932 he was appointed to the Berlin State Opera, but in 1933 both
he and his wife, the singer Tilly de Garmo, had been fired on account of the
so-called 'Law for the Restoration of the Professional Civil Service' that gave
the Nazis the legal means to expel Jews from their jobs. They had fled first to
Prague, then to France and finally to the USA, where Fritz enjoyed further
success as a conductor. Friedelind felt at home with artists such as these, for
she sensed a common bond: they too had been driven from Germany and had
been compelled to make a new living in the USA.

Friedelind then travelled to Bonn to hear Klemperer conduct his Philhar-
monia Orchestra; she invested much time in maintaining her artistic contacts.
And she enjoyed professional gossip, such as when directors and conductors
were playing musical chairs:

25 With the conductor Otto Klemperer. He too had emigrated to the US
from Nazi Germany. After the war they became friends for life.

Liebermann will resign in 1973 in Hamburg on grounds of age and See-
fehlner will succeed him. He is trying to get Abbado as musical director – someone else who has only done one opera in his life. He is very
gifted, but so is Maazel and yet I cannot stand anything he conducts.
Abbado made a sky-rocketing career ever since he won the Mitropoulos
competition in NY.[4]

She had no permanent address, practically lived in her car and spent
the night with whichever friends happened to live in the towns where she
wanted to see an opera or give a lecture. In London she often lived with Lorna
Braithwaite, the mother of the conductor Nicholas, where she could prepare
her lectures for assorted universities and other institutions such as the Wagner
Society, the Wexford Festival or the Sadler's Wells Ballet.[5] When she heard a
recording of one of her lectures, she was surprised to hear how often she could
make her audience laugh – her ironic manner went down well with people.
As a rule she spoke freely, for she hated reading a lecture from a script. She
was repeatedly asked to give radio interviews, and even the TV showed an
intermittent interest in her, mostly in the form of talk shows.

When Friedelind met Jeremy Menuhin at an evening event, the two of them talked until two in the morning. Did this son of the world-famous violinist perhaps speak to her of his troubled relationship with his own parents? He found his own childhood grotesque: he had hardly seen his parents and they had shown no interest in their children, he recalled many years later. His father was 'cold and detached', his mother domineering and volatile.[6] Friedelind had known his family since her youth, for she had stayed with Lady Crosfield in the 1930s when the Menuhins were her guests during a visit to London to give concerts. Friedelind's problems with Winifred presumably awakened her sympathy for Jeremy.

Friedelind's reputation as the *enfant terrible* of the Wagners found renewed confirmation when she gave another TV interview that offended her family. She told how Hitler had wanted to send the Bayreuth production of *Lohengrin* to London as a coronation present for Edward VIII in 1936, though the king had refused since he could not stand opera.[7] Friedelind defended herself against her family's criticism: 'I would dearly like to see the publications that have so offended you. I only know of the interview in the *Manchester Guardian*, where I spoke of plans for the future and the journalist quoted from my book. Since England is a free country, you can't forbid anyone from anything, you can only ask them.'[8] She stressed that those who had known Hitler were repeatedly an object of interest to the press and continued with a sly dig at her family: 'Should I now be made responsible for all that? I preferred to be interned in 1940 than to write lies! We can't blame the world for not having forgotten the time under Hitler or for refusing to forget it; we can't blame them for it and certainly can't stop them, though certain circles in Germany would naturally prefer that.'[9]

In early 1972 Friedelind travelled to East Berlin with Ella Lee. She saw Britten's *Midsummer Night's Dream* at the Komische Oper, which for her was 'an old Felsenstein evergreen'. She claimed to have seen the production some 50 times since 1961 – including the rehearsals she had attended. Felsenstein remained for her one of the most fascinating directors of her time, and for him she was happy to undergo the bureaucratic vexation that crossing the East-West German border entailed. She also liked visiting Joachim Herz, who invited her to his production of *Rheingold* in Leipzig: 'You'll be our guest in Leipzig.'[10] It happened at times that she had to go on stage herself to receive applause – in the East she was able to feel like a guest of honour. Herz set the *Ring* in the nineteenth century amidst all the problems of industrialization; his Leipzig production of the tetralogy thus featured a critique of capitalism that predated Patrice Chéreau's Bayreuth production by several years, but which is regrettably not documented properly.[11]

When plans to set up an International Siegfried Wagner Society (ISWS)

26 Friedelind with her lifelong friend Jeanette at Lake Lucerne
near Tribschen, where her father Siegfried was born.

became public in 1972, Friedelind expressed her readiness to take on the role of President. According to Peter Pachl, the younger founding members were happy to have her on board, not least because the ISWS was in a state of feud with the 'official' Bayreuth (Winifred and Wolfgang in particular). This actually changed when Friedelind took the helm. Winifred possessed the rights for Siegfried's music and had placed a ban on its performance, but Friedelind used a number of tricks to circumvent it. There were first concert performances of *Der Friedensengel* and *Der Kobold* in London, then performances in other cities, such as *Sternengebot* and *Sonnenflammen* in Wiesbaden, *Herzog Wildfang* in Munich and the world première of Siegfried's last opera, *Das Flüchlein, das Jeder mitbekam*, in Kiel.

It is difficult to fathom just what Friedelind really thought of her father's music. His adherence to traditional structures in his compositions has been a hindrance to efforts to bring his operas into the repertoire, either on stage or in the concert hall, and has led to negative opinions such as Béla Diòsy's comment that he wrote 'endless melody devoid of melody'.[12] Markus Kiesel has claimed that Siegfried Wagner's music suffers from 'hubris devoid of self-criticism' and that his composing methods 'left their traces in his occasional lack of inspiration and his working out of the detail'.[13] The move away from figurative art in the early 1900s (such as undertaken by Kandinsky in the visual arts and Schoenberg in music) was something that quite passed Siegfried by. And his preferred opera topics remained antiquatedly Romantic. By the 1920s, when society was straining to break out of old cultural norms, his aesthetic seemed anachronistic. To the present day, the lack of any concision in his work affords it a regressive character. Perhaps it was precisely Friedelind's hankering for an oppositional stance and her mother's repeated ban on performances that led her to champion her father's music.

As in every organization, there were differences of opinion in the Siegfried Wagner Society, too. On the whole, they were resolved again quickly. However, running the bank account proved problematical, for Friedelind had already shown a tendency to confuse 'official' and 'private' financial matters when she was running her master classes. There was no evil intent; she was simply unable to comprehend that the two must be kept separate. Of a similarly delicate nature was her endeavour to draw into the fold those who had hitherto opposed performing Siegfried's music. She had her mother then her brother appointed honorary presidents of the Society (though neither ever turned up at the meetings), and she even refused to exclude arch conservatives. She supposedly even once cried out: 'Now we've even got Hitler's last public prosecutor!'[14] Did she really think that she would be able to convert them all?

In these years, Friedelind spent more time in England than anywhere else, and her prime activity was lecturing. Her talk entitled 'Let's help Boulez burn down all the theatres' proved her 'biggest success'. Boulez had several years before caused a storm in the media by proclaiming just this – that the opera houses should be 'burnt down' – for, in his opinion, modern music theatre could not be realized in conventional theatres and, as a result, hardly any good new operas were being written. The new opera houses that were springing up often looked modern on the outside, but inside they had remained old-fashioned. 'The most expensive solution would be to blow up the opera houses. But don't you think that it would also be the most elegant solution?'[15] Provocation on this scale was just the kind of thing that appealed to Friedelind. And as someone who knew almost all the important opera houses of Europe and the USA, the notion of creating an ideal theatre was something that had occupied her for years. She presented her ideas with gusto to her audiences and the press alike. The current buildings were 'museums', she complained, that were utterly unsuited to modern productions. The ideal house would be flexible, it would offer a good view from every seat, the employees would all receive the same wage, operas and plays would both be offered, and the two genres would work in close collaboration. The proscenium arch that separated the stage curtain from the orchestra pit would have to disappear. Composers, librettists and other co-workers should settle in the area around the theatre and each of them should feel a personal connection with the works to be produced.[16] She contacted Boulez and began to develop her ideas for a variable theatre. It would also allow films to be shown and would incorporate new technologies. She drew attention to the Krupp air-inflated tent that stood on the grounds of the Hanover Trade Fair and afforded a new sensation of space because there were no columns in it. Fascinated by the idea that such a hall could be classless, un-snobbish and unpretentious,[17] she announced to the press that she would travel to any part of the world if a sponsor could be found to realize her plan. Her only condition would be that there was an adequate population density in order to draw enough creative potential to the place. Not unlike her grandfather, she ignored all practical questions regarding the cost. The financial consequences of the logistics involved in setting up such an undertaking simply did not interest her.

In the midst of all these deliberations she received a sensational piece of news from Paul R. Duffy, a member of the British Wagner Society. He told her that a cultural project was being planned in Teesside in the north-east of England that would involve building a flexible theatre. Teesside is a conurbation comprising Billingham, Stockton, Thornaby and other smaller towns grouped around Middlesbrough, the largest town of the region and the loca-

27 The French composer and conductor Pierre Boulez. He suggested
burning down opera houses; Friedelind liked the idea.

tion intended for the theatre in question. It was to be built so as to allow
cultural, sporting and business events, and work on it was due to take two-
and-a-half years, beginning soon. Duffy made two suggestions to Friedelind:
either touring cultural groups would be invited to give performances there,
or 'the alternative is to find a genius (e.g. Friedelind Wagner) to create a local
company of which a school would form an important part.'[18] In nearby Norton
there was an old vicarage where master classes could be held, for it already
had sound-proof rooms that were ideal for teaching purposes. All the other
details she received corresponded to what would be her ideal theatre: the
number of seats could be varied between 1600 and 2000, the acoustic would
be designed to the most modern standards, there would be no columns, and
the view would be good from every seat. Duffy suggested organizing a conversation with the project manager, John Pinches. Would her dream now actually
become a reality? The content of Duffy's letter went round and round in her
head: at last she might be given the opportunity to direct a cultural enterprise
that would allow her to implement the ideas that she had developed out of her
experience with the master classes.

And suddenly it all seemed within reach, for on 2 May 1973, after endless
squabbles, the long-awaited contract was signed to transfer the Wahnfried

Villa, the Festspielhaus and the Wagner archives to the city of Bayreuth, which for its part would place everything in the hands of a foundation. Friedelind had often had her lawyer represent her at the discussions about the foundation, for she had feared that the arguments involved might provoke her too much. 'I would probably commit multiple murders,' she wrote.[19] Now the hitherto private Wagner enterprise was transformed into the 'Richard Wagner Foundation Bayreuth'. The participants in the foundation were the Federal Republic of Germany, the Free State of Bavaria, the Society of Friends, the Foundation of Upper Franconia and the city of Bayreuth. Winifred had pursued this goal for years and handed over all the buildings to the state without asking for a penny. But at the same time, this freed her of all her debts. Wolfgang retained his position as the director of the festival: 'Wagner's grandson thereby transformed himself into the private entrepreneur of what he had formerly co-owned.'[20] Of the proceeds of 12.4 million marks, a fifth was given each to Friedelind, Wolfgang, Verena and Winifred, while Wieland's children divided up the remaining fifth between them. Thus, after paying back her debts to Wolfgang, Friedelind suddenly had access to more than two million marks.

As for the family's representation on the new foundation board, Winifred was given a place on it, as were her four children (in Wieland's case his vote was inherited by his heirs). Franz Wilhelm Beidler – now 72 years old – was ignored once more. If he had been offered a seat on the board, even with no possibility of setting its agenda, it would at least have provided some small satisfaction for everything that had been visited upon both him and his mother before him, Richard and Cosima's disinherited daughter Isolde.

Wolfgang Wagner was granted full artistic freedom and a lifelong appointment. It is astonishing that the family did not succeed in limiting his term as Festival Director in order to allow other family members to move up into the festival management. Reinhold Kreile was the lawyer representing the interests of Wieland's descendants, and he regarded a five-year term as director, with the option of a renewal for another five years, as a reasonable solution.[21] Bodo also suggested 'including a safety clause that would open up the doors of the Festival management to others, such as Friedelind and Wummi [Wolf Siegfried].'[22] But no one was able to push through any such clause. Wolfgang owed his lifelong position to the representatives of the state, who dominated the meetings and decided against the wishes of the rest of the family. He was allowed to make whatever decisions he deemed right, and there would later be yet another family dispute when he forbade Wieland Lafferentz from attending orchestral rehearsals, much to the annoyance of Verena and Bodo. When Bodo Lafferentz died on 17 January 1975, it was not just a personal blow to Friedelind. He had always stood by her and endeavoured to mediate within the family. In future she would have to solve her problems with Wolfgang all by herself.

Friedelind maintained close contact with her nephews and nieces. They liked to confide in her, they told her what they were studying, and for her part she would have dearly loved to see Eva, Nike, Gottfried or Wolf Siegfried involved at least in the management of the Festival, or even as the overall Director. But she sensed from the outset that any such notions would fail:

> Of course there will be a lot of harsh resistance to Wummi, because his uncle hates him (I can use no milder expression: however, in the summer of 1966, when his father was at death's door, and egged on by him, [Wolf Siegfried] regrettably behaved very badly towards his uncle. Good behaviour would hardly have helped, however. I acted properly and loyally in exemplary fashion, and it didn't help me!). But his lord and uncle ought to be mature enough at the age of 54 to forgive a few youthful sins. We weren't angels either, when we were young.[23]

Although she occasionally admitted to harbouring a continuing ambition to run the Festival,[24] Friedelind now fought for the rights of the next generation and never tired of telling the media how Wolfgang was preventing younger Wagners from directing operas in Bayreuth. She was proven right by Wolfgang Wagner himself. He gave an interview to *Playboy* magazine in which he made it clear that no one in the next generation was suitable to run the Festival: 'If I were to drop out right now, none of the younger Wagner generation would bring with them the necessary prerequisites for running Bayreuth ... my understanding of the Bayreuth Festival Direction is not primarily determined by family or patriarchal concerns.'[25]

The idea of running her master classes in England was one that Friedelind could not get out of her head. So, together with the relevant authorities and after setting up a board to oversee the venture, 'The Friedelind Wagner Masterclasses Scholarship Trust' was founded. Her aims were similar to those of her former Bayreuth master classes: she wanted to train the most talented young artists from wherever they came. Their lessons should once again encompass all possible aspects of music theatre: architecture, direction, conducting, acting, lighting, all technical matters, singing, and writing libretti. Mediocrity was again to be excluded; she was playing for high stakes.

> Everyone should have a complete understanding of each others' functions and disciplines and after three years everybody should be able to direct, light, design, stage – and, in some cases, conduct. This was done

by Piscator and the University of Pittsburgh's opera workshop – so why not by us, who preach total theatre?[26]

She had read Erwin Piscator's book *Das politische Theater* (*Political theatre*) and found it exciting:

> Whether you like him or not, he was groundbreaking. It is a shame that I knew so many of these famous artists only during our emigration and back then often did not know at all what they had achieved. Although I was already around in the 1920s I was still rather small – and I cannot imagine that my father would ever have taken me into the communist proletarian theatre, even if I had been bigger than I was.[27]

(In this last point she was surely right.) The famous Kroll Opera that had exerted such an influence on the cultural life of the 1920s had been closed down in 1931. Friedelind's cousin Franz Beidler had been close to the opera, and Otto Klemperer, who had worked there, had – like Friedelind – argued in favour of involving the members of an opera house in all aspects of the art. This was an idea he owed to Gustav Mahler.[28] So Friedelind's ideas were situated in a venerable tradition.

After organizing three concerts with Ella Lee in Stockton-on-Tees in 1973, Friedelind planned to go hunting for donations for scholarships such as she had done for her master classes in Bayreuth. She advised Dagny Beidler, the daughter of her cousin Franz, to give up teaching and work with her instead – though Dagny preferred to remain in her present profession. Friedelind was convinced that three further descendants of Wagner and Liszt would be willing to join her: Wolf Siegfried, Nike (who was busy experimenting with electronics) and Timothy Gravina, a descendant of Liszt and von Bülow, who was to be in charge of the computers.[29]

In order to accelerate the erection of the new music centre that was destined to enrich the Teesside region, Friedelind bought a small house in Ragworth Road, Norton, just north of Stockton-on-Tees, where she planned to live. In the summer of 1974 she bought the 'Southlands' villa in Eaglescliffe, a tiny town just south of Stockton. She was in euphoric mood and had both houses renovated – which was not difficult for her, given that she now possessed considerable financial resources. The 100-year-old villa offered grand rooms that looked out onto a park, plus a tower in which one could live. There were two other little houses on the estate. She imagined being able to build five to ten small houses at the far end of the park without altering its beauty. A little brook wound its way through the park, and there was a pond too. There were stables and a huge conservatory that would be ideal for further development: 'The house and the garden are ideal for the purposes of our master classes: for guests, sponsor parties, house concerts, performances in the park etc.'[30] The lecturers would live in the tower and in the two little houses, while the lower rooms would be used as studios. The building was turned upside down and much effort invested in its renovation. Friedelind plunged into it all with immense energy. Chimneys were removed, walls freed from eons of wallpaper and papered anew, bathrooms removed here and reinstalled there, double glazing added to windows, floors remade. Friedelind herself took on the task of revamping the kitchen and ended up covered in plaster that only a bath was able to remove. New electrical wiring was laid, heaters shifted about and new ones installed – at which the heating failed altogether. She bore the costs with composure – her recent inheritance meant she could afford it – but she found the local workers unreliable and annoying: 'Once you find workers, then they go drinking and either don't turn up or so many of them arrive that they flood the house.'[31]

Hanne-Lore Kuhse gave a song recital in 1975, but the beginning of the classes was postponed until 1976 on account of the continuing renovations and other necessary preparations. Friedelind accused the London authorities of delaying setting up the foundation. 'And even more time was wasted by the reorganization of the counties – that's also London's fault.'[32] Slowly but surely, she was making the same mistakes as always in the past. She confused her own expenses with those of the foundation, and in the minutes of a meeting of the foundation board of May 1975 we read that one member complained of the 'financial chaos' that he had uncovered.

The organizational restructuring of the county boundaries in England resulted in the decision that Teesside would not be building a new theatre after all. So Friedelind shifted her performances to local churches and announced that she would also be happy with an inflatable hall or a former factory building. One pleasant distraction for her was the concert performance of Siegfried Wagner's opera *Der Friedensengel* that she was able to organize in the Queen Elizabeth Hall in London and that was broadcast by the radio. She had procured the advertisements for the programme book and had provided photographs of her father. Three generations of the family came to hear the concert. Winifred and Verena were there, and even Franz Wilhelm Beidler was persuaded to come, even though he had never attended any performance in Bayreuth since his enforced departure from Germany. He had always respected his uncle Siegfried, and perhaps it was a conciliatory attempt to leave the past behind him. Beidler's daughter Dagny came as well. Wolfgang Wagner was conspicuous by his absence. In the run-up to the performance, Friedelind was unable to mention in public that her mother did not really like the opera. 'She hates the topic; she finds it terrible to be confronted with the idea of suicide, and the love triangle doesn't please her either.'[33]

The press praised the performance, especially the singers Raffaele Polani, Martha Mödl und Hanne-Lore Kuhse (though Mödl more for her dramatic talent than for her voice). Friedelind had shown courage in organizing the event, and it was a complete success. Drawing on a phrase from Thomas Mann's diaries, her niece Nike once aptly called Friedelind a 'daughter adjutant' like Erika Mann, the difference being that Friedelind could only live out her role as a 'widow' because her father died so early (Nike Wagner has also suggested that that such 'daughters of Wotan' bore no children because they were unable to take their love elsewhere).[34]

By 1976 everything was ready: the first six-week master class was to take place. Highly trained, top-quality students were selected. The local population was also involved in order to promote contact with amateur music-makers. Theatre was to be brought into the local schools, and in future the classes were intended to last the whole year through. Friedelind did not hesitate to try for the best, so she invited Cathy Berberian, Karlheinz Stockhausen, Joachim Herz, Luciano Berio and Pierre Boulez to give classes. But they all hesitated. In a brochure that she had printed, she lists H. K. Bast for stage design and costumes, Nicholas Braithwaite for conducting, Charles C. Fussell for composition, Ute Hertz for acting, Bruce Hungerford for singing coaching and Hanne-Lore Kuhse for singing and interpretation; she herself would be responsible for classes in opera direction. As one of their set tasks the students had to analyse Mozart's *Marriage of Figaro*.

Despite all her preparations, Friedelind still found time for a fortnight's journey through the country with Winifred as her companion. They drove by car to Wales and thence to Stonehenge and Stratford, and Friedelind proudly showed her mother her new house and all the building projects. Winifred was happy that her daughter had a task in life: 'That's a good thing, then she'll be diverted and won't spit in our soup!'[35]

In order to find suitable students for her master classes, Friedelind once again embarked on a feverish travel itinerary: she was in Boston in early 1977 and wrote to her mother in somewhat breathless prose that she had already chosen 20 participants and was about to travel to a performance of *Rienzi* in San Antonio, Texas:

All America is flying there, so I'll see a lot of friends. On the 29th I'm in Houston, on the 31st in Denton and then in Dallas, all of this still in Texas. Then I'll fly on to Atlanta, Georgia, and from there to Winston-

Salem, North Carolina, and from there to Washington and then either to Ottawa – New York ... then I shall stay again a little in New York and make trips to Philadelphia and New Haven ... Boulez is at present conducting four concerts each week, Lotte Klemperer is going to all of them plus the rehearsals, sadly I can't manage that because I have too much to do, but tomorrow evening I'm going there with lots of friends, I don't know yet whether I'll manage a play on Broadway on the afternoon. Sunday evening I'm being dragged off to Rockland Country, where an old friend is conducting a concert, the first half with works by Great-Grandfather, which naturally means he'd like to have me there.[36]

The list of places continues unabated and need not be reproduced in full here. Besides auditioning candidates she was also hunting for sponsors and made full use of the press, who were happy to write about her and her plans. She also felt buoyed by seeing old friends and reviving old networks.

In 1978 she held 'Saturday Night Events' in Teesside that were intended to bind her project closer to the region where it was situated. These were weekend courses at which artists would 'talk about their work, their studies, career, tasks etc. and then of course play, sing, demonstrate, exhibit, illustrate. Then there will always be discussions'.[37] At Easter there was a 'musical weekend' to which Verena and Winifred also came. The title was meant a little ironically, for the attendees comprised 'meschugge Wagnerites (35 Wagner fans from all over Great Britain), who had to listen to Boulez, Carter, Crumb etc. which they swallowed like bitter medicine'.[38] There was also an orchestral concert at which the pianist and the conductor were two young men from the region. 'I pulled a truly American stunt,' wrote Friedelind afterwards, 'by having lots of the local ladies bake for the occasion and they really outdid themselves.' In July, Hanne-Lore Kuhse gave four song recitals and eight master classes. The pianist Laurence Allix played contemporary music and works by Liszt. Friedelind planned to read from Cosima Wagner's diaries.

The master classes could not become a permanent fixture because the money available was simply insufficient. On top of everything else it transpired that the old vicarage that the town council had placed at Friedelind's disposal was unsuited for giving concerts. The low ceiling meant the acoustic was not good, so artists refused to perform there. It would have cost a lot of money to change the building. So Friedelind promptly decided to run the classes in Southlands itself, where she was also now living. But when the finances got out of hand the local authorities refused to cover the deficit. Friedelind took ill at just the time when 'the papers here are overdoing themselves in infamy and slander towards the master classes. My chairman wanted to get the local authority to guarantee the deficit for the first year, and they refused, thank God, for that prompted my whole board to resign and now I am truly freed from a nightmare and can stir again.'[39] For her new board of directors she chose Franz Wilhelm Beidler – which one might interpret as a sign of making amends – Verena Lafferentz (represented by her son Manfred), her friends Alexander Eldon and Isabella Wallich, and then herself. But the finances remained the big problem.

The end began to creep up on them when county borders were finally changed and no financial support was forthcoming from the state (quite contrary to the original plans). In March 1979 Friedelind had to acknowledge bitterly that she would have to give up. She put the blame not just on the border changes, but on 'having been driven mad, morning, noon and night by my past boards of directors in Teesside, whose "goodwill", impotence, ignorance, incompetence mixed with arrogance drove my project into the ground and who sabotaged my operating the classes up there with their constant interference, compromises and cowardice'. Her anger at others now knew no bounds. She announced to her new board that she had decided to abandon everything. Regrettably, she said, she saw no future for her project and would liquidate her household and all its contents, sell the houses and leave England. 'I will be happy to get rid of the whole responsibility for so many houses and for at least two years want to commit myself to nothing.' She was 'sick of unreliable workmen, broken promises, being cheated right and left by so-called gentlemen, being treated like a pariah because I am a woman and a foreigner'.[40] But it was really the struggles with her board that had worn her down.

Friedelind sold Southlands in 1980. Since receiving her inheritance she had been better able to indulge her natural generosity. To Bertel Meyer, her old friend from her days on the Isle of Man, she gave a holiday in Israel as a gift – for her and her husband, including a daily allowance and stopovers in Europe on the way. She paid everything, to the tune of $1575, simply because she wanted to do something to please them. They were more than surprised, and Bertel's husband wrote that 'you can't be able to make such fantastic gifts – even if you've got your inheritance from Bayreuth – without having murdered a rich Englishman. I am reading *The Times* every day with the greatest diligence but hope that you have not yet been arrested on account of murder and robbery'. She answered that she wasn't a murderess, but that her mother instead had murdered Bayreuth and everything it had proudly stood for.[41]

She paid for the medical treatment of one of her nieces, explaining that she had learnt from Toscanini that one should help the living. He had bought paintings only from living artists – 'the others had already died of hunger'. For this reason she was convinced 'that your grandfather Siegfried would surely find it more sensible and worthwhile to help out his granddaughter.'[42] Friede-lind made a far bigger investment with an offer to her friend from her youth, Isabella Wallich, when her record company 'Symphonica' got into difficulties through no fault of her own. When all seemed lost and a planned Beethoven recording with Charles Rosen was about to be cancelled because of it, 'Mausi' rang her and said that she would like to become part-owner of the label. She was interested in what Isabella and the conductor Wyn Morris were doing together, and she would rather do something worthwhile instead of investing her grandfather's monies in gold bars or shares. Isabella was overwhelmed: 'I shall never forget that astonishing gesture of generosity, nor cease to be grate-ful.'[43] So Friedelind was appointed a director of 'Symphonica Music Limited' and got involved in the team planning its releases. Charles Rosen recorded the *Diabelli Variations*, and their final recording was of Richard Wagner's rarely performed, mammoth work for orchestra and massed choirs *Das Liebesmahl der Apostel* in 1977. But when the investment company Norton Warberg went bankrupt in 1979, Isabella's financial problems returned. In the end, she had to tell Friedelind that her money, too, was lost. 'Staunch, true friend that she was, she never uttered a word of complaint, and accepted her loss philosophically, as indeed we all did,'[44] she wrote.

When she returned to Germany after the disappointments of her years in England, Friedelind brought with her an aspiring artist, the pianist Neill Thornborrow from Stockton-on-Tees, determined to help further his career. In the summer of 1979 he gave a recital with Gabriele Schnaut in Winifred's house in Bayreuth and was given a two-year contract at the opera house in Regensburg. She was delighted, for it was further proof of her ability to iden-tify talent. She would later name him her legal heir.

Back in Bayreuth, the 1970s were turbulent and scandal-ridden. In 1975 Hans-Jürgen Syberberg filmed an interview that he released under the title *Winifred Wagner und die Geschichte des Hauses Wahnfried 1914–1975* (*Wini-fred Wagner and the History of the House of Wahnfried 1914–1975*). It is five hours long. Eva Wagner-Pasquier had provided Syberberg with an introduc-tion to her grandmother, and her brother Gottfried attended the sessions. He too had long been arguing in favour of acknowledging the guilt of the Wagner family and the politicization of the Festival during the Nazi era. He was irri-tated that whenever he visited his grandmother's house, where a large painting of the 'Führer' still hung, he was not allowed to read Hitler's letters that Wini-fred kept in careful chronological order from 1923 onwards.[45] When Gottfried wanted to look at them, she rang Wolfgang to ask him – and he forbade it.

In her interview with Syberberg, Winifred admitted much that she had otherwise refrained from mentioning in public. This was especially the case in her open confession of her continuing admiration of Hitler. On his first visit to Bayreuth, she said, he had come as 'an absolutely apolitical man, a Wagner enthusiast ... anyway, he came here to enjoy our family life. There was no talk of politics at all'. He had displayed 'heartfelt tact and warmth', he had never disappointed her on a human level, 'except for what happened out there, but that didn't touch me'. 'His aura was considerable ... daemonic in the sense described by Goethe ... my National Socialism was bound up solely with the person of Adolf Hitler.' And she continued: 'I have never been able to banish the man from my mind. I reject everything that happened, but I won't let anyone take away from me what was good and human in Hitler ... I will never deny my friendship with him.' Wolfgang had been wounded and lay in the Charité Hospital when Hitler had visited him and brought him flowers. 'You don't forget things like that.' 'I am able to separate the Hitler I know from what people blame him for today. I would be just as happy and glad to see him if he walked in here today.' She knew that there were bad things, but 'for me they don't exist – I am only interested in my personal experiences ... I am a crazily faithful person. If I take a liking to someone, then it doesn't change.' She refused to see him as a mass murderer and placed the blame for this on others, such as Julius Streicher, and she summed it all up by saying: 'I was never a political person.' She rejected any criticism of the dictator. He was a friend of the Wagner family and above all an admirer of the Master. All that she would admit was that he had developed a drug dependency shortly before the capitulation. She regarded his statement that 'I hear the fluttering wings of the goddess of victory' as something from the lips of a man no longer in normal health.

Once this came out, the world media could not get enough of it. Some were horrified, others admired her for her consistency. Syberberg had made the mistake of choosing a cinematic form for his interview that by its nature conveyed an aura of veracity. He claimed that it 'guaranteed the truth of this documentation, in which honesty is everything'.[46] There was no consideration of the fact that Winifred's statements bent the truth wherever it suited her. And yet much came out of the interview that was thought-provoking. She described her daughter Friedelind as 'a very Wagnerian child: strong in will, self-assured, wilful, obstinate. An absolutely cheerful, tomboyish child. She always wanted to play first fiddle.' Her aunts had 'spoilt her', made of her a 'May Queen'. Then she spoke of her daughter's emigration and admitted that she thought it had been wrong of her. 'It was embarrassing to me that she was abroad ... Friedelind should have served her fatherland.' She was not prepared to admit that Friedelind could have made her decision on political grounds out of opposition to the Nazis, but claimed that she had let herself be influenced by people such as Frida Leider and Rudolf Deman. That, said Winifred, was where her contrariness had come from. It was through a telephone call from the Reichs Chancellery that she had learnt of Friedelind's having left for England. 'If we hadn't been members of the Wagner family, we would have landed in a concentration camp.' As for Friedelind's book, she was convinced that it had been 'written by a ghost-writer.' After her return to Germany, her brothers had allowed her to run her master classes, 'and that gave her something to do.'

In her assessment of her daughter, Winifred sounds like an absolute outsider, devoid of any trace of understanding. She simply could not take her seriously. She had nothing but criticism of Friedelind's decision to emigrate and simply would not accept that the political situation had made her leave. She defamed her autobiography and made it clear that she had been allowed to run her master classes only so as to distract her from any notion of trying to become the Festival Director. Winifred's relationship with Hitler can only be understood in psychological terms: it was a superb opportunity for self-aggrandizement to walk into the Festspielhaus at the side of the head of state. Being on first-name terms with him was perhaps some kind of erotic ersatz. She had been orphaned, abandoned and then adopted, but the mightiest man in Germany was at her feet – a man who conquered half of Europe and who took on the whole world. She held to him later, too, so as not to have to share in his ruin. In her description of the arrival of the Americans she saw herself as a victim (though she was far from the only person to see things thus). She denounced the American soldiers who had sullied Wahnfried and danced on Wagner's grave, but suppressed any thoughts of the murderous war machine of the Nazis. Instead, she created an ideal world in her head and exalted Hitler in it.

After these and other statements became generally known, Wolfgang forbade his mother from attending the Festival and from entering the Festspielhaus. He also informed the press of his decision,[47] though he was horrified less at her views than at the fact that they had become public. He had never reckoned on her revealing her innermost thoughts in this fashion. But Winifred too was aghast:

> This devious Syberberg recorded things surreptitiously that were absolutely private and were said in between his recording sessions, then he added these conversations to his film when he showed it in Paris – after having left them out when showing Wolfgang the film! ... Wolfgang once more saw a danger for the Festival (Bayreuth in the shadow of the Nazis) and decided he had to distance himself from me publicly, which he did

by forbidding me from entering the Festspielhaus except for the last four performances!!!!.[48]

Winifred was delighted, however, when she afterwards got many messages of support from her circle of friends – from those who had enjoyed the privileges afforded by her proximity during the Nazi era. After the film was shown, she got friendly telephone calls almost every day, as she wrote to Helene Roesener: 'The many approving voices about my film naturally also necessitate my thanking them in writing.'[49] Winifred was courted by people who regarded the Nazi era in positive terms and were also not prepared to alter their opinion. She took Gerdy Troost to Sternberg to visit Henry Picker, whom Winifred described as 'having one foot among the old Nazis'. Picker was the man who had published Hitler's 'table talk' of 1941–42, which was based largely on notes he had taken himself.[50] He had invited twenty people to his home, including the sister of the Bavarian president, Franz Josef Strauss, so that Winifred might get to know her. Thus Winifred was able to join fellow ultra-conservatives in celebrating memories of their supposed good old days.

At the commemoration of the 100th anniversary of the Bayreuth Festival in 1976, the Federal President Walter Scheel gave a speech, Karl Böhm conducted the *Meistersinger* and afterwards there was a public celebration around the Festspielhaus in the traditional Franconian manner. But 1976 was also the year when the young French director Patrice Chéreau staged the *Ring*. Since it was the centenary production it naturally drew much international attention. Well-known directors such as Joachim Herz and Götz Friedrich had already endeavoured to tease out the political implications of Wagner's works in their own productions, and now Chéreau did the same. Pierre Boulez conducted. They were heavily criticized. 'Boulez/Chéreau are the instigators of this first attack of the Vandals,' wrote one member of the audience. They had 'broken her heart' with their 'blasphemous' production, she said. One letter to the editor of the *Nordbayerischer Kurier* wrote of an 'experiment with a sledge-hammer'. 'To take a well-known legend and stamp it with the mark of our own times is something that only the unimaginative bigots of this young group can achieve.'[51] Friedelind was of a very different opinion: 'Every time there is an innovation, needless to say, there are howls of protests from the old-timers.'[52]

When Chéreau's *Ring* was recorded for US television, Friedelind offered her services as a 'hostess' and added a commentary in which she openly spoke of Hitler's visits to Bayreuth. This brought her much sympathy in the USA. When the ethnomusicologist Fritz A. Kuttner from the Jewish organization B'nai B'rith was asked to report on the production, he claimed that Chéreau's production in the first and second acts of *Siegfried* was 'scandalous, shabby anti-Semitic exploitation.'[53] But Friedelind disagreed, and wrote back to say that 'It is a quite grandiose, human document and precisely the opposite of what you accuse it of being ... Neither he [Chéreau] nor Boulez are anti-Semites – I would put my hand in the fire for both of them every day – indeed, I'd gladly climb the burning pyre to convince the doubters of their integrity – the anti-Semite was my grandfather and all too many people around him.' This acknowledgement is somewhat surprising, given her denial of any such tendencies in her father Siegfried. Always ready for a fight, Friedelind offered to take part in any debate in the matter. She also asked Kuttner to meet Peter Weinberg of Channel 13 and John Ardoin from the *Dallas Morning News,* who were both involved in the TV production.

Wolfgang was not happy about Friedelind's presence in Bayreuth during the centenary celebrations. When Frederick Haupt asked him for an interview, he wrote back that 'As a rule, I do not receive groups who wish to inform themselves equally through me and through one or more members of my family who have nothing to do with the management of the Festival.'[54] But it was not just Friedelind who was treated harshly. In 1976 Wolfgang married his secretary Gudrun Mack and fired his daughter Eva, who had worked in the Festspielhaus from 1968 to 1975 and who had taken her mother's side in the matter. He could almost have quoted from Wotan's words to his daughter Brünnhilde in the *Walküre*: 'Wish-maid art thou no more'.

Friedelind was able to understand why her mother might dislike the Chéreau *Ring,* for she belonged to a different generation that rejected new interpretations. But she was angry when Winifred made her opinions known in public. So she introduced Chéreau to her mother in person – Winifred had hitherto given him a wide berth – and said 'Although you wanted to shoot him at your first meeting, he insists on getting to know you.' Out of necessity, Winifred found a few things to praise, but finished by saying 'And now, Herr Chéreau, go and find a composer for your piece.'[55] In a letter to Friedelind she stressed once again that 'The sets and costumes for the Ring are completely impossible to my mind – but this parody, this blasphemy, this crime, this desecration of the temple is presumably what people want today. *I* won't have anything more to do with it!'[56]

The vehemence with which Friedelind was able to defend Chéreau's conception of the *Ring* was matched by the vehemence of her criticism when she didn't like something. She found Götz Friedrich's production of *Lohengrin* 'ugly, ugly' and quoted a visitor who swore never to eat cake in the bedroom any more because the director had designed the bridal bed as a giant wedding cake.[57]

When the city of Bayreuth celebrated Wolfgang's 60th birthday in Wahn-

fried, no one from the family was invited except for Winifred. Verena and Friedelind then requested that the rest of the family be invited too, but only they
were then issued with invitations. So Verena declined to attend. The family
of Wolfgang's second wife Gudrun was there *en masse*, but from the Wagner
side of the family Friedelind was the sole representative. The media was continually focussed on members of the next generation when there was talk of
a successor for Wolfgang, and for this reason Friedelind found it unfortunate
that none of them was present at the celebration. Furthermore, Wieland's
son Wolf Siegfried was preparing six different productions in Germany and
abroad. Friedelind advised him to show his face more in Bayreuth, 'because
the question of the succession is on everyone's lips and your name is well-
regarded everywhere. A friend of mine calls it "facial care".'[58] On the evening
before the party she was invited to visit Wolfgang and Gudrun, though she was
ill at ease there because she did not like people smoking and disliked having
to see how lobsters were boiled alive.[59]

There was much surprise when the Siegfried Wagner Society announced
in 1980 that Friedelind had found the score of Siegfried's symphonic poem
Sehnsucht in a storage room at the Festspielhaus (though it was not in fact the
autograph but a printed score). The Northwest German Philharmonic gave the
work's world première in 1981.[60]

Despite her good contacts in the media, Friedelind was also capable of
being curt when she did not want to do something. When the Bavarian radio
asked her to take part in a programme on 'Women in the Third Reich' and
added that Eva Wagner-Pasquier had already intimated that Friedelind would
refuse, her answer was short and sweet: 'My niece is quite right.'[61] And the fate
of the Festival under her brother's management remained for her a wound that
would not heal. When she received an invitation to speak about Wagner in
New York, she replied in her typically brusque manner: 'I no longer talk about
Bayreuth. And if I were to talk about Wagner, how could I NOT talk about
Bayreuth? I hope the day will not be far off that I CAN talk about it again.
Right now it is too painful.'[62] Instead she kept herself informed about developments in modern music and visited Pierre Boulez's IRCAM Institute in Paris.
She was delighted to see how Boulez was able to alter the different segments
of the concert hall according to his acoustic requirements – the ceiling, the
walls and the floor. It was just such a hall that she had dreamt of for Teesside.
'If this flexibility is extended to the performing area, the future of opera would
indeed be exciting.'[63]

Chapter 16

'A foster mother, a guiding light'
The 1980s

WINIFRED WAGNER died on 5 March 1980. No one could claim that in running the Festival she had in any way squandered the legacy of Cosima and Siegfried, for by engaging Tietjen, Preetorius and Furtwängler, and by retaining Toscanini, she had maintained and even expanded the Festival's importance as an institution that set the benchmark for theatres all over the world. One could hardly blame her for possessing neither the artistic talent nor the erudition of her mother-in-law Cosima. Even her blind enthusiasm for Hitler in the 1920s might be regarded as having been determined by the exigencies of the time. It is always problematical to sit at a safe chronological distance and indulge in moral judgements over people who had to live in times of dictatorship – not least because Winifred could claim, with some justification, to have helped people in need during the Nazi era, including several Jews.

What remained incomprehensible to Friedelind was her mother's steadfast fidelity to one of the most heinous criminals in world history – a fidelity that she maintained to the very end. But for all her anger at her unreconstructed mother, Friedelind was unable as a daughter to distance herself completely from her, and their relationship remained characterized by conflicting emotions. Both women possessed an iron will. If Winifred had condemned Nazi ideology after the fact, then she would have had to have rehabilitated the daughter who had fled from it. But instead, Winifred saw Friedelind almost solely as the person who had irritated the Nazis by emigrating, and who, on top of this, had become an American citizen and had attacked her in her book. While Friedelind could never forgive her mother for her uncritical approach to her past, Winifred could never overcome the ignominy to which her daughter had subjected her. Friedelind always remained the renegade daughter and a traitor, despite all the niceties that they later exchanged in the years when they corresponded again.[1]

Winifred's death brought Friedelind to Bayreuth for a full three years, during which she emptied her mother's house and ordered her archives. Since she was still unsure about her own future, this was a welcome activity. The city was interested in buying the dining room of the Siegfried House, and the discussions with the heirs proved arduous. There was much to negotiate and to arbitrate. When the Festival was turned into a foundation Winifred had been given over two million marks and much of it was still untouched. Then there was all the furniture, plus valuable objects from the time of Richard and Siegfried Wagner that had been among Winifred's personal belongings. Given the divergent interests of the different family members and the general atmosphere between them, it was inevitable that a legal dispute would arise. Lawyers of the various family members endeavoured to plot a course through the tangled mess in order to try and find some form of general agreement that would satisfy everyone. At one meeting on 14 February 1981, no fewer than seven lawyers were present. Since inheriting money herself, Friedelind had tried to stand by the younger generation and to mediate for them. Winifred's surviving portion of the profit from the sale of the archives was supposed to be divided up between her four children (thus Wolfgang, Verena, Friedelind and then Wieland's children Iris, Daphne, Nike and Wolf Siegfried), but Friedelind suggested that the amount should be altered in order for Richard Wagner's great-grandchildren to receive a larger share (Wagner's great-granddaughter Dagny Beidler was automatically excluded, as had become customary). The dispute escalated when Wolfgang insisted that the sum requested by his daughter Eva should be deducted from her later inheritance. Her lawyer rejected this out of hand, for the one matter had nothing to do with the other.[2]

Winifred had arranged for certain documents, including Hitler's letters to her, 'to be spirited away from Bayreuth in a cloak-and-dagger operation', as Friedelind later described it. Winifred had given these documents – also including Friedelind's letters to her from the 1940s, when things were difficult – to her favourite granddaughter Amélie Hohmann, a daughter of Bodo and Verena Lafferentz and by profession a historian. She possesses these documents down to the present day and ignores all requests to make them available for scholarly purposes. In the meantime, a company called 'Festspiele Ltd' had been founded, apparently without the knowledge of the Bayreuth Foundation Board. Both these *faits accomplis* appalled Friedelind and she wrote to her lawyer:

> In light of the fact that I am one of the founders and a member of the Foundation Board and yet, despite repeated requests, have to the present day received no information about the so-called 'Festspiele Ltd', nor a list of the 'intellectual property' that my brother has sold (to whom???), I have forbidden Amélie from giving my brother any information until I am informed 100% about his machinations and those of the Foundation. Then one can determine to whom that 'intellectual property' truly belongs, and whether the gentlemen who have founded the company were actually entitled to do so.[3]

Friedelind wanted to prevent Wolfgang from getting his hands on the material that Winifred had given to Amélie for safe-keeping – at least not until he, for his part, had provided information about the new 'Festival' company.

Even after the end of her Bayreuth master classes and her courses in Teesside, Friedelind continued to support young artists wherever she could. These included the young Chinese conductor Muhai Tang, who had applied for and received a scholarship from the Society of Friends of Bayreuth. In 1982 he suddenly became famous when he won the Karajan Competition and was invited to conduct the Berlin Philharmonic as part of his prize. One of the works proposed by the orchestra was Siegfried Wagner's *Sehnsucht*. Friedelind was delighted about this, decided to help Tang, and so introduced him to Daniel Barenboim in Berlin, whom she had known for years. Tang admired her readiness to help, her humour and her openness.

Friedelind kept in touch with many of the artists with whom she had become acquainted over the years, attending their performances whenever she could. Joachim Herz wrote to her of his experiences in New York and invited her to productions in Europe. She was Christoph Eschenbach's guest at concerts in Zurich; the director Peter Konwitschny visited her and she showed him round the Tribschen Villa; and Lord Harewood, the then director of the English National Opera, trusted her judgement to such an extent that he would ask her opinion of singers, conductors and directors whom she had seen and heard on her travels. Whenever she attended an opera performance she could always be found in the artists' dressing rooms afterwards. Her remarkable facial similarity to Richard Wagner and the wit and intelligence that she exuded in conversation altogether afforded her a special status.

However, Friedelind's scepticism towards Bayreuth remained, and she enjoyed a little *schadenfreude* whenever things went awry there. Thus she once wrote to the opera director Markus Kiesel to say 'It will amuse you that Dr Eger mixed up the death mask of Weber and the life mask of Liszt and had a "hot argument" with Neill, insisting that Weber had to be Liszt, because he had warts.'[4]

In 1983 Isabella Wallich flew to Paris to meet Friedelind and to attend rehearsals of Siegfried Wagner's symphonic poem *Die Sehnsucht* under Daniel Barenboim. On the evening, so Wallich recalled, there was a reception in Friedelind's honour held by Princess Ruspoli. Barenboim managed an excellent performance, despite the fact that the musicians had never played the work before. Friedelind was very fond of Barenboim. She had known him since he was 12 and had written of him in glowing terms to Walter Felsenstein back in 1963, calling him a 'phenomenal talent ... equally talented as conductor, composer, in languages and mathematics. And he can mimic people wonderfully.

He is completely unspoilt ...'[5] Now he was 40 years old, and she travelled to hear him perform whenever she could.

When Gottfried travelled to Bayreuth in August 1983 along with his second wife Teresina and his mother-in-law, Wolfgang refused to receive him. So Friedelind invited them to dinner in the Schloss Tiergarten Hotel. She also procured Festival tickets for them by ringing up Wolfgang and getting him to put three aside for them.[6] Her emotional support and sympathy were also important to the nephews and nieces who were trying to build up their own careers. Whenever Wolf Siegfried or Gottfried directed an opera or Wieland Lafferentz conducted, she would be there to support them. When a director was needed in Leipzig for a production of *Rienzi*, she made sure to drop Wolf Siegfried's name. She promoted the next generation at every opportunity. 'Up to her death in 1991 she was always interested in my professional career and usually came to the opening nights of my productions, full of touching pride,' wrote Gottfried.[7] Her niece Eva was also full of praise for her: 'Without your advice, your help and your generosity in the past year I would surely have despaired of our family many a time.'[8] Nike Wagner was working on her book *Wagner Theater* and thanked her for her hospitality in Lucerne:

> I slept excellently on your real and metaphorical mattress and you were able to help me a lot with your elephantine memory and your 'illuminated' [sic] precision. It is important to me, and a pleasure, to gain insights into your life in the world (in contrast to those who 'stayed at home'). You say little of its travails and difficulties, but many a thing shimmers through. You will surely understand, too, how happy I am that you exist as a counterpoint within the cultural-political development of Bayreuth – without any resentment driving you into anti-Wagnerism.[9]

Friedelind gave her nieces and nephews cars and money, plus furniture that had been given to her from Winifred's estate. But there were times when she also took offence at them. Loans were not repaid, visits cancelled: 'No phone calls, no visits. Just demands for money!' And she tried to organize a meeting that everyone could attend in order to put an end to the smouldering tensions regarding the Bayreuth inheritance.[10]

In celebration of Richard Wagner's 100th birthday in 1983, the city of Bayreuth and the Bavarian Radio planned a commemorative event in the Margravial Opera House at which Pierre Boulez was due to conduct. Friedelind heard of it only through her friend Lotte Klemperer. When she confronted Wolfgang about it, he told her that there were no seats available for family members.[11] She immediately addressed her complaint to the two institutions responsible for the concert: 'It is hardly to be believed that two public organizations – of whom one lives solely from the fame of our family – quite simply ignore the descendants of Richard Wagner at this event and thus make fools of themselves before the whole world!' She included the addresses of all her relatives.[12] But the organizers remained intransigent and invited only Friedelind and Verena, both of whom stayed away in protest. Nor was Friedelind alone in having problems with Wolfgang. 'Just look at yourself: haven't you, too, capitulated before him in his position of power?' asked her sister-in-law Gertrud when Friedelind asked her about the whereabouts of several drawings and pastels by Wieland. She had lent Wolfgang several of Wieland's sketches for *Parsifal* from the 1930s and had not received them back.[13]

When Friedelind was asked to take part in a podium discussion during a Wagner conference in Leipzig alongside Martin Gregor-Dellin, Martin Geck and others, she refused in her typically brusque fashion:

> I would not be caught dead with such people on the same platform. I refused to go to N.Y. for a symposium. I am really sick and tired of all the talk about Wagner and don't enjoy his operas any more, either, the way they are butchered by the singers and most conductors, not to speak of the producers! Wolfgang was quite relieved to hear that I don't want to participate in any public debates any more, although the reasons I named shocked him. I recommended my nieces and nephews, I believe that Nike will take part in New York. He refuses to take the Schirmherrschaft [i.e. to act as patron] in New York because of Nike and what she wrote in Wummi's book [Wolf Siegfried's 1976 photo book about the Wagner family]. Er hat ein langes Gedächtnis [he has a long memory] and no one around here has yet learned what freedom of speech really means.[14]

Friedelind did not desire to participate in public discussions any more, but she gladly agreed to attend when the Bayreuth antiquarian book dealer Peer Baedeker invited her to a matinee centring on the collection of documents he had gathered together on the topic of 'Wagner interpreters in exile'. Her own book (in the English original) was the centrepiece of his collection. The participants included the Canadian writer on music Philip M. Wults (to whom Friedelind had given material for a Wagner biography that has still not appeared), Wagner's great-granddaughter Dagny Beidler and her husband Hans Hablützel. 'Friedelind had experienced at first hand the bitterness of being cast out and of having to emigrate, and she drew Dagny into things and was cordial towards her,' wrote Nike Wagner. 'She was aware of the historical injustice that had occurred and she was perhaps also driven by her old delight in resisting the self-righteous Wahnfried establishment.'[15]

In his speech, Wults described Bayreuth as a hotbed of National Socialism and stressed that Friedelind had rebelled against it. Afterwards they went to the grave of a Jewish citizen and laid flowers – a gesture also intended as a silent protest against the recent electoral successes of the neo-fascist NPD. In Bayreuth, Friedelind felt truly 'in exile', for she once again feared the advent of the far right. She admitted to a reporter that her dispute with her family had come about because she had made friends with anti-Nazis when living in the USA; she added that she was still regarded in the family as a 'traitor'.[16]

When she was accused of 'deserting the German flag' by an ex-Nazi in 1984, it served her as an official reason to step down as president of the Siegfried Wagner Society – an office of which she was in any case already tired. She also wanted to dissolve the Society itself. She was not a person suited to societies, and certainly not of a Wagnerian kind, for the name Wagner repeatedly acted as a magnet to those on the far right of the political spectrum. 'It is with indignation that I must distance myself from a society in which I am being mobbed by old Nazis and I hope that all decent thinking people will follow my example.'[17] She was referring to a letter from Franz Ehgartner, who had a role in the Austrian Siegfried Wagner Society, based in Graz. He expressed his joy at her resignation and added. 'Siegfried Wagner – deeply connected to Graz – was a German man who stood by his people, just like his wife did, our noble Winifred!'[18]

The Society could only be dissolved by means of written confirmation from three-quarters of its members. But the majority desired by Friedelind was not reached, although numerous members did indeed leave as a result of her announcement (ironically, these were mostly members from the far right who had only recently joined). Verena Lafferentz took on the office of president for a brief time, but soon all the family members left. After new elections for the committee, a new society newsletter was created, several old members joined again, new ones were won over and the International Siegfried Wagner Society enjoyed an upturn in its fortunes.[19]

'Drama, as all things Wagnerian!' wrote Friedelind when her family was annoying her.[20] She needed distance, so it was logical that she now decided to move to Lucerne. At last she was able to arrange her books and furniture as she wished, in an apartment where she could enjoy the family objects that had been acquired after so many battles. She liked everything in Lucerne: the air, her nice landlords, the 'magnificent view over the lake, the Alps and Tribschen – what more could a Wagner ask for?'[21] She often lay on the terrace of the upper floor in her large, flowery Hawaiian sack dress,[22] gazing out at the lake and the mountains. She could even see her grandparents' house in Tribschen, that same house where she had spent hours with Toscanini, Ellen Beerli and her aunts Eva and Daniela – hours fondly remembered despite all their arguments.

She now knew where she belonged. Her half-hearted attempts to bring order to her archives were in vain (part of her archive still lies in storage in the Festspielhaus). 'Her meticulous memory was her main archive, and she could draw names, dates and events from it as if out of a giant drawer,' recalled Nike.[23] Friedelind had rented her apartment from a Mr and Mrs Marfurt, and she became good friends with them. When she went on her travels she would leave them her keys and blank cheques. Since the Marfurts were keener on *bel canto* than on Wagner, Friedelind called them 'the Donizettis downstairs' and organized them opera tickets in London, Milan and Paris. She enjoyed Switzerland's rich music scene and continued to travel much in order to hear artists she knew or to get to know new ones. Her relationship to her sister became cooler, for she felt that she was attending too many Wagner Society events – 'What she gets out of it, I wouldn't know, because I cannot stand any of them.'[24]

In 1983 Bayreuth presented a new *Ring*, this time directed by Peter Hall and conducted by Georg Solti. The three Rhinemaidens had to swim naked in a huge pool, with mirrors employed to make it look as if they were floating, and there were technical problems. The final scene of *Götterdämmerung* was still being rehearsed just a few hours before opening night – something that had hitherto been an unimaginable state of affairs. Friedelind was horrified by the production and a few months later gave one of her by now infamous interviews. This resulted in an article published on 4 May 1984 by the *Münchener Abendzeitung*, entitled: 'Bayreuth today is scandalous!' Once again, she did not mince her words. Peter Hall had no idea at all about the *Ring*, she claimed. He was turning it into a huge 'amateur show' and could not speak a word of German. 'When I see how many talented great-grandchildren of Wagner's are around who are not allowed to work in Bayreuth, it's scandalous.' And she went even further: 'Since the Solti *Ring*, my brother has been intellectually out of his depth.'[25] Wolfgang presumably filed a complaint after this, for she asked the editor of the newspaper, Werner Meyer, to publish a correction – though it was one designed to infuriate Wolfgang even more: 'My brother was not "intellectually" out of his depth with the Solti-Hall *Ring*, for there was no trace of any intellect to be found anywhere in this fiasco.'[26]

Friedelind's complaint about the exclusion of the next generation was later taken up by the *New York Times*:

Wolfgang, who turns 70 next year, will be succeeded by someone chosen by the foundation, with preference given to qualified members of the Wagner family. But who measures quality? Several members of the next generation, including some of Wolfgang's and Wieland's children, are active in the theater, as directors, administrators or scholars. However, if Friedelind Wagner, Wolfgang's sister, is to be fully believed, Wolfgang has been merciless in discouraging their careers and involvement with – or even attendance at – the festival. Perhaps he is merely paranoid; perhaps he honestly considers them untalented layabouts; perhaps he is attempting to subject them to a trial from which only the hardiest will emerge. As of now, in any case, the Bayreuth succession is cloudy indeed.[27]

Despite her departure from the Siegfried Wagner Society, Friedelind travelled to Kiel to see the world première of her father's opera *Das Flüchlein, das Jeder mitbekam* and to help with a documentary exhibition in the theatre. In 1985 she called Isabella Wallich from Lucerne and surprised her with the news that she wanted to pay for recordings of three works by her father: his Symphony in C Major and the two symphonic poems *Sehnsucht* and *Und wenn die Welt voll Teufel wär*. For this she engaged the Aalborg Symphony Orchestra in Denmark and its conductor Peter Erös. It was typical of Friedelind that she even took on the extra hotel and living costs for Isabella's recording team in Denmark, because she had known Erös for a long time and trusted him (he had been an assistant of Klemperer's). Isabella gladly accepted the offer.

However, problems were inevitable, for the Danish musicians' union had learnt that Friedelind was blithely ignoring their rules. Together with Isabella she took part in negotiations with the union but in the end banged her fist on the table and declared that they would all pack their things and go if no solution was found, and then the orchestra would lose the extra income they had anticipated from the project. That worked. The recordings took place in the city hall. After four days everything had been recorded to everyone's satisfaction and the works were published by Isabella's company Delysé.[28] In 1989 Isabella's company went bankrupt and Friedelind bought up all the remaining records. She paid for the CDs from her own pocket, and the project ended more than CHF 100,000 in the red.[29]

A special occasion for Friedelind was the inauguration of Richard Wagner's Erard piano in Tribschen. She had paid for its restoration and when the instrument came back it was placed in the Tribschen Museum. As it happened, the pianist Jeffrey Swann (born 1951) was there and so he was the first to be allowed to play it. The 'official' inauguration of the piano was, however,

28 She loved playing the piano, although she had to give up piano lessons
on account of neuralgic pain at the age of 15.

assigned to Friedelind's friend Daniel Barenboim, who once said of her that
she had hair like Franz Liszt and the profile of Richard Wagner.[30]

In 1986 Friedelind was invited to San Francisco for a showing of Tony
Palmer's film *Wagner* starring Richard Burton and Vanessa Redgrave. The
proceeds were to go to the local opera house as a contribution to the costs
of its *Ring* production planned for 1990. Friedelind's answer was to the point:
'I am neither a "Rent-a-Wagner", nor am I a glutton for punishment and will,
under no circumstances, be available for the showing of the Burton "Wagner"
film, nor will I permit my name to be used in connection with it.'[31] It seems
unlikely that she actually saw the film, for it would hardly have prompted such
a refusal. Perhaps it was the great effort involved in getting there that failed
to appeal to her.

For other serious enquiries, however, Friedelind remained as open as ever.
In 1988 she was back in Bayreuth and spent an evening there with the Baren-
boims (Daniel, his mother Elena and the nurse of his wife Jacqueline du Pré
who had died just a year earlier). When financial wrangling led to Barenboim's
dismissal as the artistic director of the Bastille Opera in Paris a year later,
Friedelind was horrified. 'No doubt you must have felt as if the entire edifice
of the new Bastille came crashing down on you last Friday – a beautiful dream

shattered – 18 months of hard work, agonies, hopes, expectations smashed. I feel that you ought to be congratulated – for this would have turned into an eternal nightmare.'[32]

One year before Friedelind's death, the cabaret artiste Eva Busch admitted in an interview for the first time that her father was Franz Beidler, the same who had married Friedelind's aunt Isolde. During Isolde's bout of tuberculosis he had fallen in love with the singer Emmy Zimmermann and had a child by her. Friedelind immediately made contact with Eva Busch and together they visited Dagny Beidler in Zurich, Beidler's granddaughter and thus Eva Busch's niece. Not unlike Friedelind, Eva had been a non-conformist all her life. She had sung songs of Tucholsky and Bertolt Brecht in cabarets and had openly sympathized with the anti-fascist resistance as had her husband, the singer and actor Ernst Busch. She had lost her German citizenship in 1937 and was living in Paris when the Nazis invaded. They took her prisoner and she later spent three-and-a-half years in the Ravensbrück concentration camp.[33]

Friedelind thought of making a new translation of her autobiography, about which she had received numerous enquiries. She was convinced that her family would try everything to block its publication, so she wanted to stay with a Swiss publisher. 'Nothing has changed and I'm still being persecuted like a criminal in the land of the Nazis.'[34] But when her publisher announced plans to put Hitler on the front of the book and to arrange a pre-publication deal with the *Spiegel* magazine, Friedelind refused both suggestions. She did not want her memoir to be seen primarily as settling scores with the Nazi era – that had indeed been important to her once, but she had now put it behind her.

She had little desire to hold back her opinions these days, as we can see from a draft letter in her archives, addressed to the President of the State of Schleswig-Holstein. She had been invited to join the board of trustees of the Schleswig-Holstein Music Festival, but declined. 'In a country in which I am ever more ostracized, defamed, hounded, persecuted and condemned because I had the courage to leave Hitler's Germany in 1937 at the age of 19 and to fight against it, there is nothing for me to do. I owe this to Hitler's victims. Nevertheless, I wish you much happiness and success with the Music festival.'[35] She thus took a quite contrary position from her friend of many years Leonard Bernstein, who happily went to conduct in Schleswig-Holstein and felt comfortable there.

On his way from his last TV recordings in Waldsassen, Bernstein stopped off in Bayreuth on 6 April 1990 in order to see the Wagner archives, the Wagner Museum in Wahnfried and the Festspielhaus. He came at Friedelind's invitation and she fetched him in Waldsassen herself. They had known each other since 1944. Wolfgang had cancelled his planned meeting with Bernstein, which was a matter of deep disappointment to Friedelind. The conductor was seriously ill and was in great pain every time he breathed (he would die just six months later). He had been no friend of abstinence, and when his fans had held up placards begging him 'We love you, Lenny. Please stop smoking' after Alan Jay Lerner's death from lung cancer, he had replied: 'I smoke. I drink. I stay up all night. I screw around. I'm over committed on all fronts' – which was quoted liberally in *USA Today* as documented proof of his *joie de vivre*.[36]

It was only out of affection for Bernstein that Friedelind now returned to the haunts of her childhood and youth and where she had later held the master classes that had meant so much to her. It was his first visit, and her last; for both it was a kind of farewell. Bernstein was moved to see the Festspielhaus, and he descended into the pit to stand at the podium where he would have conducted *Tristan und Isolde*, had Wieland not died so young. They visited Wahnfried where Bernstein, never without his sense of humour, acted out the role of King Ludwig and Friedelind that of her grandfather, leading his royal patron through the house. Bernstein was fascinated by the Steinway grand piano made of rosewood that had belonged to Wagner. He played the Prelude to *Tristan* on it, followed by excerpts from the love duet in the second act. 'You could create a whole orchestral sound on this instrument,' he said. He at first did not want to visit the composer's grave, but let Friedelind talk him into it. As they stood before the sober, stone slab out in the garden, he suggested that it was big enough for one to dance upon. With her at his side he now felt that he had somehow made his peace with a musician whom he had hated for so long – though 'on my knees'.[37] Friedelind also took him to the Bayreuth synagogue, where Bernstein made jokes about both their 'Jewish noses', – a reference, too, to Friedelind's time back in New York when, with her many Jewish friends, she had enjoyed a milieu very different from that of Bayreuth. Even now, the vestiges of the Nazi era had not died out in her home town. Afterwards she accompanied Bernstein to Munich.

Shortly before Friedelind's death, the conflict intensified between her nephew Gottfried and his father. Gottfried had been demanding that the influence of Bayreuth on Nazi policies (and vice versa) should be discussed openly and no longer suppressed. In January 1990 he learnt that Wolfgang had threatened to distance himself publicly from all Richard Wagner societies, if they did not rescind any and all speaking invitations they had made to his son. Gottfried promptly confronted his father about this – though in full awareness that he could not win the power struggle. Wolfgang astutely had numerous newspaper quotes at the ready to justify his stance (thus, for example, Gottfried had said that, after Wieland's death, the Festival had turned into 'something between a stock exchange and a scrap iron market').

The Festival Director was thus able to utilize his position to suppress debate.[38] Certainly it would have been unpleasant for him to have to argue with his own son and it would have required a degree of composure that he could no longer muster. Gottfried had not forgotten how Wolfgang had refused to receive his second wife Teresina ten years earlier, and found this particularly wounding: 'He wants nothing more to do with us – and we have to live with that.'[39] From here on, Gottfried saw his aunt Friedelind as his only ally in the family. Her sympathies were in any case always on the side of the outsiders and of those who had been cast out – it was simply part of her make up.

Friedelind had since her youth tormented her body with starvation diets, and she now took ill with pancreatic cancer. She first tried to ignore the symptoms, and having little faith in conventional medicine she put her trust in homeopathic methods. Her landlords, the Marfurts, helped to look after her, and her family rallied round. But after the disease had progressed inexorably and painfully she asked to be transferred to a special clinic in Herdecke in Westphalia in Germany. The end was by now inevitable, and she died on 8 May 1991 at the age of 73. She left her whole estate to Neill Thornborrow, the young pianist she had got to know in England and whose career she had helped to further. He works today as a theatre agent in Düsseldorf.

Although Friedelind had not asked for any service of commemoration in Bayreuth, Wolfgang organized a commemoration for 17 May to which only members of the family and Friedelind's close friends were invited.[40] The decision to invite only an inner circle explains why the city of Bayreuth did not send any representatives. However, no reason has ever been given why the city has thus far refrained from naming any of its streets after its famous émigré. (In May 2013, by contrast, the square in front of the Festspielhaus was officially named the 'Wolfgang Wagner Platz'). The music at the commemoration comprised 'Elsa's Dream' from *Lohengrin* and 'Verena's Song' from Siegfried Wagner's opera *Der Kobold*, sung by Carmen Reppel and accompanied by Klaus Arp. Between these two pieces Wolfgang gave a speech. He sketched out his sister's life, work and nature, and stressed that she had never made things easy, either for herself or for those around her. Like the life of her grandfather, hers had been an 'ocean of contradictions'. A rejection of the current state of things and opposition to the established order were, he said, the most prominent characteristics of her 'eternally rebellious spirit'.

Wolfgang thus depoliticized Friedelind's propensity to criticize, interpreting it instead as a fundamental aspect of her character. 'Non-acceptance and contrariness were a vital source of what drove her, but so was her burning desire to achieve an ideal that was strong and pure.' A degree of utopianism was fundamental to her character, he continued – something else that she would surely not have agreed with. The fact that Siegfried had pampered her, and that Winifred had felt compelled to compensate for this was interpreted by Wolfgang as a cause of her early rejection of her mother and her great love for her father. He thus made of her a victim of the circumstances into which she had been born and trivialized her conflict with her mother by explaining it as a consequence of her upbringing (and thus quite unconnected with Winifred's political beliefs). Wolfgang also described the book *Heritage of Fire* as a document of subjective experience rather than of objective truth. It was, he claimed, a concoction largely invented by Friedelind's 'American ghostwriter' (though as we have elaborated above, her co-authoress had merely made cuts and corrections and improved the language). He further maintained that Friedelind had requested that her book not be used as documentary evidence against Winifred in her denazification proceedings – by which means Wolfgang emphasized its supposed untrustworthiness (in fact, as we have seen above, Friedelind had done no such thing but had instead sent the court a telegram to ask for a delay until she could attend the hearings).[41]

Another mistake – or perhaps an intentional falsification – was Wolfgang's claim that by taking over the Festival, he and Wieland had acted 'completely in line with Siegfried Wagner's will' – whereas Siegfried had in fact made his four children equal heirs. And finally, he maintained that Friedelind had 'made claim to the direction of the Festival', though there is no documentary proof of it. It was in fact the then Mayor of Bayreuth, Dr Meyer, who had in vain urged her to return and manage the Festival.

With regard to the failure of her master classes, Wolfgang asked 'whether her plans were too grandly conceived or whether the real world was in fact too small for them' – without mentioning that it was he who had thrown her out in 1968, albeit on account of the debts that she had accumulated. He came to the conclusion that she was an 'unconventional thinker', not a 'black sheep of the family'. He unreservedly praised her commitment to their father's music, and closed thus:

> Public opinion paid attention almost solely to the controversies between mother and daughter and, to a lesser extent, to those between [Friedelind] and me, and they used these to judge my sister. But we should all endeavour to recognize her true significance, far from all the clichés.

That was a skilful summing up, for it conveyed the impression that Wolfgang had indeed spoken of her 'true significance'. But in reality he had offered up a mixture of criticism and phoney facts: her conflict with her mother had thus been merely the result of her upbringing; her book was a fiction; she had not left Germany for political reasons; and Siegfried's will had been respected in full by his two sons.[42]

Three years after her death, Wolfgang published his autobiography *Lebens-Akte* and it was much discussed in the media. 'Why did the old man Wolfgang do this to himself?' asked the reviewer of *Die Zeit*, who pointed out that the Bayreuth Festival was without peer in the world and was in artistic, legal and financial terms perfectly healthy. Wasn't it superfluous to bring this book into the world? He criticized Wolfgang's artless depiction of Hitler's connection to Bayreuth and quoted him thus: 'My brother and I thankfully had no reason to wear sackcloth and ashes and beat our breasts in penitence because our past had been too brief and too insignificant.'[43] A comparison between Wolfgang's mention of his sister in his autobiography and his words at her commemoration service show that the divide between brother and sister was bigger than one might have thought. He delights in offering ironic commentary on her book, and writes that her 'irrepressible busyness' had 'only brought financial burdens' to Bayreuth. Had Friedelind still been alive, she would never have let all that go uncontested.

Friedelind's death was the close of a life that had begun and ended with a great love for her father and that had been marked by restlessness and rootlessness. Bayreuth remained for ever at the core of who she was and what she did – even if she seldom went there late in life, it was a place of innumerable memories that had helped to define her. Her colourful, erratic life had taken her from Germany to England to Argentina to the USA and towards the end to Switzerland – and finally back to Germany to die. Her ashes were taken to her beloved Lucerne, the town where her grandfather had completed *Tristan*, where her grandparents Richard and Cosima had been so happy and had begun a new, peaceful phase of their life, and where she, Friedelind, had in her youth enjoyed carefree holidays with her aunts. At her own request, her ashes were scattered there in an unmarked spot.

'Wild Mausi or the black sheep' was the title of an article that appeared in 1994 when Friedelind's memoir was published again for the first time in 50 years. Another called her 'The oddest family offshoot who couldn't hold her tongue.'[44] Her 'oppositional' status thus remained in currency long after her death, and decades after her autobiography had first been published. If one considers her life from a historical perspective then, as a young woman, Friedelind achieved far more than her politically subservient brothers. To go into exile without any qualifications to her name, to separate herself for years from her homeland, from the cultural riches of the Festival and from her family was a deed that deserves much respect. She belonged neither here nor there, and no one thanked her for campaigning for another Germany when she was abroad.

On the contrary: after 1945 the most recent past was glossed over and denied among the perpetrators in Germany. There was no adequate acknowledgement of all that the émigrés had taken upon themselves. Friedelind too was branded an outsider and had to live with this, right down to the point where she was thrown out of a Bayreuth hotel in 1968. The transition from denazification to anti-communism coincided with a remarkably swift upturn in Germany – an upturn reflected, too, in its cultural life – which also meant that many people with a Nazi past were allowed to retain their former positions. Despite her anger at this conservative volte-face, Friedelind refused to indulge in assigning collective guilt. But she could protest just as strongly whenever she felt that the demons of Nazism were on the rise again in Germany. She was never able to reconcile herself with the fact that the Germans, to her mind, had never distanced themselves adequately from the rupture in civilization caused by the attempted genocide of the Jews. Her critical, resigned stance towards the democratic achievements of the post-war Federal Republic was perhaps a result of her act of emigration having been condemned by so many Germans. There were certainly errors of judgement made on both sides. But she remained fearless and rebutted all attempts to impose any discipline on her. Her ability to assert herself and to take herself seriously was something that many women of her generation found difficult on account of their upbringing. But these were traits that she had developed early on, and they remained with her for good, as is proven by her retort to a female Christian missionary who came knocking at her door in Lucerne: '*I* shall decide the time and the dialect for me to enter paradise.'[45]

If Friedelind had taken the risk of returning in 1947 to take over the Festival, its future would surely have been very different (the question remains hypothetical, since the Festspielhaus was in the end not confiscated by the authorities to dispose of as they saw fit; but she would perhaps have acquired a management position alongside her brothers). Power-hunger on various sides has overshadowed the history of the Festival and all questions of succession right down to the present day. But it is clear that Friedelind missed her opportunity – just as so much else in life passed her by or remained unrealized. Her separation from her family, her oppositional spirit, her struggles in exile, her imprisonment, adapting to a foreign culture and worrying about how to make ends meet – such challenges were not expected to be met by women born in the early twentieth century. She uttered no public criticism of her mother and brothers for their having never admitted to their close collaboration with the Nazis. But she remained convinced that there had been no real effort to come to terms with the past in Germany. Had those who remained helped to stabilize the system, as she so often supposed? Were those who participated despite their lack of conviction still Nazis, and did they thereby strengthen the influence of Nazi ideology? These were questions that occupied many survivors and that led them to very different conclusions. They also reflect in the end the unsolvable problems of the twentieth century.

'Despite all their ideological differences and their opposing opinions, Friedelind by no means feels estranged from her family,' wrote Kadidja Wedekind on one occasion.[46] As a daughter of the writer Frank Wedekind, Kadidja knew all about such ambivalence. Friedelind's relationship with her mother was strained, but their bond was strong. Time and again she tried to build up a real connection to her, but she was just as given to criticizing her in the press, which then ruined everything again. She never lost her adoration for her father, even when documents surfaced and were published in her lifetime that testified to his enthusiasm for Hitler that ought to have shattered her image of him as an unpolitical composer and Festival Director – an image she had constructed in prose in her own autobiography.[47] Rather like Erika Mann, who devoted herself to her father's archives, Friedelind also saw herself as the executor of Siegfried's artistic legacy towards the end of her life. She did all she could to wrest his compositional oeuvre from oblivion and return his stage works to the operatic canon. She had also been the patroness of the 'International Liszt Centre for Nineteenth-Century Music'. But above everything in her life there hovered Richard Wagner, whose music had been as mother's milk to her. Whether being a Wagner sufficed as a calling in life, whether it was a curse or a blessing, is something that we cannot answer definitively; but it was an attachment that she could not and would not sever. She returned time and again to Bayreuth, and only in her final years did she stay away. Viola Roggenkamp's description of Erika Mann is also apt in Friedelind's case: 'If she was at home anywhere, then it was in her exclusion.'[48] Perhaps she also denied her own desires in trying to serve her grandfather, to whom she seemed to cling because he afforded her an identity as his granddaughter that always opened doors and seemed to give sense to her life.

Friedelind's character seems to have borne a striking resemblance to that of her aunt Isolde, as Daniela and Eva had often claimed. Isolde was Cosima's favourite daughter, Richard Wagner's first child, and her mother described her as follows:

There is nothing brilliant about her, though she has a certain genius (at least what I understand by genius). Possessed of an innocence that no man out in the world could even begin to comprehend, the world's influence can only serve to confuse her; she lacks the sharpness necessary to see through it; she has only senses and no real thoughts ... many talents and no joy in exercising them ... I wish for her to find a husband who loves her. But that will be difficult, for she only understands the absolute masculine, nothing else attracts her, and since she desires nothing I fear that my wish will remain an empty one.[49]

Friedelind, too, failed to develop all her talents. She could not keep to a budget, and perhaps she lacked the analytical faculties that would have been needed to deal confidently with the many conflicts that confronted her. Nor did she ever find a partner for life.

'I admire her sincerity, her openness, her rectitude and her steadfastness, though it all means she will forge a difficult path for herself,' wrote Daniela once of her niece.[50] Verena Lafferentz has spoken of her sister's 'great talent, her effervescent personality, her readiness to help, her benevolence, love, friendship and her great heart.'[51] 'She wore her generous heart on her tongue,' quipped the *Nordbayerische Kurier*, 'Her almost fanatical love of truth could be as refreshing as it was disarming.'[52]

'The world of music from Sydney to Toronto and Stockholm owes Friedelind's master classes outstanding singers, conductors and instrumentalists,' wrote one newspaper in her obituary. It was right; one of her former students, Patricia Sage, has written of those classes as follows:

I hold tightly to all those incredible Master Class memories, to those magic times when we were all crouched down in the rehearsals, so Wieland wouldn't see us and throw us out, when the music of Wagner was flowing forth – I am grateful to God that Friedelind was the great lady she was (no matter how difficult!) and saw to it that we all had the best she could provide – it put all our lives – and careers – in an uplifted orbit.[53]

Mateo Lettunich wrote that Friedelind was 'fanatically devoted to her ideals,' and 'utterly unselfish'. He continued:

I have known and been fond of Friedelind for a long time and I have watched her wonderful work with the Master Classes from their beginnings in Bayreuth to her present headquarters in the north of England ... despite all obstacles she has managed to launch a number of wonderful careers and she never completely ceases her help to those who pass muster at the Master Classes.[54]

The music critic Martin Bernheimer found her 'brilliant, opinionated to a high degree, capable of playing favorites, and not terribly trustworthy in matters of planning and finance',[55] while her friend Isabella Wallich wrote:

> I could see much of her father in the meticulous care and concentration that Mausi displayed when she undertook any task, and also in her impatience with inefficiency. Happily, she also inherited her father's warmth, which made her such a delightful friend. Her character was both resolute and courageous, and she never flinched at doing what she believed was right, even if the price she had to pay was high.[56]

The singer Anja Silja praised her 'clinical sense of justice'; 'she fought against everything that seemed unjust to her. When she put her trust in someone, it stayed that way. She was in human terms unique and always stood up for others.'[57] Friedelind's niece Dagny, with whom she enjoyed a friendship of many years, described her as

> an extremely interesting, independent, courageous, combative, generous woman who tackled and initiated many things. A woman who possessed intuition and empathy, who could get enthusiastic, who took on much, was barely aware of her limits and thus expected much of others too. But she was also withdrawn, someone who hesitated to trust completely, who was afraid that others might get too close to her.[58]

The musicologist Markus Kiesel wrote: 'With Friedelind Wagner, the world of music and theatre has lost a foster mother, a role model, an adviser and an inconvenient contemporary of stature. But it is possible that the world will once again not notice.'[59] And he continued: 'What I myself owe to her is something that I hope I show, unremarked upon, every day: the right mixture of integrity, personal responsibility and human kindness.'[60]

To her nephew Gottfried too she was a role model: 'With her readiness to confront family history – especially in the era of the Third Reich – she sent a message to all descendants of Wagner that they must take on personal responsibility when dealing with their own history and the history of Germany.'[61]

And indeed, her life seems to be a mirror of the boundless contradictions and burdens that Germany imposed upon its citizens in the twentieth century – and half the world with them – convulsing the moral compass of several generations to come. Thomas Mann's famous claim that there was 'a lot of Hitler in Wagner' is justified on the one hand because of the ideological links between the composer and the racial policies of the Nazis,[62] but on the other hand it is also uncannily accurate when we consider Wagner's chronological proximity to the crimes of National Socialism. Thus the same Elsa Bernstein with whom Wagner once shook hands – the daughter of his friend Heinrich Porges – was deported to Theresienstadt.[63] The illegitimate daughter of Wagner's son-in-law Franz Beidler, Eva Busch, was sent to the Ravensbrück concentration camp and Wagner's grandson Franz Beidler – for sixteen years the heir to all of Bayreuth – was politically imperilled and had to flee abroad. All this makes evident Wagner's own direct proximity to Germany's descent into barbarism. As mentioned above, the chairwoman of the 'Richard Wagner Women's Group' in Heidelberg, Violetta von Waldberg, committed suicide when she was about to be deported to a camp in Poland. Winifred had refused to help her – was this because Frau Waldberg had been close to Daniela, Winifred's inconvenient sister-in-law and a source of increasing conflict since Siegfried's death? Winifred is proven to have helped numerous fellow human beings whose Jewish origins endangered them in the Third Reich, but there were also those for whom she did nothing. How could an English orphan presume to decide wilfully whether others should live or die? To be sure, one could ask a similar question of Hitler, a sometime picture-postcard painter living on the breadline in Vienna who three decades later would send millions to their deaths.

The historian Ian Kershaw recently asked why the German population accepted the carpet bombing of their cities without daring to rise up and shorten a war that caused endless misery to so many.[64] It is all too easy for those born later to point a finger and to sit in judgement, and it is all the more difficult to put oneself in the shoes of those who had to live in those difficult times. It is hard to imagine how it was back in 1947 when Friedelind very nearly took the witness stand against her mother in order to defend her own identity as an émigré and the integrity of her book. Was Wieland's early death somehow linked to his having suppressed his own role in Germany – a role into which he was catapulted as a young man and which had suited him so well for so long? And as for Wolfgang's lifelong obstinacy towards the younger generation of Wagners and his shrewdness in drawing up contracts so as to protect himself from attack in the family: was this also a result of the wounds that the Nazi period and its sham promises had inflicted on so many young people? Was Friedelind's decision to vilify her cousin Beidler to General Clay a token of an unshakeable bond with her mother and siblings, a bond she was unable to sever, far away from home as she was, despite all her conflict with them?

The close connections between Hitler and Wagner have been the subject of many books and articles, and yet there remain issues that must be clarified.

There is no doubt that by courting Hitler, the Bayreuth Festival bestowed a higher social status on him, and when he sought to bolster his rule by recourse to the might of tradition, Bayreuth allowed him to acquire a cultural aura that radiated out among the population at large.

It is not for us to excuse or to bemoan; but we must ask questions so that we might hope they may never have to be asked again. In Friedelind's life story there lie reflected the misfortunes suffered by her whole generation. And it is not least for this reason that it has been important for us to retrace it here.

Notes

⫸ Intro

1 *FonoForum* 10 (1998), p. 25.

2 The first German-language edition was published in Switzerland in 1948; a reprint was published in Cologne in Germany in 1994.

3 *Die Zeit* 27 (2007).

4 Wolfgang Wagner 1994, p. 138.

5 Wieland and Wolfgang Wagner to FW, 8.7.1950 (WWS).

6 HoF 197–199. Brigitte Hamann established the facts; see BH pp. 356–359.

7 Carr 2007, p. 206.

8 Janet Malcolm: *Two Lives. Gertrude and Alice.* New Haven/London, 2007, p. 223.

9 Ebermayer 1951, pp. 217, 218f.

10 Wolfgang Wagner 1994, 73; BH is of the opinion that Friedelind unjustly portrayed herself as a 'great figure of opposition to Hitler'. See Doris Stoisser: Radio feature 'Friedelind Wagner'.

11 Schostack 1998, p. 309.

12 See Eva Weissweiler, afterword to the new edition of *Nacht über Bayreuth*, pp. 337–346.

13 For example, VL claimed that Friedelind had known Siegfried Wagner's music intimately, while a former student of her master classes believed that she only had a superficial knowledge of it. There are many more, similarly contradictory reports about Friedelind.

14 *Neue Zürcher Zeitung*, 31.10.2010, p. 67.

⫸ Chapter 1

1 Cosima Wagner: *Die Tagebücher*. Munich/Zurich: Piper, 1976, Vol. I, pp. 107, 168, 13.

2 Quoted in Mack 1980, p. 11.

3 Mack 1980, pp. 12 and 15.

4 Karbaum 1976, Part I, p. 55.

5 Pachl 1988, pp. 83, 98f., 111.

6 Mack 1980, p. 870 (19.12.1915).

7 WW in Syberberg, n.d.

8 Mack 1980, p. 741.

9 WW to HR, n.d. (April 1918, VLA).

10 Von Kraft 1969, p. 217 (to Rosa Eidam).

11 Humperdinck 1999, p. 321 (with reproduction of the postcard).

12 WW to HR, 17.8.1919 (VLA).

13 Information from VL.

14 WW to HR, n.d. (ca 1920, VLA).

15 Letter from Cosima Wagner to Houston S. Chamberlain of 23.11.1891, in Paul Pretzsch, ed.: *Cosima Wagner und Houston S. Chamberlain im Briefwechsel.* Leipzig: Reclam, 1934, p. 253.

16 HoF, p. xi.

17 Isolde's son, Franz W. Beidler, left Germany in 1933 together with his wife (see Borchmeyer 2011, p. 365ff.).

18 N. Wagner in Friedländer/Rüsen 2000, p. 191.

19 FW, typoscript 'Wahnfried', p. 27 (NTh).

20 Syberberg.

21 FW, manuscript 'Enter Hitler', p. 40 (NTh).

22 Quoted in BH, p. 90.

23 BH, pp. 91 and 94.

24 In Zelinsky 1976, p. 169.

25 Hans Conrad: *Der Führer und Bayreuth* (1936), quoted in Karbaum 1976, Part II, p. 68f.

26 BH, p. 99.

27 BH, p. 96.

28 5.5.1924, reproduced in Karbaum 1976, Part II, p. 65f.

29 Henry Picker: *Hitlers Tischgespräche im Führerhauptquartier* (1963). Stuttgart: Propyläen, 1976, p. 115f.

30 Quoted in BH, 86.

31 N. Wagner: 'Für uns war er überhaupt nicht der Führer', in Friedländer/Rüsen 2000, pp. 179–193.

⦚ *Chapter 2*

1 Wolfgang Wagner 1994, p. 138.

2 FW: 'From my Life and Work', in: LiS, p. 20.

3 Statement made by VL on: *The Wagner Family*, DVD directed by Tony Palmer, 2011.

4 Written statement by VL.

5 Schostack 1998, pp. 82 and 94.

6 Schostack 1998, p. 82.

7 VL, letter to the author (October 2011).

8 Waldberg 1933, p. 26 (11.6.1869).

9 FW: Manuscript 'Wahnfried' (NTh). Where not otherwise mentioned, the descriptions here come from this source and from HoF.

10 Warburg 1989, p. 48.

11 Interview with VL.

12 FW: 'Lauritz Melchior zum 100. Geburtstag', manuscript (NTh).

13 FW to Sabine Rapp, 12.1.1956 (NTh).

14 Wolfgang Wagner 1994, pp. 63, 66, 168.

15 FW: 'A Price on my Head'. Manuscript, 15.3.1943 (NTh).

16 Schostack 1998, p. 79.

17 Syberberg.

18 HoF, p. 23.

19 WW to HR, 20.2.1920 (VLA).

20 Hans Wegener: 'Freundschaften', in: *Die Sonne* 1924, p. 695; it is included in her letter of 20.2.1920 (VLA).

21 Daniela Thode to A. Zinsstag, 24.9.1934 (MUB).

22 Schostack 1997, p. 84f.

23 Interview with VL in: *The Wagner Family*. DVD, 2011.

24 WW to HR, 27.2.1926 (VLA).

25 Winifred Wagner, 'Denkschrift 1946', quoted in Karbaum 1976, Part II, p. 114.

26 Quoted in BH, 85.

27 WW to Helene Boy (after her marriage: Helene Rösener), 8.4.1925 (NTh).

28 9.9.1926, quoted in Karbaum 1976, Part II, p. 67, and BH, p. 155.

29 HoF, p. 17.

30 Anna Bahr-Mildenburg/Hermann Bahr: *Bayreuth*. Leipzig, 1912, p. 17.

31 FW: 'From my Life and Work', in: LiS, p. 20.

32 Typescript 'A Price on my Head' of 15.3.1943 (NTh); HoF, p. 23

33 Letter of 21.12.1926, offered for sale by the online vendor www.z.vab.de on 8.9.2008.

34 HoF, p. 45.

35 HoF, p. 46.

36 HoF, p. 48.

37 Gertrud Wagner, in Wolf S. Wagner 1976, n.p.

38 WW to HR, 27.3.1928 (VLA).

39 WW to HR, 24.5.1928 (VLA).

40 Von Kraft 1969, p. 269.

41 WW to HR, 6.2.1929 (VLA).

42 FW to I. Kolodin, 20.8.1953 (NTh).

43 LS, 30.7.1929.

44 Pachl 1988, p. 424.

45 Richard Wagner. *Sämtliche Briefe*, ed. Hans-Joachim Bauer and Johannes Forner. Leipzig, 1988. Vol. VII, p. 97 (7.4.1855).

46 WW to HR, 25.2.1930 (VLA).

47 Letter from Dorothy Stead, 4.12.1940 (NA).

48 WW to HR, 25.2.1930 (VLA).

49 Pachl 1988, p. 429.

50 VL, written statement.

51 Leider 1959, p. 104.

52 Geissmar 1944, pp. 205 and 296. Friedelind was already 13.

53 11.2.1931 (LS).

54 LS, 24.1.1931.

55 WW to HR, 15.11.1930 (VLA).

56 LS, 24.1.1931.

57 Heer/von Haken 2010, p. 32.

58 LS, 7.6.1931.

59 Syberberg, n.d. (RWA).

60 25.4.1947 (NTh). 'Meanwhile he's sitting in prison, God bless him.'

61 22.2.1932 (WWS).

62 25.1.1956 (NTh).

⫸ Chapter 3

1 LS, 18.1.1931.

2 FW typescript 'Meine Schulzeit' (NTh).

3 Miss Sarhage, 4.2.1931 (NTh).

4 Albert Knittel, n.d. (NTh)

5 LS, 14.1.1931.

6 LS, 8.3.1932.

7 LS, March 1932.

8 LS, 19.4.1932.

9 LS, 3.5.1932.

10 WW to HR, 30.7.1933 (VLA).

11 LS, 13.5.1932.

12 See BH, pp. 220–223.

13 WW to HR, 23.2.1936 (VLA).

14 VL on 18.1.2011 on the occasion of her 90th birthday in the Bayreuth Town Hall.

15 HoF, p. 64.

16 WW to HR, 14.12. and 16.7.1932 (VLA).

17 Schostack 1998, p. 120.

18 LS, 14(7). The page has been cut and is in places illegible.

19 Postcard of 23.7.32, RWA.

20 Christa Winsloe: 'Zu meinem Stück', in Programme book for the world première at the Leipzig Schauspielhaus on 30.11.1930 (with thanks to Doris Hermanns for bringing this to my attention).

21 Report by Barbara Böhnke, Vol. 1/56, Heiligengrabe Archives. The following quotations are from reports by pupils such as Gisa von Barsewisch and others who were in Heiligengrabe at the same time (or almost) as Friedelind (source: Heiligengrabe Archives) and from Friedelind's own descriptions (HoF). A similarly atmospheric description can be found in Erika von Hornstein: *Adieu Potsdam*. Cologne/Berlin 1969, p. 89ff.

22 Interview with Helga Dolega-Kozierowski (Frankfurt am Main).

23 WW to HR, 12.10.1932 (VLA).

24 HoF, p. 121.

25 LS, September 1932 (RWA).

26 LS to FW, 6.9.1932 (NTh).

27 Christa Winsloe (see fn. 19).

28 WW to HR, 14.12.1932 (VLA). See *Tannhäuser*, 1st Act: 'Zieh hin, Wannsinniger, zieh hin! Verräter, sieh, nicht halt ich dich!'

29 Contract of 28.12.1933 (NTh).

30 13.9.1939 (RWA).

31 WW to HR, 24.3. and 15.4.1933 (VLA).

32 No author or editor: *Bayreuth im Dritten Reich. Ein Buch des Dankes und der Erinnerung.* Hamburg 1933, 13f.

33 WW to HR, 25.6.1933 (VLA).

34 WW to HR, 8.10.1933 (VLA).

35 WW to HR, 2.1.1934 (VLA).

36 FW: 'Ein Teil der Schulzeit –Heiligengrabe'. Typescript, p. 68 (NTh).

37 Stiftsarchiv Heiligengrabe, chronicle, p. 444.

38 WW to HR, 10.10.1934 (VLA). According to VL these were long conversations, conducted 'with seriousness and humour'. Letter to the present writer, 10.11.2008.

39 HoF, p. 63.

40 WW to HR, 24.5.1935 (VLA).

41 WW to HR, 10.10.1934 (VLA).

42 WW to HR, 19.9.1934 (VLA).

43 WW to HR, 20.2.1935 (VLA).

44 Address unknown (NTh).

45 WW to HR, 12.12.1934 (VLA).

46 WW to HR, 29.11.1934 (VLA).

47 Wörner-Heil 1997, 7.

48 WW to HR, 14.5.1935 (VLA).

49 HoF, p. 125.

50 WW to HR, 2.2.1936 (VLA).

51 WW an HR, 17.11.1935 (VLA).

52 FW an HR, 16.12.1935 (VLA).

53 LS, quoted in Skelton 1971.

54 WW to HR, 25.12.1935 (VLA).

⚜ *Chapter 4*

1 HoF, p. 4.

2 Card from Tietjen to FW, 27.1. (no year), (NTh).

3 FW: Typescript 'Wahnfried', p. 20 (NTh).

4 Waldberg 1933, pp. 240, 248, 307.

5 Daniela Thode: 'Mitteilungen an die Freundin über Bayreuther Kostümfragen' in *Festspielführer 1931*, pp. 34–36. (Originally in *Der Bazar. Illustrirte Damen-Zeitung* 77, 1932).

6 See also Carnegy 2006, p. 154.

7 19.10.1937 (RWA).

8 Waldberg 1933, p. 135.

9 20.9.1935 (BG).

10 Daniela Thode: 'Bayreuth seit 1930'. Manuscript, 1935, pp. 9, 10 (RWA Hs 93/127).

11 Karbaum 1976, Part II, p. 87.

12 WW to HR, 17.1.1936 (VLA).

13 WW to HR, 5.4.1936 (VLA). According to Friedelind, 'neuralgia' forced her to abandon playing the piano at the age of 15 (interview in *Arbeiter-Zeitung*, 28.5.1953).

14 HoF, p. 159.

15 26.1.38 (RWA).

16 12.6.1936 (RWA, Hs 26).

17 WW to HR, 28.3.1936 (VLA).

18 Karbaum 1976, Part I, p. 87.

19 See Karl D. Bracher: 'Stufen totalitärer Gleichschaltung', in *Vierteljahrshefte für Zeitgeschichte* 4 (1956), p. 42.

20 WW to HR, 5.8.1936 (VLA).

21 FW, radio manuscript, n.d. (NTh).

22 HoF, p. 157.

23 Paul Schultze-Naumburg: *Nordische Schönheit.* Berlin 1937, p. 33.

24 GSt, 13.11.40, 17.6. and 27.8.1941.

25 Interview with VL, 2009.

26 WW to HR, 26.10.1936 (VLA).

27 24.11.1936 (NTh).

28 19.1. and 7.2.1937 (RWA).

29 HoF, p. 172.

30 BH, p. 330.

31 11.6.1937 (RWA).

32 7.2.1937 (RWA).

33 HoF, p. 174.

34 WW to HR, 2.4.1937 (VLA).

35 Leider 1959, p. 104f.

36 Eva Chamberlain to FW, 4.7.1937 (RWA).

37 To Eva Chamberlain, 3.8.1937 (RWA).

38 To her aunts, 19.6.1937 (RWA).

39 Geissmar 1944, p. 296f.

40 Arturo Toscanini (1867–1957) was variously the chief conductor of La Scala Milan, the Metropolitan Opera in New York, the New York Philharmonic and then from 1937 to 1954 of the NBC Symphony Orchestra. He conducted in Bayreuth in 1930 and 1931, from 1935 to 1937 at the Salzburg Festival and in 1939 at the Lucerne Festival.

41 11.6.1937 (RWA).

42 To her aunts, 4.11.1937 (RWA).

43 Toscanini to FW, July 1937; copy made by FW (NTh).

44 To Daniela, 16.8.1937 (RWA).

45 19.6.1937 (RWA).

46 11.11.1937 (RWA). 'Dem ewig Jungen weicht in Wonne der Gott' (Akt III of *Siegfried*).

47 Quoted in Sachs 1980, p. 31.

48 11.8.1937 (RWA).

49 Antek 1964, p. 73.

50 13.9.1939 (RWA).

51 9.8.1937 to her aunts (RWA). The three Norns weave the rope of fate in the *Ring des Nibelungen*.

52 Geissmar 1944, p. 205f.

53 Wallich 2001, p. 49. Fred Gaisberg had engaged Siegfried Wagner to record the *Siegfried Idyll* in England in 1927.

54 Wallich 2001, p. 52.

55 18.8.1937 (RWA).

56 31.7. and 1.8.1937 (RWA).

57 27.8.1937 (RWA).

58 Mack 1976, p. 102.

59 27.8.1937 (RWA).

60 23.7.1937 (RWA).

61 10.4.1988 to Dieter (NTh.) See also the *Nordbayerischer Kurier*, 28./29.3.1988, p. 17. The photo is reproduced in the photo book by Wolf Siegfried Wagner, p. 125.

62 WW to HR, 24.3.1938 (VLA).

◢◣ Chapter 5

1 WW to HR, 29.1.1938 (VLA).

2 FW to Daniela, 24.1.1938 (RWA).

3 12.2.1938 (NTh).

4 23.2.1938 (RWA).

5 FW's handwritten commentary on the obituary notice for Lady Cholmondeley in 1989 (Harvey Sachs Archive).

6 Peter Stansky: *Sassoon. The Worlds of Philip and Sybil*. New Haven/London 2003, 211f., 280.

7 Eva to WW, early 1938 (RWA).

8 To her aunts, 4.4.1938 (RWA).

9 HoF, p. 192.

10 WW to HR, 24.6.1938 (VLA).

11 4.4.1938 (RWA).

12 Leider 1959, p. 184.

13 Dok. 11a (NA).

14 Leider 1959, p. 283f.

15 H. Tietjen to Gertrud Beckel, quoted in BH, p. 376.

16 LS, 27.7.1938 (RWA).

17 FW, typescript 'A Price on my Head', 15.3.1943 (NTh).

18 Kropf 1978, p. 39.

19 Unity to Diana Mitford, 4.8.1938, in: *The Mitfords. Letters between six sisters*, ed. Charlotte Mosley. London etc., 2007, p. 131.

20 26.1.1938 (RWA).

21 See Naegele 2005.

22 12.5.1938 (RWA).

23 v. Einem 1995, p. 67. 'We were close friends – he was madly in love': FW to Bernard Servatius, 2.12.1968 (NTh).

24 Beerli-Hottinger 2008, p. 19.

25 Beerli-Hottinger 2008. p. 15.

26 Beerli-Hottinger 2008, p. 20.

27 Review of the Victor-LP-Albums *Toscanini dirigiert Wagner*, typescript 1947 (NTh).

28 Von Einem 1995, p. 67. Von Einem adds that this door was open. VL remains convinced, however, that for Friedelind their relationship remained platonic (interview 2009).

29 14.9.1938 (RWA).

30 14.9.1938 (RWA).

31 27.9.1938 (RWA).

32 Jörg Osterloh: *Nationalsozialistische Judenverfolgung im Reichsgau Sudetenland 1938–45*. Munich 2006, p. 170f.

33 19.10.1938 (RWA).

34 FW to her aunts, 17.11.1938 (RWA); Isabella Wallich: 'Friedelind Wagner. "Mausi". Memoirs of a friend' in LiS, p. 12.

35 Hitler's speech before the German press, quoted in: *Vierteljahrshefte für Zeitgeschichte* 2 (1958), p. 183.

36 HoF, p. 215.

37 WW to FW, 14.6.1939 (NTh).

38 FW to her aunts, 1.7.1939 (RWA).

39 FW to her aunts, 25.1.1940 (RWA).

40 Telegram of 20.8.1939 (NTh). The date is odd, for FW was already in Lucerne.

41 FW to her aunts, 1.7.1939 (RWA). The aunts shared her dislike of Tietjen.

42 Beerli-Hottinger 2008, p. 21.

43 Potter 2010, Vol. 2, p. 700.

44 Blubacher 2008, p. 286f.

45 Taubman 1951, p. 242. Beerli does not mention this in her memoirs, but FW writes of it.

46 Undated manuscript by FW: 'Meine Beziehungen zu Luzern und der Schweiz' (NTh).

47 E.g. Eitel Dobert Graf Prebentow: 'Statt SA – Emigrantenleben' in Zadek 1981, pp. 46–53.

48 D. Thode to A. Zinsstag, 26.2 and 22.4.1939 (MUB).

49 Reported by Thornborrow, quoting reminiscences of Friedelind.

50 Beerli-Hottinger 2008, p. 23.

51 Daniela Thode to A. Zinsstag, 30.8.1939 (MUB).

52 To Daniela Thode, 23.9.1939 (RWA).

53 See Baxter's speech in the House of Commons of 3.12.1940.

54 17.12.1939 (NYPL).

55 Letter from VL to the present writer (10.11.2008).

56 10.7.1939 (RWA).

57 10.9.1939 (NTh).

58 Beerli-Hottinger 2008, p. 22.

59 Interview with VL (10.11.2008).

60 17.1.1939 (MUB, Zinsstag archives).

61 HoF, p. 105f.

62 25.1.1940 (NTh).

63 German General Consulate, 10.11.1939 (PA).

64 Letter from L. Lafferentz to the present writer (10.11.2008).

65 10.1.1940 (RWA).

66 13.1.1940 (MUB).

67 Zinsstag to Thode, 25.1.1940 (MUB) and 6.2.1940 (Lucerne City Archives).

68 Adolf Zinsstag to Daniela Thode, 25.1.1940 (MUB).

⚓ *Chapter 6*

1   To Daniela, 25.1.1940 (RWA).

2   25.1.1940 (NTh).

3   FW: 'Nazis or Non-Nazis? – Is Our "Screening" a Success?' in *Musical Courier*, 15.3.1946.

4   To WW, 21.12.1939 (WWS).

5   26.1.1940 (RWA).

6   Wieland to FW, 26.1.1940 (WWS).

7   To Adolf Zinsstag, 2.2.1940 (MUB).

8   Daniela to Wieland, 10.1.1940 (WWS).

9   WoWa to Wieland Wagner, n.d., ca 1940 (WWS).

10 WoWa to Wieland, 12.2.1940 (WWS).

11 Interview with VL.

12 FW to WW, 14.1.1940 (NTh).

13 24.1. and 6.1.1940 (NTh).

14 HoF, p. 218.

15 FW, undated manuscript (NTh).

16 Letter from VL to the present writer, 4.5.2011. There would thus be no reason for Winifred having denied her words, as she did in her interview with Syberberg. VL's answer to Himmler was apparently: 'Reichsführer, my sister will not return during the war.'

17 WoWa to Wieland W., 16.4.1940 (WWS).

18 NYPL, 13.2.1940.

19 April 1940 (NYPL).

20 Kurt Overhoff: Open letter to the *Spiegel* on their edition No. 53 (1967); manuscript version (NTh).

21 9.2.1940 (NTh).

22 FW to WW 29.2.1940, copy (WWS).

23 WoWa to Wieland, 25.1.1940 (WWS).

24 HOF, p. xiv.

25 GSt, 4.2.1940; FW to Toscanini, 13.2.1940 (NY, Toscanini Legacy L88D).

26 WW to FW, 23.2.1940 (NTh).

27 WW to FW, 6.1.1940 (NTh).

28 *Der Spiegel* No. 25 of 21.6.1947. VL says, however, that Hitler paid no attention to Friedelind's emigration.

29 3.3.1940 (RWA).

30 11.3.1940 (NTh).

31 18.3.1940 (Lucerne City Archives).

32 6.3.1940 (Lucerne City Archives).

33 27.3.1940 (Lucerne City Archives). The 'child' was at this time almost 22 years old.

34 Letter of 2.1.1940 to Zinsstag (DBA).

35 Gilbert Finnegan 2007, p. 42.

36 Eva Chamberlain: 'Mein letzter Wille'. Manuscript will and testament (NTh).

37 Her archives contain telegrams that prove Baxter's efforts to get her into Britain.

38 Newman 1963, p. 194.

39 As evident from a letter, sender unknown, of 29.4.1949 (Lucerne City Archives).

40 FW to Gisela, 3.11.1987 (NTh).

41 Where not otherwise stated, this is taken from the FW File (NA).

42 6.11.1939 (RWA).

43 7.3.1940 (AGM).

44 Wallich 2001, p. 68.

45 Alan Blackwood: *Sir Thomas Beecham. The Man and the Music*. London 1994, p. 177.

46 FW to her aunts, 4.11.1937 (RWA).

47 Syberberg interview with Winifred Wagner, p. 69.

48 *Daily Sketch*, 7.-16.5.1940 (NTh).

49 'How Wagner came to Stockton' in *The Observer*, 5.10.1975.

50 To W.H. Woolley, 5.1.1942 (NTh).

51 Isabella Wallich: 'Friedelind Wagner. Mausi. Memoirs of a Friend', in LiS, p. 12.

52 Peter Stansky: *Sassoon. The Worlds of Philip and Sybil*. New Haven/London 2003, pp. 225 and 242.

53 'Ask [Mrs Wolff] also whether all the documents have arrived to do with Lord Kemsley and Mr Woolley.' FW to Jeanette Simon, 16.11.1950 (NTh).

54 Wilhelm Lenz/Lothar Kettenacker: 'Lord Kemsleys Gespräch mit Hitler Ende Juli 1939' in *Vierteljahreshefte für Zeitgeschichte* 6/3.19 (1971), pp. 305–321.

55 Emery Reves to FW, 10.10.1941 and 4.12.1944 (NTh).

56 Dok 18B (NA).

57 11.9.1939 (NA).

58 Isabella Wallich claims that Friedelind was interned in Holloway Prison (Wallich 2001, 70), though there is no other reference to this.

⁜ *Chapter 7*

1 Nelki 1981.

2 Ramati 1980, p. 94.

3 Ramati 1980, pp. 195 and 123.

4 Goodall 2004, p. 249.

5 Connery Chappell: *Island of Barbed Wire.* Reading, 1986

6 www.aussing.com.au/madame_marianne_mathy.htm, accessed 2011.

7 To Jeanette Simon, 29.9.1940 (NTh).

8 29.9.1942 to Helen (NTh).

9 8.5.1948 to Jeanette Simon: 'You have become thin – it suits you wonderfully – and all admirers on the Isle of Man at the Friday Night Concerts will stare at you' (NTh).

10 Brinson 2003, p. 73.

11 Charmian Brinson: 'Musik im britischen Fraueninternierungslager Rushen', in: Rhode-Jüchtern/Kulitz-Kramer 2004, p. 259f.

12 Sophie Rützow: *Richard Wagner und Bayreuth.* Munich 1943, p. 105.

13 GSt, 21, 22 and 23.7.1940.

14 WoWa did not want to be dependent on the Nazi association 'Kraft durch Freude'.

15 WoWa to Wieland, 15.11.1940 (WWS).

16 WoWa to WW, 5.11.1940 (WWS).

17 Walter 1984, p. 122.

18 7.9.1940 (NA).

19 FW to Toscanini, 19.5.1940 (NYPL, L88D).

20 BH, p. 319

21 BH, p. 318f.

22 Goodall 2004, p. 98.

23 Joseph Goebbels: *Tagebücher*, Vol. 4: 1940–1942. Munich/Zurich, 1992, p. 1471.

24 Phyllis Warner, quote in Goodall 2004, p. 120.

25 Dok 19A (NA).

26 20.9.1940 (NTh).

27 KV4, pp. 141ff and 339ff. (NA).

28 To Jeanette Simon, 24.9.1940 (NTh).

29 11.12.1940 (NTh).

30 19.9., 24.9. and 27.9.1940 (NTh).

31 19.9.1940 (NTh).

32 1.11.1940 (NTh).

33 19.9 and 8.11.1940 (NTh).

34 Elias Canetti: *Party in the Blitz. The English Years.* New York: A New Directions Book, 2005.

35 34 32A, 24.1.1941 (NA).

36 Manuscript without title, n.d. (NTh).

37 *New York Herald Tribune*, 4.12.1940. See also Stent 1980, p. 196.

38 Dok. 22ab4 of 27.12.1940 (NA).

39 GSt. 5.12.1940 (RWA).

40 *Der Spiegel* of 24.3.1954. There is no reference to this in the archives of the British secret services.

41 Information from Roger Sims, librarian of the MNH.

42 NYPL (L 88B); Mortimer H. Frank: *Arturo Toscanini. The NBC Years.* Portland, Oregon, 2002, p. 47.

43 6.2. and 31.1.1941 (NTh).

44 13.2.1941 (NYPL).

45 NA (22ab4).

46 Report on a lecture by FW, in *The Free Lance-Star*, Fredericksburg, 4.5.1945.

47 FW to Toscanini from the Blue Star Line, n.d. (NYPL L 93J).

48 25.2.1941 (RWA).

Chapter 8

1 FW to Toscanini, April 1940 (NYPL).
2 Robert Schopflocher: *Weit von wo. Mein Leben zwischen drei Welten*. Munich, 2010, p. 88f.
3 World telegram of 28.1.1944 (NTh).
4 Eick 2008.
5 29.12.1941 to Jeanette Simon (NTh).
6 5.12.1949 to Alfhild Brickbauer (ERA).
7 See Spotts 1994, p. 147; however, VL disputes this (letter to the present writer).
8 E. and K. Mann 1991, p. 214.
9 Heer/Haken 2010, p. 40.
10 Quote in Russell 1958, p. 205f.
11 FW to Peter Weinberg, 7.6.1984 (NTh).
12 Horowitz 1982, p. 209.
13 FW to Scherz Verlag, 2.11.1984 (NTh).
14 FW to A. Brickbauer, 5.12.1949 (ERA).
15 FW to Toscanini, 26.5.1941 (NYPL, L 93L).
16 N.d. (NYPL, L93K).
17 Russell 1958, p. 224.
18 29.12.1941 (NTh).
19 FW, notes on her encounter with Toscanini, 20.6.1941 (NTh).
20 FW to Jeanette Simon, 29.12.1941 (NTh).
21 To her aunts, 4.11.1937 (NTh).
22 E. and K. Mann 1991, p. 285.
23 Alexander Kipnis: Booklet for the Music & Arts CD 1119.
24 FW, manuscript (see fn. 19), 20.6.1941 (NTh).
25 21.3.1990 to Gudrun (NTh).
26 29.12.1941 to Jeanette Simon (NTh).
27 29.12.1941 to Jeanette Simon (NTh).
28 Brinkmann/Wolff 1999, p. xiii.
29 Eva Schweitzer: *Amerika und der Holocaust. Die verschwiegene Geschichte*. Munich 2004, p. 26.
30 FW diary, 30.7.1941 (NTh).
31 29.12. 1941 (NTh).
32 Thus Harvey Sachs.
33 To the lawyer W.H. Woolley, 27.8.1941 (NTh).
34 GSt 25.12.1941.
35 Landshoff-Yorck 1963, p. 205; Pascal 2007, p. 5.
36 See Gilbert 2007, p. 82f.
37 Taubman 1951, p. 326.
38 Statement by Walfredo Toscanini, 4.11.2009.
39 Taubman 1951, p. 315.
40 This information is from her diary of 1941 (NTh).
41 Quoted in Blubacher 2008, p. 292.
42 Davenport 1967, p. 467.
43 Pascal 2007, p. 7.
44 Blubacher 2008, p. 298.
45 To Frau Kayersling, 7.1.1942 (NTh).
46 4.8.1947 (NTh)
47 Pascal 2007, p. 44.
48 To Miss Wilson, 31.10.1944 (NTh).
49 She was thus of one opinion with German émigrés such as Adolf Busch, who found the noise of the US bombers 'a beautiful, comforting thing'. See Potter Vol. 2, p. 736.
50 Blubacher 2008, p. 218.
51 Lehmann/Faber 2003, p. 90.
52 Information from NTh.
53 Monika Mann: *Das fahrende Haus. Aus dem Leben einer Weltbürgerin*. Reinbek, 2007, p. 49.
54 *Münchner Illustrierte* 31 (1951)
55 Letter of 18.4.1942 to Erika Mann, in *Klaus-Mann-Schriftenreihe*, Vol. 5: *Trauma Amerika. 1937–1942*, ed. Fredric Kroll. Wiesbaden 1986, p. 371.
56 To 'Darlings', 24.7.1943 (NTh).
57 *The Free Lance-Star*, 4.5.1945 (NTh).
58 Mann 1996, p. 162f.
59 Quoted in von der Lühe 1994, p. 195.
60 Von der Lühe/Naumann 2005, 163. 'Übscher' was an expression used in the Mann family.
61 A.-I. Berndt to WW, 1.3.1942 (NTh). Winifred's letter is no longer extant.
62 Fischer, in Friedländer/Rüsen 2000, p. 146f.
63 N. Wagner 1998, p. 171.
64 BH, p. 369f.
65 GSt, 9.4.1942.

⚡ *Chapter 9*

1   29.9.1942 to Helen (NTh).

2   Arrau 1984, p. 122.

3   23.8.1942 to Herbert and Erna Janssen, 29.9.1942 to Helen (NTh).

4   See Kolodin 1953, pp. 518 and 510.

5   31.10.1944 to Coggie Margetson (NTh).

6   FW to Jeanette Simon, 29.12.1941 (NTh).

7   FW to the Lafferentzes, 10.1.1973 (NTh).

8   Letter of 2.4.1942 from Edmund Stinnes to James P. Warburg (NTh).

9   Secret memorandum of the US Coordinator of Information of 2.4.1942 (NTh).

10   18.1.1979 to Walter (NTh).

11   Kater 2008, p. 150f.

12   De Vries, Willem: 'Von St. Leu nach Lakeville – das Exil der Wanda Landowska', in Rhode-Jüchtern/Kublitz-Kramer 2004, p. 212.

13   Claudia Maurer Zenck: 'Gedanken zu einer "Leerstelle". Versuch, ein Forschungsfeld abzustecken' in Rhode-Jüchtern/Kublitz-Kramer 2004, p. 40f.

14   FW, manuscript (NTh).

15   FW to Coggie Margetson, 21.10.1944 (NTh).

16   GSt, 4.12.1941 (RWA).

17   N. Wagner 1998, p. 319. However, Geoffrey Skelton had already pointed out in 1971 that Flossenbürg was a concentration camp. See Skelton 1971, p. 78f.

18   Bald/Skriebeleit 2003, p. 64. VL denies this.

19   Karbaum 1976, Part I, p. 95.

20   Skelton 1971, p. 77 (with a reproduction of Wieland's letter).

21   Winifred Wagner to Heinz Drewes, 3.6.1944 (PA). She still writes of the time 'when this fateful struggle will have ended happily'. It is signed: 'Heil Hitler! Your Winifred Wagner.'

22   Information from VL.

23   Schostack 1998, p. 204.

24   WW to K. Overhoff, 15.1.1945 (RWA HS 122/V).

25   N. Wagner 1998, p. 171.

26   See Maurizio Bach: 'Staat und Weltkrieg aus dem Stegreif geführt' in *Frankfurter Allgemeine Zeitung*, 7.12.2011.

27   Mayer/Paulus 2008, p. 9.

28   To FW, 28.9.1945 (NTh).

29   FW to Erna and Herbert Janssen, 28.8.1945 (NTh).

30   23.7.1945 to Mausi, Jennerl and Katzi (NTh).

31   FW to Wieland Wagner, 5.11.1945 (NTh).

32   WW to Colonel Fiori, 3.8.1945 (NTh).

33   Drüner 2009, introduction.

34   Beidler 1997, p. 333.

35   Beidler 1997, p. 341.

36   Nicole Nottelmann: *Ich liebe dich. Für immer. Greta Garbo und Salka Viertel.* Berlin, 2011, p. 221.

37   Robert Hanzlik, ed., *Augenblicke europäischer Musikgeschichte in Briefen.* Hamburg, 2007, p. 134f.

38   Quoted in Melina Gehring: *Alfred Einstein. Ein Musikwissenschaftler im Exil.* Hamburg, 2007, p. 85.

39   Busch 1949, p. 164.

40   Allende-Blin 1993, p. 9.

41   2.9.1945 (NTh).

42   11.2.1948 to the Beerlis (NTh).

43   20.1.1948 to Jeanette Simon (i.e. Jeanette Eisex), (NTh).

44   Inge and Walter Jens: *Frau Thomas Mann. Das Leben der Katharina Pringsheim.* Reinbek, 2002, p. 232f.

45   WW to FW, 27.11.1948 (NTh).

46   WW to O. Wiinholt, 20.4. and 19.6.1948 (RWA).

47   Heinz Tietjen, in *Das bin ich*, ed. Hannes Reinhardt. Munich 1970, p. 203.

48   FW to Erna and Herbert Janssen, 31.7.1945 (NTh).

49   GSt of 8.8.1945, letter from Wieland to Dr Deubzer.

50   *Mittelbayer. Zeitung* of 14.5.1946.

51   Wieland W. to Toscanini, 31.9.1945 (NTh).

52   Wieland W. to FW, 29.9.1945 (NTh)

53   FW to Wieland W., 5.11.1945 (NTh).

54   Wieland W. to Kurt Overhoff, March 1946 (RWA, Hs 122/V).

55   *Lebens-Akte*, p. 146f.

⫸ Chapter 10

1 Oswald Bauer III/1991, p. 8.

2 WW to HR, 10.3.1949 (GGA).

3 Quoted in Schostack, p. 228.

4 Bauer III/1991, p. 15.

5 GSt, 1947 (RWA).

6 *Volksrecht.* 16.10.1946.

7 WW to FW, 7.4.1946 (NTh).

8 WW to FW, 10.10.1946 (NTh).

9 *Neue Auslese* 2. (2) 1947, pp. 87–92.

10 E. Preetorius to H. Tietjen, 15.10.1946 (AdK).

11 Heinz Tietjen to Hallwag Verlag, 5.3.1947 (NTh)

12 WW to FW, 6.8.1947 (NTh).

13 August Roesener to FW, 19.7.1947 (NTh).

14 See e.g. Wolfgang Wagner 1994, p. 138; N. Wagner 1998, p. 322. VL has also stated that Friedelind made a telephone call to insist on this.

15 Telegram printed in Mayer/Paulus 2008, p. 118.

16 21.6.1947 (STM).

17 WW to FW, 16.03.1947 (NTh).

18 Mayer/Paulus 2008, p. 116.

19 To WoWa, 11.7.1947 (WWS).

20 Wieland W. to FW, n.d., ca July 1947 (WWS). At the top there is the hand-written comment: 'Was not sent off, by mistake'.

21 Heer/von Haken 2010, p. 44f. In the 'scholarly literature on the resistance, neither Tietjen's name nor his contribution is mentioned anywhere'.

22 Statement by Tietjen, in RG 260 OMGUS 5/347–3/5 (IfZ).

23 Winifred Wagner file (STM).

24 Winifred Wagner file (STM).

25 WW to FW, 8.5.1947 (NTh).

26 Bald/Skriebeleit 2003, pp. 57, 66f.

27 Warburg 1989, p. 371.

28 WW to FW, 1.8.1948 (NTh).

29 WW to FW, 26.6.1948 (NTh).

30 WW to FW, 1.8.1948 (NTh).

31 Blubacher 2008, p. 258.

32 Rosamond Chapin, 27.3.1946 to Ted Shawn, in Ted Shawn Collection (NYPL).

33 FW to Erszi, 11.8.1946 (NTh).

34 H. Gump to FW, 28.1.1947 (NTh).

35 FW to Jeanette Eisex, 23.8.1947 and 14.4.1948 (NTh).

36 FW to Wieland Wagner, 20.3.1948 (NTh).

37 FW to Jeanette Eisex, 13.1. and 26.3.1948 (NTh).

38 FW to Jeanette Eisex, 29.6.1948 (NTh).

39 GSt, 6.11.1947.

40 Schostack 1998, 251.

41 Quoted in BH 417 (WoWa archive).

42 Quoted in BH 526 (WoWa archive).

43 WW to FW, 8.5.1947 (NTh).

44 6.11.1944 to Leonard Liebling (NTh).

45 Gillis 1970, 69 and 88; Herbert Haffner: *Furtwängler.* Berlin 2003, p. 380f.

46 'McClure Explains Allies' Boycott of Furtwaengler as Conductor' in *New York Times,* 22.2.1946.

47 FW: 'Nazis or Non-Nazis? Is our "Screening" a Success?' in *Musical Courier,* 15.3.1946.

48 Prieberg 1986, p. 351.

49 Howard Taubman in *New York Times,* 6.1.1949.

50 See Curt Riess: *Furtwängler. Musik und Politik.* Bern 1953, p. 301.

51 *New York Times,* 13.1.1949.

52 Wieland Wagner: 'Plan zur Gründung eines ausländischen Festspielunternehmens' (ca 1946), quoted in Karbaum 1976, Part II, p. 125.

53 9.7.1946 (NTh).

54 9.7.1946 (NTh).

55 Oskar Meyer: 'Bayreuth, die deutsche Festspielstadt!' n.d., ca Januar 1947 (IfZ, MK 50451).

56 FW to Jeanette Simon, 6.9.1946 (NTh).

57 FW to Jeanette Eisex, 27.3.1947 and 14.4.1948 (NTh).

58 WW, 136; see also Bauer IV, p. 3.

59 *New York Times,* 6.4.1947.

60 *Aufbau,* 25.4.1947, see Henze-Döhring 1994, p. 50.

61 22.5.1949 to Tankred (NTh).

62 *The Detroit Times,* 11.2.1948.

63 Statement, n.d. (NTh).

64 5.2.1947 (NTh).

65 WW to FW, 16.3.1947 (NTh).

66 WW to FW, 16.3.1947 (NTh).

67 Wieland W. to FW, 22.6.1947 (NTh).

68 WW to August Roesener, 7.3.1947, quoted in BH, p. 539.

69 6.3.1947 (NTh).

70 12.7.1947 (NTh).

71 Hans Rudolf Vaget: *Thomas Mann, der Amerikaner.* Frankfurt/M. 2011, p. 339.

72 FW to Nike Wagner, 4.12.1989 (NTh). She confirmed her visit to Thomas Mann in a letter to Inge Jens of 4.12.1989 (NTh).

73 Friedelind Wagner to Geoffrey Skelton, 15 January 1970 (FWA).

74 FW to WoWa, 22.4.1947 (WWS).

75 VL, written communication.

76 9.6.1948, BHA (10/120–2/2).

77 F. Beidler to A. Landau, 5.10.1946 (Landau archives, AdK9).

78 10.3.1947 (NTh).

79 4.2.1938 (MUB AII 81,124–154).

80 FW to Geoffrey Skelton, 15.1.1970 (NTh). See also her interview in *Der Brücken-bauer*, 5.12.1975.

81 FW to WoWa and Wieland, 11.7.1947 (WWS). See also FW to Geoffrey Skelton, 15.1.1970 (NTh).

82 WoWa to FW, 23.3.1948 (NTh).

83 WoWa to FW, 23.3.1948 (NTh).

84 WoWa, Entwurf 20.6.1948 (WoWa archives), quoted in BH, p. 562.

85 WW to FW, 5.8.1948 (NTh).

86 BH, p. 488.

87 Monod 2005, 255. She tactlessly compared the strength of her will to the 'Wehrmacht's blitzkrieg'.

88 WW to FW, 1.8.1948 (NTh). Tietjen regarded Wieland as unfit to manage the Festival.

89 14.4.1948 to Jeanette Eisex (NTh).

90 Schostack 1998, p. 271f.

91 WW to HR, 5.8.1949 (GGA).

92 Lebens-Akte, p. 158.

93 Lebens-Akte, p. 142.

94 Lebens-Akte, p. 141.

95 Syberberg n.d. (RWA).

96 WW to FW, 1.5.1948 (NTh).

97 Wieland to FW, 4.12.1946 (NTh).

98 To A. Brickbauer, 25.11.1947 (ERA).

99 To Jeanette Eisex, 23.8.1947 (NTh).

100 To A. Brickbauer, 12.12.1947 (ERA).

101 19.3.1948 (NTh).

102 Letter to Jeanette Eisex, 13.1.1948 (NTh).

⫚ *Chapter 11*

1 To Alfhild Brickbauer, 11.5.1950 (ERA).

2 FW to Marguerite Wolff, 26.1.1950 (NTh).

3 To Jeanette Eisex (23.8.1947) (NTh).

4 FW to Jeanette Eisex, 12.5.1950 (NTh).

5 FW: manuscript 'To the *Musical Courier*', 11.11.1949 (NTh).

6 See BH, p. 276.

7 In *Aufbau*, 30.6.1950, p. 10.

8 Ross Parmenter: 'Wagner´s Manuscripts' in *New York Times*, 11.6.1950.

9 FW to her family, 7.6.1950, in *Aufbau*, 30.6.1950, p. 10.

10 FW to VL ('Nickel'), 30.11.1950 (NTh).

11 To Alfhild Brickbauer, 26.6.1950 (ERA).

12 Wieland and Wolfgang to FW, 10.07.1950 (NTh).

13 7.6.1950 (WWS).

14 *Lady's Home Journal*, ca September/October 1953; copy in FW's archives without date (NTh).

15 Jens Malte Fischer: 'Wagner-Interpretation im Dritten Reich' in Friedländer/Rüsen 2000, p. 161.

16 12.1.1934, in: Karbaum 1976, Part II, p. 96.

17 8.6.1949 (AdK). Alois Hundhammer was at the time State Minister for Education and Culture.

18 Quoted in BH, p. 442.

19 FW to VL, 30.11.1950 (NTh). The letter she mentions is not extant in her archives.

20 WW to Ilse Ernst, 23.4.1950, quoted in BH, p. 450.

21 WW to FW, 21.3.1950 (NTh).

22 WW to FW, 19.12.1950, and WoWa to FW, 23.3.1948 (NTh).

23 Lebens-Akte, p. 162f.

24 Howard Taubman: 'Wagner Brothers reopen Baireuth' in *NY Times*, 5.8.1951.

25 15.8.1950 (AdK).

26 Overhoff, letter to the *Spiegel*, n.d. (NTh).

27 Silja 2000, p. 125

28 Wieland Wagner 1962, p. 235.

29 Nicholas Vazsonyi in Vazsonyi, ed.: *Wagner's Meistersinger. Performance, History, Representation*. Rochester, 2003, p. 15.

30 Eichner 1952, p. 8.

31 Eichner 1952, p. 158. Mayor Meyer had long been replaced.

32 Eichner 1952, pp. 21, 158, 108, 8, 10.

33 Published in Beidler 1997, pp. 298–302.

34 Eichner 1952, pp. 30 and 36.

35 *NY Times*, 5.8.1951.

36 Rental contract of 15.5.1955 (NTh). According to VL, Winifred was only allowed to spend DM 200 of this per month. The rest was to be given to her heirs after her death.

37 N. Wagner 1998, p. 343; Schostack 1998, p. 301.

38 WW to HR, 7.3.1950 (GGA).

39 WW to WoWa and Wieland, 12.11.1951 (WWS).

40 WW to FW, 27.6.1953 (NTh).

41 O. Wiinholt, 28.12.1951 (RWA).

42 Lebens-Akte, p. 288.

43 Lebens-Akte, p. 287.

44 Nike Wagner 1998, p. 344.

45 According to Nike Wagner, Friedelind kept the income from the sales because she needed the money (interview).

46 Statement by Gottfried Wagner (interview).

47 WW to HR, 19.4.1953 (GGA).

48 To Alfhild Brickbauer, 11.6.1953 (ERA).

49 To Alfhild Brickbauer, 4.3.1953 and 10.6.1951 (ERA).

50 WW to FW, 27.6.1953 (NTh).

51 '"Flammenerbe". Begegnung mit Friedelind Wagner' in *Arbeiter-Zeitung*, 28.5.1953.

52 'Bayreuth: Kult auf der Koch-Platte' in *Der Spiegel*, 12.8.1953, p. 27.

53 Schostack 1998, p. 308.

54 FW to Alfhild Brickbauer, 4.10.1953 (ERA).

55 *Ibid.*

56 G. Wagner 1998, p. 39.

57 FW to Irving Kolodin, 20.8.1953 (NTh).

58 N. Wagner 1998, p. 416f.

59 FW to Lee Jones, 7.8.1953 (NTh).

60 See Monod 2005, pp. 256 and 259.

61 *AZ*, 27.7.1953.

62 According to VL. But perhaps Toscanini did not want to meet Winifred Wagner for political reasons.

63 WW to HR, 4.9.1953 (GGA). FW mentioned the music journalist Harald Taubman, whom she knew well.

64 FW to Kolodin, 14.12.1953 (NTh).

65 Newman 1963, p. 243.

66 WW to HR, 23.10.1953 (GGA); WW to Maude, 10.1.1954 (A 2010/II–A2–96) RWA.

67 Sachs 1978, p. 310.

68 WW to FW, 26.1.1954 (NTh).

69 Nike Wagner, p. 42.

70 VL to FW, beginning of 1953 (NTh).

71 16.7.1952; a copy is in the WW-HR correspondence (GGA).

72 *New York Times*, 10.2.1954; FW to Wolfgang Wagner, 10.2.1954 (NTh).

73 30.3.1954.

74 FW to Wolfgang W., 27.2.1954 (NTh).

75 FW to Verena and Bodo, 3.3.1954 (NTh).

76 FW to Lady Crosfield, 10.7.1954 (NTh).

77 FW to George (presumably Brickbauer), 19.6.1949 (NTh).

78 The copy is in Friedelind's archives (NTh.).

79 FW to George 6.2.1954: letter from FW to Verena (NTh).

80 Wieland to FW, 24.8.1950 (NTh).

81 See *Der Spiegel* 24.3.1954: 'Kummer in Bayreuth'.

82 Lebens-Akte, p. 386.

83 *Bayreuther Tagblatt*, 17.9.1954.

84 VL, written communication with the present writer.

85 FW to Jeanette Eisex, 8.6.1954 (NTh).

86 FW to Frida Leider, 7.9.1954 (NTh).

87 According to Gottfried von Einem, Wolfgang Wagner promised to make up the loss by handing over a sketch of Richard Wagner. However, Wolfgang denied it and published a press release stating that the Festival managers were under no obligations of any kind to Gottfried or his mother. FW to Frida Leider, 7.9.1954 (NTh). See also N. Wagner 1998, p. 390.

88 FW to Herbert and Erna Janssen, 1.8.1954 (NTh).

89 FW to Irving Kolodin, 30.7.1954 (NTh).

90 FW to Irving Kolodin, 7.8.1954.

91 FW to Herbert and Erna Janssen, 1.8.1954 (NTh).

92 Jeanette Eisex to FW, 29.7.1954 (NTh).

93 *Bayreuther Tageblatt*, 30.9.1955.

⚙ Chapter 12

1 WW to HR, 14.3.1956 (GGA).

2 FW to I. Kolodin, 19.6.1955 (NTh).

3 E. and K. Mann 1991, p. 178.

4 FW to Jeanette Eisex, 11.1.1956 (NTh).

5 11.3.1956 to Sabine Rapp (NTh).

6 Quoted in Ingrid Kapsamer: *Wieland Wagner. Wegbereiter und Weltwirkung.* Vienna etc. 2010, p. 188.

7 Quoted in Spotts 1994, 221; *Die Meistersinger und Richard Wagner*, ed. Germanisches Nationalmuseum. Nürnberg 1981, p. 326.

8 2.10.1956 (NTh). 7.5.1956 to Jeanette Eisex.

9 See *Lebens-Akte*, p. 179.

10 24.12.1960 (NTh).

11 6.11.1957 to Marianne Kasel. It remains unclear what the topic of the lecture was and who was responsible for hounding Friedelind. The Düsseldorf Wagner Association has no archival documents for 1957. With thanks to Dr Elisabeth Scheeben of the Düsseldorf City Archives for this information.

12 WW to Ilse Ernst, 1957 (Musikantiquariat Dr. Ulrich Drüner, internet list, January 2010).

13 6.11.1957 to Sabine Rapp (NTh).

14 Contract pledge from the revisionary heir of 13.11.1957 (NTh).

15 Schostack 1998, p. 310. (Schostack wrote this biography in close collaboration with Gertrud Wagner and used her sources).

16 Taubman 1951, pp. 194 and 205.

17 April 1958 to Madeleine Conn (NTh).

18 5.3.1959 to WW (NTh).

19 18.1.1959 to Howard Taubman (NTh).

20 7.1.1956 to Irving Kolodin (NTh).

21 Inge and Walter Jens: *Frau Thomas Mann. Das Leben der Katharina Pringsheim.* Reinbek 2003, p. 289.

22 See Weissweiler 2010, p. 242.

23 23.2.1959 to Marianne (NTh).

24 Wolfgang Wagner, no title, 30.9.1959 (NTh).

25 3.5.1959 to Fred (NTh).

26 5.3.1959 to WW (NTh).

27 30.11.1958 (Felsenstein Archives, AdK).

28 16.3.1959 to Bolte (NTh).

29 1.6.1959 to Fred Haupt (NTh).

30 April 1958 to Madeleine (NTh).

31 8.2.1959 to Hans (NTh).

32 15.6.1959 to Fred Haupt (NTh).

33 Howard Taubman: 'New Wagnerites. Students to Learn Operatic Skills in Master Classes at Bayreuth' in *The New York Times*, 8.2.1959.

34 FW to Matteo Lettunich, 2.1.1961 (NTh).

35 See Michael H. Kater: *Never sang for Hitler. The Life and Times of Lotte Lehmann*. Cambridge, 2008, p. 253f.

36 Martin Bernheimer: 'The Master Classes of Bayreuth' in *Saturday Review*, 30.4.1960.

37 24.9.1959 to Lys, Randy and Vicky (NTh).

38 25.10.1959 to Herrn Walter (NTh).

39 26.10.1959 to Robert Gutman (NTh).

40 2.7.1959 to 'Sascha' and Jeremiah Gutman (NTh).

41 25.7.1959 from Sascha (NTh).

42 7.8.1959 to Sascha (NTh).

43 Jeremiah Gutman to FW, 9.9.1959 (NTh).

44 Jeremiah Gutman and Sascha Merovitch to FW, 17.11.1959 (NTh).

45 26.10.1959 Martin Hirsch to FW (NTh).

46 24.01.1969 from Martin Hirsch (NTh).

47 To Marianne, 29.12.59 (NTh).

48 To Alfhild Brickbauer, 24.12.1960 (ERA).

49 4.9.1959 to Jeanette Eisex (NTh).

50 Robert Gutman to FW, 21.9.1959.

51 13.11.1957 (recte 1959) to Mrs. Pandit (NTh).

52 21.4.1959 to Alfhild Brickbauer (ERA).

53 8.12.1959 (NTh).

54 10.12.59 to Frances Martin (NTh). See also the *New York Times*, 8.12.1959.

55 26.10.1959 to FW (NTh).

56 2.11.1959 to Felsenstein (NTh).

57 13.11.1959 to FW (NTh).

⫻ *Chapter 13*

1   *Bayreuther Tagblatt*, 24.6.1960.

2   Report (author unknown) to Matteo Lettunich of 4.11.1960 (NTh).

3   24.12.1960 (NTh).

4   20.8.1960 to W. Felsenstein (NTh).

5   Reinhard Mieke to FW, 15.8.1960 (NTh).

6   Letter from Alfred Kaine to the present writer, 15.6.2009.

7   *Fränkische Presse*, 24.8.1962.

8   Thomson 1997 (as also the ensuing quotations).

9   Interview with Michael Tilson Thomas, 13.9.2010, Lucerne.

10 W. Felsenstein, recordings.

11 To Marion Saerchinger, 11.10.1959 (NTh).

12 To Walter Felsenstein, 6.8.1957 (AdK).

13 WW to HR, 15.2.1963 (GGA).

14 Julia Rothhaas/Alexandros Stefanidis: 'Der Mann für's Leben' in *Süddeutsche Zeitung Magazin* 21 (2009).

15 FW to Alfred Kaine, 14.10.1961 (NTh).

16 FW to A. Kaine, 26.3.1964 (NTh); A. Kaine to FW, 23.4.1964 (ERA).

17 Jonathan Dudley, interview, 5.11.2009, New York.

18 Email to the present writer of 14.4.2010.

19 Email from Patricia Sage, 10.7.2010, conversation with Jonathan Dudley on 5.11.2009.

20 Letter to the present writer, 11.11.2011.

21 Conversation with Jonathan Dudley on 5.11.2009.

22 Abe Polakoff: 'Remembering Friedelind Wagner' in LiS, p. 16.

23 Mansouri 2010, p. 54.

24 Dudley, interview, 5.11.2009.

25 Interview with Michael Tilson Thomas, 13.9.2010, Lucerne.

26 FW to Edward Downes, 21.12.1960 (NTh).

27 FW to Alfhild Brickbauer, 11.1.1962.

28 To Walter Legge, 17.1.1962 (NTh).

29 2.5.1961 to Floris (NTh).

30 FW to 'Mr Mehner', 9.4.1962 (AFB).

31 According to Alfred Kaine, 15.6.2009.

32 FW to Felsenstein, 7.5.1963 (AdK).

33 FW to Sarah-Maud and Bob, 4.5.1966 (NTh).

34 Report by John Dew, 11.11.2011.

35 Silja 2000, p. 176.

36 *The Times*, 24.12.1966.

37 *Die Zeit*, 17.10.1966.

38 FW to Verena, Bodo and their children (n.d.).

39 Lebens-Akte, p. 289.

40 February 1968 (NTh).

41 Lebens-Akte, p. 289.

42 19.4.1966 to Laux (NTh).

43 26.2.1966 to WW (NTh).

44 Undated manuscript (interview with FW) (NTh). Since she mentions that Wieland had died a few months before, the manuscript must date from early 1967 or thereabouts.

45 FW to Harvey Sachs, 2.1.1967 (Harvey Sachs Archive).

46 *Westfalen-Blatt*, 18.7.1968.

47 FW to Martin Hirsch, 20.3.1969 (NTh).

⌁ *Chapter 14*

1   WW to Gerdy Troost, 23.11.1966, quoted in BH, p. 604.

2   WW to HR, 22.1.1965 (GGA).

3   Harro Zimmermann: *Günter Grass unter den Deutschen. Chronik eines Verhält-nisses*. Göttingen 2006, p. 168.

4   WW to Verena and Bodo Lafferentz, 9.6.1967 (NTh).

5   Bodo L. to FW, 18.11.1968 (NTh).

6   In 1938, Mayor Schmidt of Bayreuth had drawn up guidelines for a 'German centre for Richard Wagner research', which was, however, only set up in 1943.

7   Memorandum by B. Conz 17.11.1966 (SLB).

8   FW: 'Staging Wagner Operas' in *Musical America*, February 1946.

9   *Neue Westfälische Zeitung*, 11.12.1967.

10 *Neue Westfälische Zeitung*, 11.12.1967.

11 *Neue Westfälische Zeitung*, 11.12.1967, *Die Glocke*, 7.12.1967.

12 'Oper: Friedelind Wagner. Endlich Mensch' in *Der Spiegel* 53 (1967), p. 100.

13 *Neue Westfälische Zeitung*, 12.12.1967.

14 Conz to FW, 6.9.1967 (NTh).

15 *Der Spiegel* 53 (1967).

16 Typescript 'Bayreuth and Dream Theatres', n.d. (NTh).

17 Reinhold Brinkmann: 'Wagners Aktu-alität für den Nationalsozialismus' in Friedländer/Rüsen 2000, p. 131.

18 6.11.1957 to Marianne (NTh).

19 Wallich 2001, p. 204.

20 From a lecture given by Friedelind, quoted in *Westfalenblatt*, 11.12.1967.

21 G. Wagner 2010, p. 153.

22 Interview with V. Lafferentz, September 2009.

23 Quoted in the *Westfalenblatt*, 6.1.1968.

24 Quoted in N. Wagner 1998, p. 381.

25 *Die Zeit* 1 (1968).

26 *Westfalenblatt*, 6.1.1968.

27 Frida Leider to FW, 2.3.1968 (NTh).

28 E.g. *Die Musikdramen Richard Wagners. Eine thematisch-musikalische Interpre-tation*. Salzburg, 1967. This study was based on the lessons that Overhoff gave Wieland.

29 Kurt Overhoff: 'Die Wahrheit über die künstlerische Ausbildung Wieland Wagners'. Manuscript (RWA).

30 FW, unpublished manuscript, ca 1970 (NTh).

31 Joseph Wechsberg: 'A Reporter at Large. My Grandfather would be all for it' (Conversation with Wieland Wagner) in *The New Yorker*, 18.8.1956, p. 68.

32 Wallich 2001, p. 206.

33 FW to Dr Wolfram, n.d. (NTh).

34 BH, p. 478.

35 3.3.1968 (NTh).

36 To Jeanette Eisex, 9.4.1968.

37 Berndt W. Wessling to N. Thornborrow, 17.4.1996 (NTh).

38 Statement by the city of Bayreuth: 'Im Zorn über Unwahrheiten', n.d. (RWA).

39 Julia Spinola: 'Frischer Wind in Bayreuth' in *Frankfurter Allgemein Zeitung*, 25.7.2009: 'Already the illegal intervention by the public administration last year in the succession process, which was torpedoed when State Minister Neumann and the then Bavarian Culture Minister Thomas Goppel decided without further ado to push through the coronation of Katharina Wagner, shows how closely the future of Bayreuth is linked to election campaign interests.'

40 To B. Servatius 3.12.1968 (NTh).

41 WW to 'Putt', 16.4.1968 (ERA).

42 Pöhner to the family lawyer Dr Gottfried Breit, 14.6.1968 (NTh).

43 WoWa to FW, 1.7.1968 (NTh). Brigitte Hamann's claim that Wolfgang called Friedelind a 'Miststück' ('bitch'), see the German edition of BH, p. 603f., cannot be proven.

44 WoWa to Bernhard Servatius, 18.7.1968.

45 19.7.1968 (AdK).

46 Written communcation to the present writer, November 2011.

47 To Dr Wolfram, n.d. (1968) (NTh).

48 To Dr Bernard Servatius, 10.6.1968 (NTh).

49 To Alfhild Brickbauer, 22.9.1968 (ERA).

50 Quoted in: *Der Brückenbauer*, 5.12.1975.

51 Servatius to WoWa, 1.11.1968 (NTh). In fact, Friedelind did not go to the Festival in 1969.

52 Servatius to FW, 30.4.1969 (NTh).

53 Silja 2000, p. 224.

54 10.10.1969.

55 FW to Alan Young, 7.9.1969 (NTh).

56 FW to Dorothy, 9.9.1969 (NTh).

57 FW to Servatius, 4.12.1969 (NTh).

58 FW to Gerard Semon, 22.01.1969 (NTh).

59 FW: 'Lauritz Melchior on his 100th birthday', manuscript (NTh).

∿ *Chapter 15*

1 FW to Servatius, 28.9.1970 (NTh).

2 FW to John, 3.10.1970 (NTh).

3 FW to Mateo Lettunich, 21.11.1978 (NTh).

4 FW to Richard (Martell?), 14.9.1970 (NTh).

5 *Manchester Guardian*, 29.8.1972.

6 Jeremy Menuhin: 'I only felt loved when I played well'. Interview in *Daily Telegraph*, 21.2.2005.

7 The family's letter is no longer extant; the report about Hitler is given in the *Manchester Guardian*, 29.8.1972.

8 FW to Verena, Bodo Lafferentz and family, 9.1.1973 (NTh). She wrote a second version of the letter on 10.1.73.

9 FW to Verena, Bodo Lafferentz and family, 10.1.1973 (NTh).

10 Joachim Herz to FW, telegram, 15.1.1973 (NTh).

11 *Oper mit Herz*, vol. 1, eds Joachim Herz, Michael Heinemann and Kristel Pappel-Herz. Bergheim, 2011.

12 Quoted in Kiesel 1994, p. 188.

13 Kiesel 1994, p. 189.

14 Information from Peter Pachl.

15 *Der Spiegel* 40 (25.9.1967).

16 *The Guardian*, 29.8.1972.

17 FW to Pierre Boulez, 20.8.1971 (NTh).

18 Paul R. Duffy to FW, 5.4.1972 (NTh).

19 FW to John, 11.4.1972 (NTh).

20 Nike Wagner 1998, p. 393. The wording of the foundation document is given in Lebens-Akte, p. 446ff.

21 Reinhold Kreile to B. Servatius, 6.11.1972 (NTh).

22 Bodo Lafferentz to B. Servatius, 23.3.1972 (NTh).

23 FW to Servatius, 24.1.1974 (NTh).

24 In a German TV programme of 2.3.1968 (typescript) she refused to rule out the possibility of one day running the Festival.

25 Lebens-Akte, p. 374f.

26 FW: autograph corrections to an article by N. Braithwaite, n.d., ca 1976 (NTh).

27 FW to a 'dear quartet', 15.10.1970 (NTh).

28 Peter Heyworth: *Conversations with Klemperer*. London 1973.

29 24.1.1974 to Servatius (NTh).

30 To Bodo Lafferentz, 7.4.1974 (NTh).

31 To Servatius, 24.1.1974 (NTh).

32 29.4.1974 to the Modesti family.

33 *Der Brückenbauer*, 5.12.1975.

34 Nike Wagner: '"Es war ein Verhältnis". Thomas Mann and Richard Wagner' in *Vom weltläufigen Erzählen. Die Vorträge des Kongresses in Zürich 2006*, eds Manfred Papst and Thomas Sprecher, Frankfurt am Main, 2008, p. 57f.

35 WW to Fritz Kempfler, 25.6.1974, quoted in BH (German version), p. 629.

36 To WW, 21.1.1977 (NTh).

37 15.1.1978 to Ilse Laux, 7.6.1978 (NTh).

38 31.5.1978 to Lotte Klemperer (NTh). The audience paid £15 each.

39 31.5.1978 to Lotte Klemperer (NTh).

40 22.3.1979 to Ray, 1.10.1979 to Hertha, 5.9.1979 to Erzsi and Delia (NTh).

41 Bertel Meyer and husband to FW, 27.1.1974; FW to Judy Sullivan, 14.2.1974 (NTh).

42 3.11.1979 (NTh).

43 Wallich 2001, p. 267.

44 Wallich 2001, p. 277.

45 Interview with Gottfried Wagner.

46 Hans Jürgen Syberberg, ed.: *Syberbergs Filmbuch*. Munich, 1976, p. 149.

47 Kropf 1978, p. 19.

48 WW to Lieselotte Tietjen, 13.9.1975 (AdK).

49 WW to HR, 17.1.1976 (GGA).

50 WW to FW, 24.4.1978 (NTh). A new edition was published by Werner Jochmann in 1980.

51 Quoted in Kropf 1978, p. 7.

52 FW: 'From my Life and Work' in LiS, p. 20.

53 Fritz A. Kuttner to FW, 21.5.1983 (NTh).

54 Frederick Haupt to FW, 21.5.1983 (NTh).

55 Written statement from VL.

56 21.7.1976 (NTh).

57 3.9.1979 to Judy Sullivan (NTh).

58 FW to Wolf Siegfried Wagner, 19.10.1979 (NTh).

59 To Judy Sullivan, 3.9.1979 (NTh).

60 Pachl 1988, p. 135.

61 Waltraud Ehrhardt to FW, 1.6.1983, with a handwritten note by FW, dated 15.6.1983 (NTh).

62 9.10.1970 to Delia (NTh).

63 FW: 'From my Life and Work' in LiS, p. 21.

⫘ *Chapter 16*

1 Winifred's granddaughter Nike has offered a comprehensive analysis of her character in N. Wagner, 2000.

2 Minutes made at the meeting, 14.2.1981 (NTh).

3 21.1.1987 to B. Servatius (NTh).

4 8.6.1988 to M. Kiesel.

5 FW to Felsenstein, 7.5.1963 (AdK).

6 G. Wagner 1998, p. 193.

7 G. Wagner 1998, p. 39.

8 Eva Wagner-Pasquier to FW, 23.3.1981 (NTh).

9 Nike Wagner to FW, 30.8.1989 (NTh).

10 6.10.1983 to B. Servatius (NTh).

11 FW to Ph. Wults, 5.2.1983 (NTh).

12 29.12.1982 (NTh).

13 Gertrud Wagner to FW, 24.7.1986 (NTh).

14 5.1.1983 to Philip Wults (NTh).

15 N. Wagner 1998, p. 371f.

16 '"Rebell" von Bayreuth' in *Münchener AZ*, 12.8.1983.

17 1.8.1984 (NTh).

18 28.6.1984 to Frau Hildebrand (NTh).

19 Information from Peter Pachl. Despite occasional criticism of Friedelind, he remained 'full of gratitude' for all she had done.

20 FW to Oscar A. Beuselinck, 2.9.1977 (NTh).

21 FW to Hans Sulzer, 18.12.1984 (NTh).

22 N. Wagner 1998, p. 415.

23 N. Wagner 1998, p. 416.

24 To Craig, 27.6.1989 (NTh).

25 *Münchener Abendzeitung*, 4.5.1984.

26 14.5.1984 (NTh).

27 *New York Times*, 14.8.1988.

28 Wallich 2001, p. 279f.

29 FW to Joachim (publisher), n.d. (probably January 1989) (NTh).

30 Busch 1991, p. 345.

31 FW to Werner H. Kraus, 1.2.1986 (NTh).

32 FW to Daniel Barenboim, letter draft, n.d. (NTh).

33 Busch 1991, p. 345.

34 Letter to Ilse and Konrad Wolff, 14.1.1988 (NTh).

35 FW, draft letter, ca January 1986 (NTh). The year 1937 was incorrect, as is explained earlier in this book.

36 Burton 1994, p. 484.

37 Burton 1994, p. 514.

38 Gottfried Wagner to WoWa, 30.1.1990 and WoWa's answer of 1.2.1990 (NTh).

39 Gottfried Wagner to FW, 16.4.1981 (NTh).

40 '"Maus" had expressly forbidden any commemorative service to be held for her in Bayreuth' (Gottfried Wagner 2010, p. 48). Gottfried was not invited to the commemoration (interview with Gottfried Wagner).

41 See Mayer/Paulus 2008, p. 118, where the telegram is given in facsimile.

42 VL also found the speech 'unfair' (written communication to the present writer).

43 Anon., in *Die Zeit* 31 (1994).

44 *Nordbayerischer Kurier*, 13/14.8.1994; *Der Spiegel* 21/1991.

45 20.1.1984 to Lorna Braithwaite (NTh).

46 Kadidja Wedekind: 'Sie rettete die Ehre der Familie Wagner' in *Neue Münchner Illustrierte*, 4.8.1951.

47 See Karbaum 1976, Part I, p. 73f.

48 Viola Roggenkamp: *Erika Mann. Eine jüdische Tochter*. Frankfurt am Main 2008, p. 228.

49 Paul Pretzsch, ed.: *Cosima Wagner and Houston S. Chamberlain im Briefwechsel 1888–1908*. Leipzig, 1934, p. 253.

50 To Adolf Zinsstag, 12.11.1939 (MUB).

51 Letter to the Marfurts, 2.7.1991 (privately owned by the Marfurts).

52 11/12.5.1991.

53 Patricia Sage, email of 12.2.2009 to NTh.

54 30.7.1978 (NTh).

55 Email, 27.5.2010.

56 Wallich 2001, p. 207.

57 Interview, 9.1.2012.

58 Email, 2.1.2009.

59 Markus Kiesel: 'Friedelind Wagner: Würdigung' in *Musica* 4 (1991), p. 269.

60 Markus Kiesel, manuscript (NTh).

61 Gottfried Wagner, email, 9.1.2012.

62 See Friedländer/Rüsen 2000.

63 Elsa Bernstein ed. Rita Bake and Birgit Kiupel: *Das Leben als Drama. Erinnerungen an Theresienstadt*. Hamburg 1999, p. 15.

64 Ian Kershaw: *The End. Hitler´s Germany, 1944–45*. London 2011.

Bibliography

Allende-Blin, Juan, ed., 1993. *Musiktradition im Exil. Zurück aus dem Vergessen.* Cologne: Bund.

Angenete, Hildegard, 1994. 'Geschichte der Landfrauenschule Groß-Sachsenheim' in *Die Mörin* 2, (March) 1994.

Antek, Samuel, 1963. *This was Toscanini.* New York: Vanguard Press.

Ardoin, John, 1983. 'A Ring Diary' in *The Opera Quarterly* Vol. 1, No. 2.

Bald, Albrecht/Jörg Skriebeleit, 2003. *Das Außenlager Bayreuth des KZ Flossenbürg. Wieland Wagner und Bodo Lafferentz im 'Institut für physikalische Forschung'.* Bayreuth: C. & C. Rabenstein.

Bauer, Oswald Georg, 1991. 'Vierzig Jahre Neubayreuth' in Programmhefte III *Rheingold*, pp. 1–19, IV *Die Walküre*, pp. 1–15, V *Siegfried*, pp. 1–23, VI *Die Götterdämmerung*, pp. 1–15. Bayreuth.

Beerli-Hottinger, Ellen, 2008. *Richard Wagners Nachfahren auf Tribschen*, ed. Katja Fleischer. Lucerne: Museum Tribschen.

Beidler, Franz W, 1997. *Cosima Wagner-Liszt. Der Weg zum Wagner-Mythos*, ed. Dieter Borchmeyer. Bielefeld: Pendragon. 2nd ed. Würzburg: Königshausen & Neumann 2011.

Blubacher, Thomas, 2008. *Gibt es etwas Schöneres als Sehnsucht? Die Geschwister Eleonora und Francesco von Mendelssohn.* Leipzig: Henschel.

Brinkmann, Reinhold/Christoph Wolff, 1999. *Driven into Paradise: The Musical Migration from Nazi Germany to the United States.* Berkeley, CA: University of California Press.

Brinson, Charmian, 2003. 'In the "Exile of Internment", or "Von Versuchen, aus einer Not eine Tugend zu machen": German-speaking women interned by the British during the Second World War', in *Politics and Culture in Twentieth-Century Germany*, eds William Niven and James Jordan. Rochester, N.Y.: Camden House, pp. 63–87.

Brinson, Charmian, 2004. 'Keine verlorene Zeit: Musik im britischen Fraueninternierungslager Rushen' in *Echolos*, eds Anna-Christine Rhode-Jüchtern/Maria Kublitz-Kramer. Bielefeld: Aisthesis, pp. 243–264.

Burton, Humphrey, 1994. *Leonard Bernstein.* New York: Doubleday.

Busch, Eva, 1991. *Und trotzdem. Eine Autobiographie.* Munich: Knaus.

Busch, Fritz, 1953. *Pages from a Musician's Life.* London: Hogarth Press.

Carnegy, Patrick, 2006. *Wagner and the Art of the Theatre.* New Haven/London: Yale University Press.

Carr, Jonathan, 2007. *The Wagner Clan. The Saga of Germany's most Illustrious and Infamous Family.* New York: Atlantic Monthly Press.

Chappell, Connery, 1984. *Island of Barbed Wire.* London: Robert Hale.

Davenport, Marcia, 1968. *Too strong for fantasy.* London: Collins.

Ebermayer, Erich, 1951. *Magisches Bayreuth.* Stuttgart: Steingrüben.

Eichner, Walter, ed., 1952. *Weltdiskussion um Bayreuth. Im Auftrag der 'Gesellschaft der Freunde von Bayreuth.'* Bayreuth: Selbstverlag.

Eick, Simone, ed., 2008. *Nach Buenos Aires! Deutsche Auswanderer und Flüchtlinge im 20. Jahrhundert.* Bremerhaven: Deutsches Auswandererhaus.

Einem, Gottfried von/Schmidt, Manfred A., 1995. *Ich hab' unendlich viel erlebt.* Vienna: Ibera-&-Molden.

Felsenstein, Walter/Melchinger, Siegfried, 1961. *Musiktheater.* Bremen: Schünemann.

Fischer, Jens Malte, 2000. 'Wagner-Interpretation im Dritten Reich. Musik und Szene zwischen Politisierung und Kunstanspruch' in Friedländer/Rüsen 2000, pp. 142–164.

Friedländer, Saul/Jörn Rüsen, eds, 2000. *Richard Wagner im Dritten Reich. Ein Schloss Elmau-Symposium.* München: Beck.

Geissmar, Berta, 1944. *The Baton and the Jackboot. Recollections of Musical Life.* London: Hamish Hamilton.

Gilbert Finnegan, Marianne, 2002. *Memories of a Mischling: Becoming an American.* Philadelphia: Xlibris Corp.

Gilbert, Pia, 1993. 'Rückblicke in die Gegenwart' in Allende-Blin, pp. 134–147.

Gillis, Daniel, 1970. *Furtwängler and America.* New York: Maryland Books.

Gillman, Peter and Leni, 1980. *'Collar the Lot!' How Britain interned and expelled its wartime refugees.* London: Quartet Books.

Glass, Beaumont, 1988. *Lotte Lehmann. A Life in Opera & Song.* Santa Barbara: Capra Press.

Goodall, Felicity, 2004. *Voices from the Home Front.* Newton Abbot: David & Charles Publishers.

Hamann, Brigitte, 2005. *Winifred Wagner. A Life at the Heart of Hitler's Bayreuth.* Orlando et al.: Harcourt.

Heer, Hannes/Boris von Haken, ed., 2010. 'Der Überläufer. Heinz Tietjen. Der Generalintendant der Preußischen Staatstheater im Dritten Reich' in *Zeitschrift für Geschichtswissenschaft* 58.1, pp. 28–53.

Henze-Döhring, Sabine, 1997. 'Kulturelle Zentren in der amerikanischen Besatzungszone: der Fall Bayreuth' in *Kulturpolitik im besetzten Deutschland 1945–1949*, ed. Gabriele Clemens. Stuttgart: Steiner, pp. 39–54.

Horowitz, Joseph, 1982. *Conversations with Arrau.* London: Collins.

Humperdinck, Eva, 1999. *Engelbert Humperdinck in seinen persönlichen Beziehungen zu Richard Wagner, Cosima Wagner, Siegfried Wagner.* Vol. III: 1905–1921. Koblenz: Görres.

Karbaum, Michael, 1976. *Studien zur Geschichte der Bayreuther Festspiele.* Regensburg: Bosse.

Kater, Michael H., 2000. *Composers of the Nazi Era. Eight Portraits.* New York: Oxford University Press.

Kater, Michael H., 2008. *Never Sang for Hitler. The Life and Times of Lotte Lehmann, 1888–1976.* Cambridge: Cambridge University Press.

Kiesel, Markus, 1994. *Studien zur Instrumentalmusik Siegfried Wagners.* Frankfurt/M. u.a.: Lang.

Kolodin, Irving, 1953. *The Story of the Metropolitan Opera 1883–1950: A Candid History.* New York: Alfred A. Knopf.

Kraft, Zdenko von, 1969. *Der Sohn. Siegfried Wagner's Leben und Umwelt.* Graz: Stocker.

Kropf, Meta, 1978. *Bayreuther Festspielsommer von damals (1936–1944).* (1977). Bayreuth.

Landshoff-Yorck, Ruth, 1963. *Klatsch, Ruhm und kleine Feuer. Biographische Impressionen.* Cologne: Kiepenheuer & Witsch.

Lehmann, Stephen/Marion Faber, 2003. *Rudolf Serkin. A Life.* New York: Oxford University Press.

Lerman, Leo, 2007. *The Grand Surprise. The Journals of Leo Lerman,* ed. Stephen Pascal. New York: Alfred A. Knopf.

Lühe, Irmela von der, 1994. *Erika Mann. Eine Biographie.* Frankfurt/New York: Fischer

Mack, Dietrich, 1976. *Der Bayreuther Inszenierungsstil.* München: Prestel.

Mack, Dietrich, ed., 1980. *Cosima Wagner. Das zweite Leben. Briefe und Aufzeichnungen.* Munich/Zurich: Piper.

Mann, Erika, 2005. *Mein Vater, der Zauberer,* eds Irmela von der Lühe /Uwe Naumann (2nd ed.). Reinbek: Rowohlt.

Mann, Erika and Klaus, 1939. *Escape to Life.* Boston: Houghton Mifflin.

Mansouri, Lotfi/Donald Arthur, 2010. *Lotfi Mansouri. An Operatic Journey.* Lebanon: University Press of New England.

Mayer, Bernd/Helmut Paulus, 2008. *Eine Stadt wird entnazifiziert. Die Gauhauptstadt Bayreuth vor der Spruchkammer.* Bayreuth: Ellwanger.

Monod, David, 2005. *Settling Scores. German music, denazification, and the Americans, 1945–1953.* Chapel Hill, N.C.: University of North Carolina Press.

Naegele, Verena, 2005. 'Luzern als "Gegenfestival". Mythos und Realität' in *Musik im Exil. Die Schweiz und das Ausland 1918–1945,* eds Chris Walton and Antonio Baldassarre. Bern et al.: Lang, pp. 237–254.

Nelki, Erna, 1981. 'Eingesperrt im englischen Frauenlager' in Zadek, 120–126.

Newman, Vera, 1963. *Ernest Newman. A Memoir.* London: Putnam.

Northrop Moore, Jerrold, 1976. *A Voice in Time: The Gramophone of Fred Gaisberg 1873–1951.* London: Hamilton.

Oelker, Simone/Astrid Reuter, eds, 2002. *Lebenswerke. Frauen im Kloster Stift zum Heiligengrabe zwischen 1847 und 1945.* Bonn: Deutsche Stiftung Denkmalschutz.

Pachl, Peter P., 1988. *Siegfried Wagner. Genie im Schatten.* München: Nymphenburger.

Potter, Tully, 2010. *Adolf Busch. The Life of an Honest Musician.* 2 vols. London: Toccata.

Prieberg, Fred K., 1986. *Kraftprobe. Wilhelm Furtwängler im Dritten Reich.* Wiesbaden: Brockhaus.

Ramati, Alexander, 1980. *Barbed Wire on the Isle of Man.* New York: Harcourt Brace Jovanovich.

Rhode-Jüchtern, Anna-Christine/ Maria Kublitz-Kramer, eds, 2004. *Echolos. Klangwelten verfolgter Musikerinnen in der NS-Zeit.* Bielefeld: Aisthesis.

Rockwell, John, 2006. *Outsider. John Rockwell on the Arts, 1967–2006.* Pompton Plains, NJ: Limelight Editions.

Russell, John, 1957. *Erich Kleiber. A memoir*. London: Andre Deutsch.

Sachs, Harvey, 1978. *Toscanini*. Philadelphia & New York: J. B. Lippincott.

Schaefer, Hans Joachim, 2007. *Du hast vielleicht noch nicht alles versucht: Erinnerungen*. Kassel: University Press (Studia Cassellana, Vol. 17).

Schopflocher, Robert, 2010. *Weit von wo. Mein Leben zwischen drei Welten*. München: LangenMüller.

Schostack, Renate, 1998. *Hinter Wahnfrieds Mauern. Gertrud Wagner. Ein Leben*. Hamburg: Hoffmann und Campe.

Schulenburg, Tisa von der, 1993. *Des Kaisers weibliche Kadetten. Schulzeit in Heiligengrabe – zwischen Kaiserreich und Revolution*. Freiburg: Herder.

Silja, Anja, 2000. *Die Sehnsucht nach dem Unerreichbaren. Wege und Irrwege*. (1999). Berlin: Parthas.

Skelton, Geoffrey, 1971. *Wieland Wagner. A Positive Sceptic*. London: Gollancz.

Spotts, Frederic, 1994. *Bayreuth. A History of the Wagner Festival*. New Haven/London: Yale University Press.

Stent, Ronald, 1980. *A Bespattered Page? The Internment of 'His Majesty's most Loyal Enemy Aliens'.* London: Andre Deutsch.

Syberberg, Hans-Jürgen. *Winifred Wagner und die Geschichte des Hauses Wahnfried von 1914–1975*. Transcript of Film (Richard-Wagner-Archive Bayreuth).

Taubman, Howard, 1951. *The Maestro. The Life of Arturo Toscanini*. New York: Simon und Schuster.

Thomson, John Mansfield, 1997. 'The Path to Bayreuth: Friedelind Wagner's 1962 Master class and the Influence of Walter Felsenstein (1901–1973)' in *Liber Amicorum John Steele. A musicological tribute*, ed. Warren Drake. Stuyvesant: Pendragon Press, pp. 453–467.

Wagner, Friedelind/Page, Cooper, 1945. *Heritage of Fire*. New York/London: Harper & Brothers Publishers.

Wagner, Gertrud 1976. 'Ein Blick zurück', in Wolf Siegfried Wagner (unpaginated)

Wagner, Gottfried, 1999. *Twilight of the Wagners: The Unveiling of a Family's Legacy*. New York: Picador.

Wagner, Nike, 1998. *Wagner Theater*. Frankfurt/M.: Suhrkamp.

Wagner, Nike, 2000. 'Für uns war er überhaupt nicht der Führer. Zu Winifred Wagner' in Friedländer/Rüsen, 179–193.

Wagner, Wieland, ed., 1962. *Richard Wagner und das neue Bayreuth*. Munich: Paul List.

Wagner, Wolf Siegfried, ed., 1976. *Wagner. Die Geschichte unserer Familie in Bildern*. Bayreuth 1876–1976. Munich: Rogner & Bernhard.

Wagner, Wolfgang, 1994. *Lebens-Akte*. Munich: Albrecht Knaus.

Waldberg, Max Freiherr von, ed., 1933. *Cosima Wagners Briefe an ihre Tochter Daniela von Bülow 1866–1885*. Stuttgart/Berlin: J.G. Cotta'sche Buchhandlung Nachfolger.

Wallich, Isabella, 2001. *Recording My Life*, London: Sanctuary.

Walter, Hans-Albert, 1984. *Deutsche Exilliteratur 1933–50*. Vol 2: *Europäisches Appeasement und überseeische Asylpraxis*. Stuttgart: Metzler.

Warburg, Lotte, 1989. *Eine vollkommene Närrin durch meine ewigen Gefühle. Aus den Tagebüchern der Lotte Warburg 1925 bis 1947*. Bayreuth: Druckhaus Bayreuth.

Wörner-Heil, Ortrud. *Frauenschulen auf dem Lande. Reifensteiner Verband (1897–1997)*, Kassel, 2. ed. 1997 (= *Schriftenreihe des Archivs der deutschen Frauenbewegung* 11).

Zadek, Walter, ed., 1981. *Sie flohen vor dem Hakenkreuz. Selbstzeugnisse der Emigranten*, Reinbek: Rowohlt.

Zelinsky, Hartmut, 1976. *Richard Wagner – ein deutsches Thema. Eine Dokumentation zur Wirkungsgeschichte Richard Wagners 1876–1976*, Frankfurt: Zweitausendundeins.

Index